Supreme Court
Watch—1996

Other Books by David M. O'Brien
STORM CENTER:
THE SUPREME COURT IN AMERICAN POLITICS
FOURTH EDITION

CONSTITUTIONAL LAW AND POLITICS:
Vol. 1, STRUGGLES FOR POWER AND GOVERNMENTAL
ACCOUNTABILITY
Vol. 2, CIVIL RIGHTS AND CIVIL LIBERTIES
SECOND EDITION

ABORTION AND AMERICAN POLITICS
(co-authored)

JUDICIAL ROULETTE

WHAT PROCESS IS DUE?
COURTS AND SCIENCE-POLICY DISPUTES

VIEWS FROM THE BENCH:
THE JUDICIARY AND CONSTITUTIONAL POLITICS
(co-authored)

THE POLITICS OF TECHNOLOGY ASSESSMENT:
INSTITUTIONS, PROCESSES, AND POLICY DISPUTES
(co-authored)

THE PUBLIC'S RIGHT TO KNOW:
THE SUPREME COURT AND THE FIRST AMENDMENT

PRIVACY, LAW, AND PUBLIC POLICY

THE POLITICS OF AMERICAN GOVERNMENT
(co-authored)

TO DREAM OF DREAMS:
RELIGIOUS FREEDOM AND CONSTITUTIONAL POLITICS IN
POSTWAR JAPAN

JUDGES ON JUDGING

SUPREME COURT WATCH—1996

Highlights of the 1993–1996 Terms
Preview of the 1996–1997 Term

DAVID M. O'BRIEN

UNIVERSITY OF VIRGINIA

W. W. NORTON & COMPANY
New York London

W. W. Norton & Company, Inc., 500 Fifth Avenue, New York, NY 10110
        http://www.wwnorton.com
W. W. Norton & Company Ltd., 10 Coptic Street, London WC1A 1PU

1 2 3 4 5 6 7 8 9 0

CONTENTS

Cases in italics only are excerpted; cases within brackets are discussed and
extensively quoted in the chapter introductions.

PREFACE

Changes in the composition of the Supreme Court often bring changes in constitutional law as well. The dynamics of the Court, of course, also change with each new appointee. Major changes in constitutional law and politics, moreover, are not uncommon when there are several changes on the high bench in a brief period of time. The Court's 1993–1994 term opened with the seating of Justice Ruth Bader Ginsburg, the second woman and seventh Jewish justice to sit on the high bench, and the first appointee of a Democratic president in over a quarter of a century. The 1993–1994 term then ended with the retirement of Justice Harry Blackmun and the 1994–1995 term began with the addition of President Bill Clinton's second appointee, Justice Stephen Breyer.

Supreme Court Watch—1996 is intended to examine the changes and decisions made during the Supreme Court's 1993, 1994, and 1995 terms. Besides highlighting the major rulings in excerpts from leading cases, I discuss in section-by-section introductions other important decisions as well as analyze recent developments in various areas of constitutional law. I preview here some of the important cases that the Court has granted review and will decide in its 1996–1997 term. To offer even more information in an efficient format, I have included special boxes titled "The Development of Law" and "Inside the Court."

The favorable reception of and comments received on previous editions of the *Watch* have been gratifying, and I hope this 1996 edition will further contribute to students' understanding of constitutional law, politics, and history, as well as to their appreciation for how the politics of constitutional interpretation turn on differing interpretations of constitutional politics. Ms. Deborah Gerish did a terrific job copyediting the manuscript, and I am grateful to her and Steve Dunn.

D. M. O.
July 1, 1996

VOLUME ONE

VOLUME ONE

2

LAW AND POLITICS IN THE SUPREME COURT: JURISDICTION AND DECISION-MAKING PROCESS

AFTER ALMOST A QUARTER of a century in which Republican presidents made ten consecutive appointments to the Supreme Court, Democratic President Bill Clinton had the opportunity to fill two vacancies. Midway through the 1992 term, Justice Byron White announced his decision to resign at the end of the term. Appointed by John F. Kennedy in 1962 at age forty-four, Justice White served for thirty-one years on the bench and remained the last appointee of a Democratic president. In his time on the bench, he established a staunch, though by no means uniformly, conservative track record. On some of the most controversial social-civil rights issues, he voted with conservatives. Justice White dissented from the landmark decision in *Roe v. Wade*, 410 U.S. 113 (1973) (see Vol. 2, Ch. 11),[1] and all subsequent rulings affirming a woman's right to have an abortion, as well as authoring the opinion for a bare majority rejecting an extension of the right of privacy to protect private consensual sexual relations in *Bowers v. Hardwick*, 478 U.S. 186 (1986) (see Vol. 2, Ch. 11). Except for upholding Congress's power to enact affirmative action programs, Justice White opposed such state and local programs, unless adopted to remedy specific policies of past discrimination (see Vol. 2, Ch. 12). With respect to the rights of the accused and criminal justice

---

[1] References to Vol. 1 or 2 are to the author's two-volume *Constitutional Law and Politics* (Norton, 2d ed., 1995).

matters, he also generally sided with conservatives, dissenting from the watershed ruling in *Miranda v. Arizona*, 384 U.S. 436 (1966) (in Vol. 2, Ch. 8), for instance. Although supportive of First Amendment free speech claims in many cases, Justice White often dissented from the Court's decisions enforcing a rigid "separation of church and state" under the First Amendment's (dis)establishment clause (see Vol. 2, Ch. 6).

In announcing his decision to retire almost four months in advance of the end of the Court's term, Justice White gave President Clinton not only a chance to fill his seat but ample time to select his successor. Among others on the Court, Justice White reportedly lamented how the televised coverage of the Senate confirmation hearings for controversial nominees—in particular, the ill-fated 1987 nomination of Robert H. Bork and the bitter 1991 struggle over Justice Thomas's confirmation—denigrated the Court. Besides considerations for the Court's institutional prestige, Justice White may have wanted to ensure that Clinton had ample time to pick a suitable successor, given the spats over the withdrawal of Clinton's first two nominees for attorney general and the extraordinary battle that had doomed the last Democratic president's opportunity to affect the Court. In 1968 President Lyndon Johnson's proposed elevation of Justice Abe Fortas to the seat of chief justice was defeated when Republicans and conservative Southern Democrats in the Senate forced Fortas to withdraw from consideration. In any event, Justice White's announcement gave Clinton the first of several possible opportunities during his time in the Oval Office to fill seats on the high bench and to shift the Court's direction on abortion, the right of privacy, affirmative action, and religious freedom, among other matters.

For his part, President Clinton immediately announced that he would search for a nominee who possessed "a fine mind, good judgment, wide experience in the law and the problems of real people . . . and who has a big heart." Yet over three months passed before Clinton finally settled on Judge Ruth Bader Ginsburg as the 107th justice of the Supreme Court. Clinton had wanted a politician—a "consensus builder"—for the Court. But several prominent and potential nominees withdrew from consideration: New York's governor Mario M. Cuomo and that state's chief judge Judith Kaye, as well as the secretary of the Department of Education, Richard Riley. From a list of over fifty potential nominees (including federal judges Jose Cabranes, Jon O. Newman, Amalya Kearse, and Patricia Wald, along with Tennessee's supreme court justice Gilbert Merritt), the president narrowed the contenders to a handful.

In the week before the announcement of his nominee, Clinton vacillated between elevating his secretary of the Department of Interior, Bruce Babbitt—a friend and former Arizona governor—or naming one of two federal appellate court judges, Ruth Bader Ginsburg or Stephen

G. Breyer. Environmentalists wanted Babbitt to stay at Interior, and he faced strong opposition from the senior minority member on the Senate Judiciary Committee, Orrin Hatch (R.-Utah). By contrast, both Ginsburg and Breyer had the support of Hatch and Senator Edward Kennedy (D.-Mass.). Moreover, each had won seats on the federal bench as last-minute appointees of President Jimmy Carter in 1980. Breyer had been serving as chief counsel to the Senate Judiciary Committee when it was chaired by Senator Kennedy, and Hatch had been instrumental in pushing Ginsburg's appointment through in 1980, when Republicans threatened to block all further Carter judicial nominees. At that time, Hatch agreed to meet her at the request of H. Ross Perot, who was asked to arrange the meeting by his Washington tax attorney and Ginsburg's husband, Martin. Ginsburg impressed Hatch then and later with thirteen years of service on the Court of Appeals for the District of Columbia Circuit, during which time she served with future Justices Scalia and Thomas, as well as Judge Bork. In 1993, though, New York's senator Daniel Patrick Moynihan, leaders of prominent women's groups, and her husband were among Ginsburg's strongest supporters.

After meeting Judge Breyer for a widely publicized luncheon amid speculation that he would get the nod, Clinton met with Ginsburg the next day. He was plainly touched by the charm and strength of the sixty-year-old Jewish grandmother, jurist, and leader of the women's movement in law in the 1970s. When subsequently announcing his selection, Clinton praised Ginsburg's "pragmatism" and called her the Thurgood Marshall of the women's movement. That comparison, however, was initially drawn by former solicitor general Erwin Griswold when, at the fiftieth anniversary of the Supreme Court Building in 1985, he observed that "in modern times two appellate advocates altered the nation's course . . . Thurgood Marshall and Ruth Ginsburg."

Born in Brooklyn, Ginsburg went to Cornell University as an undergraduate, where she also met her future husband. Both Ginsburgs went on to Harvard Law School, but following her husband's graduation and acceptance of a position in a New York law firm, Ginsburg finished her third year at Columbia Law School, where she tied for first in the class. Following graduation, Ginsburg worked as a law clerk for two years for a federal judge, but then could not find a New York law firm that would hire her in 1961 because she was a woman. After two more years working as a research assistant, Ginsburg was hired by Rutgers University School of Law, where she taught until 1972, when she became the first woman law professor at Columbia.

Because no Jewish justice had sat on the high bench in almost a quarter of a century (since Justice Fortas resigned in 1969), Jewish groups welcomed Ginsburg's nomination, while also rejecting the mythology of a "Jewish seat" and emphasizing that her selection was based on merit. Women's groups were also generally pleased, though some voiced concerns about Ginsburg's criticisms of *Roe v. Wade*. In a 1993 speech at New York University Law School, Ginsburg expressed reservations about the scope, though not the result, of that controversial ruling. In her words:

> [W]ithout taking giant strides and thereby risking a backlash too forceful to contain, the Court, through constitutional adjudication, can reinforce or signal a green light for a social change. In most of the post-1970 gender classification cases, unlike Roe, the Court functioned in just that way. It approved the direction of change through a temperate brand of decision-making, one that was not extravagant or divisive.
>
> *Roe v. Wade*, on the other hand, halted a political process that was moving in a reform direction and thereby, I believe, prolonged divisiveness and deterred stable settlement of the issue. The most recent *Planned Parenthood [of Southeastern Pennsylvania v. Casey* (1992) (see Vol. 2, Ch. 11)] decision, although a retreat from *Roe*, appears to have prompted a renewed dialogue, a revival of the political movement in progress in the early 1970s. That renewed dialogue, one may hope, will, within a relatively short span, yield an enduring resolution of this vital matter.[2]

Despite that measured criticism of *Roe*, Ginsburg had been at the forefront of the women's movement in law in the 1970s. Besides teaching at Rutgers and Columbia law schools, in the 1970s Ginsburg also served as the director of the ACLU's Women's Rights Project, arguing six (and winning five) important gender-based discrimination cases before the Supreme Court. Ginsburg championed a legal strategy of chipping away at precedents on a piecemeal basis and building on new principles of equal protection that exposed the irrationality of gender discriminations that often resulted in men receiving benefits they would not have otherwise received. Although ultimately failing to persuade the Court to recognize gender as a "suspect category" under the Fourteenth Amendment, Ginsburg was victorious before the Court in *Frontiero v. Richardson*, 411 U.S. 677 (1973), which overturned regulations that discriminated on the basis of gender in conferring benefits on dependents of military personnel; *Weinberger v. Wiesenfeld*, 420 U.S. 636 (1975), which struck down a Social Security Act provision that gave greater survivor benefits to women with children; *Edwards v. Healy*, 421 U.S. 772 (1975), which invalidated a Louisiana law exempting women from jury service; *Califano v. Goldfarb*, 430 U.S. 199 (1977), which invalidated a Social Security Act provision that automatically awarded survivors' benefits to women, but not to men; and *Duren v. Missouri*, 439 U.S. 357 (1979), which struck

---

2 Ruth Bader Ginsburg, "Speaking in a Judicial Voice," *New York University Law Review* 67 (1992): 1885.

down a state law exempting women from jury service upon request of attorneys. With little opposition from Republicans and guarded responses during her confirmation hearings, Ginsburg's nomination sailed through the Senate with a final vote of ninety-six to three. On the bench in her first term, Justice Ginsburg proved to be an aggressive questioner during oral argument sessions and gave no sign of experiencing the so-called "freshman effect" in undertaking her share of the Court's workload. By contrast, since his appointment in 1991, Justice Thomas has remained the most reticent member of the bench during oral arguments. Indeed, during the ninety-one hours of oral arguments that the Court heard during its 1993–1994 term, Justice Thomas failed to ask a single question.

On April 6, 1994, Justice Harry Blackmun announced that he would retire at the end of the term. The eighty-five-year-old justice had served on the Court for almost a quarter of a century. Appointed as a "law and order jurist" by Republican President Richard M. Nixon in 1970, at the suggestion of Blackmun's high school friend, Chief Justice Warren Burger, Justice Blackmun initially voted with Burger, which earned them the label "the Minnesota twins." But Justice Blackmun soon asserted his own independence and over the course of his tenure on the bench came to vote more often on social-civil rights issues with the Court's last liberals, Justices William J. Brennan and Thurgood Marshall. Justice Blackmun authored the controversial landmark ruling on abortion, *Roe v. Wade*, 410 U.S. 113 (1973) (in Vol. 2, Ch. 11), for which he received thousands of letters attacking him, including death threats, and of which he repeatedly said he would carry *Roe* to "his grave." Although *Roe* will overshadow his other opinions, Justice Blackmun handed down several important rulings, including *Garcia v. San Antonio Metropolitan Transit Authority*, 469 U.S. 528 (1985) (see Vol. 1, Ch. 7), on the Tenth Amendment. He also championed the Court's extending First Amendment protection to commercial speech (see Vol. 2, Ch. 5). On most matters of criminal procedure, however, Justice Blackmun remained a steadfast conservative, writing several significant opinions for the Court that cut back on the scope of the Fourth Amendment; for example, see *California v. Acevedo*, 500 U.S. 565 (1991) (in Vol. 2, Ch. 7). The principal exception to his stand on criminal justice matters was a reconsideration of his position on capital punishment shortly before announcing his retirement.

Justice Blackmun and President Clinton had become friends over the years, attending annual gatherings of the Renaissance Club in Hilton Head, South Carolina. In announcing that he would retire at the end of the term, as Justice White had almost a year earlier, Justice Blackmun gave the president ample time to choose a successor. Clinton in turn took less time in selecting his second nominee to the Court, taking only thirty-seven days in contrast with the eighty-seven days that passed before he announced his first appointee. Clinton, though, once again agonized and vacillated in making his decision. In the end, he finally settled on the noncontroversial federal judge Stephen Breyer, whom he had passed over a year earlier. Apparently, Clinton picked Breyer because his other top two candidates would have proven more controversial and might have set off a confirmation fight in the Senate.

Clinton had said he wanted a nominee who was an experienced "politician" with a "big heart," but he again passed over his Secretary of the Interior, claiming that he "could not bear to lose him from the Cabinet." In fact, Bruce Babbitt was the most liberal of Clinton's top three final candidates and would have confronted strong opposition from the Senate Judiciary Committee's ranking Republican, Orrin Hatch. Conservative groups were also certain to come out in opposition to his views and his attack in 1987 on Robert Bork, President Reagan's controversial and ill-fated nominee to the Court. Clinton's other favored candidate and long-time friend, federal appellate judge Richard Arnold, presented other political problems. Judge Arnold, a Harvard-trained former law clerk to Justice William J. Brennan, had lymphoma cancer and had recently undergone low-level radiation therapy. While Judge Arnold's cancer was not life-threatening, it could have been used as a basis for senators' voting against his confirmation. Clinton cited Judge Arnold's health as the reason for bypassing him, but the judge's record on the federal bench would have invited attacks from both the right and the left. In particular, liberal women's groups were likely to come out against Judge Arnold because of some of his rulings on all-male clubs and abortion rights.

The fifty-six-year-old Judge Breyer was trained as an undergraduate at Stanford and Oxford universities and later received his law degree from Harvard Law School, where he subsequently taught administrative law for over a decade. In 1979–1980 he served briefly as chief counsel to the Senate Judiciary Committee, before becoming a federal judge on the First Circuit Court of Appeals. After graduating from law school, he also served as a law clerk to Justice Arthur J. Goldberg. During that year the justice handed down his controversial and visionary opinion on the Ninth Amendment in *Griswold v. Connecticut*, 391 U.S. 145 (1965) (in Vol. 2, Ch. 4). Unlike that former very liberal justice, however, Breyer was more moderate and much more of a legal technician. Breyer's academic writings, moreover, concern primarily issues of administrative law and regulatory policy. And for that reason the president's advisers anticipated relatively low-key confirmation hearings for Clinton's second nominee and the 108th member of the Court.

INSIDE THE COURT

Voting Alignments in the Rehnquist Court, 1987–1994 Terms

	Rehnquist	White	Blackmun	Stevens	O'Connor	Scalia	Kennedy	Souter	Thomas	Brennan	Marshall	Ginsburg	Breyer
Rehnquist	—	80.2	55.4	53.0	78.7	77.6	81.1	70.5	77.9	49.9	48.2	66.9	67.1
White	80.2	—	62.3	60.8	72.5	68.4	75.7	73.5	67.7	54.8	54.7	68.2	
Blackmun	55.4	62.3	—	72.1	50.6	41.8	57.6	64.8	44.4	77.1	76.3	68.2	
Stevens	53.0	60.8	72.1	—	57.3	48.2	57.0	63.6	42.3	70.7	72.5	75.4	70.7
O'Connor	78.7	72.5	50.6	57.3	—	70.4	77.5	73.6	65.9	50.9	49.1	67.2	74.4
Scalia	77.6	68.4	41.8	48.2	70.4	—	77.4	64.6	85.7	49.4	46.1	60.8	59.3
Kennedy	81.1	75.7	57.6	57.0	77.5	77.4	—	74.7	72.2	53.7	51.2	70.4	72.0
Souter	70.5	73.5	64.8	63.6	73.6	64.6	74.7	—	59.0		54.6	78.5	82.9
Thomas	77.9	67.7	44.4	42.3	65.9	85.7	72.2	59.0	—			53.5	58.5
Brennan	49.9	54.8	77.1	70.7	50.9	49.4	53.7			—	94.0		
Marshall	48.2	54.7	76.3	72.5	49.1	46.1	51.2	54.6		94.0	—		
Ginsburg	66.9	68.2	68.2	75.4	67.2	60.8	70.4	78.5	53.5			—	82.7
Breyer	67.1			70.7	74.4	59.3	72.0	82.9	58.5			82.7	—

The above are average percentages. The percentages for each term are from Table 1(B) of the *Harvard Law Review's* annual review of the Court's term in volumes 102–109 (1988–1996).

A. JURISDICTION AND JUSTICIABLE CONTROVERSIES

In an important ruling on judicial independence and the separation of powers, but otherwise without far-reaching consequences, the Court struck down a 1991 congressional enactment in *Plaut v. Spendthrift Farm, Inc.*, 115 S.Ct. 1447 (1995). That enactment aimed at reviving a group of securities fraud suits and tried to get around a 1991 Supreme Court ruling that securities fraud cases must be brought within one year of the discovery of the questionable conduct and within three years of when the events took place. Moreover, the Court had given its 1991 ruling retroactive effect, resulting in lower courts' dismissals of a number of pending suits. Congress in turn promptly responded by amending the Securities Exchange Act of 1934 and basically directing federal courts to reopen past lawsuits. Writing for a majority of seven justices, Justice Scalia advanced his categorical view of separation of powers, including its guarantee for judicial independence and judicial review. The principle of separation of powers was, in his words, a "structural safeguard . . . establishing high walls and clear distinctions because low walls and vague distinctions will not be judicially defensible in the heat of interbranch conflict." Justice Stevens dissented and was joined by Justice Ginsburg.

B. THE COURT'S DOCKET AND SCREENING CASES

With a docket continuing to grow steadily, the Rehnquist Court has nonetheless pressed ahead in granting fewer and fewer cases plenary consideration. In its 1992–1993 term, for the first time in the Court's history, the docket rose above 7,000 cases. And in the 1994–1995 term, the docket rose to over 8,000 cases.

Rehnquist Court Terms	Total Cases on the Docket	Number of Cases Granted and Decided	Percentage
1986	5,123	175	3.4
1987	5,268	167	3.1
1988	5,657	164	2.8
1989	5,746	146	2.5
1990	6,316	125	1.9
1991	6,770	127	1.8
1992	7,245	116	1.6
1993	7,786	90	1.1
1994	8,100	94	1.1

The Court heard only eighty-six hours of oral arguments during its 1993–1994 term, eighty-three hours of oral arguments in its 1994–1995 term, and only seventy-seven hours in the 1995–1996 term. Chief Justice Rehnquist is credited with cutting back on the Court's workload in spite of an increasing caseload. However, due to the dramatic rise in the number of annual filings, the expansion of the Court's discretionary jurisdiction in 1988, and the Rehnquist Court's decision to grant fewer cases review, less than two percent of the cases coming to the Court are now given plenary consideration. By comparison, in 1953, the first year of Chief Justice Earl Warren's tenure, the Court had only 1,463 cases on its docket and decided 76 (or 5.1 percent) by written opinion. Sixteen years later in Chief Justice Warren Burger's first year on the bench, the Court faced a docket of 4,202 cases and decided 108 (or 2.5 percent). In the 1985 term, Chief Justice Burger's last term, the Court had a docket of 5,158 cases and decided 171 (or 3.3 percent). The growth in the Court's docket is due primarily to an increase in the number of unpaid petitions, which has almost doubled in the last decade, rising from 2,352 in the 1982–1983 term to 5,574 in the 1994–1995 term.

The overwhelming number of petitions are never reviewed by the justices, since (with the sole exception of Justice Stevens) eight justices—including Justice Ginsburg—rely on "*cert.* memos," written by their collective law clerks, and study, as well as discuss in conference, only those cases that they and their law clerks deem important (see Vols. 1 or 2, Ch. 2).

INSIDE THE COURT

The Business of the Supreme Court in the 1995–1996 Term

Subject of Court Opinions	Summary	Plenary
Admiralty		3
Antitrust		1
Bankruptcy	2	2
Bill of Rights (other than rights of accused and equal protection		9
Commerce Clause		
1. Constitutionality and construction of federal regulation	1	1
2. Constitutionality of state regulation		2
Common law		
Misc. statutory construction	3	11
Due process		
1. Economic interests		3
2. Procedure and rights of accused	4	12
3. Substantive due process (noneconomic)		
Impairment of contract and just compensation		1
International law, war, and peace	1	1
Jurisdiction, procedure, and practice	6	10
Land legislation		
Native Americans		1
Patents, copyright, and trademarks	1	1
Other suits against the government		3
Suits by states		4
Taxation (federal and state)		1
Totals	18	66

The categorizations here are adapted from Felix Frankfurter and James Landis, *Th Business of the Supreme Court* (New York: Macmillan, 1927). The classification o cases is that of the author, and necessarily invites differences of opinion as to th dominant issue in some cases. For further discussion, see David M. O'Brien, *Stor Center: The Supreme Court in American Politics*, 4th ed. (New York: Norton, 1996) The table includes opinions in cases whether decided summarily or given plenar consideration, but not cases summarily disposed of by simple orders, opinion dissenting from the denial of review, and those dismissing cases as improvidentl granted.

INSIDE THE COURT

Opinion Writing during the 1995–1996 Term

Opinions	Majority	Concurring	Dissenting	Separate	Totals
Per curiam	10				10
Rehnquist	10	3	1		14
Stevens	8	4	19	3	34
O'Connor	8	2	1	3	14
Scalia	9	6	9		24
Kennedy	8	5	5	2	20
Souter	8	6	3	2	19
Thomas	8	5	5	3	21
Ginsburg	8	6	1	1	16
Breyer	8	4	4	3	19
Totals:	85	41	48	17	191

Court opinions disposing of two or more companion cases are counted only onc here. In addition, this table includes cases disposed of either summarily or upo plenary consideration, but does not include concurring or dissenting opinions fro the denial of *certiorari*. Note also that Justices Stevens and Breyer delivere plurality opinions announcing the Court's decision in *Morse v. Republican Party o Virginia* and each opinion is counted here as an "opinion for the majority."

I. THE IMPACT OF SUPREME COURT DECISIONS: COMPLIANCE AND IMPLEMENTATION

In *Powell v. Nevada*, 114 S.Ct. 1280 (1994), the Court unanimously held that its earlier ruling, requiring probable-cause hearings to be held within forty-eight hours for defendants arrested without a warrant, in *County of Riverside v. McLaughlin*, 500 U.S. 44 (1991) (in Vol. 2, Ch. 7), applied retroactively to all other pending cases. (For a further discussion of the doctrine of retroactivity, see Vol. 1 or 2, Ch. 2.) Writing for the Court, however, Justice Ginsburg held that a violation of the forty-eight-hour rule need not always result in a reversal of a conviction, if other factors in a case rendered the violation of the rule a "harmless rule." Justice Clarence Thomas, joined by Chief Justice Rehnquist, dissented from the part of the Court's decision remanding *Powell* back to the Nevada supreme court, which had ruled against ap-plying *McLaughlin* retroactively. Remanding the case, in Justice Thomas's words, would "merely require the needless expenditure of further judicial resources" since Powell's underlying claim "lacks merit."

As the Court has moved over the last two decades in more conservative directions in areas of civil rights and liberties, state supreme courts increasingly have refused to follow the high court's construction of federal law and have recognized new rights or extended protection on the basis of state constitutions to claims that the Supreme Court has declined to embrace (see Vols. 1 or 2, Ch. 2, as well as Vol. 1, Ch. 7). Among the recent decisions, in *Torre Jenkins v. Chief Justice of the District Court Department*, 416 Mass. 221 (1993), the Massachusetts supreme court refused to follow the Supreme Court's ruling in *County of Riverside v. McLaughlin*, 500 U.S. 44 (1991) (see Vol. 2, Ch. 7), that following a warrantless arrest individuals may be incarcerated for up to forty-eight hours before being given a hearing to determine the probable cause for their arrest. In *Rick Sitz v. Michigan Department of State Police*, 443 Mich. 744 (1993), the supreme court of Michigan likewise departed from the Supreme Court's upholding of Michigan state police's use of sobriety checkpoints under the Fourth Amendment, in *Michigan Department of State Police v. Sitz*, 496 U.S. 444 (1990). When that case was remanded back to the state appellate court, the state court held that the state's policy of indiscriminate suspicionless stopping of automobiles violates Michigan's state constitution's prohibition against unreasonable searches and seizures.

Finally, in *Florida v. White*, 660 So.2d 664 (1995) (excerpted below), the Florida state supreme court denied to follow the Court's ruling just months earlier in *Arizona v. Evans*, 115 S.Ct. 1185 (1995) (excerpted here in Vol. 2, Ch. 7), that the "good faith exception" to the exclusionary rule extends to police officers' reliance on mistaken computer records of outstanding arrest warrants.

Florida v. White
660 So.2d 664 (1995)

David White was stopped in his car by a police officer for driving with a defective taillight. The officer subsequently ran his driver's license number through the department's computer and found a record of an outstanding civil arrest warrant for White's failure to pay child support. On that basis, White was arrested and his car was searched by the officer, who discovered contraband. At his trial, White's lawyer moved to exclude the contraband as evidence on the ground that the search was illegal because the warrant had in fact been served four days before and thus, contrary to the computer record, there was no outstanding warrant. The trial court agreed and the government appealed to the Florida state supreme court.

The court's decision was five to one. Justice Shaw announced the majority's opinion and Justice Overton filed a dissenting opinion.

Justice SHAW delivered the opinion of the Court.

We approve the decision of the court below, but in so doing we address important facts which, though absent from the stipulation, are nonetheless critical to this case's resolution. During the hearing on the motion to suppress it became clear that the arrest was premised upon the assumption that there was an outstanding warrant against White. The assumption resulted from a computer in the Sheriff's Office incorrectly showing the warrant against White as active. In sum, the computer reflected an outstanding active warrant when, in point of fact, the warrant had been served four days previously and was no longer valid when White was arrested.

The "computer age" has had a profound impact upon the lives of most if not all of us. Law enforcement agencies are no exception. The computer's ability to assemble information is undoubtedly of great benefit to police agencies that are burdened with arduous record-keeping tasks. The accuracy of the information generated by the computer, however, is only as precise as data supplied. If the computer is given inaccurate data, the computer-generated results will likewise be inaccurate. As is well known in computer jargon, "junk in equals junk out." The United States Supreme Court recently addressed this issue when it granted *certiorari* to "determine whether the exclusionary rule requires suppression of evidence seized incident to an arrest resulting from an inaccurate computer record, regardless of whether police personnel or court personnel were responsible for the record's continued presence in the police computer." *Arizona v. Evans*, 115 S.Ct. 1185 (1995). The Court held that the rule does not require evidence suppression where the erroneous computer information results from clerical errors committed by court employees. The issue of whether the exclusionary rule bars the use of evidence obtained as the result of an illegal arrest resulting from police error was left unanswered. *Evans* does not speak to this precise issue. . . .

The purpose of the Fourth Amendment is to prohibit unreasonable governmental incursion into one's person, home, papers, or effects. *United States v. Calandra*, 414 U.S. 338 (1974). The exclusionary rule inhibits governmental breach of the principles embodied in the Fourth Amendment by prohibiting governmental use of evidence seized in violation of the rule. As written in *Calandra*, "the rule's prime purpose is to deter future unlawful police conduct and thereby effectuate the guarantee of the Fourth Amendment against unreasonable searches and seizures: 'The rule is calculated to prevent, not to repair. . . .'" The rule is not all-encompassing, and its use has been historically limited to the deterrence of police misconduct. Even within the realm of deterring police misconduct, the rule is not ironclad, as is demonstrated by its "good faith" exception enunciated in *United States v. Leon*, 468 U.S. 897 (1984). The *Leon* court modified the exclusionary rule to allow prosecutorial "case-in-chief" use of evidence obtained by officers reasonably relying on a search warrant issued by a detached and neutral magistrate, even though the warrant was subsequently found to be unsupported by probable cause. Although the issue in *Leon* concerned judicial error, the opinion provided insight into the purpose and goals of the exclusionary rule relative to police error. We find the following passage particularly insightful: "The deterrent purpose of the exclusionary rule necessarily assumes that the police have engaged in willful, or at the very least negligent, conduct which has deprived the defendant of some right. By refusing to admit evidence gained as a result of such conduct, the courts hope to instill in those particular investigating officers, or in their future counterparts, a greater degree of care toward the rights of an accused. Where the official conduct was pursued in complete good faith, however, the deterrence rationale loses much of its force." *Leon* (quoting *Michigan v. Tucker*, 417 U.S. 433 (1974)).

A police officer has knowledge, or may be properly charged with knowledge, of an unconstitutional search under what is commonly called the "fellow officer" or "collective knowledge" rule. The rule generally works to the officer's advantage by providing that when making an arrest, an officer may rely upon information supplied by fellow officers. However, if the information fails to support a legal arrest, evidence seized as a result of the arrest cannot be insulated from challenge on the grounds that the instigating officer relied on information furnished by fellow officers. *Whiteley v. Warden, Wyoming State Penitentiary*, 401 U.S. 560 (1971). . . . The *Evans* court, in recognizing the ongoing validity of this rule, stated that "*Whiteley* clearly retains relevance in determining whether police officers have violated the Fourth Amendment."

Turning to the instant case, we find that the error under review boils down to one unmistakable fact—failure of the police to maintain up-to-date and accurate computer records resulted in an illegal arrest and search. This type of police negligence fits squarely within the class of governmental action that the exclusionary rule was designed to deter, i.e., police negligence or misconduct that is likely to be thwarted if the evidence seized is suppressed. Suppression of evidence seized pursuant to police computer error will encourage law enforcement agencies to diligently maintain accurate and current computer records. We find that the following automation error concerns expressed by [the state supreme court in] *Arizona v. Evans* are germane to our opinion: "It is repugnant to the principles of a free society that a person should ever be taken into police custody because of a computer error precipitated by government carelessness. As automation increasingly invades modern life, the potential for Orwellian mischief grows. Under such circumstances, the exclusionary rule is a 'cost' we cannot afford to be without." The good faith exception is inapplicable in this instance since it was within the collective knowledge of the sheriff's office that the warrant was void. In essence, the arresting officers are charged with knowledge that they had no authority to arrest the defendant. Evidence obtained as a result of the illegal arrest is subject to the exclusionary rule. . . .

THE DEVELOPMENT OF LAW

Congress Overrides the Court:
The Religious Freedom Restoration Act of 1993

Congress overrode the controversial ruling in *Employment Division, Department of Human Resources of Oregon v. Smith*, 494 U.S. 872 (1990) (see Vol. 2, Ch. 6), with the enactment of the Religious Freedom Restoration Act of 1993. Writing for the majority in *Smith*, Justice Scalia rejected the Warren Court's analysis of the First Amendment's protection for religious freedom in *Sherbert v. Verner*, 374 U.S. 398 (1963) (see Vol. 2, Ch. 6). In *Sherbert* the Court advanced a "balancing test," requiring states to show a compelling interest in regulations that justifies overriding free exercise claims. By contrast, *Smith* held that there should be no exemption from otherwise "generally applicable laws" for individuals claiming they are denied the First Amendment's protection for the free exercise of religion. That ruling angered and united a broad range of religious organizations, who in turn succeeded in pushing Congress to enact the Religious Freedom Restoration Act.

The coalition that pushed for the enactment of the Religious Freedom Restoration Act included liberal, conservative, and religious organizations such as the National Association of Evangelicals, the Southern Baptist Convention, the National Council of Churches, the American Jewish Congress, the National Conference of Catholic Bishops, the Mormon Church, the Traditional Values Coalition, and the American Civil Liberties Union. In support of the legislation, sponsors pointed out that following the 1990 ruling in *Smith*, lower courts had denied exemptions for religious minorities, such as the Amish, in over fifty cases.

The Religious Freedom Restoration Act basically rewrote *Sherbert v. Verner*'s analysis and "balancing test" back into federal law, thereby overriding the Rehnquist Court's decision in *Smith*. The act forbids any federal agency or state government from burdening a person's free exercise of religion, even if the burden results from a law of general applicability, unless the agency or state government demonstrates that the regulation or law burdening an individual's religious freedom (1) "furthers a compelling governmental interest" and (2) "is the least restrictive means of furthering that compelling governmental interest."

4

THE PRESIDENT AS CHIEF
EXECUTIVE IN DOMESTIC
AFFAIRS

B. APPOINTMENT AND REMOVAL POWERS

In *Weiss v. United States*, 114 S.Ct. 752 (1994), the Court confronted
a challenge under the appointments clause of Article II and the Fifth
Amendment's due process clause to the way judges are appointed in
military courts. Article II authorizes the president to

> nominate, and by and with the Advice and Consent of the Senate . . . appoint
> Ambassadors, other public Ministers and Consuls, Judges of the supreme
> Court, and all other Officers of the United States, whose Appointments are
> not herein otherwise provided for, and which shall be established by Law;
> but the Congress may by law vest the Appointment of such inferior Officers,
> as they think proper, in the President alone, in the Courts of Law, or in the
> Heads of Departments.

Under the Uniform Code of Military Justice (UCMJ), a special and
general court martial trial is heard before a military judge and from
three to five court martial members, all of whom are temporarily assigned by the Judge Advocate General. Weiss, a marine who was found
guilty of larceny at a special court martial, appealed on the grounds that
the UCMJ's prescribed appointment method violated Article II and the
due process clause.

Writing for the majority, Chief Justice Rehnquist rejected the contentions that the appointment as judges of commissioned military
officers runs afoul of Article II. Neither did he find any merit to the
claim that the position of a military judge is so similar to other positions specified in Article II as to require Senate confirmation, nor did
he agree that military judges are akin to other high government offi-

cials, such as the Chairman of the Joint Chiefs of Staff, subject to a second appointment proceeding under Article II. In the chief justice's words: "It is quite clear that Congress has not required a separate appointment to the position of military judge, and we believe it equally clear that the Appointments Clause by its own force does not require a second appointment before military officers may discharge the duties of such a judge."

In addition, *Weiss* laid to rest the claim that military judges' fixed terms of tenure and provisions for independence fall short of ensuring the kind of judicial independence enjoyed by federal judges and required by the due process clause. "Although a fixed term of office is a traditional component of the Anglo-American civilian judicial system," Rehnquist added that "it has never been a part of the military justice tradition." That historical fact should be accorded great weight, according to Rehnquist. "A fixed term of office," as the chief justice put it, "is not an end in itself. It is a means of promoting judicial independence, which in turn helps to ensure judicial impartiality. We believe the applicable provisions of the UCMJ, and corresponding regulations, by insulating military judges from the effects of command influence, sufficiently preserve judicial impartiality so as to satisfy the Due Process Clause." In separate opinions, Justices Ginsburg, Souter, and Scalia concurred.

C. LEGISLATIVE POWERS IN THE ADMINISTRATIVE STATE

With the collapse of the Soviet Union and the end of the Cold War era, Congress finally agreed on a plan for closing U.S. military bases and getting around the vexing problem of members of Congress fighting to preserve bases located in their home districts and states. Under the 1990 Defense Base Closure and Realignment Act, an independent commission was created to hold public hearings, consider proposals made by the Secretary of Defense, and to make recommendations for base closings. The president then had to approve or reject the entire list of proposed closings and Congress had forty-five days to veto his action. Accordingly, neither the president nor members of Congress could remove or add individual bases to the package.

When the decision to close the 193-year-old Philadelphia Naval Shipyard was subsequently made, however, Pennsylvania's Republican senator Arlen Specter sued and claimed that it was improperly slated for closure. He also argued that federal courts should review the commission's procedures in order to determine their fairness. A federal district court initially dismissed his suit, but the Court of Appeals for the Third Circuit reversed and the federal government appealed its decision to the Supreme Court.

Writing for the Court in *Dalton v. Specter*, 114 S.Ct. 1719 (1994), Chief Justice Rehnquist rejected Senator Specter's claims of standing to sue under the Administrative Procedure Act (APA) and on the basis of a constitutional claim. Relying on an earlier ruling in *Franklin v. Massachusetts*, 505 U.S. 788 (1992), which limited judicial review under the APA only to governmental agencies' "final" decisions, the chief justice dismissed Specter's challenge to the independent commission's procedures. The commission's recommendations were not technically "final," reasoned Rehnquist, since they remained subject to the president's approval. "Without the President's approval," the chief justice emphasized, "no bases are closed under the act." Turning next to Specter's claim that the president had violated the 1990 act by accepting flawed recommendations, Chief Justice Rehnquist rejected out of hand the contention that the senator had raised a "constitutional" claim meriting judicial review. In the chief justice's words:

> Our cases do not support the proposition that every action by the President, or by another executive official, in excess of his statutory authority is *ipso facto* in violation of the Constitution. On the contrary, we have often distinguished between claims of constitutional violations and claims that an official has acted in excess of his statutory authority. . . . [C]laims simply alleging that the President has exceeded his statutory authority are not "constitutional" claims, subject to judicial review under the exception recognized in *Franklin* [v. *Massachusetts*, 505 U.S. 788 (1992)]. . . .
>
> So the claim raised here is a statutory one: The President is said to have violated the terms of the 1990 Act by accepting procedurally flawed recommendations. The exception identified in *Franklin* for review of constitutional claims thus does not apply in this case. We may assume for the sake of argument that some claims that the President has violated a statutory mandate are judicially reviewable outside the framework of the APA. See *Dames & Moore v. Regan*, 453 U.S. 654 (1981). But longstanding authority holds that such review is not available when the statute in question commits the decision to the discretion of the President. . . .
>
> How the President chooses to exercise the discretion Congress has granted him is not a matter for our review. As we stated in [*United States v.*] *George S. Bush & Co.*, [310 U.S. 371 (1940)], "no question of law is raised when the exercise of [the President's] discretion is challenged."
>
> In sum, we hold that the actions of the Secretary and the Commission cannot be reviewed under the APA because they are not "final agency actions." The actions of the President cannot be reviewed under the APA because the President is not an "agency" under that Act. The claim that the President exceeded his authority under the 1990 Act is not a constitutional claim, but a statutory one. Where a statute, such as the 1990 Act, commits decisionmaking to the discretion of the President, judicial review of the President's decision is not available.

In a separate opinion joined by Justices Blackmun, Ginsburg, and Stevens, however, Justice Souter pointed out that

It is not necessary to reach the question the Court answers in Part I, whether the Commission's report is final agency action, because the text, structure, and purpose of the Act compel the conclusion that judicial review of the Commission's or the Secretary's compliance with it is precluded. There is, to be sure, a "strong presumption that Congress did not mean to prohibit all judicial review." But although no one feature of the Act, taken alone, is enough to overcome that strong presumption, I believe that the combination present in this unusual legislative scheme suffices.

In adopting the Act, Congress was intimately familiar with repeated, un-successful, efforts to close military bases in a rational and timely manner. That history of frustration is reflected in the Act's text and intricate structure, which plainly express congressional intent that action on a base-closing package be quick and final, or no action be taken at all. . . . While no one aspect of the Act, standing alone, would suffice to overcome the strong presumption in favor of judicial review, this structure (combined with the Act's provision for Executive and congressional review, and its requirement of time-constrained judicial review of implementation under NEPA) can be understood no other way than as precluding judicial review of a base-closing decision under the scheme that Congress, out of its doleful experience, chose to enact. I conclude accordingly that the Act forecloses such judicial review.

D. ACCOUNTABILITY AND IMMUNITIES

In its 1996–1997 term, the Court will decide the important issue of whether the president has immunity from private lawsuits. *Clinton v. Jones* stems from a suit seeking $700,000 in damages for sexual harassment filed by Paula Corbin Jones in 1994. Jones claims that in 1991 then-governor Bill Clinton asked her to come to his hotel room and then made unwanted sexual advances there. The case before the Court appeals a decision by the Court of Appeals for the Eighth Circuit that held that the President could be sued and that trial over Jones's claims could begin. The President's attorney counters that, "No president has ever before been compelled to submit to a civil damages action, directed personally against him, during his term in office." Such lawsuits against the president, while in office, would violate the principle of separation of powers because they "increasingly would enmesh presidents in the judicial process, and the courts in the political arena, to the detriment of both." The Court has never decided whether an incumbent president is immune from private lawsuits for alleged activities before taking office. In *Nixon v. Fitzgerald*, 457 U.S. 731 (1982) (see Vol. 1, Ch. 4), a bare majority of the Court held that the president "is entitled to absolute immunity from damages liability predicated on his official acts." The appellate court distinguished that ruling on the ground that Jones's suit is not related to Clinton's official duties as president.

5

CONGRESS: MEMBERSHIP, IMMUNITIES, AND INVESTIGATORY POWERS

A. MEMBERSHIP AND IMMUNITIES

During its 1994–1995 term, the Court took up one of the most hotly contested contemporary political issues, namely, whether states may impose term limits on representatives elected to Congress. Since 1990, a grass-roots movement has succeeded in persuading twenty-three states to adopt term limits. The issue of term limits was also a prominent feature of the House of Representatives Republicans' "Contract With America" in the 1994 elections; however, in March 1995 the House defeated four different versions of a constitutional amendment imposing term limits. A bare majority of the Court subsequently struck down state-imposed term limits in *U.S. Term Limits, Inc. v. Thornton* (excerpted below). In his sixty-one-page opinion for the Court, Justice Stevens declared unconstitutional such limits on membership in Congress and left no doubt that any term limitations on members of Congress requires amending the Constitution. By contrast, Chief Justice Rehnquist and Justices O'Connor and Scalia joined Justice Thomas's eighty-eight-page dissent, maintaining that the Constitution was silent on the matter and that the states retained authority to add qualifications for their representatives in Congress beyond those specified in Article I for members' age, citizenship, and residency.

U.S. Term Limits, Inc. v. Thornton
115 S.Ct. 1842 (1995)

In 1992, Arkansas voters approved Amendment 73 to their state constitution and imposed term limits on three categories of elected officials. Section 1 provides that no elected official in the executive branch of the state government may serve for more than two terms. Section 2 provides that no member of the state house of representatives may serve for more than three two-year terms and no state senator may serve for more than two four-year terms. Section 3 further specified that state representatives to the U.S. House of Representatives may not be certified as candidates or be eligible for having their names placed on the ballot after having served for three or more terms. That section similarly limited candidates from running for the U.S. Senate after they served two or more terms there.

Within weeks of the adoption of Arkansas's term-limitation amendment, the League of Women Voters sought a declaratory judgment that Section 3 was an unconstitutional additional qualification under Article 1 of the U.S. Constitution. A state lower court and the Arkansas state supreme court agreed, whereupon U.S. Term Limits, Inc., an organization advocating term limits for elected officials, appealed to the Supreme Court.

The Court's decision was five to four and the majority's opinion was announced by Justice Stevens. Justice Kennedy filed a concurring opinion. Justice Thomas filed a dissenting opinion, joined by Chief Justice Rehnquist and Justices O'Connor and Scalia.

Justice STEVENS delivered the opinion of the Court.

The Constitution sets forth qualifications for membership in the Congress of the United States. Article I, Sec. 2, cl. 2, which applies to the House of Representatives, provides: "No Person shall be a Representative who shall not have attained to the Age of twenty-five Years, and been seven Years a Citizen of the United States, and who shall not, when elected, be an Inhabitant of that State in which he shall be chosen." Article I, Sec. 3, cl. 3, which applies to the Senate, similarly provides: "No Person shall be a Senator who shall not have attained to the Age of thirty Years, and been nine Years a Citizen of the United States, and who shall not, when elected, be an Inhabitant of that State for which he shall be chosen."

Today's cases present a challenge to an amendment to the Arkansas State Constitution that prohibits the name of an otherwise-eligible candidate for Congress from appearing on the general election ballot if that candidate has already served three terms in the House of Representatives or two terms in the Senate. The Arkansas Supreme Court held that the amendment violates the Federal Constitution. We agree with that holding. Such a state-imposed restriction is contrary to the "fundamental principle of our representative democracy," embodied in the Constitution, that "the people should choose whom they please to govern them." *Powell v. McCormack*, 395 U.S. 486 (1969). Allowing individual States to adopt their own qualifications for congressional service would be inconsistent with the Framers' vision of a uniform National Legislature representing the people of the United States. If the qualifications set forth in the text of the Constitution are to be changed, that text must be amended. . . .

Twenty-six years ago, in *Powell v. McCormack*, we reviewed the history and text of the Qualifications Clauses in a case involving an attempted exclusion of a duly elected Member of Congress. The principal issue was whether the power granted to each House in Art. I, Sec. 5, to judge the "Qualifications of its own Members" includes the power to impose qualifications other than those set forth in the text of the Constitution. In an opinion by Chief Justice WARREN for eight Members of the Court, we held that it does not. . . .

We started our analysis in *Powell* by examining the British experience with qualifications for membership in Parliament, focusing in particular on the experience of John Wilkes. While serving as a member of Parliament, Wilkes had published an attack on a peace treaty with France. This literary endeavor earned Wilkes a conviction for seditious libel and a 22-month prison sentence. In addition, Parliament declared Wilkes ineligible for membership and ordered him expelled. Despite (or perhaps because of) these difficulties, Wilkes was reelected several times. Parliament, however, persisted in its refusal to seat him. After several years of Wilkes' efforts, the House of Commons voted to expunge the resolutions that had expelled Wilkes and had declared him ineligible, labeling those prior actions "'subversive of the rights of the whole body of electors of this kingdom.'" After reviewing Wilkes' "long and bitter struggle for the right of the British electorate to be represented by men of their own choice," we concluded in *Powell* that "on the eve of the Constitutional Convention, English precedent stood for the proposition that 'the law of the land had regulated the qualifications of members to serve in parliament' and those qualifications were 'not occasional but fixed.'"

Against this historical background, we viewed the Convention debates as manifesting the Framers' intent that the qualifications in the Constitution be fixed and exclusive. We found particularly revealing the debate concerning a proposal made by the Committee of Detail that would have given Congress the power to add property qualifications. James Madison argued that such a power would vest "'an improper & dangerous power in the Legislature,'" by which the Legislature "'can by degrees subvert the Constitution.'" . . .

We also recognized in *Powell* that the post-Convention ratification debates confirmed that the Framers understood the qualifications in the Constitution to be fixed and unalterable by Congress. . . . Moreover, we reviewed the debates at the state conventions and found that they "also demonstrate the Framers' understanding that the qualifications for members of Congress had been fixed in the Constitution."

The exercise by Congress of its power to judge the qualifications of its Members further confirmed this understanding. We concluded that, during the first 100 years of its existence, "Congress strictly limited its power to judge the qualifications of its members to those enumerated in the Constitution."

As this elaborate summary reveals, our historical analysis in *Powell* was both detailed and persuasive. We thus conclude now, as we did in *Powell*, that history shows that, with respect to Congress, the Framers intended the Constitution to establish fixed qualifications. . . .

Our reaffirmation of *Powell* does not necessarily resolve the specific questions presented in these cases. For petitioners argue that whatever the constitutionality of additional qualifications for membership imposed by Congress, the historical and textual materials discussed in *Powell* do not support the conclusion that the Constitution prohibits additional qualifications imposed by States. In the absence of such a constitutional prohibition, petitioners argue, the Tenth Amendment and the principle of reserved powers require that States be allowed to add such qualifications. . . .

Contrary to petitioners' assertions, the power to add qualifications is not part of the original powers of sovereignty that the Tenth Amendment reserved to the States. Petitioners' Tenth Amendment argument misconceives the nature of the right at issue because that Amendment could only "reserve" that which existed before. As Justice STORY recognized, "the states can exercise no powers whatsoever, which exclusively spring out of the existence of the national government, which the constitution does not delegate to them. . . . No state can say, that it has reserved, what it never possessed." Justice STORY's position thus echoes that of Chief Justice MARSHALL in *McCulloch v. Maryland*, 17 U.S. 316 (1819). In *McCulloch*, the Court rejected the argument that the Constitution's silence on the subject of state power to tax corporations chartered by Congress implies that the States have "reserved" power to tax such federal instrumentalities. . . .

With respect to setting qualifications for service in Congress, no such right existed before the Constitution was ratified. The contrary argument overlooks the revolutionary character of the government that the Framers conceived. Prior to the adoption of the Constitution, the States had joined together under the Articles of Confederation. In that system, "the States retained most of their sovereignty, like independent nations bound together only by treaties." *Wesberry v. Sanders*, 376 U.S. 1 (1964). After the Constitutional Convention convened, the Framers were presented with, and eventually adopted a variation of, "a plan not merely to amend the Articles of Confederation but to create an entirely new National Government with a National Executive, National Judiciary, and a National Legislature." In adopting that plan, the Framers envisioned a uniform national system, rejecting the notion that the Nation was a collection of States, and instead creating a direct link between the National Government and the people of the United States. In that National Government, representatives owe primary allegiance not to the people of a State, but to the people of the Nation. . . .

Two other sections of the Constitution further support our view of the Framers' vision. First, consistent with STORY's view, the Constitution provides that the salaries of representatives should "be ascertained by Law, and paid out of the Treasury of the United States," Art. I, Sec. 6, rather than by individual States. The salary provisions reflect the view that representatives owe their allegiance to the people, and not to States. Second, the provisions governing elections reveal the Framers' understanding that powers over the election of federal officers had to be delegated to, rather than reserved by, the States. It is surely no coincidence that the context of federal elections provides one of the few areas in which the Constitution expressly requires action by the States, namely that "the Times, Places and Manner of holding Elections for Senators and Representatives, shall be prescribed in each State by the legislature thereof." This duty parallels the duty under Article II that "Each State shall appoint, in such Manner as the Legislature thereof may direct, a Number of Electors." Art. II., Sec. 1, cl. 2. These Clauses are express delegations of power to the States to act with respect to federal elections.

This conclusion is consistent with our previous recognition that, in certain limited contexts, the power to regulate the incidents of the federal system is not a reserved power of the States, but rather is delegated by the Constitution. . . .

We find further evidence of the Framers' intent in Art. 1, Sec. 5, cl. 1, which provides: "Each House shall be the Judge of the Elections, Returns and Qualifications of its own Members." That Art. I, Sec. 5 vests a federal tribunal with ultimate authority to judge a Member's qualifications is fully consistent with the understanding that those qualifications are fixed in the Federal Constitution, but not with the understanding that they can be altered by the States. If the States had the right to prescribe additional qualifications—such as property, educational, or professional qualifications —for their own representatives, state law would provide the standard for judging a Member's eligibility. As we concluded in *Murdock v. Memphis*, 87 U.S. 590 (1875), federal questions are generally answered finally by federal tribunals because rights which depend on federal law "should be the same everywhere" and "their construction should be uniform." . . . The Constitution's provision for each House to be the judge of its own qualifications thus provides further evidence that the Framers believed that the primary source of those qualifications would be federal law. . . .

Our conclusion that States lack the power to impose qualifications vindicates the same "fundamental principle of our representative democracy" that we recognized in *Powell*, namely that "the people should choose whom they please to govern them." As we noted earlier, the *Powell* Court recognized that an egalitarian ideal—that election to the National Legislature should be open to all people of merit—provided a critical foundation for the Constitutional structure. . . .

Similarly, we believe that state-imposed qualifications, as much as congressionally imposed qualifications, would undermine the second critical idea recognized in *Powell*: that an aspect of sovereignty is the right of the people to vote for whom they wish. Again, the source of the qualification is of little moment in assessing the qualification's restrictive impact.

Finally, state-imposed restrictions, unlike the congressionally imposed restrictions at issue in *Powell*, violate a third idea central to this basic principle: that the right to choose representatives belongs not to the States, but to the people. From the start, the Framers recognized that the "great and radical vice" of the Articles of Confederation was "the principle of LEGISLATION for STATES or GOVERNMENTS, in their CORPORATE or COLLECTIVE CAPACITIES, and as contradistinguished from the INDI-

VIDUALS of whom they consist." *The Federalist* No. 15 (Hamilton). Thus the Framers, in perhaps their most important contribution, conceived of a Federal Government directly responsible to the people, possessed of direct power over the people, and chosen directly, not by States, but by the people. The Framers implemented this ideal most clearly in the provision, extant from the beginning of the Republic, that calls for the Members of the House of Representatives to be "chosen every second Year by the People of the several States." Art. I, Sec. 2, cl. 1. Following the adoption of the 17th Amendment in 1913, this ideal was extended to elections for the Senate. The Congress of the United States, therefore, is not a confederation of nations in which separate sovereigns are represented by appointed delegates, but is instead a body composed of representatives of the people. . . .

Petitioners argue that, even if States may not add qualifications, Amendment 73 is constitutional because it is not such a qualification, and because Amendment 73 is a permissible exercise of state power to regulate the "Times, Places and Manner of Holding Elections." We reject these contentions.

Unlike Sections 1 and 2 of Amendment 73, which create absolute bars to service for long-term incumbents running for state office, Section 3 merely provides that certain Senators and Representatives shall not be certified as candidates and shall not have their names appear on the ballot. They may run as write-in candidates and, if elected, they may serve. Petitioners contend that only a legal bar to service creates an impermissible qualification, and that Amendment 73 is therefore consistent with the Constitution. . . .

The merits of term limits, or "rotation," have been the subject of debate since the formation of our Constitution, when the Framers unanimously rejected a proposal to add such limits to the Constitution. The cogent arguments on both sides of the question that were articulated during the process of ratification largely retain their force today. Over half the States have adopted measures that impose such limits on some offices either directly or indirectly, and the Nation as a whole, notably by constitutional amendment, has imposed a limit on the number of terms that the President may serve. Term limits, like any other qualification for office, unquestionably restrict the ability of voters to vote for whom they wish. On the other hand, such limits may provide for the infusion of fresh ideas and new perspectives, and may decrease the likelihood that representatives will lose touch with their constituents. It is not our province to resolve this longstanding debate.

We are, however, firmly convinced that allowing the several States to adopt term limits for congressional service would effect a fundamental change in the constitutional framework. Any such change must come not by legislation adopted either by Congress or by an individual State, but rather— as have other important changes in the electoral process—through the Amendment procedures set forth in Article V. The Framers decided that the qualifications for service in the Congress of the United States be fixed in the Constitution and be uniform throughout the Nation. That decision reflects the Framers' understanding that Members of Congress are chosen by separate constituencies, but that they become, when elected, servants of the people of the United States. They are not merely delegates appointed by separate, sovereign States; they occupy offices that are integral and essential components of a single National Government. In the absence of a properly passed constitutional amendment, allowing individual States to craft their own qualifications for Congress would thus erode the structure envisioned by the Framers, a structure that was designed, in the words of the Preamble to our Constitution, to form a "more perfect Union."

The judgment is affirmed.

Justice THOMAS, with whom the CHIEF JUSTICE, Justice O'CONNOR, and Justice SCALIA join, dissenting.

I dissent. Nothing in the Constitution deprives the people of each State of the power to prescribe eligibility requirements for the candidates who seek to represent them in Congress. The Constitution is simply silent on this question. And where the Constitution is silent, it raises no bar to action by the States or the people. . . .

Our system of government rests on one overriding principle: all power stems from the consent of the people. To phrase the principle in this way, however, is to be imprecise about something important to the notion of "reserved" powers. The ultimate source of the Constitution's authority is the consent of the people of each individual State, not the consent of the undifferentiated people of the Nation as a whole.

The ratification procedure erected by Article VII makes this point clear. The Constitution took effect once it had been ratified by the people gathered in convention in nine different States. But the Constitution went into effect only "between the States so ratifying the same," Art. VII; it did not bind the people of North Carolina until they had accepted it.

When they adopted the Federal Constitution, of course, the people of each State surrendered some of their authority to the United States (and hence to entities accountable to the people of other States as well as to themselves). They affirmatively deprived their States of certain powers, see, e.g., Art. I, Sec. 10, and they affirmatively conferred certain powers upon the Federal Government, see, e.g., Art. I, Sec. 8. Because the people of the several States are the only true source of power, however, the Federal Government enjoys no authority beyond what the Constitution confers: the Federal Government's powers are limited and enumerated. . . .

In each State, the remainder of the people's powers—"the powers not delegated to the United States by the Constitution, nor prohibited by it to the States," Amdt. 10—are either delegated to the state government or retained by the people. The Federal Constitution does not specify which of these two possibilities obtains; it is up to the various state constitutions to declare which powers the people of each State have delegated to their state government. As far as the Federal Constitution is concerned, then, the States can exercise all powers that the Constitution does not withhold from them. The Federal Government and the States thus face different default rules: where the Constitution is silent about the exercise of a particular power— that is, where the Constitution does not speak either expressly or by necessary implication—the Federal Government lacks that power and the States enjoy it.

These basic principles are enshrined in the Tenth Amendment, which declares that all powers neither delegated to the Federal Government nor prohibited to the States "are reserved to the States respectively, or to the people." With this careful last phrase, the Amendment avoids taking any position on the division of power between the state governments and the people of the States: it is up to the people of each State to determine which "reserved" powers their state government may exercise. But the Amendment does make clear that powers reside at the state level except where the Constitution removes them from that level. All powers that the Constitution neither delegates to the Federal Government nor prohibits to the States are controlled by the people of each State. . . .

The majority is therefore quite wrong to conclude that the people of the States cannot authorize their state governments to exercise any powers that were unknown to the States when the Federal Constitution was drafted. Indeed, the majority's position frustrates the apparent purpose of the Amendment's final phrase. The Amendment does not pre-empt any limitations on state power found in the state constitutions, as it might have done if it simply had said that the powers not delegated to the Federal Government are reserved to the States. But the Amendment also does not prevent the people of the States from amending their state constitutions to remove limitations that were in effect when the Federal Constitution and the Bill of Rights were ratified. . . .

The majority settles on "the Qualifications Clauses" as the constitutional provisions that Amendment 73 violates. Because I do not read those provisions to impose any unstated prohibitions on the States, it is unnecessary for me to decide whether the majority is correct to identify Arkansas' ballot-access restriction with laws fixing true term limits or otherwise prescribing "qualifications" for congressional office. . . . [T]he Qualifications Clauses are merely straightforward recitations of the minimum eligibility requirements that the Framers thought it essential for every Member of Congress to meet. They restrict state power only in that they prevent the States from abolishing all eligibility requirements for membership in Congress.

Because the text of the Qualifications Clauses does not support its position, the majority turns instead to its vision of the democratic principles that animated the Framers. But the majority's analysis goes to a question that is not before us: whether Congress has the power to prescribe qualifications for its own members. . . . [T]he democratic principles that contributed to the Framers' decision to withhold this power from Congress do not prove that the Framers also deprived the people of the States of their reserved authority to set eligibility requirements for their own representatives. . . .

To the extent that they bear on this case, the records of the Philadelphia Convention affirmatively support my unwillingness to find hidden meaning in the Qualifications Clauses, while the surviving records from the ratification debates help neither side. As for the postratification period, five States supplemented the constitutional disqualifications in their very first election laws. The historical evidence thus refutes any notion that the Qualifications Clauses were generally understood to be exclusive. Yet the majority must establish just such an understanding in order to justify its position that the Clauses impose unstated prohibitions on the States and the people. In my view, the historical evidence is simply inadequate to warrant the majority's conclusion that the Qualifications Clauses mean anything more than what they say. . . .

[T]oday's decision reads the Qualifications Clauses to impose substantial implicit prohibitions on the States and the people of the States. I would not draw such an expansive negative inference from the fact that the Constitution requires Members of Congress to be a certain age, to be inhabitants of the States that they represent, and to have been United States citizens for a specified period. Rather, I would read the Qualifications Clauses to do no more than what they say. I respectfully dissent.

6

CONGRESS: LEGISLATIVE, TAXING, AND SPENDING POWERS

WHEN CONGRESS ENACTED the controversial Civil Rights Act of 1991, which overrode numerous recent rulings of the Supreme Court (see "The Development of Law: Congress Reverses the Supreme Court—The Civil Rights Act of 1991," in Chapter 2 in Vols. 1 or 2), it could not agree on whether the law's provisions should apply retroactively to cases pending in the courts. Democrats argued that the law's provisions forbidding gender and racial harassment and discrimination in the workplace should apply retroactively, while Republicans and the Bush administration stood adamantly in opposition. In two rulings in 1994, the Court held eight to one that the Civil Rights Acts of 1991 does not apply retroactively. Writing for the majority in *Landgraf v. USI Film Products*, 114 S.Ct. 1483 (1994), and *Rivers v. Roadway Express*, 114 S.Ct. 1530 (1994), Justice Stevens issued a broad ruling holding that congressional legislation must explicitly state that it applies retroactively, otherwise the courts should presume that it does not. In *Landgraf*, a woman had sued a company in the mid-1980s after a co-worker repeatedly harassed her, which a trial court deemed not severe enough to force her to quit her job, and her appeal was pending when the 1991 law went into effect. In *Rivers*, two black mechanics challenged their firings as racially discriminatory, but before their suits were decided, the Supreme Court handed down decisions narrowing the scope of Section 1981 of the Civil Rights Act. When the Civil Rights Act of 1991 overrode those decisions, then, an appellate court held that the 1991 statute did not apply retroactively, and they appealed to the Supreme Court.

In Justice Stevens's words, "Since the early days of this Court, we have declined to give retroactive effect to statutes burdening private rights, unless Congress ha[s] made clear its intent." After examining the legislative history of the Civil Rights Act of 1991, Justice Stevens observed, "It seems likely that one of the compromises that made it possible to enact the 1991 version was an agreement *not* to include the kind of explicit retroactivity command found in the 1990 bill."

In a concurring opinion, however, Justice Scalia chided the majority for looking to the congressional history of the 1991 law and engaging in what he deemed "the soft science of legislative history." In his view, the Court should have rested its decision solely on the text of the statute. By contrast, dissenting Justice Blackmun argued that the majority's rulings in the two cases simply "prolongs the life of" the Court's prior rulings, which Congress had expressly repudiated, and insisted that "at no time within the last generation has an employer had a vested right to engage in or permit sexual harassment."

During its 1994–1995 term, the Court handed down an important ruling on Congress's power that signaled the emergence on the high bench of a majority willing to defend states' interests and to limit congressional power, at least in the area of expanding federal criminal law under the Commerce Clause. Writing for a bare majority in *United States v. Lopez* (excerpted below), Chief Justice Rehnquist struck down the Gun-Free School Zones Act of 1990, which had made it a federal crime to possess a firearm within 1,000 feet of a school. This was only the second ruling to limit Congress's power under the Commerce Clause in almost sixty years. Prior to the 1937 "constitutional crisis" over Franklin D. Roosevelt's "Court-packing plan," the Court struck down much of the New Deal legislation, including minimum-wage and maximum-hour regulations, as exceeding congressional power and intruding on areas of state authority (see Vol. 1, Chs. 7 and 8). While the chief justice's opinion in *Lopez* was written broadly, in a concurring opinion Justice Thomas appeared to go even further by calling into question the Court's post-1937 jurisprudence in the area. In another concurring opinion, joined by Justice O'Connor, Justice Kennedy struck a more measured tone but staunchly supported the majority's reconsideration of how to draw a line between national and state authority. Justices Stevens and Souter wrote separate dissenting opinions, while also joining, along with Justice Ginsburg, a major dissent by Justice Breyer, who sharply disagreed with both the majority's second-guessing of Congress in striking down the act and the basis for the majority's doing so, as well as its treatment of long-standing precedents upholding congressional power.

The ruling and reasoning in *Lopez* is certain to invite further litigation attacking the constitutionality of not only Congress's power to enact federal criminal law, but also legislation bearing on education, health, safety, and the environment. However, in another case handed down a week afterwards, the Court appeared to give pause. At issue in *United States v. Robertson*, 115 S.Ct. 1732 (1995), was whether the Racketeer Influenced and Corrupt Organizations Act (RICO) may be applied to a business, a small gold mine in Alaska, that operates within the borders of a single state. The RICO Act makes it a crime to invest the earnings from racketeering in a business "the activities of which affect interstate or foreign commerce." The Court of Appeals for the Ninth Circuit had reversed the conviction of Juan Robertson under the RICO Act on the ground that federal prosecutors failed to produce sufficient evidence showing that the gold mine, in which Robertson had invested money from drug-dealing, was "engaged in or affected interstate commerce." After granting the government's appeal but before hearing oral arguments, the justices reversed the appellate court's decision in a brief *per curiam* opinion, holding that there was sufficient evidence that the mine was within the RICO Act's "affecting commerce" provision, since Robertson, a resident of Arizona, had shipped equipment from out of state and had hired out-of-state workers to work at the mine. Notably, though, the Court expressly declined to address whether those activities would meet *Lopez*'s "substantially affecting commerce" requirement.

United States v. Lopez
115 S.Ct. 1624 (1995)

Shortly after the enactment of the Gun-Free School Zones Act of 1990, which made it a federal crime to possess a firearm within 1,000 feet of public or private schools, Alfonso Lopez, Jr., a twelfth-grade student, was arrested for carrying a .38 caliber handgun into Edison High School in San Antonio, Texas. Lopez was initially charged with violating Texas's law against firearm possession on school premises, but those charges were dropped after federal agents charged him with violating the Gun-Free School Zones Act. Subsequently, a federal district court found Lopez guilty and sentenced him to six months' imprisonment and two years' probation. On appeal, Lopez's attorneys challenged his conviction on the ground the Gun-Free School Zones Act was unconstitutional because Congress exceeded its power under the Commerce Clause in enacting the legislation. The Court of Appeals for the Fifth Circuit agreed and reversed his conviction. The federal government appealed that decision.

The Court's decision was five to four and the majority's opinion was announced by Chief Justice Rehnquist. Justices Kennedy and Thomas filed concurring opinions. Justices Stevens, Souter, and Breyer filed dissenting opinions, which Justice Ginsburg joined.

Chief Justice REHNQUIST delivered the opinion of the Court.

We start with first principles. The Constitution creates a Federal Government of enumerated powers. As James Madison wrote, "the powers delegated by the proposed Constitution to the federal government are few and defined. Those which are to remain in the State governments are numerous and indefinite." *The Federalist* No. 45. . . . The Constitution delegates to Congress the power "to regulate Commerce with foreign Nations, and among the several States, and with the Indian Tribes." The Court, through Chief Justice MARSHALL, first defined the nature of Congress' commerce power in *Gibbons v. Ogden*, 9 Wheat. 1 (1824): "Commerce, undoubtedly, is traffic, but it is something more: it is intercourse. It describes the commercial intercourse between nations, and parts of nations, in all its branches, and is regulated by prescribing rules for carrying on that intercourse." The commerce power "is the power to regulate; that is, to prescribe the rule by which commerce is to be governed. This power, like all others vested in Congress, is complete in itself, may be exercised to its utmost extent, and acknowledges no limitations, other than are prescribed in the constitution." The *Gibbons* Court, however, acknowledged that limitations on the commerce power are inherent in the very language of the Commerce Clause. "It is not intended to say that these words comprehend that commerce, which is completely internal, which is carried on between man and man in a State, or between different parts of the same State, and which does not extend to or affect other States. Such a power would be inconvenient, and is certainly unnecessary." "Comprehensive as the word 'among' is, it may very properly be restricted to that commerce which concerns more States than one. . . . The enumeration presupposes something not enumerated; and that something, if we regard the language or the subject of the sentence, must be the exclusively internal commerce of a State." Id.

For nearly a century thereafter, the Court's Commerce Clause decisions dealt but rarely with the extent of Congress' power, and almost entirely with the Commerce Clause as a limit on state legislation that discriminated against interstate commerce. Under this line of precedent, the Court held that certain categories of activity such as "production," "manufacturing," and "mining" were within the province of state governments, and thus beyond the power of Congress under the Commerce Clause. See *Wickard v. Filburn*, 317 U.S. 111 (1942) (describing development of Commerce Clause jurisprudence).

In 1887, Congress enacted the Interstate Commerce Act, and in 1890, Congress enacted the Sherman Antitrust Act. These laws ushered in a new era of federal regulation under the commerce power. When cases involving these laws first reached this Court, we imported from our negative Commerce Clause cases the approach that Congress could not regulate activities such as "production," "manufacturing," and "mining." See, e.g., *United States v. E. C. Knight Co.*, 156 U.S. 1 (1895) ("Commerce succeeds to manufacture, and is not part of it"); *Carter v. Carter Coal Co.*, 298 U.S. 238 (1936) ("Mining brings the subject matter of commerce into existence. Commerce disposes of it."). Simultaneously, however, the Court held that, where the interstate and intrastate aspects of commerce were so mingled together that full regulation of interstate commerce required incidental regulation of intrastate commerce, the Commerce Clause authorized such regulation.

In *A. L. A. Schecter Poultry Corp. v. United States*, 295 U.S. 495 (1935), the Court struck down regulations that fixed the hours and wages of individuals employed by an intrastate business because the activity being regulated related to interstate commerce only indirectly. In doing so, the Court characterized the distinction between direct and indirect effects of intrastate transactions upon interstate commerce as "a fundamental one, essential to the maintenance of our constitutional system." . . .

Two years later, in the watershed case of *NLRB v. Jones & Laughlin Steel Corp.*, 301 U.S. 1 (1937), the Court upheld the National Labor Relations Act against a Commerce Clause challenge, and in the process, departed from the distinction between "direct" and "indirect" effects on interstate commerce. The Court held that intrastate activities that "have such a close and substantial relation to interstate commerce that their control is essential or appropriate to protect that commerce from burdens and obstructions" are within Congress' power to regulate.

In *United States v. Darby*, 312 U.S. 100 (1941), the Court upheld the Fair Labor Standards Act, stating: "The power of Congress over interstate commerce is not confined to the regulation of commerce among the states. It extends to those activities intrastate which so affect interstate commerce or the exercise of the power of Congress over it as to make regulation of them appropriate means to the attainment of a legitimate end, the exercise of the granted power of Congress to regulate interstate commerce."

In *Wickard v. Filburn*, the Court upheld the application of amendments to the Agricultural Adjustment Act of 1938 to the production and consumption of home-grown wheat. The *Wickard* Court explicitly rejected earlier distinctions between direct and indirect effects on interstate commerce, stating: "Even if appellee's activity be local and though it may not be regarded as commerce, it may still, whatever its nature, be reached by Congress if it exerts a substantial economic effect on interstate commerce, and this irrespective of whether such effect is what might at some earlier time have been defined as 'direct' or 'indirect.'" . . .

Jones & Laughlin Steel, *Darby*, and *Wickard* ushered in an era of Commerce Clause jurisprudence that greatly expanded the previously defined authority of Congress under that Clause. In part, this was a recognition of the great changes that had occurred in the way business was carried on in this country. Enterprises that had once been local or at most regional in nature had become national in scope. But the doctrinal change also reflected a view that earlier Commerce Clause cases artificially had constrained the authority of Congress to regulate interstate commerce.

But even these modern-era precedents which have expanded congressional power under the Commerce Clause confirm that this power is subject to outer limits. In *Jones & Laughlin Steel*, the Court warned that the scope of the interstate commerce power "must be considered in the light of our dual system of government and may not be extended so as to embrace effects upon interstate commerce so indirect and remote that to embrace them, in view of our complex society, would effectually obliterate the distinction between what is national and what is local and create a completely centralized government." Since that time, the Court has heeded that warning and undertaken to decide whether a rational basis existed for concluding that a regulated activity sufficiently affected interstate commerce.

Similarly, in *Maryland v. Wirtz*, 392 U.S. 183 (1968), the Court reaffirmed that "the power to regulate commerce, though broad indeed, has limits" that "the Court has ample power" to enforce. In response to the dissent's warnings that the Court was powerless to enforce the limitations on Congress' commerce powers because "all activities affecting commerce, even in the minutest degree, [*Wickard*], may be regulated and controlled by Congress," (DOUGLAS, J., dissenting), the *Wirtz* Court replied that the dissent had misread precedent as "neither here nor in *Wickard* has the Court declared that Congress may use a relatively trivial impact on commerce as an excuse for broad general regulation of state or private activities." Rather, "the Court has said only that where a general regulatory statute bears a substantial relation to commerce, the de minimis character of individual instances arising under that statute is of no consequence."

Consistent with this structure, we have identified three broad categories of activity that Congress may regulate under its commerce power. First, Congress may regulate the use of the channels of interstate commerce. Second, Congress is empowered to regulate and protect the instrumentalities of interstate commerce, or persons or things in interstate commerce, even though the threat may come only from intrastate activities. Finally, Congress' commerce authority includes the power to regulate those activities having a substantial relation to interstate commerce, those activities that substantially affect interstate commerce.

Within this final category, admittedly, our case law has not been clear whether an activity must "affect" or "substantially affect" interstate commerce in order to be within Congress' power to regulate it under the Commerce Clause. We conclude, consistent with the great weight of our case law, that the proper test requires an analysis of whether the regulated activity "substantially affects" interstate commerce.

We now turn to consider the power of Congress, in the light of this framework, to enact Section 922(q). The first two categories of authority may be quickly disposed of: Section 922(q) is not a regulation of the use of the channels of interstate commerce, nor is it an attempt to prohibit the interstate transportation of a commodity through the channels of commerce; nor can Section 922(q) be justified as a regulation by which Congress has sought to protect an instrumentality of interstate commerce or a thing in interstate commerce. Thus, if Section 922(q) is to be sustained, it must be under the third category as a regulation of an activity that substantially affects interstate commerce.

First, we have upheld a wide variety of congressional Acts regulating intrastate economic activity where we have concluded that the activity substantially affected interstate commerce. Examples include the regulation of intrastate coal mining; intrastate extortionate credit transactions, restaurants utilizing substantial interstate supplies, inns and hotels catering to interstate guests, and production and consumption of home-grown wheat. These examples are by no means exhaustive, but the pattern is clear. Where economic activity substantially affects interstate commerce, legislation regulating that activity will be sustained. . . .

Section 922(q) is a criminal statute that by its terms has nothing to do with "commerce" or any sort of economic enterprise, however broadly one might define those terms. Section 922(q) is not an essential part of a larger regulation of economic activity, in which the regulatory scheme could be undercut unless the intrastate activity were regulated. It cannot, therefore, be sustained under our cases upholding regulations of activities that arise out of or are connected with a commercial transaction, which viewed in the aggregate, substantially affects interstate commerce. . . .

The Government's essential contention, in fine, is that we may determine here that Section 922(q) is valid because possession of a firearm in a local school zone does indeed substantially affect interstate commerce. The Government argues that possession of a firearm in a school zone may result in violent crime and that violent crime can be expected to affect the functioning of the national economy in two ways. First, the costs of violent crime are substantial, and, through the mechanism of insurance, those costs are spread throughout the population. Second, violent crime reduces the willingness of individuals to travel to areas within the country that are perceived to be unsafe. The Government also argues that the presence of guns in schools poses a substantial threat to the educational process by threatening the learning environment. A handicapped educational process, in turn, will result in a less productive citizenry. That, in turn, would have an adverse effect on the Nation's economic well-being. As a result, the Government argues that Congress could rationally have concluded that Section 922(q) substantially affects interstate commerce.

We pause to consider the implications of the Government's arguments. The Government admits, under its "costs of crime" reasoning, that Congress could regulate not only all violent crime, but all activities that might lead to violent crime, regardless of how tenuously they relate to interstate commerce. . . . [I]f we were to accept the Government's arguments, we are hard-pressed to posit any activity by an individual that Congress is without power to regulate. . . .

To uphold the Government's contentions here, we would have to pile inference upon inference in a manner that would bid fair to convert congressional authority under the Commerce Clause to a general police power of the sort retained by the States. Admittedly, some of our prior cases have taken long steps down that road, giving great deference to congressional action. The broad language in these opinions has suggested the possibility of additional expansion, but we decline here to proceed any further. To do so would require us to conclude that the Constitution's enumeration of powers does not presuppose something not enumerated, and that there never will be a distinction between what is truly national and what is truly local. This we are unwilling to do.

For the foregoing reasons the judgment of the Court of Appeals is Affirmed.

Justice THOMAS, concurring.

Although I join the majority, I write separately to observe that our case law has drifted far from the original understanding of the Commerce Clause. In a future case, we ought to temper our Commerce Clause jurisprudence in a manner that both makes sense of our more recent case law and is more faithful to the original understanding of that Clause. . . . In an appropriate case, I believe that we must further reconsider our "substantial effects" test with an eye toward constructing a standard that reflects the text and history of the Commerce Clause without totally rejecting our more recent Commerce Clause jurisprudence. . . .

At the time the original Constitution was ratified, "commerce" consisted of selling, buying, and bartering, as well as transporting for these purposes. As one would expect, the term "commerce" was used in contradistinction to productive activities such as manufacturing and agriculture. Alexander Hamilton, for example, repeatedly treated commerce, agriculture, and manufacturing as three separate endeavors. See, e.g., *The Federalist* No. 36, (referring to "agriculture, commerce, manufactures"); id., No. 21 (distinguishing commerce, arts, and industry); id., No. 12 (asserting that commerce and agriculture have shared interests).

Moreover, interjecting a modern sense of commerce into the Constitution generates significant textual and structural problems. For example, one cannot replace "commerce" with a different type of enterprise, such as manufacturing. When a manufacturer produces a car, assembly cannot take place "with a foreign nation" or "with the Indian Tribes." Parts may come from different States or other nations and hence may have been in the flow of commerce at one time, but manufacturing takes place at a discrete site. Agriculture and manufacturing involve the production of goods; commerce encompasses traffic in such articles. . . .

The Constitution not only uses the word "commerce" in a narrower sense than our case law might suggest, it also does not support the proposition that Congress has authority over all activities that "substantially affect" interstate commerce. The Commerce Clause does not state that Congress may "regulate matters that substantially affect commerce with foreign Nations, and among the several States, and with the Indian Tribes." In contrast, the Constitution itself temporarily prohibited amendments that would "affect" Congress' lack of authority to prohibit or restrict the slave trade or to enact unproportioned direct taxation. . . .

Put simply, much if not all of Art. I, Section 8 (including portions of the Commerce Clause itself) would be surplusage if Congress had been given authority over matters that substantially affect interstate commerce. An interpretation of cl. 3 that makes the rest of Section 8 superfluous simply cannot be correct. Yet this Court's Commerce Clause jurisprudence has endorsed just such an interpretation: the power we have accorded Congress has swallowed Art. I, Section 8.

Indeed, if a "substantial effects" test can be appended to the Commerce Clause, why not to every other power of the Federal Government? There is no reason for singling out the Commerce Clause for special treatment. Accordingly, Congress could regulate all matters that "substantially affect" the Army and Navy, bankruptcies, tax collection, expenditures, and so on. In that case, the clauses of Section 8 all mutually overlap, something we can assume the Founding Fathers never intended.

Our construction of the scope of congressional authority has the additional problem of coming close to turning the Tenth Amendment on its head. Our case law could be read to reserve to the United States all powers not expressly prohibited by the Constitution. Taken together, these fundamental textual problems should, at the very least, convince us that the "substantial effects" test should be reexamined. . . .

Apart from its recent vintage and its corresponding lack of any grounding in the original understanding of the Constitution, the substantial effects test suffers from the further flaw that it appears to grant Congress a police power over the Nation. When asked at oral argument if there were any limits to the Commerce Clause, the Government was at a loss for words. Likewise, the principal dissent insists that there are limits, but it cannot muster even one example. . . .

The substantial effects test suffers from this flaw, in part, because of its "aggregation principle." Under so-called "class of activities" statutes, Congress can regulate whole categories of activities that are not themselves either "interstate" or "commerce." In applying the effects test, we ask whether the class of activities as a whole substantially affects interstate commerce, not whether any specific activity within the class has such effects when considered in isolation.

The aggregation principle is clever, but has no stopping point. Suppose all would agree that gun possession within 1,000 feet of a school does not substantially affect commerce, but that possession of weapons generally (knives, brass knuckles, nunchakus, etc.) does. Under our substantial effects doctrine, even though Congress cannot single out gun possession, it can prohibit weapon possession generally. But one always can draw the circle broadly enough to cover an activity that, when taken in isolation, would not have substantial effects on commerce. Under our jurisprudence, if Congress passed an omnibus "substantially affects interstate commerce" statute, purporting to regulate every aspect of human existence, the Act apparently would be constitutional. Even though particular sections may govern only trivial activities, the statute in the aggregate regulates matters that substantially affect commerce.

This extended discussion . . . reveals that our substantial effects test is far removed from both the Constitution and from our early case law and that the Court's opinion should not be viewed as "radical" or another "wrong turn" that must be corrected in the future. . . .

Justice SOUTER, dissenting.

In reviewing congressional legislation under the Commerce Clause, we defer to what is often a merely implicit congressional judgment that its regulation addresses a subject substantially affecting interstate commerce "if there is any rational basis for such a finding." *Hodel v. Virginia Surface Mining & Reclamation Assn., Inc.*, 452 U.S. 264 (1981). If that congressional determination is within the realm of reason, "the only remaining question for judicial inquiry is whether 'the means chosen by Congress [are] reasonably adapted to the end permitted by the Constitution.'" *Hodel*, quoting *Heart of Atlanta Motel, Inc. v. United States*, 379 U.S. 241 (1964).

The practice of deferring to rationally based legislative judgments "is a paradigm of judicial restraint." In judicial review under the Commerce Clause, it reflects our respect for the institutional competence of the Congress on a subject expressly assigned to it by the Constitution and our

appreciation of the legitimacy that comes from Congress's political accountability in dealing with matters open to a wide range of possible choices.

It was not ever thus, however, as even a brief overview of Commerce
Clause history during the past century reminds us. The modern respect for
the competence and primacy of Congress in matters affecting commerce
developed only after one of this Court's most chastening experiences, when
it perforce repudiated an earlier and untenably expansive conception of
judicial review in derogation of congressional commerce power. A look at
history's sequence will serve to show how today's decision tugs the Court
off course, leading it to suggest opportunities for further developments that
would be at odds with the rule of restraint to which the Court still wisely
states adherence.

Notwithstanding the Court's recognition of a broad commerce power in
Gibbons v. Ogden, 9 Wheat. 1 (1824) (MARSHALL, C. J.), Congress saw
few occasions to exercise that power prior to Reconstruction, and it was
really the passage of the Interstate Commerce Act of 1887 that opened a new
age of congressional reliance on the Commerce Clause for authority to
exercise general police powers at the national level. Although the Court
upheld a fair amount of the ensuing legislation as being within the
commerce power, the period from the turn of the century to 1937 is better
noted for a series of cases applying highly formalistic notions of
"commerce" to invalidate federal social and economic legislation, see, e.g.,
Carter v. Carter Coal Co., 298 U.S. 238 (1936) (striking Act prohibiting
unfair labor practices in coal industry as regulation of "mining" and
"production," not "commerce"); *A. L. A. Schechter Poultry Corp. v. United
States*, 295 U.S. 495 (1935) (striking congressional regulation of activities
affecting interstate commerce only "indirectly"); *Hammer v. Dagenhart*, 247
U.S. 251 (1918) (striking Act prohibiting shipment in interstate commerce
of goods manufactured at factories using child labor because the Act
regulated "manufacturing," not "commerce"); *Adair v. United States*, 208
U.S. 161 (1908) (striking protection of labor union membership as outside
"commerce").

These restrictive views of commerce subject to congressional power
complemented the Court's activism in limiting the enforceable scope of state
economic regulation. It is most familiar history that during this same period
the Court routinely invalidated state social and economic legislation under
an expansive conception of Fourteenth Amendment substantive due process.
See, e.g., *Lochner v. New York*, 198 U.S. 45 (1905) (striking state law
establishing maximum working hours for bakers). The fulcrums of judicial
review in these cases were the notions of liberty and property characteristic
of laissez-faire economics, whereas the Commerce Clause cases turned on
what was ostensibly a structural limit of federal power, but under each
conception of judicial review the Court's character for the first third of the
century showed itself in exacting judicial scrutiny of a legislature's choice of
economic ends and of the legislative means selected to reach them.

It was not merely coincidental, then, that sea changes in the Court's con-
ceptions of its authority under the Due Process and Commerce Clauses
occurred virtually together, in 1937, with *West Coast Hotel Co. v. Parrish*,
[300 U.S. 379], and *NLRB v. Jones & Laughlin Steel Corp.*, 301 U.S. 1. . . .
In *West Coast Hotel*, the Court's rejection of a due process challenge to a

state law fixing minimum wages for women and children marked the abandonment of its expansive protection of contractual freedom. Two weeks
later, *Jones & Laughlin* affirmed congressional commerce power to authorize NLRB injunctions against unfair labor practices. The Court's finding that
the regulated activity had a direct enough effect on commerce has since been
seen as beginning the abandonment, for practical purposes, of the formalistic
distinction between direct and indirect effects.

In the years following these decisions, deference to legislative policy
judgments on commercial regulation became the powerful theme under both
the Due Process and Commerce Clauses, and in due course that deference
became articulate in the standard of rationality review. In due process
litigation, the Court's statement of a rational basis test came quickly. The
parallel formulation of the Commerce Clause test came later, only because
complete elimination of the direct/indirect effects dichotomy and acceptance
of the cumulative effects doctrine, *Wickard v. Filburn*, 317 U.S. 111 (1942),
so far settled the pressing issues of congressional power over commerce as
to leave the Court for years without any need to phrase a test explicitly
deferring to rational legislative judgments. The moment came, however,
with the challenge to congressional Commerce Clause authority to prohibit
racial discrimination in places of public accommodation, when the Court
simply made explicit what the earlier cases had implied: "where we find that
the legislators, in light of the facts and testimony before them, have a
rational basis for finding a chosen regulatory scheme necessary to the
protection of commerce, our investigation is at an end." *Katzenbach v.
McClung*, 379 U.S. 294 (1964), discussing *United States v. Darby*; see
Heart of Atlanta Motel, Inc. v. United States, 379 U.S. 241 (1964). Thus,
under commerce, as under due process, adoption of rational basis review
expressed the recognition that the Court had no sustainable basis for subjecting economic regulation as such to judicial policy judgments, and for the
past half-century the Court has no more turned back in the direction of
formalistic Commerce Clause review (as in deciding whether regulation of
commerce was sufficiently direct) than it has inclined toward reasserting the
substantive authority of *Lochner* due process (as in the inflated protection of
contractual autonomy).

There is today, however, a backward glance at both the old pitfalls, as the
Court treats deference under the rationality rule as subject to gradation
according to the commercial or noncommercial nature of the immediate
subject of the challenged regulation. The distinction between what is patently commercial and what is not looks much like the old distinction
between what directly affects commerce and what touches it only indirectly.
And the act of calibrating the level of deference by drawing a line between
what is patently commercial and what is less purely so will probably
resemble the process of deciding how much interference with contractual
freedom was fatal. Thus, it seems fair to ask whether the step taken by the
Court today does anything but portend a return to the untenable jurisprudence from which the Court extricated itself almost 60 years ago. The
answer is not reassuring. To be sure, the occasion for today's decision
reflects the century's end, not its beginning. But if it seems anomalous that
the Congress of the United States has taken to regulating school yards, the
act in question is still probably no more remarkable than state regulation of

bake shops 90 years ago. In any event, there is no reason to hope that the Court's qualification of rational basis review will be any more successful than the efforts at substantive economic review made by our predecessors as the century began. Taking the Court's opinion on its own terms, Justice BREYER has explained both the hopeless porosity of "commercial" character as a ground of Commerce Clause distinction in America's highly connected economy, and the inconsistency of this categorization with our rational basis precedents from the last 50 years. . . .

Justice BREYER, with whom Justice STEVENS, Justice SOUTER, and Justice GINSBURG join, dissenting.

In my view, the statute falls well within the scope of the commerce power as this Court has understood that power over the last half-century.

In reaching this conclusion, I apply three basic principles of Commerce Clause interpretation. First, the power to "regulate Commerce . . . among the several States" encompasses the power to regulate local activities insofar as they significantly affect interstate commerce. See, e.g., *Gibbons v. Ogden*, 9 Wheat. 1 (1824) (MARSHALL, C. J.); *Wickard v. Filburn*, 317 U.S. 111 (1942). As the majority points out, the Court, in describing how much of an effect the Clause requires, sometimes has used the word "substantial" and sometimes has not. . . . I use the word "significant" because the word "substantial" implies a somewhat narrower power than recent precedent suggests. But, to speak of "substantial effect" rather than "significant effect" would make no difference in this case.

Second, in determining whether a local activity will likely have a significant effect upon interstate commerce, a court must consider, not the effect of an individual act (a single instance of gun possession), but rather the cumulative effect of all similar instances (i.e., the effect of all guns possessed in or near schools). Third, the Constitution requires us to judge the connection between a regulated activity and interstate commerce, not directly, but at one remove. Courts must give Congress a degree of leeway in determining the existence of a significant factual connection between the regulated activity and interstate commerce—both because the Constitution delegates the commerce power directly to Congress and because the determination requires an empirical judgment of a kind that a legislature is more likely than a court to make with accuracy. The traditional words "rational basis" capture this leeway. . . .

Applying these principles to the case at hand, we must ask whether Congress could have had a rational basis for finding a significant (or substantial) connection between gun-related school violence and interstate commerce. Or, to put the question in the language of the explicit finding that Congress made when it amended this law in 1994: Could Congress rationally have found that "violent crime in school zones," through its effect on the "quality of education," significantly (or substantially) affects "interstate" or "foreign commerce"? As long as one views the commerce connection, not as a "technical legal conception," but as "a practical one," *Swift & Co. v. United States*, 196 U.S. 375 (1905) (HOLMES, J.), the answer to this question must be yes. Numerous reports and studies—generated both inside and outside government—make clear that Congress could reasonably have found the empirical connection that its law, implicitly or explicitly, asserts.

For one thing, reports, hearings, and other readily available literature make clear that the problem of guns in and around schools is widespread and extremely serious. These materials report, for example, that four percent of American high school students (and six percent of inner-city high school students) carry a gun to school at least occasionally; that 12 percent of urban high school students have had guns fired at them; that 20 percent of those students have been threatened with guns; and that, in any 6-month period, several hundred thousand schoolchildren are victims of violent crimes in or near their schools. And, they report that this widespread violence in schools throughout the Nation significantly interferes with the quality of education in those schools. Based on reports such as these, Congress obviously could have thought that guns and learning are mutually exclusive. And, Congress could therefore have found a substantial educational problem—teachers unable to teach, students unable to learn—and concluded that guns near schools contribute substantially to the size and scope of that problem.

Having found that guns in schools significantly undermine the quality of education in our Nation's classrooms, Congress could also have found, given the effect of education upon interstate and foreign commerce, that gun-related violence in and around schools is a commercial, as well as a human, problem. Education, although far more than a matter of economics, has long been inextricably intertwined with the Nation's economy. When this Nation began, most workers received their education in the workplace, typically (like Benjamin Franklin) as apprentices. As late as the 1920's, many workers still received general education directly from their employers —from large corporations, such as General Electric, Ford, and Goodyear, which created schools within their firms to help both the worker and the firm. (Throughout most of the 19th century fewer than one percent of all Americans received secondary education through attending a high school.) As public school enrollment grew in the early 20th century, the need for industry to teach basic educational skills diminished. But, the direct economic link between basic education and industrial productivity remained. Scholars estimate that nearly a quarter of America's economic growth in the early years of this century is traceable directly to increased schooling. . . . Increasing global competition also has made primary and secondary education economically more important. . . .

The economic links I have just sketched seem fairly obvious. Why then is it not equally obvious, in light of those links, that a widespread, serious, and substantial physical threat to teaching and learning also substantially threatens the commerce to which that teaching and learning is inextricably tied? That is to say, guns in the hands of six percent of inner-city high school students and gun-related violence throughout a city's schools must threaten the trade and commerce that those schools support. The only question, then, is whether the latter threat is (to use the majority's terminology) "substantial." And, the evidence of (1) the extent of the gun-related violence problem, (2) the extent of the resulting negative effect on classroom learning, and (3) the extent of the consequent negative commercial effects, when taken together, indicate a threat to trade and commerce that is "substantial." At the very least, Congress could rationally have concluded that the links are "substantial."

In sum, a holding that the particular statute before us falls within the commerce power would not expand the scope of that Clause. Rather, it simply would apply pre-existing law to changing economic circumstances. See *Heart of Atlanta Motel, Inc. v. United States*, 379 U.S. 241 (1964). It would recognize that, in today's economic world, gun-related violence near the classroom makes a significant difference to our economic, as well as our social, well-being. . . .

The majority's holding—that Section 922 falls outside the scope of the Commerce Clause—creates three serious legal problems. First, the majority's holding runs contrary to modern Supreme Court cases that have upheld congressional actions despite connections to interstate or foreign commerce that are less significant than the effect of school violence. . . .

In *Katzenbach v. McClung*, 379 U.S. 294 (1964), this Court upheld, as within the commerce power, a statute prohibiting racial discrimination at local restaurants, in part because that discrimination discouraged travel by African Americans and in part because that discrimination affected purchases of food and restaurant supplies from other States. In *Daniel v. Paul*, 395 U.S. 298 (1969), this Court found an effect on commerce caused by an amusement park located several miles down a country road in the middle of Alabama—because some customers (the Court assumed), some food, 15 paddleboats, and a jukebox had come from out of State. In both of these cases, the Court understood that the specific instance of discrimination (at a local place of accommodation) was part of a general practice that, considered as a whole, caused not only the most serious human and social harm, but had nationally significant economic dimensions as well. It is difficult to distinguish the case before us, for the same critical elements are present. . . . Most importantly, like the local racial discrimination at issue in *McClung* and *Daniel*, the local instances here, taken together and considered as a whole, create a problem that causes serious human and social harm, but also has nationally significant economic dimensions. . . .

The second legal problem the Court creates comes from its apparent belief that it can reconcile its holding with earlier cases by making a critical distinction between "commercial" and noncommercial "transaction[s]." That is to say, the Court believes the Constitution would distinguish between two local activities, each of which has an identical effect upon interstate commerce, if one, but not the other, is "commercial" in nature. As a general matter, this approach fails to heed this Court's earlier warning not to turn "questions of the power of Congress" upon "formulas" that would give "controlling force to nomenclature such as 'production' and 'indirect' and foreclose consideration of the actual effects of the activity in question upon interstate commerce." *Wickard*. Moreover, the majority's test is not consistent with what the Court saw as the point of the cases that the majority now characterizes. Although the majority today attempts to categorize *Perez* [*v. United States*, 402 U.S. 146 (1971)], *McClung*, and *Wickard* as involving intrastate "economic activity," the Courts that decided each of those cases did not focus upon the economic nature of the activity regulated. Rather, they focused upon whether that activity affected interstate or foreign commerce. In fact, the *Wickard* Court expressly held that *Wickard's* consumption of home grown wheat, "though it may not be regarded as commerce," could nevertheless be regulated—"whatever its nature"—so long as "it exerts a substantial economic effect on interstate commerce." . . .

Regardless, if there is a principled distinction that could work both here and in future cases, Congress (even in the absence of vocational classes, industry involvement, and private management) could rationally conclude that schools fall on the commercial side of the line. In 1990, the year Congress enacted the statute before us, primary and secondary schools spent $230 billion—that is, nearly a quarter of a trillion dollars—which accounts for a significant portion of our $5.5 trillion Gross Domestic Product for that year. . . . Certainly, Congress has often analyzed school expenditure as if it were a commercial investment, closely analyzing whether schools are efficient, whether they justify the significant resources they spend, and whether they can be restructured to achieve greater returns. Why could Congress, for Commerce Clause purposes, not consider schools as roughly analogous to commercial investments from which the Nation derives the benefit of an educated work force?

The third legal problem created by the Court's holding is that it threatens legal uncertainty in an area of law that, until this case, seemed reasonably well settled. Congress has enacted many statutes (more than 100 sections of the United States Code), including criminal statutes (at least 25 sections), that use the words "affecting commerce" to define their scope. Do these, or similar, statutes regulate noncommercial activities? If so, would that alter the meaning of "affecting commerce" in a jurisdictional element? More importantly, in the absence of a jurisdictional element, are the courts nevertheless to take *Wickard* (and later similar cases) as inapplicable, and to judge the effect of a single noncommercial activity on interstate commerce without considering similar instances of the forbidden conduct? However these questions are eventually resolved, the legal uncertainty now created will restrict Congress' ability to enact criminal laws aimed at criminal behavior that, considered problem by problem rather than instance by instance, seriously threatens the economic, as well as social, well-being of Americans. . . .

7

THE STATES AND
AMERICAN FEDERALISM

A. STATES' POWER OVER COMMERCE
AND REGULATION

As usual, the Court took a fair number of commerce clause cases in its 1993–1995 terms. (See "The Development of Law" boxes in this chapter.) In particular, and as has become more common since the late 1980s, the Court again confronted challenges to state and local attempts to regulate the disposal of hazardous waste. In *Oregon Waste Systems, Inc. v. Department of Environmental Quality of the State of Oregon*, 114 S.Ct. 1345 (1994), the Court again struck down a state law imposing a surcharge on the disposal of solid waste generated outside of the state's borders as a violation of the dormant commerce clause. Under a 1989 law, Oregon imposed a fee of $3.10 per ton on the disposal of out-of-state waste in its landfills. Writing for the Court, Justice Thomas overturned the law as economic protectionism that unconstitutionally discriminated against interstate commerce. "Discrimination simply means differential treatment of in-state and out-of-state economic interests that benefits the former and burdens the latter," Justice Thomas observed when holding that "if a restriction on commerce is discriminatory, it is virtually per se invalid."

Chief Justice Rehnquist, joined by Justice Blackmun, dissented and countered that "Oregon should be applauded" for developing a comprehensive plan for its solid-waste disposal problem. "The Court today leaves states with only two options," argued the chief justice, "become a dumper and ship as much waste as possible to a less populated state or become a dumpee, and stoically accept waste from more densely populated states." Concluding, Chief Justice Rehnquist added, "I see nothing in the commerce clause that compels less densely populated states to serve as the low-cost dumping grounds for their neighbors."

46

As in *United States v. Lopez*, 115 S.Ct. 1624 (1995) (see Chapter 6), in the 1995–1996 term Chief Justice Rehnquist mustered a bare majority for limiting congressional power and defending states' autonomy. Writing for the Court in *Seminole Tribe of Florida v. Florida* (excerpted below), Chief Justice Rehnquist held that the Eleventh Amendment limits congressional power over regulating commerce with Indian tribes, under Article 1, Section 10, clause 3. And Congress, therefore, impermissibly gave Indian tribes standing to sue states in federal courts in order to force them to negotiate compacts for their running casinos and other gambling activities on reservations. As in *Lopez*, Justices Souter, Stevens, Ginsburg, and Breyer dissented.

Finally, in its 1996–1997 term, the Court will take up another major challenge to congressional power and one of the hottest contemporary political issues, namely, federal and state powers over gun control. At issue in *Mack v. United States* and *Printz v. United States* is the constitutionality of requirements of the 1993 Brady Handgun Violence Prevention Act, which is named for former White House press secretary James Brady, who was wounded in the 1981 assassination attempt on President Ronald Reagan. That law established a five-day waiting period for the purchase of handguns and requires local law enforcement officials to make a "reasonable effort" in that time to determine whether the buyer has a felony record or a history of mental illness or drug use. The law also requires a national instant-check system to be in place by November 1998, at which time local officials would no longer have to do the background checks. Sheriffs in Arizona and Montana, as well as elsewhere, challenged the constitutionality of the requirements on the ground that the law "commandeers" local officials by forcing them to run a federal program, thereby diverting local law enforcement resources and usurping the power of the states. Although the Court of Appeals for the Ninth Circuit upheld the constitutionality of the law in *Mack* and *Printz*, other appellate courts have found the requirements unconstitutional. The Court will also hear in its 1996–1997 term another dormant Commerce Clause case, *Camp Newfound/Owatonna v. Harrison, Maine*. A Christian Science summer camp challenged Maine's law denying charitable organizations a property tax exemption if they serve primarily nonresidents. Attorneys for the camp argue that the law unconstitutionally discriminates against interstate commerce and seek a refund of about $60,000, which it had paid in taxes during the preceding three years. A trial court's decision agreeing with the camp was reversed by the Maine supreme judicial court, which ruled that the law had only an "incidental" impact on interstate commerce.

Seminole Tribe of Florida v. Florida
116 S.Ct. 1114 (1996)

In 1988, Congress enacted the Indian Gaming Regulatory Act, authorizing Indian tribes to conduct gaming activities in conformance with compacts agreed to by the tribe and the state in which the gaming activities are located. The act also imposed on the states a duty to negotiate in "good faith" compacts with Indian tribes and authorized tribes to bring suits in federal courts against a state that failed to negotiate a gaming compact. Subsequently, after negotiations between Florida and the Seminole Tribe broke down in 1991, the tribe sued the state in federal court. Attorneys for Florida, however, moved to have the suit dismissed on the grounds that the act violated the Eleventh Amendment and that the suit violated the state's sovereign immunity from suits in federal court. The federal district court dismissed that motion and the state's attorneys appealed to the Court of Appeals for the Eleventh Circuit, which reversed the lower court upon concluding that the Eleventh Amendment bars Congress from abrogating a state's Eleventh Amendment immunity from suits in federal courts. The Seminole Tribe appealed that decision to the Supreme Court, which granted review.

The Court's decision was five to four. Chief Justice Rehnquist announced the opinion for the majority and Justices Stevens and Souter filed dissenting opinion. Justices Ginsburg and Breyer joined the latter justice's dissent.

CHIEF JUSTICE REHNQUIST delivered the opinion of the Court.

The Indian Gaming Regulatory Act provides that an Indian tribe may conduct certain gaming activities only in conformance with a valid compact between the tribe and the State in which the gaming activities are located. The Act, passed by Congress under the Indian Commerce Clause, U.S. Const., Art. I, sec. 10, cl. 3, imposes upon the States a duty to negotiate in good faith with an Indian tribe toward the formation of a compact, and authorizes a tribe to bring suit in federal court against a State in order to compel performance of that duty. We hold that notwithstanding Congress' clear intent to abrogate the States' sovereign immunity, the Indian Commerce Clause does not grant Congress that power, and therefore [provisions of the act] cannot grant jurisdiction over a State that does not consent to be sued. We further hold that the doctrine of *Ex parte Young*, 209 U.S. 123 (1908), may not be used to enforce [the act's provisions] against a state official. . . .

The Eleventh Amendment provides: "The Judicial power of the United States shall not be construed to extend to any suit in law or equity, commenced or prosecuted against one of the United States by Citizens of another State, or by Citizens or Subjects of any Foreign State." Although the text of the Amendment would appear to restrict only the Article III diversity jurisdiction of the federal courts, "we have understood the Eleventh Amendment to stand not so much for what it says, but for the presupposition . . . which it confirms." *Blatchford v. Native Village of Noatak,* 501 U.S. 775 (1991). That presupposition, first observed over a century ago in *Hans v. Louisiana,* 134 U.S. 1 (1890), has two parts: first, that each State is a sovereign entity in our federal system; and second, that "'it is inherent in the nature of sovereignty not to be amenable to the suit of an individual without its consent.'" . . .

[O]ur inquiry into whether Congress has the power to abrogate unilaterally the States' immunity from suit is narrowly focused on one question: Was the Act in question passed pursuant to a constitutional provision granting Congress the power to abrogate? Previously, in conducting that inquiry, we have found authority to abrogate under only two provisions of the Constitution. In *Fitzpatrick* [*v. Bitzer,* 427 U.S. 445 (1976)], we recognized that the Fourteenth Amendment, by expanding federal power at the expense of state autonomy, had fundamentally altered the balance of state and federal power struck by the Constitution. We noted that Section 1 of the Fourteenth Amendment contained prohibitions expressly directed at the States and that Section 5 of the Amendment expressly provided that "The Congress shall have the power to enforce, by appropriate legislation, the provisions of this article." We held that through the Fourteenth Amendment, federal power extended to intrude upon the province of the Eleventh Amendment and therefore that Section 5 of the Fourteenth Amendment allowed Congress to abrogate the immunity from suit guaranteed by that Amendment.

In only one other case has congressional abrogation of the States' Eleventh Amendment immunity been upheld. In *Pennsylvania v. Union Gas Co.,* 491 U.S. 1 (1989), a plurality of the Court found that the Interstate Commerce Clause granted Congress the power to abrogate state sovereign immunity, stating that the power to regulate interstate commerce would be "incomplete without the authority to render States liable in damages." Justice WHITE added the fifth vote necessary to the result in that case, but wrote separately in order to express that he "[did] not agree with much of [the plurality's] reasoning." . . .

Both parties make their arguments from the plurality decision in *Union Gas,* and we, too, begin there. We think it clear that Justice BRENNAN's opinion finds Congress' power to abrogate under the Interstate Commerce Clause from the States' cession of their sovereignty when they gave Congress plenary power to regulate interstate commerce. Respondents' focus elsewhere is misplaced. While the plurality decision states that Congress' power under the Interstate Commerce Clause would be incomplete without the power to abrogate, that statement is made solely in order to emphasize the broad scope of Congress' authority over interstate commerce. Moreover, respondents' rationale would mean that where Congress has less authority, and the States have more, Congress' means for exercising that power must be greater. We read the plurality opinion to provide just the opposite. Indeed, it was in those circumstances where Congress exercised complete authority that Justice BRENNAN thought the power to abrogate most necessary.

Following the rationale of the *Union Gas* plurality, our inquiry is limited to determining whether the Indian Commerce Clause, like the Interstate Commerce Clause, is a grant of authority to the Federal Government at the expense of the States. The answer to that question is obvious. If anything, the Indian Commerce Clause accomplishes a greater transfer of power from the States to the Federal Government than does the Interstate Commerce Clause. This is clear enough from the fact that the States still exercise some authority over interstate trade but have been divested of virtually all authority over Indian commerce and Indian tribes. Under the rationale of *Union Gas*, if the States' partial cession of authority over a particular area includes cession of the immunity from suit, then their virtually total cession of authority over a different area must also include cession of the immunity from suit. We agree with the petitioner that the plurality opinion in *Union Gas* allows no principled distinction in favor of the States to be drawn between the Indian Commerce Clause and the Interstate Commerce Clause.

Never before the decision in *Union Gas* had we suggested that the bounds of Article III could be expanded by Congress operating pursuant to any constitutional provision other than the Fourteenth Amendment. Indeed, it had seemed fundamental that Congress could not expand the jurisdiction of the federal courts beyond the bounds of Article III. The plurality's citation of prior decisions for support was based upon what we believe to be a misreading of precedent. The plurality claimed support for its decision from a case holding the unremarkable, and completely unrelated, proposition that the States may waive their sovereign immunity, and cited as precedent propositions that had been merely assumed for the sake of argument in earlier cases.

Reconsidering the decision in *Union Gas*, we conclude that none of the policies underlying *stare decisis* require our continuing adherence to its holding. The decision has, since its issuance, been of questionable precedential value, largely because a majority of the Court expressly disagreed with the rationale of the plurality. The case involved the interpretation of the Constitution and therefore may be altered only by constitutional amendment or revision by this Court. Finally, both the result in *Union Gas* and the plurality's rationale depart from our established understanding of the Eleventh Amendment and undermine the accepted function of Article III. We feel bound to conclude that *Union Gas* was wrongly decided and that it should be, and now is, overruled. . . .

In overruling *Union Gas* today, we reconfirm that the background principle of state sovereign immunity embodied in the Eleventh Amendment is not so ephemeral as to dissipate when the subject of the suit is an area, like the regulation of Indian commerce, that is under the exclusive control of the Federal Government. Even when the Constitution vests in Congress complete law-making authority over a particular area, the Eleventh Amendment prevents congressional authorization of suits by private parties against unconsenting States. The Eleventh Amendment restricts the judicial power under Article III, and Article I cannot be used to circumvent the constitutional limitations placed upon federal jurisdiction. Petitioner's suit against the State of Florida must be dismissed for a lack of jurisdiction. . . .

Justice SOUTER, with whom Justice GINSBURG and Justice BREYER join, dissenting.

I part company from the Court because I am convinced that its decision is fundamentally mistaken, and for that reason I respectfully dissent.

It is useful to separate three questions: (1) whether the States enjoyed sovereign immunity if sued in their own courts in the period prior to ratification of the National Constitution; (2) if so, whether after ratification the States were entitled to claim some such immunity when sued in a federal court exercising jurisdiction either because the suit was between a State and a non-state litigant who was not its citizen, or because the issue in the case raised a federal question; and (3) whether any state sovereign immunity recognized in federal court may be abrogated by Congress.

The answer to the first question is not clear, although some of the Framers assumed that States did enjoy immunity in their own courts. The second question was not debated at the time of ratification, except as to citizen-state diversity jurisdiction; there was no unanimity, but in due course the Court in *Chisholm v. Georgia,* [2 Dall. 419 (1793),] answered that a state defendant enjoyed no such immunity. As to federal question jurisdiction, state sovereign immunity seems not to have been debated prior to ratification, the silence probably showing a general understanding at the time that the States would have no immunity in such cases.

The adoption of the Eleventh Amendment soon changed the result in *Chisholm,* not by mentioning sovereign immunity, but by eliminating citizen-state diversity jurisdiction over cases with state defendants. I will explain why the Eleventh Amendment did not affect federal question jurisdiction, a notion that needs to be understood for the light it casts on the soundness of *Hans*'s holding that States did enjoy sovereign immunity in federal question suits. The *Hans* Court erroneously assumed that a State could plead sovereign immunity against a noncitizen suing under federal question jurisdiction, and for that reason held that a State must enjoy the same protection in a suit by one of its citizens. The error of *Hans*'s reasoning is underscored by its clear inconsistency with the Founders' hostility to the implicit reception of common-law doctrine as federal law, and with the Founders' conception of sovereign power as divided between the States and the National Government for the sake of very practical objectives.

The Court's answer today to the third question is likewise at odds with the Founders' view that common law, when it was received into the new American legal systems, was always subject to legislative amendment. In ignoring the reasons for this pervasive understanding at the time of the ratification, and in holding that a nontextual common-law rule limits a clear grant of congressional power under Article I, the Court follows a course that has brought it to grief before in our history, and promises to do so again.

Beyond this third question that elicits today's holding, there is one further issue. To reach the Court's result, it must not only hold the *Hans* doctrine to be outside the reach of Congress, but must also displace the doctrine of *Ex parte Young*, 209 U.S. 123 (1908), that an officer of the government may be ordered prospectively to follow federal law, in cases in which the government may not itself be sued directly. None of its reasons for displacing *Young's* jurisdictional doctrine withstand scrutiny.

The doctrine of sovereign immunity comprises two distinct rules, which are not always separately recognized. The one rule holds that the King or the Crown, as the font of law, is not bound by the law's provisions; the other provides that the King or Crown, as the font of justice, is not subject to suit in its own courts. The one rule limits the reach of substantive law; the other, the jurisdiction of the courts. We are concerned here only with the latter rule, which took its common-law form in the high middle ages. . . .

Whatever the scope of sovereign immunity might have been in the Colonies, however, or during the period of Confederation, the proposal to establish a National Government under the Constitution drafted in 1787 presented a prospect unknown to the common law prior to the American experience: the States would become parts of a system in which sovereignty over even domestic matters would be divided or parcelled out between the States and the Nation, the latter to be invested with its own judicial power and the right to prevail against the States whenever their respective substantive laws might be in conflict. With this prospect in mind, the 1787 Constitution might have addressed state sovereign immunity by eliminating whatever sovereign immunity the States previously had, as to any matter subject to federal law or jurisdiction; by recognizing an analogue to the old immunity in the new context of federal jurisdiction, but subject to abrogation as to any matter within that jurisdiction; or by enshrining a doctrine of inviolable state sovereign immunity in the text, thereby giving it constitutional protection in the new federal jurisdiction.

The 1787 draft in fact said nothing on the subject, and it was this very silence that occasioned some, though apparently not widespread, dispute among the Framers and others over whether ratification of the Constitution would preclude a State sued in federal court from asserting sovereign immunity as it could have done on any matter of nonfederal law litigated in its own courts. . . .

The argument among the Framers and their friends about sovereign immunity in federal citizen-state diversity cases, in any event, was short lived and ended when this Court, in *Chisholm v. Georgia*, chose between the constitutional alternatives of abrogation and recognition of the immunity enjoyed at common law. The 4-to-1 majority adopted the reasonable (although not compelled) interpretation that the first of the two Citizen-State Diversity Clauses abrogated for purposes of federal jurisdiction any immunity the States might have enjoyed in their own courts, and Georgia was accordingly held subject to the judicial power in a common-law *assumpsit* action by a South Carolina citizen suing to collect a debt. . . .

The Eleventh Amendment, of course, repudiated *Chisholm* and clearly divested federal courts of some jurisdiction as to cases against state parties: "The Judicial power of the United States shall not be construed to extend to any suit in law or equity, commenced or prosecuted against one of the United States by Citizens of another State, or by Citizens or Subjects of any Foreign State." There are two plausible readings of this provision's text. Under the first, it simply repeals the Citizen-State Diversity Clauses of Article III for all cases in which the State appears as a defendant. Under the second, it strips the federal courts of jurisdiction in any case in which a state defendant is sued by a citizen not its own, even if jurisdiction might otherwise rest on the existence of a federal question in the suit. Neither reading of the Amendment, of course, furnishes authority for the Court's view in today's case, but we need to choose between the competing readings for the light that will be shed on the *Hans* doctrine and the legitimacy of inflating that doctrine to the point of constitutional immutability as the Court has chosen to do.

The history and structure of the Eleventh Amendment convincingly show that it reaches only to suits subject to federal jurisdiction exclusively under the Citizen-State Diversity Clauses. In precisely tracking the language in Article III providing for citizen-state diversity jurisdiction, the text of the Amendment does, after all, suggest to common sense that only the Diversity Clauses are being addressed. . . . If the Framers of the Eleventh Amendment had meant it to immunize States from federal question suits like those that might be brought to enforce the Treaty of Paris, they would surely have drafted the Amendment differently.

It should accordingly come as no surprise that the weightiest commentary following the amendment's adoption described it simply as constricting the scope of the Citizen-State Diversity Clauses. In *Cohens v. Virginia*, 6 Wheat. 264 (1821), for instance, Chief Justice Marshall, writing for the Court, emphasized that the amendment had no effect on federal courts' jurisdiction grounded on the "arising under" provision of Article III and concluded that "a case arising under the constitution or laws of the United States, is cognizable in the Courts of the Union, whoever may be the parties to that case." The point of the Eleventh Amendment, according to *Cohens*, was to bar jurisdiction in suits at common law by Revolutionary War debt creditors, not "to strip the government of the means of protecting, by the instrumentality of its Courts, the constitution and laws from active violation." In sum, reading the Eleventh Amendment solely as a limit on citizen-state diversity jurisdiction has the virtue of coherence with this Court's practice, with the views of John Marshall, with the history of the Amendment's drafting, and with its allusive language. Today's majority does not appear to disagree, at least insofar as the constitutional text is concerned; the Court concedes, after all, that "the text of the Amendment would appear to restrict only the Article III diversity jurisdiction of the federal courts." . . .

Hans was indeed a leap in the direction of today's holding, even though it does not take the Court all the way. The parties in *Hans* raised, and the Court in that case answered, only what I have called the second question, that is, whether the Constitution, without more, permits a State to plead sovereign immunity to bar the exercise of federal question jurisdiction. Although the Court invoked a principle of sovereign immunity to cure what it took to be the Eleventh Amendment's anomaly of barring only those state suits brought by noncitizen plaintiffs, the *Hans* Court had no occasion to consider whether Congress could abrogate that background immunity by statute. Indeed (except in the special circumstance of Congress's power to enforce the Civil War Amendments), this question never came before our Court until *Union Gas*, and any intimations of an answer in prior cases were mere *dicta*. In *Union Gas* the Court held that the immunity recognized in *Hans* had no constitutional status and was subject to congressional abrogation. Today the Court overrules *Union Gas* and holds just the opposite. In deciding how to choose between these two positions, the place to begin is with *Hans*'s holding that a principle of sovereign immunity derived from the common law insulates a state from federal question jurisdiction at the suit of its own citizen. A critical examination of that case will show that it was wrongly decided, as virtually every recent commentator has concluded. It follows that the Court's further step today of constitutionalizing *Hans*'s rule against abrogation by Congress compounds and immensely magnifies the century-old mistake of *Hans* itself and takes its place with other historic examples of textually untethered elevations of judicially derived rules to the status of inviolable constitutional law. . . .

Three critical errors in *Hans* weigh against constitutionalizing its holding as the majority does today. The first we have already seen: the *Hans* Court misread the Eleventh Amendment. It also misunderstood the conditions under which common-law doctrines were received or rejected at the time of the Founding, and it fundamentally mistook the very nature of sovereignty in the young Republic that was supposed to entail a State's immunity to federal question jurisdiction in a federal court. . . .

While the States had limited their reception of English common law to principles appropriate to American conditions, the 1787 draft Constitution contained no provision for adopting the common law at all. This omission stood in sharp contrast to the state constitutions then extant, virtually all of which contained explicit provisions dealing with common-law reception. Since the experience in the States set the stage for thinking at the national level, this failure to address the notion of common-law reception could not have been inadvertent. Instead, the Framers chose to recognize only particular common-law concepts, such as the writ of *habeas corpus*, U.S. Const., Art. I, sec. 9, cl. 2, and the distinction between law and equity, U.S. Const., Amdt. VII, by specific reference in the constitutional text. This approach reflected widespread agreement that ratification would not itself entail a general reception of the common law of England.

The Framers also recognized that the diverse development of the common law in the several states made a general federal reception impossible. "The common law was not the same in any two of the Colonies," Madison observed; "in some the modifications were materially and extensively different." Report on Resolutions, House of Delegates, Session of 1799–1800, Concerning Alien and Sedition Laws. In particular, although there is little evidence regarding the immunity enjoyed by the various colonial governments prior to the Revolution, the profound differences as to the source of colonial authority between chartered colonies, royal colonies, and so on seems unlikely, wholly apart from other differences in circumstance, to have given rise to a uniform body of immunity law. There was not, then, any unified "Common Law" in America that the Federal Constitution could adopt, and, in particular, probably no common principle of sovereign immunity. The Framers may, as Madison, Hamilton, and Marshall argued, have contemplated that federal courts would respect state immunity law in diversity cases, but the generalized principle of immunity that today's majority would graft onto the Constitution itself may well never have developed with any common clarity and, in any event, has not been shown to have existed. . . .

Given the refusal to entertain any wholesale reception of common law, given the failure of the new Constitution to make any provision for adoption of common law as such, and given the protests already quoted that no general reception had occurred, the *Hans* Court and the Court today cannot reasonably argue that something like the old immunity doctrine somehow slipped in as a tacit but enforceable background principle. The evidence is even more specific, however, that there was no pervasive understanding that sovereign immunity had limited federal question jurisdiction. . . .

As a matter of political theory, this federal arrangement of dual delegated sovereign powers truly was a more revolutionary turn than the late war had been. Before the new federal scheme appeared, 18th-century political theorists had assumed that "there must reside somewhere in every political unit a single, undivided, final power, higher in legal authority than any other power, subject to no law, a law unto itself." The American development of divided sovereign powers, which "shattered . . . the categories of government that had dominated Western thinking for centuries," was made possible only by a recognition that the ultimate sovereignty rests in the people themselves. The people possessing this plenary bundle of specific powers were free to parcel them out to different governments and different branches of the same government as they saw fit. . . .

Given this metamorphosis of the idea of sovereignty in the years leading up to 1789, the question whether the old immunity doctrine might have been received as something suitable for the new world of federal question jurisdiction is a crucial one. The answer is that sovereign immunity as it would have been known to the Framers before ratification thereafter became inapplicable as a matter of logic in a federal suit raising a federal question. The old doctrine, after all, barred the involuntary subjection of a sovereign to the system of justice and law of which it was itself the font, since to do otherwise would have struck the common-law mind from the Middle Ages onward as both impractical and absurd. But the ratification demonstrated that state governments were subject to a superior regime of law in a judicial system established, not by the State, but by the people through a specific delegation of their sovereign power to a National Government that was paramount within its delegated sphere. When individuals sued States to enforce federal rights, the Government that corresponded to the "sovereign" in the traditional common-law sense was not the State but the National Government, and any state immunity from the jurisdiction of the Nation's courts would have required a grant from the true sovereign, the people, in their Constitution, or from the Congress that the Constitution had empowered. . . .

State immunity to federal question jurisdiction would, moreover, have run up against the common understanding of the practical necessity for the new federal relationship. According to Madison, the "multiplicity," "mutability," and "injustice" of then-extant state laws were prime factors requiring the formation of a new government. These factors, Madison wrote to Jefferson, "contributed more to that uneasiness which produced the Convention, and prepared the Public mind for a general reform, than those which accrued to our national character and interest from the inadequacy of the Confederation to its immediate objects." These concerns ultimately found concrete expression in a number of specific limitations on state power, including provisions barring the States from enacting bills of attainder or ex post facto laws, coining money or emitting bills of credit, denying the privileges and immunities of out-of-staters, or impairing the obligation of contracts. But the proposed Constitution also dealt with the old problems affirmatively by granting the powers to Congress enumerated in Article I, Section 8, and by providing through the Supremacy Clause that Congress could preempt State action in areas of concurrent state and federal authority.

Given the Framers' general concern with curbing abuses by state governments, it would be amazing if the scheme of delegated powers embodied in the Constitution had left the National Government powerless to render the States judicially accountable for violations of federal rights. And of course the Framers did not understand the scheme to leave the government powerless. . . .

Without citing a single source to the contrary, the Court dismisses the historical evidence regarding the Framers' vision of the relationship between national and state sovereignty, and reassures us that "the Nation survived for nearly two centuries without the question of the existence of [the abrogation] power ever being presented to this Court." But we are concerned here not with the survival of the Nation but the opportunity of its citizens to enforce federal rights in a way that Congress provides. The absence of any general federal question statute for nearly a century following ratification of Article III (with a brief exception in 1800) hardly counts against the importance of that jurisdiction either in the Framers' conception or in current reality; likewise, the fact that Congress has not often seen fit to use its power of abrogation (outside the Fourteenth Amendment context, at least) does not compel a conclusion that the power is not important to the federal scheme. In the end, is it plausible to contend that the plan of the convention was meant to leave the National Government without any way to render individuals capable of enforcing their federal rights directly against an intransigent state?

The considerations expressed so far, based on text, *Chisholm*, caution in common-law reception, and sovereignty theory, have pointed both to the mistakes inherent in *Hans* and, even more strongly, to the error of today's holding. Although for reasons of *stare decisis* I would not today disturb the century-old precedent, I surely would not extend its error by placing the common-law immunity it mistakenly recognized beyond the power of Congress to abrogate. In doing just that, however, today's decision declaring state sovereign immunity itself immune from abrogation in federal question cases is open to a further set of objections peculiar to itself. For today's decision stands condemned alike by the Framers' abhorrence of any notion that such common-law rules as might be received into the new legal systems would be beyond the legislative power to alter or repeal, and by its resonance with this Court's previous essays in constitutionalizing common-law rules at the expense of legislative authority. . . .

History confirms the wisdom of Madison's abhorrence of constitutionalizing common-law rules to place them beyond the reach of congressional amendment. The Framers feared judicial power over substantive policy and the ossification of law that would result from transforming common law into constitutional law, and their fears have been borne out every time the Court has ignored Madison's counsel on subjects that we generally group under economic and social policy. It is, in fact, remarkable that as we near the end of this century the Court should choose to open a new constitutional chapter in confining legislative judgments on these matters by resort to textually unwarranted common-law rules, for it was just this practice in the century's early decades that brought this Court to the nadir of competence that we identify with *Lochner v. New York*, 198 U.S. 45 (1905).

It was the defining characteristic of the *Lochner* era, and its characteristic vice, that the Court treated the common-law background (in those days, common-law property rights and contractual autonomy) as paramount, while regarding congressional legislation to abrogate the common law on these economic matters as constitutionally suspect. See, e.g., *Adkins v. Childrens Hospital of D.C.*, 261 U.S. 525 (1923) (finding abrogation of common-law freedom to contract for any wage an unconstitutional "compulsory exaction"). And yet the superseding lesson that seemed clear after *West Coast Hotel Co. v. Parrish*, 300 U.S. 379 (1937), that action within the legislative power is not subject to greater scrutiny merely because it trenches upon the case law's ordering of economic and social relationships, seems to have been lost on the Court.

The majority today, indeed, seems to be going *Lochner* one better. When the Court has previously constrained the express Article I powers by resort to common-law or background principles, it has done so at least in an ostensible effort to give content to some other written provision of the Constitution, like the Due Process Clause, the very object of which is to limit the exercise of governmental power. . . . Today, however, the Court is not struggling to fulfill a responsibility to reconcile two arguably conflicting and Delphic constitutional provisions, nor is it struggling with any Delphic text at all. For even the Court concedes that the Constitution's grant to Congress of plenary power over relations with Indian tribes at the expense of any state claim to the contrary is unmistakably clear, and this case does not even arguably implicate a textual trump to the grant of federal question jurisdiction. . . .

In *Ex parte Young*, this Court held that a federal court has jurisdiction in a suit against a state officer to enjoin official actions violating federal law, even though the State itself may be immune. Under *Young*, "a federal court, consistent with the Eleventh Amendment, may enjoin state officials to conform their future conduct to the requirements of federal law." . . .

[I]n the years since *Young* was decided, the Court has recognized only one limitation on the scope of its doctrine: under *Edelman v. Jordon*, 415 U.S. 651 (1974), *Young* permits prospective relief only and may not be applied to authorize suits for retrospective monetary relief.

It should be no cause for surprise that *Young* itself appeared when it did in the national law. It followed as a matter of course after the *Hans* Court's broad recognition of immunity in federal question cases, simply because "remedies designed to end a continuing violation of federal law are necessary to vindicate the federal interest in assuring the supremacy of that law." *Green v. Mansour*, 474 U.S. 64 (1985). *Young* provided, as it does today, a sensible way to reconcile the Court's expansive view of immunity expressed in *Hans* with the principles embodied in the Supremacy Clause and Article III. . . .

There is no question that by its own terms *Young*'s indispensable rule authorizes the exercise of federal jurisdiction over respondent Chiles. Since this case does not, of course, involve retrospective relief, *Edelman*'s limit is irrelevant, and there is no other jurisdictional limitation. Obviously, for jurisdictional purposes it makes no difference in principle whether the injunction orders an official not to act, as in *Young*, or requires the official to take some positive step, as in *Milliken* [*v. Bradley*, 433 U.S. 267 (1977) (*Milliken II*)]. Nothing, then, in this case renders *Young* unsuitable as a jurisdictional basis for determining on the merits whether the petitioners are entitled to an order against a state official under general equitable doctrine. The Court does not say otherwise, and yet it refuses to apply *Young*. There is no adequate reason for its refusal. . . .

Absent the application of *Ex parte Young*, I would, of course, follow *Union Gas* in recognizing congressional power under Article I to abrogate *Hans* immunity. . . .

In being ready to hold that the relationship [between the states and the national government] may still be altered, not by the Court but by Congress, I would tread the course laid out elsewhere in our cases. The Court has repeatedly stated its assumption that insofar as the relative positions of States and Nation may be affected consistently with the Tenth Amendment, they would not be modified without deliberately expressed intent. See *Gregory v. Ashcroft*, 501 U.S. [452 (1992)]. The plain statement rule, which "assures that the legislature has in fact faced, and intended to bring into issue, the critical matters involved in the judicial decision," is particularly appropriate in light of our primary reliance on "the effectiveness of the federal political process in preserving the States' interests." *Garcia v. San Antonio Metropolitan Authority*, 469 U.S. 528 (1985). Hence, we have required such a plain statement when Congress pre-empts the historic powers of the States, *Rice v. Santa Fe Elevator Corp.*, 331 U.S. 218 (1947), imposes a condition on the grant of federal moneys, *South Dakota v. Dole*, 483 U.S. 203 (1987), or seeks to regulate a State's ability to determine the qualifications of its own officials.

When judging legislation passed under unmistakable Article I powers, no further restriction could be required. Nor does the Court explain why more could be demanded. In the past, we have assumed that a plain statement requirement is sufficient to protect the States from undue federal encroachments upon their traditional immunity from suit. It is hard to contend that this rule has set the bar too low, for (except in *Union Gas*) we have never found the requirement to be met outside the context of laws passed under Section 5 of the Fourteenth Amendment. The exception I would recognize today proves the rule, moreover, because the federal abrogation of state immunity comes as part of a regulatory scheme which is itself designed to invest the States with regulatory powers that Congress need not extend to them. This fact suggests to me that the political safeguards of federalism are working, that a plain statement rule is an adequate check on congressional overreaching, and that today's abandonment of that approach is wholly unwarranted. . . .

THE DEVELOPMENT OF LAW

Rulings on State Regulatory Powers in Alleged Conflict with Federal Legislation

Case	Vote	Ruling
Northwest Airlines, Inc. v. County of Kent, Michigan, 114 S.Ct. 855 (1994)	7:1	Rebuffed a challenge to a airport system of collectin fees based on charging com

mercial airlines 100 percent of their square footage allocation costs, but onl 20 percent of the same costs incurred by general aviation. Writing for th majority, Justice Ginsburg held that that system did not violate the Anti-Hea Tax Act or burden interstate commerce. Justice Thomas dissented.

Livades v. Bradshaw, 114 S.Ct. 2068 (1994)	9:0	Writing for the Court, Jus tice Souter held that a collec tive-bargain agreement wa

preempted under provisions of the National Labor Relations Act.

Doctor's Associates, Inc. v. Casarotto, 116 S.Ct. 1653 (1996)	8:1	Writing for the Court, Justic Ginsburg struck down Montana law governing ar

bitration agreements as preempted by the Federal Arbitration Act. Justic Thomas dissented.

Medtronic, Inc. v. Lohr, 116 S.Ct. — (1996)	5:4	Writing for the Court, Justic Stevens held that the Med ical Device Amendments o

1976 did not preempt state law tort claims for the recovery of damages cause by a defective pacemaker. Justice O'Connor filed an opinion in part concurrin and dissenting, which Chief Justice Rehnquist and Justices Scalia and Thoma joined.

THE DEVELOPMENT OF LAW

Rulings on State Regulations of Commerce in the Absence of
Federal Legislation

Case	Vote	Ruling
Northwest Airlines, Inc. v. County of Kent, Michigan, 114 S.Ct. 855 (1994)	7:1	Rejected a dormant com merce clause challenge to a airport fee scheme that dis

criminated between commercial airlines and general aviation by assessin
higher fees on the former. Justice Thomas dissented.

Oregon Waste Systems, Inc. v. Department of Environmental Quality of the State of Oregon, 114 S.Ct. 1345 (1994)	7:2	Struck down Oregon's sur charge on the disposal o out-of-state solid waste in it landfills as discriminator economic protectionism i

violation of the dormant commerce clause. Chief Justice Rehnquist and Justic
Blackmun dissented.

C&A Carbone, Inc. v. Town of Clarkstown, New York, 114 S.Ct. 1677 (1994)	7:2	Struck down an ordinanc requiring all nonhazardou solid waste within the tow to be deposited at a loca

transfer station. Writing for the majority, Justice Kennedy held that th
ordinance deprived out-of-state businesses of access to the local market an
thereby unconstitutionally discriminated in favor of local businesses. Chie
Justice Rehnquist and Justice Souter dissented.

Associated Industries of Missouri v. Lohman, 114 S.Ct. 1815 (1994)	9:0	Writing for the Court, Just ice Thomas invalidated statewide "additional use tax"

on goods purchased outside of the state for impermissibly discriminatin
against interstate commerce.

West Lynn Creamery, Inc. v. Healy, 114 S.Ct. 2205 (1994)	7:2	Struck down a Massachu setts pricing order on al milk sold within the state an

subsidy for in-state dairy farmers as economically discriminatory and
violation of the commerce clause. Justice Stevens wrote for the majority an
Chief Justice Rehnquist, joined by Justice Thomas, dissented.

Barclays Bank PLC v. Franchise Tax 7:2 Writing for the Court'
Board of California and *Colgate-* majority, Justice Ginsbur
Palmolive Co. v. Franchise Tax Board upheld a controversial stat
of California, 114 S.Ct. 2268 (1994) policy of taxing multination
al corporations based on thei
worldwide income, rather than on their earnings within the state, ove
objections that the policy discriminates against foreign and interstate com
merce. The majority reaffirmed that state tax policies may run afoul of th
commerce clause if the tax (1) applies to an activity lacking a "substantia
nexus to the taxing state"; (2) is not fairly apportioned; (3) discriminate
against interstate commerce; or (4) is not fairly related to the services provide
by a state. In addition, in cases involving the taxation of foreign commerce, th
Court examines (5) whether there is an "enhanced risk of multiple taxation,"
and (6) whether a state's tax interferes with the federal government's capacit
to "speak with one voice when regulating commercial relations with foreig
governments." Justice Ginsburg found California's "worldwide combine
reporting" method of taxation to survive all but the third criteria. However, th
justice concluded that Barclays had failed to show that the state's method o
taxation in fact operated to impose an inordinate burden on multinationa
corporations. Justice O'Connor, joined by Justice Thomas, dissented.

Oklahoma Tax Commission v. 7:2 Writing for the majority
Jefferson Lines, Inc., Justice Souter upheld a stat
115 S.Ct. 1331 (1995) sales tax on bus tickets fo
interstate travel sold withi
the state over the objection that the tax imposed on an undue burden o
interstate commerce and was inconsistent with the commerce clause. Justice
Breyer and O'Connor dissented.

Fulton Corporation v. Faulkner, 9:0 Writing for the Court, Jus
116 S.Ct. 848 (1996) tice Souter struck dow
North Carolina's tax o
state residents who own stock in companies that do no business within th
state, while exempting residents who own stock in companies doing busi
ness within the state, as a violation of the dormant commerce clause.

8

REPRESENTATIVE GOVERNMENT, VOTING RIGHTS, AND ELECTORAL POLITICS

B. VOTING RIGHTS AND THE REAPPORTIONMENT REVOLUTION

In *Shaw v. Reno,* 509 U.S. 630 (1993) (see Vol. 1, Ch. 8), a bare majority of the Rehnquist Court ruled that the Fourteenth Amendment forbids racial gerrymandering in electoral redistricting unless the government demonstrates a "compelling reason" for creating so-called majority-minority districts. Justice O'Connor's opinion for the majority was so sweeping that it called into question the permissibility of race-conscious redistricting. But on the last day of the 1993–1994 term, in two rulings on the Voting Rights Act, a majority of the Court took a different course and badly fragmented the Court, as well as drawing an angry and lengthy opinion from Justice Thomas, who was joined by Justice Scalia.

In *Johnson v. De Grandy,* 114 S.Ct. 2647 (1994), the Court overruled a court-ordered redistricting plan for Florida's house of representatives. The plan would have increased the number of Hispanic-majority voting districts from nine to eleven out of a total of twenty districts. Writing for the Court, Justice Souter held that such majority-minority districts are permissible under the Voting Rights Act and sometimes necessary in order to increase minorities' representation, but ruled that the act does not require creating the greatest possible number of majority-minority districts. Once a minority group has achieved representation in "rough proportion" to its population, said Justice Souter, the Voting Rights Act requires nothing more. In this case, he concluded: "Treating equal political opportunity as the focus of the inquiry, we do not see how these district lines, apparently providing political effectiveness in proportion to voting-age numbers, deny equal political opportunity." Notably, Justice Souter avoided ruling on such related issues as how to measure the size of minority groups, whether as part of the overall population, the voting-age population, or the number of citizens eligible to vote. Specifying a "magic parameter," claimed the justice, was not necessary here. His opinion was joined by the chief justice and Justices Blackmun, Stevens, O'Connor, and Ginsburg, while Justice Kennedy joined only in part. Justices Scalia and Thomas dissented for reasons set forth more fully in their opinion in *Holder v. Hall.*

In the second case, *Holder v. Hall*, 114 S.Ct. 2581 (1994), the Court not only split five to four, but the bare majority splintered three ways in different opinions. The result, nonetheless, was a reversal of an appellate court's decision ordering the change from a single-member county commission to a five-member commission with districts drawn so that at least one black commissioner could be elected. The case had originally been brought by black voters under Section 2 of the Voting Rights Act, which forbids any voting practice that denies or abridges the right to vote on the basis of race. They challenged the permissibility of the single-member commission in rural Bleckley, Georgia, where twenty percent of the county's population is black but where a black commissioner has never been elected.

With only Chief Justice Rehnquist and Justice O'Connor joining his opinion announcing the Court's decision in *Holder v. Hall*, Justice Kennedy rejected the claim that the Voting Rights Act permits challenges to the size of a governmental body or organization. He did so upon concluding that it was impossible to determine what size or structure would be best. Justice Kennedy's plurality opinion emphasized, for instance, that California has an eighty-member assembly, while New Hampshire has 400 members in its house of representatives. In a concurring opinion, Justice O'Connor further explained that there was no "limiting principle" for courts to insist on one size or another for a governing body. The result reached by these three justices was joined by concurring Justices Scalia and Thomas, though for different reasons and in order to form a bare majority for the outcome. They agreed with the result, but because they would have held that the Voting Rights Act does not govern race-conscious districting in the first place.

The four dissenters in *Holder v. Hall* countered that it was "clear" from the history of Bleckley County that the single-member commission had the effect of diluting the voting power of blacks. Justices Ginsburg, Stevens, and Souter joined Justice Blackmun's dissenting opinion. They maintained that the Voting Rights Act should remain available for attacking "subtler, more complex means of infringing minority voting strength" in cases such as here. In another opinion also joined by the three other dissenters, Justice Stevens rebutted what he termed the "radical reinterpretation" of the Voting Rights Act advanced by Justices Scalia and Thomas.

With Justice Scalia joining him in a fifty-nine-page concurring opinion in *Holder v. Hall*, Justice Thomas expressly rejected over two decades of the Court's jurisprudence in the area of voting rights. The concept of minority-vote dilution has been central to the Court's analysis and interpretation of the Voting Rights Act. Yet Thomas dismissed it as "a disastrous misadventure in judicial policymaking." "Our current practice should not continue," he claimed, "not for another term, not until the next case, not for another day." Instead, Thomas proposed that the Voting Rights Act should be reinterpreted to allow challenges solely to classical and overtly racially discriminatory practices bearing on voter qualifications. The Court's decision in *Allen v. State Board of Elections*, 393 U.S. 544 (1969), and other cases rejecting such a narrow reading of the Voting Rights Act, Thomas said, should simply be overturned and abandoned. The Court's approach to voting rights under the Voting Rights Act and the Fourteenth Amendment, in Thomas's words, had "given credence to the view that race defines political interest" and "should be repugnant to any nation that strives for the ideal of a color-blind Constitution."

In its 1994–1995 term, the justices continued to grapple with the fallout from their 1993 ruling in *Shaw v. Reno*. Following that decision, white voters have attacked the permissiblity of racially gerrymandered districts in Florida, Georgia, Louisiana, North Carolina, and Texas. Since 1990, the number of so-called majority-minority districts in the U.S. House of Representatives has doubled. Although blacks constitute twelve percent of the U.S. population, in 1994 they held seven percent of the seats in Congress; Hispanics, accounting for ten percent of the total population, had won three percent of the congressional seats.

In order to revisit the issue and to clarify its prior ruling, the Court granted two consolidated cases, *Louisiana v. Hays* and *United States v. Hays*, 115 S.Ct. 2431 (1995), which appealed a lower federal court's invalidation of the redistricting of Louisiana's fourth congressional district. In the lower court's view, the district, which stretches diagonally across the state, was not only "bizarre and irregular" but impermissible "racial gerrymandering" under the "principles of racial equality" proclaimed by the bare majority in *Shaw v. Reno*. But the Court held that the appellees had no standing to sue. Writing for the Court, Justice O'Connor explained,

We held in *Shaw v. Reno* (1993), that a plaintiff may state a claim for relief under the Equal Protection Clause of the Fourteenth Amendment by alleging that a State adopted a reapportionment scheme so irrational on its face that it can be understood only as an effort to segregate voters into separate voting districts because of their race, and that the separation lacks sufficient justification. Appellees Ray Hays, Edward Adams, Susan Shaw Singleton, and Gary Stokley claim that the State of Louisiana's congressional districting plan is such a racial gerrymander, and that it violates the Fourteenth Amendment. But appellees do not live in the district that is the primary focus of their racial gerrymandering claim, and they have not otherwise demonstrated that they, personally, have been subjected to a racial classification. For that reason, we conclude that appellees lack standing to bring this lawsuit. . . .

It is by now well settled that the irreducible constitutional minimum of standing contains three elements. First, the plaintiff must have suffered an "injury in fact," an invasion of a legally protected interest which is (a) concrete and particularized, and (b) actual or imminent, not conjectural or hypothetical. Second, there must be a causal connection between the injury and the conduct complained of. . . . Third, it must be likely, as opposed to merely speculative, that the injury will be redressed by a favorable decision. *Lujan v. Defenders of Wildlife*, 504 U.S. 555 (1992). In light of these principles, we have repeatedly refused to recognize a generalized grievance against allegedly illegal governmental conduct as sufficient for standing to invoke the federal judicial power. . . .

The rule against generalized grievances applies with as much force in the equal protection context as in any other. *Allen v. Wright*, [468 U.S. 737 (1984)], made clear that even if a governmental actor is discriminating on the basis of race, the resulting injury accords a basis for standing only to "those persons who are personally denied equal treatment" by the challenged discriminatory conduct. We therefore reject appellees' position that anybody in the State has a claim, and adhere instead to the principles outlined above.

However, in still another voting-rights case, *Miller v. Johnson* (excerpted below), the justices split five to four in reaffirming that racial gerrymandering violates the Fourteenth Amendment's equal protection clause.

By the same five-to-four vote, the Rehnquist Court struck down the creation of majority-minority congressional districts in Texas and North Carolina, in *Bush v. Vera* and *Shaw v. Hunt* (both are excerpted below).

Finally, in its 1995–1996 term, the Court unanimously held that the federal government did not have to adjust 1990 census figures that undercounted blacks, Hispanics, and other minorities in some metropolitan areas and along the country's borders. New York City challenged the census figures, which are used in congressional redistricting and to calculate federal funding for the states, as a violation of minority voting rights. Although acknowledging that blacks were undercounted by 4.8 percent, Hispanics by 5.2, Native Americans by 5 percent, and Asian-Pacific Islanders by 3.1 percent, the secretary of the Department of Commerce, who oversees the Census Bureau, decided that it was not worth statistically adjusting the headcount so as to make the population headcount more accurate. Subsequently, Wisconsin and Oklahoma entered the suit on side of the Commerce Department, in order to preserve their federal funding under the 1990 census. A federal court of appeals, however, concluded that the department had failed to make a good-faith effort to obtain an accurate population count. But the Supreme Court reversed that decision on the grounds that Congress, which delegated its authority to the commerce secretary, has virtually unlimited discretion in deciding how to conduct the decennial census. Writing for the Court in *Wisconsin v. City of New York*, 116 S.Ct. 1091 (1996), Chief Justice Rehnquist observed that the Census Bureau had "made an extraordinary effort to conduct an accurate enumeration, and was successful in counting 98.4 percent of the population."

In its 1995–1996 term, a bare majority of the Court also ruled that provisions of the Voting Rights Act of 1965, which forbids discrimination in elections and requires Southern states to obtain preclearance of changes in election laws from the Department of Justice (DoJ), extend to changes made in political parties' requirements for primary elections. Virginia has delegated its authority in primary elections to the major political parties in the state. And in 1994 the Virginia Republican Party decided to charge a fee of $45 per person to attend its convention that nominated Oliver L. North as the party's candidate for the U.S. Senate. Three University of Virginia law students in turn filed a suit contending that the party should have obtained the Justice Department's approval of the fee and that the fee constituted a poll tax in violation of the Voting Rights Act. Although not reaching the merits of whether the convention fees amounted to a poll tax in *Morse v. Republican Party of Virginia*, 116 S.Ct. 1186 (1996), the Court held that the party's nominating convention effectively constituted a state primary election and thus was subject to the provisions of the Voting Rights Act. Joined only by Justice Ginsburg, Justice Stevens noted that the nominating convention and fees limits participation and undercuts the influence of voters on the nomination of candidates and observed that, "If the party chooses to avail itself of this delegated power over the electoral process it necessarily becomes subject to the regulation of [the Voting Rights Act]." Although joining the judgment, Justice Breyer wrote a separate opinion, joined by Justices O'Connor and Souter, that was more narrowly drawn but nonetheless stressed that the Voting Right Act was meant to cover all political party activities that substitute for primary elections. In contrast, the four dissenters—Chief Justice Rehnquist and Justices Kennedy, Scalia, and Thomas—countered that the act did not extend to parties' nominating conventions, because political parties are not "state actors," and that the majority's ruling infringed on political parties' freedom of association, as guaranteed by the First Amendment.

In its 1996–1997 term, the Court will consider another challenge to electoral methods in *Lopez v. Monterey County*. In this case, Hispanic voters challenge the method used to elect municipal court judges in Monterey, California. But the Court's ruling could affect local judicial elections nationwide. The Court will also hear an important case, *Reno v. Bossier Parish School Board*, No. 95-1455, involving the Department of Justice's standards for approving changes in voting district boundaries and procedures. Section 5 of the Voting Rights Act, which applies to much of the South, requires state and local governments to receive the DoJ's preclearance of changes in election laws and a showing that the proposed change has neither a discriminatory purpose nor discriminatory effect. Under Section 2 of that act, which applies nationwide, any voting practice that has a discriminatory effect, regardless of its purpose, is prohibited. At issue is the DoJ's policy, adopted in 1987, that any practice violating Section 2 is automatically disqualified from preclearance under Section 5. The case originated in Bossier Parish, Louisiana, where twenty percent of the population is black but which has never elected a black member to its twelve-member school board. After the 1990 census, the school board redistricted and rejected a plan advanced by the local chapter of the National Association for the Advancement of Colored People that would have provided for two majority-minority districts. Instead, the board adopted a plan already in place for jury selection. The DoJ found the plan to violate Section 2 and declined to give it preclearance approval under Section 5. A three-judge panel of the federal district court overturned that decision and held that the DoJ must show not only that a challenged plan fails to improve the lot of black voters but also that they are made worse off. The DoJ appealed that decision to the Supreme Court.

Miller v. Johnson
115 S.Ct. 2475 (1995)

Following the 1990 census, it was determined that Georgia's population, twenty-seven percent of whom are black, merited an additional eleventh congressional district. Accordingly, in 1991 Georgia's general assembly redrew district lines so as to create two majority-minority districts and another in which blacks comprised over thirty-five percent of the voting age population. As required under the Voting Rights Act, Georgia, like other southern states that once discriminated against blacks, then submitted its redistricting plan to the Department of Justice (DoJ) for preclearance approval. Although the plan increased the number of majority-minority districts from one to two, the DoJ rejected the plan for failing to recognize certain black populations. The general assembly again redrew the lines but its second plan was rejected as well, in part because the DoJ relied on an alternative "Max-Black plan" proposing the creation of three majority-minority districts. The key to this plan was a "Macon/Savannah trade," in which Macon's dense black population would be transferred from the eleventh district to the second district, which then became a majority-minority district, and the eleventh district's loss of black population would be offset by extending that district to include Savannah's black populations. For a third time, Georgia's general assembly redrew its congressional district lines. This time, though, it created three majority-minority districts by utilizing the "Macon/Savannah trade."

In 1992, elections were held under the new congressional redistricting plan and black candidates were elected to Congress from all three majority-minority districts. Subsequently, in 1994 five white voters from the eleventh district filed a lawsuit challenging the constitutionality of the redistricting. They relied on the Supreme Court's recent ruling in *Shaw v. Reno*, 509 U.S. 630 (1993) (see Vol. 1, Ch. 8), in arguing that the redistricting constituted racial gerrymandering and violated the Fourteenth Amendment's equal protection clause. A three-judge federal district court agreed and held that the creation of three majority-minority districts was not required under the Voting Rights Act, whereupon an appeal of that decision was made to the Supreme Court.

The Court's decision was five to four and opinion announced by Justice Kennedy. Justice O'Connor filed a concurring opinion. Justices Stevens and Ginsburg filed dissenting opinions, and the latter's was joined by Justices Breyer, Souter, and Stevens.

Justice KENNEDY delivered the opinion of the Court.

The constitutionality of Georgia's congressional redistricting plan is at issue here. In *Shaw v. Reno* (1993), we held that a plaintiff states a claim under the Equal Protection Clause by alleging that a state redistricting plan, on its face, has no rational explanation save as an effort to separate voters on the basis of race. The question we now decide is whether Georgia's new Eleventh District gives rise to a valid equal protection claim under the principles announced in *Shaw*, and, if so, whether it can be sustained nonetheless as narrowly tailored to serve a compelling governmental interest.

The Equal Protection Clause of the Fourteenth Amendment provides that no State shall "deny to any person within its jurisdiction the equal protection of the laws." Its central mandate is racial neutrality in governmental decisionmaking. Though application of this imperative raises difficult questions, the basic principle is straightforward: "Racial and ethnic distinctions of any sort are inherently suspect and thus call for the most exacting judicial examination. . . . This perception of racial and ethnic distinctions is rooted in our Nation's constitutional and demographic history." *Regents of Univ. of California v. Bakke*, 438 U.S. 265 (1978). This rule obtains with equal force regardless of "the race of those burdened or benefited by a particular classification." [*City of*] *Richmond v. J. A. Croson Co.*, 488 U.S. 469 (1989). Laws classifying citizens on the basis of race cannot be upheld unless they are narrowly tailored to achieving a compelling state interest.

In *Shaw v. Reno*, we recognized that these equal protection principles govern a State's drawing of congressional districts, though, as our cautious approach there discloses, application of these principles to electoral districting is a most delicate task. . . . This case requires us to apply the principles articulated in *Shaw* to the most recent congressional redistricting plan enacted by the State of Georgia. . . .

Finding that the "evidence of the General Assembly's intent to racially gerrymander the Eleventh District is overwhelming, and practically stipulated by the parties involved," the District Court held that race was the predominant, overriding factor in drawing the Eleventh District. Appellants do not take issue with the court's factual finding of this racial motivation. Rather, they contend that evidence of a legislature's deliberate classification of voters on the basis of race cannot alone suffice to state a claim under *Shaw*. They argue that, regardless of the legislature's purposes, a plaintiff must demonstrate that a district's shape is so bizarre that it is unexplainable other than on the basis of race, and that appellees failed to make that showing here. Appellants' conception of the constitutional violation misapprehends our holding in *Shaw* and the Equal Protection precedent upon which *Shaw* relied.

Shaw recognized a claim "analytically distinct" from a vote dilution claim. Whereas a vote dilution claim alleges that the State has enacted a particular voting scheme as a purposeful device "to minimize or cancel out the voting potential of racial or ethnic minorities," *Mobile v. Bolden*, 446 U.S. 55 (1980), an action disadvantaging voters of a particular race, the essence of the equal protection claim recognized in *Shaw* is that the State has used race as a basis for separating voters into districts. Just as the State may not, absent extraordinary justification, segregate citizens on the basis of race in its public parks, *New Orleans City Park Improvement Assn. v. Detiege*, 358 U.S. 54 (1958), buses, *Gayle v. Browder*, 352 U.S. 903 (1956), golf courses, *Holmes v. Atlanta*, 350 U.S. 879 (1955), beaches, *Mayor and City Council of Baltimore v. Dawson*, 350 U.S. 877 (1955), and schools, *Brown v. Board of Education*, 347 U.S. 483 (1954), so did we recognize in *Shaw* that it may not separate its citizens into different voting districts on the basis of race. The idea is a simple one: "At the heart of the Constitution's guarantee of equal protection lies the simple command that the Government must treat citizens 'as individuals, not "as simply components of a racial, religious, sexual or national class."'" *Metro Broadcasting, Inc. v.* [*Federal Communications Commission*], 497 U.S. 547 (1990) (O'CONNOR, J., dissenting). When the State assigns voters on the basis of race, it engages in the offensive and demeaning assumption that voters of a particular race, because of their race, "think alike, share the same political interests, and will prefer the same candidates at the polls." *Shaw*. Race-based assignments "embody stereotypes that treat individuals as the product of their race, evaluating their thoughts and efforts—their very worth as citizens—according to a criterion barred to the Government by history and the Constitution." *Metro Broadcasting* (O'CONNOR, J., dissenting). They also cause society serious harm. . . .

Our observation in *Shaw* of the consequences of racial stereotyping was not meant to suggest that a district must be bizarre on its face before there is a constitutional violation. Nor was our conclusion in *Shaw* that in certain instances a district's appearance (or, to be more precise, its appearance in combination with certain demographic evidence) can give rise to an equal protection claim, a holding that bizarreness was a threshold showing, as appellants believe it to be. Our circumspect approach and narrow holding in *Shaw* did not erect an artificial rule barring accepted equal protection analysis in other redistricting cases. Shape is relevant not because bizarreness is a necessary element of the constitutional wrong or a threshold requirement of proof, but because it may be persuasive circumstantial evidence that race for its own sake, and not other districting principles, was the legislature's dominant and controlling rationale in drawing its district lines. The logical implication, as courts applying *Shaw* have recognized, is that parties may rely on evidence other than bizarreness to establish race-based districting.

Our reasoning in *Shaw* compels this conclusion. We recognized in *Shaw* that, outside the districting context, statutes are subject to strict scrutiny under the Equal Protection Clause not just when they contain express racial classifications, but also when, though race neutral on their face, they are motivated by a racial purpose or object. . . .

Appellants and some of their *amici* argue that the Equal Protection Clause's general proscription on race-based decisionmaking does not obtain in the districting context because redistricting by definition involves racial considerations. Underlying their argument are the very stereotypical assumptions the Equal Protection Clause forbids. It is true that redistricting in most cases will implicate a political calculus in which various interests compete for recognition, but it does not follow from this that individuals of the same race share a single political interest. The view that they do is "based on the demeaning notion that members of the defined racial groups ascribe to certain 'minority views' that must be different from those of other citizens," *Metro Broadcasting* (KENNEDY, J., dissenting), the precise use of race as a proxy the Constitution prohibits. . . .

In sum, we make clear that parties alleging that a State has assigned voters on the basis of race are neither confined in their proof to evidence regarding the district's geometry and makeup nor required to make a threshold showing of bizarreness. Today's case requires us further to consider the requirements of the proof necessary to sustain this equal protection challenge. . . .

In our view, the District Court applied the correct analysis, and its finding that race was the predominant factor motivating the drawing of the Eleventh District was not clearly erroneous. The court found it was "exceedingly obvious" from the shape of the Eleventh District, together with the relevant racial demographics, that the drawing of narrow land bridges to incorporate within the District outlying appendages containing nearly 80% of the district's total black population was a deliberate attempt to bring black populations into the district. Although by comparison with other districts the geometric shape of the Eleventh District may not seem bizarre on its face, when its shape is considered in conjunction with its racial and population densities, the story of racial gerrymandering seen by the District Court becomes much clearer. Although this evidence is quite compelling, we need not determine whether it was, standing alone, sufficient to establish a *Shaw* claim that the Eleventh District is unexplainable other than by race. The District Court had before it considerable additional evidence showing that the General Assembly was motivated by a predominant, overriding desire to assign black populations to the Eleventh District and thereby permit the creation of a third majority-black district in the Second. . . .

Race was, as the District Court found, the predominant, overriding factor explaining the General Assembly's decision to attach to the Eleventh District various appendages containing dense majority-black populations. As a result, Georgia's congressional redistricting plan cannot be upheld unless it satisfies strict scrutiny, our most rigorous and exacting standard of constitutional review.

To satisfy strict scrutiny, the State must demonstrate that its districting legislation is narrowly tailored to achieve a compelling interest. There is a "significant state interest in eradicating the effects of past racial discrimination." *Shaw.* The State does not argue, however, that it created the Eleventh District to remedy past discrimination, and with good reason: there is little doubt that the State's true interest in designing the Eleventh District was creating a third majority-black district to satisfy the Justice Department's preclearance demands. Whether or not in some cases compliance with the Voting Rights Act, standing alone, can provide a compelling interest independent of any interest in remedying past discrimination, it cannot do so here. . . .

We do not accept the contention that the State has a compelling interest in complying with whatever preclearance mandates the Justice Department issues. When a state governmental entity seeks to justify race-based remedies to cure the effects of past discrimination, we do not accept the government's mere assertion that the remedial action is required. Rather, we insist on a strong basis in evidence of the harm being remedied. Our presumptive skepticism of all racial classifications prohibits us as well from accepting on its face the Justice Department's conclusion that racial districting is necessary under the Voting Rights Act. Where a State relies on the Department's determination that race-based districting is necessary to comply with the Voting Rights Act, the judiciary retains an independent obligation in adjudicating consequent equal protection challenges to ensure that the State's actions are narrowly tailored to achieve a compelling interest. . . .

For the same reasons, we think it inappropriate for a court engaged in constitutional scrutiny to accord deference to the Justice Department's interpretation of the Act. Although we have deferred to the Department's interpretation in certain statutory cases, we have rejected agency interpretations to which we would otherwise defer where they raise serious constitutional questions. When the Justice Department's interpretation of the Act compels race-based districting, it by definition raises a serious constitutional question, and should not receive deference. . . .

The Voting Rights Act, and its grant of authority to the federal courts to uncover official efforts to abridge minorities' right to vote, has been of vital importance in eradicating invidious discrimination from the electoral process and enhancing the legitimacy of our political institutions. Only if our political system and our society cleanse themselves of that discrimination will all members of the polity share an equal opportunity to gain public office regardless of race. As a Nation we share both the obligation and the aspiration of working toward this end. The end is neither assured nor well served, however, by carving electorates into racial blocs. . . . It takes a shortsighted and unauthorized view of the Voting Rights Act to invoke that statute, which has played a decisive role in redressing some of our worst forms of discrimination, to demand the very racial stereotyping the Fourteenth Amendment forbids.

The judgment of the District Court is affirmed, and the case is remanded for further proceedings consistent with this decision.

Justice GINSBURG, with whom Justices STEVENS and BREYER join, and with whom Justice SOUTER joins except as to Part III-B, dissenting.

Legislative districting is highly political. business. This Court has generally respected the competence of state legislatures to attend to the task. When race is the issue, however, we have recognized the need for judicial intervention to prevent dilution of minority voting strength. Generations of rank discrimination against African-Americans, as citizens and voters, account for that surveillance.

Two Terms ago, in *Shaw v. Reno* (1993), this Court took up a claim "analytically distinct" from a vote dilution claim. *Shaw* authorized judicial intervention in "extremely irregular" apportionments, in which the legislature cast aside traditional districting practices to consider race alone—in the *Shaw* case, to create a district in North Carolina in which African-Americans would compose a majority of the voters.

Today the Court expands the judicial role, announcing that federal courts are to undertake searching review of any district with contours "predominantly motivated" by race: "strict scrutiny" will be triggered not only when traditional districting practices are abandoned, but also when those practices are "subordinated to"—given less weight than—race. . . . Because I do not endorse the Court's new standard and would not upset Georgia's plan, I dissent.

I

At the outset, it may be useful to note points on which the Court does not divide. First, we agree that federalism and the slim judicial competence to draw district lines weigh heavily against judicial intervention in apportionment decisions; as a rule, the task should remain within the domain of state legislatures. Second, for most of our Nation's history, the franchise has not been enjoyed equally by black citizens and white voters. To redress past wrongs and to avert any recurrence of exclusion of blacks from political processes, federal courts now respond to Equal Protection Clause and Voting Rights Act complaints of state action that dilutes minority voting strength. Third, to meet statutory requirements, state legislatures must sometimes consider race as a factor highly relevant to the drawing of district lines. Finally, state legislatures may recognize communities that have a particular racial or ethnic makeup, even in the absence of any compulsion to do so, in order to account for interests common to or shared by the persons grouped together.

Therefore, the fact that the Georgia General Assembly took account of race in drawing district lines—a fact not in dispute—does not render the State's plan invalid. To offend the Equal Protection Clause, all agree, the legislature had to do more than consider race. How much more, is the issue that divides the Court today. . . .

Federal courts have ventured into the political thicket of apportionment when necessary to secure to members of racial minorities equal voting rights—rights denied in many States, including Georgia, until not long ago.

The Fifteenth Amendment, ratified in 1870, declares that the right to vote "shall not be denied . . . by any State on account of race." That declaration, for generations, was often honored in the breach; it was greeted by a near century of "unremitting and ingenious defiance" in several States, including Georgia. *South Carolina v. Katzenbach*, 383 U.S. 301 (1966). After a brief interlude of black suffrage enforced by federal troops but accompanied by rampant violence against blacks, Georgia held a constitutional convention in 1877. Its purpose, according to the convention's leader, was to "fix it so that the people shall rule and the Negro shall never be heard from." In pursuit of this objective, Georgia enacted a cumulative poll tax, requiring voters to show they had paid past as well as current poll taxes; one historian described this tax as the "most effective bar to Negro suffrage ever devised."

In 1890, the Georgia General Assembly authorized "white primaries"; keeping blacks out of the Democratic primary effectively excluded them from Georgia's political life, for victory in the Democratic primary was tantamount to election. Early in this century, Georgia governor Hoke Smith persuaded the legislature to pass the "Disenfranchisement Act of 1908"; true to its title, this measure added various property, "good character," and literacy requirements that, as administered, served to keep blacks from voting. The result, as one commentator observed 25 years later, was an "almost absolute exclusion of the Negro voice in state and federal elections."

Faced with a political situation scarcely open to self-correction—disenfranchised blacks had no electoral influence, hence no muscle to lobby the legislature for change—the Court intervened. It invalidated white primaries, see *Smith v. Allwright*, 321 U.S. 649 (1944), and other burdens on minority voting.

It was against this backdrop that the Court, construing the Equal Protection Clause, undertook to ensure that apportionment plans do not dilute minority voting strength. By enacting the Voting Rights Act of 1965, Congress heightened federal judicial involvement in apportionment, and also fashioned a role for the Attorney General. Section 2 creates a federal right of action to challenge vote dilution. Section 5 requires States with a history of discrimination to preclear any changes in voting practices with either a federal court (a three-judge United States District Court for the District of Columbia) or the Attorney General.

These Court decisions and congressional directions significantly reduced voting discrimination against minorities. In the 1972 election, Georgia gained its first black Member of Congress since Reconstruction, and the

1981 apportionment created the State's first majority-minority district. This voting district, however, was not gained easily. Georgia created it only after the United States District Court for the District of Columbia refused to preclear a predecessor apportionment plan that included no such district — an omission due in part to the influence of Joe Mack Wilson, then Chairman of the Georgia House Reapportionment Committee. As Wilson put it only 14 years ago, "'I don't want to draw nigger districts.'" *Busbee v. Smith*, 549 F. Supp. 494 (DC 1982).

II

Before *Shaw v. Reno*, this Court invoked the Equal Protection Clause to justify intervention in the quintessentially political task of legislative districting in two circumstances: to enforce the one-person-one-vote requirement, and to prevent dilution of a minority group's voting strength.

In *Shaw*, the Court recognized a third basis for an equal protection challenge to a State's apportionment plan. The Court wrote cautiously, emphasizing that judicial intervention is exceptional: "Strict [judicial] scrutiny" is in order, the Court declared, if a district is "so extremely irregular on its face that it rationally can be viewed only as an effort to segregate the races for purposes of voting." . . . The problem in *Shaw* was not the plan architects' consideration of race as relevant in redistricting. Rather, in the Court's estimation, it was the virtual exclusion of other factors from the calculus. Traditional districting practices were cast aside, the Court concluded, with race alone steering placement of district lines.

The record before us does not show that race similarly overwhelmed traditional districting practices in Georgia. Although the Georgia General Assembly prominently considered race in shaping the Eleventh District, race did not crowd out all other factors, as the Court found it did in North Carolina's delineation of the *Shaw* district.

In contrast to the snake-like North Carolina district inspected in *Shaw*, Georgia's Eleventh District is hardly "bizarre," "extremely irregular," or "irrational on its face." Instead, the Eleventh District's design reflects significant consideration of "traditional districting factors (such as keeping political subdivisions intact) and the usual political process of compromise and trades for a variety of nonracial reasons." The District covers a core area in central and eastern Georgia, and its total land area of 6,780 square miles is about average for the State. The border of the Eleventh District runs 1,184 miles, in line with Georgia's Second District, which has a 1,243-mile border, and the State's Eighth District, with a border running 1,155 miles.

Nor does the Eleventh District disrespect the boundaries of political subdivisions. Of the 22 counties in the District, 14 are intact and 8 are divided. That puts the Eleventh District at about the state average in divided counties. . . .

Evidence at trial similarly shows that considerations other than race went into determining the Eleventh District's boundaries. For a "political reason"—to accommodate the request of an incumbent State Senator regarding the placement of the precinct in which his son lived—the DeKalb County portion of the Eleventh District was drawn to include a particular (largely white) precinct. The corridor through Effingham County was substantially narrowed at the request of a (white) State Representative. In Chatham County, the District was trimmed to exclude a heavily black community in Garden City because a State Representative wanted to keep the city intact inside the neighboring First District. The Savannah extension was configured by "the narrowest means possible" to avoid splitting the city of Port Wentworth.

Georgia's Eleventh District, in sum, is not an outlier district shaped without reference to familiar districting techniques. . . .

III

To separate permissible and impermissible use of race in legislative apportionment, the Court orders strict scrutiny for districting plans "predominantly motivated" by race. No longer can a State avoid judicial oversight by giving—as in this case—genuine and measurable consideration to traditional districting practices. Instead, a federal case can be mounted whenever plaintiffs plausibly allege that other factors carried less weight than race. This invitation to litigate against the State seems to me neither necessary nor proper. . . .

B

Under the Court's approach, judicial review of the same intensity, i.e., strict scrutiny, is in order once it is determined that an apportionment is predominantly motivated by race. It matters not at all, in this new regime, whether the apportionment dilutes or enhances minority voting strength. As very recently observed, however, "there is no moral or constitutional equivalence between a policy that is designed to perpetuate a caste system and one that seeks to eradicate racial subordination." *Adarand Constructors, Inc. v. Pena,* [115 S.Ct. 2097 (1995)] (STEVENS, J., dissenting).

Special circumstances justify vigilant judicial inspection to protect minority voters—circumstances that do not apply to majority voters. A history of exclusion from state politics left racial minorities without clout to extract provisions for fair representation in the lawmaking forum. The equal protection rights of minority voters thus could have remained unrealized absent the Judiciary's close surveillance. The majority, by definition, encounters no such blockage. White voters in Georgia do not lack means to exert strong pressure on their state legislators. The force of their numbers is itself a powerful determiner of what the legislature will do that does not coincide with perceived majority interests. . . .

The reapportionment plan that resulted from Georgia's political process merited this Court's approbation, not its condemnation. Accordingly, I dissent.

Bush v. Vera
116 S.Ct. — (1996)

The 1990 census indicated that, due to an increase in population in urban areas, Texas was entitled to three additional congressional seats. In response and with a view to complying with the Voting Rights Act, the Texas legislature proposed a redistricting plan that created District 30, a majority–African-American district in Dallas; District 29, a majority-Hispanic district in and around Houston; and reconfigured District 18 in order to make it a majority–African-American district. The Department of Justice precleared the plan under Section 5 of the Voting Rights Act. Subsequently, several voters challenged the plan in federal court, alleging that twenty-four of Texas's thirty congressional seats constituted racial gerrymanders in violation of the Fourteenth Amendment. A three-judge district court held that Districts 18, 29, and 30 were unconstitutional in 1994, whereupon the state's governor, George W. Bush, appealed that ruling to the Supreme Court.

The Court's decision was five to four and its opinion was delivered by Justice O'Connor. Only Chief Justice Rehnquist and Justice Kennedy joined Justice O'Connor's opinion. Justice O'Connor also issued a concurring opinion. Justice Thomas, joined by Justice Scalia, filed a concurring opinion. Justices Stevens and Souter issued dissenting opinions, which were joined by Justices Ginsburg and Breyer.

Justice O'CONNOR announced the judgment of the Court and delivered an opinion, in which the CHIEF JUSTICE and Justice KENNEDY join.

We must now determine whether those districts are subject to strict scrutiny. Our precedents have used a variety of formulations to describe the threshold for the application of strict scrutiny. Strict scrutiny applies where "redistricting legislation . . . is so extremely irregular on its face that it rationally can be viewed only as an effort to segregate the races for purposes of voting, without regard for traditional districting principles," [*Shaw v. Reno*, 509 U.S. 630 (1993)], *Shaw I*, or where "race for its own sake, and not other districting principles, was the legislature's dominant and controlling rationale in drawing its district lines," *Miller* [*v. Johnson*, 115 S.Ct. 2475 (1995)], and "the legislature subordinated traditional race-neutral districting principles . . . to racial considerations," id.

Strict scrutiny does not apply merely because redistricting is performed with consciousness of race. Nor does it apply to all cases of intentional creation of majority-minority districts. Electoral district lines are "facially race neutral," so a more searching inquiry is necessary before strict scrutiny can be found applicable in redistricting cases than in cases of "classifications based explicitly on race." See *Adarand Constructors, Inc. v. Pena,* [115 S.Ct. 2097 (1995)]. For strict scrutiny to apply, the plaintiffs must prove that other, legitimate districting principles were "subordinated" to race. *Miller.* By that, we mean that race must be "the predominant factor motivating the legislature's [redistricting] decision." We thus differ from Justice THOMAS, who would apparently hold that it suffices that racial considerations be a motivation for the drawing of a majority-minority district.

The present case is a mixed motive case. The appellants concede that one of Texas' goals in creating the three districts at issue was to produce majority-minority districts, but they also cite evidence that other goals, particularly incumbency protection, also played a role in the drawing of the district lines. The record does not reflect a history of "purely race-based" districting revisions. . . .

The District Court began its analysis by rejecting the factual basis for appellants' claim that Texas' challenged "districts cannot be unconstitutionally bizarre in shape because Texas does not have and never has used traditional redistricting principles such as natural geographical boundaries, contiguity, compactness, and conformity to political subdivisions." The court instead found that "generally, Texas has not intentionally disregarded traditional districting criteria," and that only one pre-1991 congressional district in Texas was comparable in its irregularity and noncompactness to the three challenged districts. . . .

The District Court also found substantial direct evidence of the legislature's racial motivations. The State's submission to the Department of Justice for preclearance under [Voting Rights Act (VRA)] Section 5 reports a consensus within the legislature that the three new congressional districts "'should be configured in such a way as to allow members of racial, ethnic, and language minorities to elect Congressional representatives. Accordingly, the three new districts include a predominantly black district drawn in the Dallas County area [District 30] and predominantly Hispanic districts in the Harris County area [District 29] and in the South Texas region. In addition to creating the three new minority districts, the proposed Congressional redistricting plan increases the black voting strength of the current District 18 (Harris County) by increasing the population to assure that the black community may continue to elect a candidate of its choice.'" . . .

The means that Texas used to make its redistricting decisions provides further evidence of the importance of race. The primary tool used in drawing district lines was a computer program called "REDAPPL." REDAPPL permitted redistricters to manipulate district lines on computer maps, on which racial and other socioeconomic data were superimposed. At each change in configuration of the district lines being drafted, REDAPPL displayed updated racial composition statistics for the district as drawn. REDAPPL contained racial data at the block-by-block level, whereas other data, such as party registration and past voting statistics, were only available at the level of voter tabulation districts (which approximate election precincts). The availability and use of block-by-block racial data was unprecedented; before the 1990 census, data were not broken down beyond the census tract level. By providing uniquely detailed racial data, REDAPPL enabled districters to make more intricate refinements on the basis of race than on the basis of other demographic information. . . .

These findings—that the State substantially neglected traditional districting criteria such as compactness, that it was committed from the outset to creating majority-minority districts, and that it manipulated district lines to exploit unprecedentedly detailed racial data—together weigh in favor of the application of strict scrutiny. We do not hold that any one of these factors is independently sufficient to require strict scrutiny. The Constitution does not mandate regularity of district shape, see *Shaw I*, and the neglect of traditional districting criteria is merely necessary, not sufficient. For strict scrutiny to apply, traditional districting criteria must be subordinated to race. *Miller.* Nor, as we have emphasized, is the decision to create a majority-minority district objectionable in and of itself. The direct evidence of that decision is not, as Justice STEVENS suggests, "the real key" to our decision; it is merely one of several essential ingredients. . . .

Several factors other than race were at work in the drawing of the districts. Traditional districting criteria were not entirely neglected: Districts 18 and 29 maintain the integrity of county lines; each of the three districts takes its character from a principal city and the surrounding urban area; and none of the districts is as widely dispersed as the North Carolina district held unconstitutional in [*Shaw v. Hunt*, 116 S.Ct. — (1996) (*Shaw II*)]. . . .

Strict scrutiny would not be appropriate if race-neutral, traditional districting considerations predominated over racial ones. We have not subjected political gerrymandering to strict scrutiny. See *Davis v. Bandemer*, 478 U.S. 109 (1986). . . .

The population of District 30 is 50% African-American and 17.1% Hispanic. Fifty percent of the district's population is located in a compact, albeit irregularly shaped, core in south Dallas, which is 69% African-American. But the remainder of the district consists of narrow and bizarrely shaped tentacles—the State identifies seven "segments"—extending primarily to the north and west. Over 98% of the district's population is within Dallas County, but it crosses two county lines at its western and northern extremities. Its western excursion into Tarrant County grabs a small community that is 61.9% African-American, its northern excursion into Collin County occupies a hook-like shape mapping exactly onto the only area in the southern half of that county with a combined African-American and Hispanic percentage population in excess of 50%. . . .

Finally, and most significantly, the objective evidence provided by the district plans and demographic maps suggests strongly the predominance of race. Given that the districting software used by the State provided only racial data at the block-by-block level, the fact that District 30, unlike Johnson's original proposal, splits voter tabulation districts and even individual streets in many places, suggests that racial criteria predominated over other districting criteria in determining the district's boundaries. And, despite the strong correlation between race and political affiliation, the maps reveal that political considerations were subordinated to racial classification in the drawing of many of the most extreme and bizarre district lines. For example, the northernmost hook of the district, where it ventures into Collin County, is tailored perfectly to maximize minority population (all whole and parts of 1992 voter tabulation districts within District 30's Collin County hook have a combined African-American and Hispanic population in excess of 50%, with an average African-American population of 19.8%, while the combined African-American and Hispanic population in all surrounding voter tabulation districts, and the other parts of split districts, in Collin County is less than 25%), whereas it is far from the shape that would be necessary to maximize the Democratic vote in that area (showing a Republican majority, based on 1990 voting patterns in seven of the eight 1990 voter tabulation districts wholly or partly included in District 30 in Collin County).

The combination of these factors compels us to agree with the District Court that "the contours of Congressional District 30 are unexplainable in terms other than race." It is true that District 30 does not evince a consistent, single-minded effort to "segregate" voters on the basis of race, and does not represent "apartheid" (SOUTER, J., dissenting). But the fact that racial data were used in complex ways, and for multiple objectives, does not mean that race did not predominate over other considerations. . . .

In Harris County, centered on the city of Houston, Districts 18 and 29 interlock "like a jigsaw puzzle . . . in which it might be impossible to get the pieces apart." As the District Court noted, "these districts are so finely 'crafted' that one cannot visualize their exact boundaries without looking at a map at least three feet square." According to the leading statistical study of relative district compactness and regularity, they are two of the three least regular districts in the country.

District 18's population is 51% African-American and 15% Hispanic. It "has some of the most irregular boundaries of any congressional district in the country[,] . . . boundaries that squiggle north toward Intercontinental Airport and northwest out radial highways, then spurt south on one side toward the port and on the other toward the Astrodome." Its "many narrow corridors, wings, or fingers . . . reach out to enclose black voters, while excluding nearby Hispanic residents."

District 29 has a 61% Hispanic and 10% African-American population. . . . Not only are the shapes of the districts bizarre; they also exhibit utter disregard of city limits, local election precincts, and voter tabulation district lines. This caused a severe disruption of traditional forms of political activity. Campaigners seeking to visit their constituents "had to carry a map to identify the district lines, because so often the borders would move from block to block"; voters "did not know the candidates running for office" because they did not know which district they lived in. In light of Texas' requirement that voting be arranged by precinct, with each precinct representing a community which shares local, state, and federal representatives, it also created administrative headaches for local election officials. . . .

Having concluded that strict scrutiny applies, we must determine whether the racial classifications embodied in any of the three districts are narrowly tailored to further a compelling state interest. Appellants point to three compelling interests: the interest in avoiding liability under the "results" test of VRA Section 2(b), the interest in remedying past and present racial discrimination, and the "nonretrogression" principle of VRA Section 5 (for District 18 only). We consider them in turn.

Section 2(a) of the VRA prohibits the imposition of any electoral practice or procedure that "results in a denial or abridgment of the right of any citizen . . . to vote on account of race or color." In 1982, Congress amended the VRA by changing the language of Section 2(a) and adding Section 2(b), which provides a "results" test for violation of Section 2(a). A violation exists if, "based on the totality of circumstances, it is shown that the political processes leading to nomination or election in the State or political subdivision are not equally open to participation by members of a class of citizens protected by subsection (a) of this section in that its members have less opportunity than other members of the electorate to participate in the political process and to elect representatives of their choice." Appellants contend that creation of each of the three majority-minority districts at issue was justified by Texas' compelling state interest in complying with this results test.

As we have done in each of our previous cases in which this argument has been raised as a defense to charges of racial gerrymandering, we assume without deciding that compliance with the results test, as interpreted by our precedents, can be a compelling state interest. See *Shaw II*; *Miller*. . . .

A Section 2 district that is reasonably compact and regular, taking into account traditional districting principles such as maintaining communities of interest and traditional boundaries, may pass strict scrutiny without having to defeat rival compact districts designed by plaintiffs' experts in endless "beauty contests." . . .

We assume, without deciding, that the State had a "strong basis in evidence" for finding the second and third threshold conditions for Section 2 liability to be present. We have, however, already found that all three districts are bizarrely shaped and far from compact, and that those characteristics are predominantly attributable to gerrymandering that was racially motivated and/or achieved by the use of race as a proxy. . . .

These characteristics defeat any claim that the districts are narrowly tailored to serve the State's interest in avoiding liability under Section 2, because Section 2 does not require a State to create, on predominantly racial lines, a district that is not "reasonably compact." See *Johnson v. De Grandy*, [114 S.Ct. 2647] (1994). If, because of the dispersion of the minority population, a reasonably compact majority-minority district cannot be created, Section 2 does not require a majority-minority district; if a reasonably compact district can be created, nothing in Section 2 requires the race-based creation of a district that is far from compact. . . .

The United States and the State next contend that the district lines at issue are justified by the State's compelling interest in "ameliorating the effects of racially polarized voting attributable to past and present racial discrimination." In support of that contention, they cite Texas' long history of discrimination against minorities in electoral processes, stretching from the Reconstruction to modern times, including violations of the Constitution and of the VRA.

A State's interest in remedying discrimination is compelling when two conditions are satisfied. First, the discrimination that the State seeks to remedy must be specific, "identified discrimination"; second, the State "must have had a 'strong basis in evidence' to conclude that remedial action was necessary, 'before it embarks on an affirmative action program.'" *Shaw*

II. Here, the only current problem that appellants cite as in need of remediation is alleged vote dilution as a consequence of racial bloc voting, the same concern that underlies their VRA Section 2 compliance defense, which we have assumed to be valid for purposes of this opinion. We have indicated that such problems will not justify race-based districting unless "the State employs sound districting principles, and . . . the affected racial group's residential patterns afford the opportunity of creating districts in which they will be in the majority." *Shaw I.* Once that standard is applied, our agreement with the District Court's finding that these districts are not narrowly tailored to comply with Section 2 forecloses this line of defense.

The final contention offered by the State and private appellants is that creation of District 18 (only) was justified by a compelling state interest in complying with VRA Section 5. We have made clear that Section 5 has a limited substantive goal: "'to insure that no voting-procedure changes would be made that would lead to a retrogression in the position of racial minorities with respect to their effective exercise of the electoral franchise.'" *Miller.* Appellants contend that this "nonretrogression" principle is implicated because Harris County had, for two decades, contained a congressional district in which African-American voters had succeeded in selecting representatives of their choice, all of whom were African-Americans.

The problem with the State's argument is that it seeks to justify not maintenance, but substantial augmentation, of the African-American population percentage in District 18. At the previous redistricting, in 1980, District 18's population was 40.8% African-American. Plaintiffs' Exh. 13B, p. 55. As a result of Hispanic population increases and African-American emigration from the district, its population had reached 35.1% African-American and 42.2% Hispanic at the time of the 1990 census. The State has shown no basis for concluding that the increase to a 50.9% African-American population in 1991 was necessary to insure nonretrogression. Nonretrogression is not a license for the State to do whatever it deems necessary to insure continued electoral success; it merely mandates that the minority's opportunity to elect representatives of its choice not be diminished, directly or indirectly, by the State's actions. We anticipated this problem in *Shaw I*: "A reapportionment plan would not be narrowly tailored to the goal of avoiding retrogression if the State went beyond what was reasonably necessary to avoid retrogression." Applying that principle, it is clear that District 18 is not narrowly tailored to the avoidance of Section 5 liability. . . .

Justice O'CONNOR, concurring.

I write separately to express my view on two points. First, compliance with the results test of Section 2 of the Voting Rights Act (VRA) is a compelling state interest. Second, that test can co-exist in principle and in practice with *Shaw v. Reno*, 509 U.S. 630 (1993), and its progeny, as elaborated in today's opinions. . . .

The results test is violated if, "based on the totality of circumstances, it is shown that the political processes leading to nomination or election in the

State or political subdivision are not equally open to participation by members of [e.g., a racial minority group] in that its members have less opportunity than other members of the electorate to participate in the political process and to elect representatives of their choice."

In the 14 years since the enactment of Section 2(b), we have interpreted and enforced the obligations that it places on States in a succession of cases, assuming but never directly addressing its constitutionality. . . . Against this background, it would be irresponsible for a State to disregard the Section 2 results test. The Supremacy Clause obliges the States to comply with all constitutional exercises of Congress' power. . . . We should allow States to assume the constitutionality of Section 2 of the Voting Rights Act, including the 1982 amendments. . . .

Although I agree with the dissenters about Section 2's role as part of our national commitment to racial equality, I differ from them in my belief that that commitment can and must be reconciled with the complementary commitment of our Fourteenth Amendment jurisprudence to eliminate the unjustified use of racial stereotypes. At the same time that we combat the symptoms of racial polarization in politics, we must strive to eliminate unnecessary race-based state action that appears to endorse the disease. . . .

Justice KENNEDY, concurring.

I join the plurality opinion, but the statements in the opinion that strict scrutiny would not apply to all cases of intentional creation of majority-minority districts, require comment. Those statements are unnecessary to our decision, for strict scrutiny applies here. I do not consider these *dicta* to commit me to any position on the question whether race is predominant whenever a State, in redistricting, foreordains that one race be the majority in a certain number of districts or in a certain part of the State. In my view, we would no doubt apply strict scrutiny if a State decreed that certain districts had to be at least 50 percent white, and our analysis should be no different if the State so favors minority races. . . .

Justice THOMAS, with whom Justice SCALIA joins, concurring in the judgment.

I cannot agree with Justice O'CONNOR's assertion that strict scrutiny is not invoked by the intentional creation of majority-minority districts. Though *Shaw v. Reno*, 509 U.S. 630 (1993) (*Shaw I*), expressly reserved that question, we effectively resolved it in subsequent cases. Only last Term, in *Adarand Constructors, Inc. v. Pena*, [115 S.Ct. 2097] (1995), we vigorously asserted that all governmental racial classifications must be strictly scrutinized. And in *Miller v. Johnson*, [115 S.Ct. 2475] (1995), Georgia's concession that it intentionally created majority-minority districts was sufficient to show that race was a predominant, motivating factor in its redistricting.

Strict scrutiny applies to all governmental classifications based on race, and we have expressly held that there is no exception for race-based redistricting. . . . I concur in the judgment.

Justice STEVENS, with whom Justice GINSBURG and Justice BREYER join, dissenting.

For two reasons, I believe that the Court errs in striking down those districts.

First, I believe that the Court has misapplied its own tests for racial gerrymandering, both by applying strict scrutiny to all three of these districts, and then by concluding that none can meet that scrutiny. In asking whether strict scrutiny should apply, the Court improperly ignores the "complex interplay" of political and geographical considerations that went into the creation of Texas' new congressional districts, and focuses exclusively on the role that race played in the State's decisions to adjust the shape of its districts. A quick comparison of the unconstitutional majority-minority districts with three equally bizarre majority-Anglo districts, demonstrates that race was not necessarily the predominant factor contorting the district lines. I would follow the fair implications of the District Court's findings, and conclude that Texas' entire map is a political, not a racial, gerrymander. . . .

Second, even if I concluded that these districts failed an appropriate application of this still-developing law to appropriately read facts, I would not uphold the District Court decision. The decisions issued today serve merely to reinforce my conviction that the Court has, with its "analytically distinct" jurisprudence of racial gerrymandering, *Shaw v. Reno* (*Shaw I*), struck out into a jurisprudential wilderness that lacks a definable constitutional core and threatens to create harms more significant than any suffered by the individual plaintiffs challenging these districts. Though we travel ever farther from it with each passing decision, I would return to the well-traveled path that we left in *Shaw I*. The factors motivating Texas' redistricting plan are clearly revealed in the results of the 1992 elections. Both before and immediately after the 1990 census, the Democratic Party was in control of the Texas Legislature. Under the new map in 1992, more than two-thirds of the Districts—including each of the new ones—elected Democrats, even though Texas voters are arguably more likely to vote Republican than Democrat. Incumbents of both parties were just as successful: 26 of the 27 incumbents were reelected, while each of the three new districts elected a state legislator who had essentially acted as an incumbent in the districting process, giving "incumbents" a 97 percent success rate.

It was not easy for the State to achieve these results while simultaneously guaranteeing that each district enclosed the residence of its incumbent, contained the same number of people, and complied with other federal and state districting requirements. Much of Dallas and Houston, for example, was already represented in Congress by Democrats, and creating new Democratic districts in each city while ensuring politically safe seats for sitting Representatives required significant political gerrymandering. This task was aided by technological and informational advances that allowed the State to adjust lines on the scale of city blocks, thereby guaranteeing twists and turns that would have been essentially impossible in any earlier redistricting. . . .

It is clear that race also played a role in Texas' redistricting decisions. According to the 1990 Census, Texas contained 16,986,510 residents, of whom 22.5% were of Hispanic origin, and 11.6% were non-Hispanic African-American. Under the pre-1990 districting scheme, Texas' 27-member delegation included four Hispanics and one African-American. In Harris County, a concentrated Hispanic community was divided among several majority-Anglo districts as well as the majority-minority District 18. In Dallas County, the majority-black community in South Dallas was split down the middle between two majority-Anglo districts. The legislature was well aware, after the 1990 census, that the minority communities in each county were disproportionately responsible for the growth in population that gained three representatives for the State. Given the omnipresence of Section 2 of the Voting Rights Act, the demographics of the two communities, and the pressure from leaders of the minority communities in those cities, it was not unreasonable—and certainly not invidious discrimination of any sort— for the State to accede to calls for the creation of majority-minority districts in both cities. . . .

To determine whether the Court correctly affirms [the lower court's] decision, I begin, as does the plurality, by asking whether "strict scrutiny" should be applied to the State's consideration of race in the creation of these majority-minority districts.

We have traditionally applied strict scrutiny to state action that discriminates on the basis of race. Prior to *Shaw I*, however, we did so only in cases in which that discrimination harmed an individual or set of individuals because of their race. In contrast, the harm identified in *Shaw I* and its progeny is much more diffuse. Racial gerrymandering of the sort being addressed in these cases is "discrimination" only in the sense that the lines are drawn based on race, not in the sense that harm is imposed on a given person on account of their race.

Aware of this distinction, a majority of this Court has endorsed a position crucial to a proper evaluation of Texas' congressional districts: neither the Equal Protection Clause nor any other provision of the Constitution was offended merely because the legislature considered race when it deliberately created three majority-minority districts. The plurality's statement that strict scrutiny "does [not] apply to all cases of intentional creation of majority-minority districts," merely caps a long line of discussions, stretching from *Shaw I* to *Shaw II*, which have both expressly and implicitly set forth precisely that conclusion. . . .

Of course, determining the "predominant" motive of the Texas Legislature is not a simple matter. The members of that body faced many unrelenting pressures when they negotiated the creation of the contested districts. They had to ensure that there was no deviation in population from district to district. They reasonably believed that they had to create districts that would comply with the Voting Rights Act. If the redistricting legislation was to be enacted, they had to secure the support of incumbent Congressmen of both parties by drawing districts that would ensure their election. And all of these desires had to be achieved within a single contiguous district. Every time a district line was shifted from one place to another, each of these considerations was implicated, and additional, compensating shifts were necessary to ensure that all competing goals were simultaneously accomplished. In such a constrained environment, there will rarely be one "dominant and controlling" influence. Nowhere is this better illustrated than in Dallas' District 30 where, at the very least, it is clear that race was not such an overriding factor.

The Court lists several considerations which, when taken in combination, lead it to conclude that race, and no other cause, was the predominant factor influencing District 30's configuration. First, there is the shape itself. Second, there is evidence that the districts were intentionally drawn with consciousness of race in an effort to comply with the Voting Rights Act. Third, the Court dismisses two race-neutral considerations (communities of interest and incumbency protection) that petitioners advanced as race-neutral considerations that led to the odd shape of the districts. Finally, the plurality concludes that race was impermissibly used as a proxy for political affiliation during the course of redistricting. In my opinion, an appropriate reading of the record demonstrates that none of these factors—either singly or in combination—suggests that racial considerations "subordinated" race-neutral districting principles. . . .

I cannot profess to know how the Court's developing jurisprudence of racial gerrymandering will alter the political and racial landscape in this Nation—although it certainly will alter that landscape. As the Court's law in this area has developed, it has become ever more apparent to me that the Court's approach to these cases creates certain perverse incentives and (I presume) unanticipated effects that serve to highlight the essentially unknown territory into which it strides. Because I believe that the social and political risks created by the Court's decisions are not required by the Constitution, my first choice would be to avoid the preceding analysis altogether, and leave these considerations to the political branches of our Government.

The first unintended outcome of the legal reasoning in *Shaw II* and *Bush [v. Vera*, 116 S.Ct. — (1996),] is the very result that those decisions seek to avoid: The predominance of race in the districting process, over all other principles of importance. Given the Court's unwillingness to recognize the role that race-neutral districting principles played in the creation of the bizarrely shaped districts in both this case and *Shaw II*, it now seems clear that the only way that a State can both create a majority-minority district and avoid a racial gerrymander is by drawing, "without much conscious thought" (opinion of O'CONNOR, J.), and within the "limited degree of leeway" granted by the Court, the precise compact district that a court would impose in a successful Section 2 challenge. After the Court's decisions today, therefore, minority voters can make up a majority only in compact districts, whether intentionally or accidentally drawn, while white voters can be placed into districts as bizarre as the State desires. . . .

In light of this Court's recent work extolling the importance of state sovereignty in our federal scheme, *Seminole Tribe of Fla. v. Florida*, [116 S.Ct. 1114] (1996), I would have expected the Court's sensibilities to steer a course rather more deferential to the States than the one that it charts with its decisions today. . . .

The results are not inconsequential. After *Miller* and today's decisions, States may find it extremely difficult to avoid litigation flowing from decennial redistricting. On one hand, States will risk violating the Voting Rights Act if they fail to create majority-minority districts. If they create those districts, however, they may open themselves to liability under *Shaw* and its progeny. . . .

Regardless of the route taken by the States, the Court has guaranteed that federal courts will have a hand—and perhaps the only hand—in the "abrasive task of drawing district lines." *Wells v. Rockefeller*, 394 U.S. 542 (1969) (WHITE, J., dissenting). Given the uniquely political nature of the redistricting process, I fear the impact this new role will have on the public's perception of the impartiality of the federal judiciary. . . .

Justice SOUTER, with whom Justice GINSBURG and Justice BREYER join, dissenting.

When the Court devises a new cause of action to enforce a constitutional provision, it ought to identify an injury distinguishable from the consequences of concededly constitutional conduct, and it should describe the elements necessary and sufficient to make out such a claim. Nothing less can give notice to those whose conduct may give rise to liability or provide standards for courts charged with enforcing the Constitution. Those principles of justification, fair notice, and guidance, have never been satisfied in the instance of the action announced three Terms ago in *Shaw v. Reno*, 509 U.S. 630 (1993) (*Shaw I*), when a majority of this Court decided that a State violates the Fourteenth Amendment's Equal Protection Clause by excessive consideration of race in drawing the boundaries of voting districts, even when the resulting plan does not dilute the voting strength of any voters and so would not otherwise give rise to liability under the Fourteenth or Fifteenth Amendments, or under the Voting Rights Act.

Far from addressing any injury to members of a class subjected to differential treatment, the standard presupposition of an equal protection violation, *Shaw I* addressed a putative harm subject to complaint by any voter objecting to an untoward consideration of race in the political process. Although the Court has repeatedly disclaimed any intent to go as far as to outlaw all conscious consideration of race in districting, after three rounds of appellate litigation seeking to describe the elements and define the contours of the *Shaw* cause of action, a helpful statement of a *Shaw* claim still eludes this Court. This is so for reasons that go to the conceptual bone.

The result of this failure to provide a practical standard for distinguishing between the lawful and unlawful use of race has not only been inevitable confusion in state houses and courthouses, but a consequent shift in responsibility for setting district boundaries from the state legislatures, which are invested with front-line authority by Article I of the Constitution, to the courts, and truly to this Court, which is left to superintend the drawing of every legislative district in the land.

Today's opinions do little to solve *Shaw*'s puzzles or return districting responsibility to the States. . . . The price of *Shaw I*, indeed, may turn out to be the practical elimination of a State's discretion to apply traditional districting principles, widely accepted in States without racial districting issues as well as in States confronting them.

As the flaws of *Shaw I* persist, and as the burdens placed on the States and the courts by *Shaw* litigation loom larger with the approach of a new census and a new round of redistricting, the Court has to recognize that *Shaw*'s problems result from a basic misconception about the relation between race and districting principles, a mistake that no amount of case-by-case tinkering can eliminate. There is, therefore, no reason for confidence that the Court will eventually bring much order out of the confusion created by *Shaw I*, and because it has not, in any case, done so yet, I respectfully dissent. . . .

Shaw v. Hunt
116 S.Ct. — (1996)

Following the 1990 census, North Carolina's congressional seats increased from eleven to twelve. The state general assembly adopted a reapportionment plan that included one majority-black district, District 1, and submitted the plan to the Department of Justice (DoJ) for preclearance under Section 5 of the Voting Rights Act. The DoJ objected to the plan because it failed "to give effect to black and Native American voting strength" in "the south-central to southeastern part of the state," and viewed the state's reasons for not creating a second majority-minority district "to be pretextual." Thereafter, the legislature revised its districting scheme to include a second majority-black district. The new plan, Chapter 7, located the minority district, District 12, in the north-central or Piedmont region, not in the south-central or southeastern region identified in the DoJ objection letter. The department nonetheless precleared the revised plan. Five residents subsequently challenged the constitutionality of the redistricting. A federal district court dismissed the complaint, but was reversed by the Supreme Court in *Shaw v. Reno*, 503 U.S. 630 (1993) (*Shaw I*). On remand, a majority of the three-judge district court held that the plan did not violate the Fourteenth Amendment equal protection clause because it was narrowly tailored to further the state's compelling interests in complying with Sections 2 and 5 of the Voting Rights Act. That decision was in turn appealed to the Supreme Court.

The Court's decision was five to four and opinion delivered by Chief Justice Rehnquist. Justices Stevens and Souter filed dissenting opinions, in which Justices Ginsburg and Breyer joined.

CHIEF JUSTICE REHNQUIST delivered the opinion of the Court.

We explained in *Miller v. Johnson*, [115 S.Ct. 2475 (1995)], that a racially gerrymandered districting scheme, like all laws that classify citizens on the basis of race, is constitutionally suspect. Applying traditional equal protection principles in the voting-rights context is "a most delicate task," however, because a legislature may be conscious of the voters' races without using race as a basis for assigning voters to districts. The constitutional wrong occurs when race becomes the "dominant and controlling" consideration. . . .

[W]e think that the District Court's findings, read in the light of the evidence that it had before it, comport with the *Miller* standard.

First, the District Court had evidence of the district's shape and demographics. The court observed "the obvious fact" that the district's shape is "highly irregular and geographically non-compact by any objective standard that can be conceived." In fact, the serpentine district has been dubbed the least geographically compact district in the Nation.

The District Court also had direct evidence of the legislature's objective. The State's submission for preclearance expressly acknowledged that the Chapter 7's "overriding purpose was to comply with the dictates of the Attorney General's December 18, 1991, letter and to create two congressional districts with effective black voting majorities." . . .

Racial classifications are antithetical to the Fourteenth Amendment, whose "central purpose" was "to eliminate racial discrimination emanating from official sources in the States." *MacLaughlin v. Florida*, 379 U.S. 184 (1964); [*City of*] *Richmond v. J. A. Croson Co.*, 488 U.S. 469 (1989). While appreciating that a racial classification causes "fundamental injury" to the "individual rights of a person," *Goodman v. Lukens Steel Co.*, 482 U.S. 656 (1987), we have recognized that, under certain circumstances, drawing racial distinctions is permissible where a governmental body is pursuing a "compelling state interest." A State, however, is constrained in how it may pursue that end: "The means chosen to accomplish the State's asserted purpose must be specifically and narrowly framed to accomplish that purpose." *Wygant v. Jackson Bd. of Ed.*, 476 U.S. 267 (1986). North Carolina, therefore, must show not only that its redistricting plan was in pursuit of a compelling state interest, but also that "its districting legislation is narrowly tailored to achieve [that] compelling interest." *Miller.*

Appellees point to three separate compelling interests to sustain District 12: to eradicate the effects of past and present discrimination; to comply with Section 5 of the Voting Rights Act; and to comply with Section 2 of that Act. We address each in turn.

A State's interest in remedying the effects of past or present racial discrimination may in the proper case justify a government's use of racial distinctions. For that interest to rise to the level of a compelling state interest, it must satisfy two conditions. First, the discrimination must be "'identified discrimination.'" *Croson*. A generalized assertion of past discrimination in a particular industry or region is not adequate because it "provides no guidance for a legislative body to determine the precise scope of the injury it seeks to remedy." Accordingly, an effort to alleviate the effects of societal discrimination is not a compelling interest. Second, the institution that makes the racial distinction must have had a "strong basis in evidence" to conclude that remedial action was necessary, "before it embarks on an affirmative-action program."

In this case, the District Court found that an interest in ameliorating past discrimination did not actually precipitate the use of race in the redistricting plan. While some legislators invoked the State's history of discrimination as an argument for creating a second majority-black district, the court found that these members did not have enough voting power to have caused the creation of the second district on that basis alone. . . .

Appellees devote most of their efforts to arguing that the race-based redistricting was constitutionally justified by the State's duty to comply with the Voting Rights Act. The District Court agreed and held that compliance with Sections 2 and 5 of the Act could be, and in this case was, a compelling state interest. In *Miller*, we expressly left open the question whether under the proper circumstances compliance with the Voting Rights Act, on its own, could be a compelling interest. Here once again we do not reach that question because we find that creating an additional majority-black district was not required under a correct reading of Section 5 and that District 12, as drawn, is not a remedy narrowly tailored to the State's professed interest in avoiding Section 2 liability. . . .

It appears that the Justice Department was pursuing in North Carolina the same policy of maximizing the number of majority-black districts that it pursued in Georgia. See *Miller*. . . . We explained in *Miller* that this maximization policy is not properly grounded in Section 5 and the Department's authority thereunder.

With respect to Section 2, appellees contend, and the District Court found, that failure to enact a plan with a second majority-black district would have left the State vulnerable to a lawsuit under this section. Our precedent establishes that a plaintiff may allege a Section 2 violation in a single-member district if the manipulation of districting lines fragments politically cohesive minority voters among several districts or packs them into one district or a small number of districts, and thereby dilutes the voting strength of members of the minority population. To prevail on such a claim, a plaintiff must prove that the minority group "is sufficiently large and geographically compact to constitute a majority in a single-member district"; that the minority group "is politically cohesive"; and that "the white majority votes sufficiently as a bloc to enable it . . . usually to defeat the minority's preferred candidate." *Thornburg v. Gingles*, 478 U.S. 30 (1986). A court must also consider all other relevant circumstances and must ultimately find based on the totality of those circumstances that members of a protected class "have less opportunity than other members of the electorate to participate in the political process and to elect representatives of their choice."

We assume, *arguendo*, for the purpose of resolving this case, that compliance with Section 2 could be a compelling interest, and we likewise assume, *arguendo*, that the General Assembly believed a second majority-minority district was needed in order not to violate Section 2, and that the legislature at the time it acted had a strong basis in evidence to support that conclusion. We hold that even with the benefit of these assumptions, the

North Carolina plan does not survive strict scrutiny because the remedy—the creation of District 12—is not narrowly tailored to the asserted end. . . .

Appellees . . . contend, and a majority of the District Court agreed, that once a legislature has a strong basis in evidence for concluding that a Section 2 violation exists in the State, it may draw a majority-minority district anywhere, even if the district is in no way coincident with the compact *Gingles* district, as long as racially polarized voting exists where the district is ultimately drawn.

We find this position singularly unpersuasive. We do not see how a district so drawn would avoid Section 2 liability. If a Section 2 violation is proven for a particular area, it flows from the fact that individuals in this area "have less opportunity than other members of the electorate to participate in the political process and to elect representatives of their choice." The vote dilution injuries suffered by these persons are not remedied by creating a safe majority-black district somewhere else in the State. For example, if a geographically compact, cohesive minority population lives in south-central to southeastern North Carolina, as the Justice Department's objection letter suggested, District 12 which spans the Piedmont Crescent would not address that Section 2 violation. The black voters of the south-central to southeastern region would still be suffering precisely the same injury that they suffered before District 12 was drawn. District 12 would not address the professed interest of relieving the vote dilution, much less be narrowly tailored to accomplish the goal. . . .

For the foregoing reasons, the judgment of the District Court is Reversed.

Justice STEVENS, with whom Justice GINSBURG and Justice BREYER join as to Part II-V, dissenting.

As the Court analyzes the case, it raises three distinct questions: (1) Should North Carolina's decision to create two congressional districts in which a majority of the voters are African-American be subject to strict constitutional scrutiny?; (2) If so, did North Carolina have a compelling interest in creating such districts?; and (3) If so, was the creation of those districts "narrowly tailored" to further the asserted compelling interest? The Court inadequately explains its answer to the first question, and it avoids answering the second because it concludes that its answer to the third disposes of the case. In my estimation, the Court's disposition of all three questions is most unsatisfactory. . . .

Subsequent to the District Court's decision, we handed down *Miller v. Johnson*. As I understand the *Miller* test, state legislatures may take racial and ethnic characteristics of voters into account when they are drawing district boundaries without triggering strict scrutiny so long as race is not the "predominant" consideration guiding their deliberations. To show that race has been "predominant," a plaintiff must show that "the legislature subordinated traditional race-neutral districting principles . . . to racial considerations" in drawing that district.

Indeed, the principal opinion in *Bush v. Vera*, [116 S.Ct. — (1996)], issued this same day makes clear that the deliberate consideration of race in drawing district lines does not in and of itself invite constitutional suspicion. . . . Rather, strict scrutiny should apply only upon a demonstration that "'race for its own sake, and not other districting principles, was the legislature's dominant and controlling rationale in drawing its district lines.'" . . .

In holding that the present record shows race to have been the "predominant" consideration in the creation of District 12, the Court relies on two pieces of evidence: the State's admission that its "overriding" purpose was to "'create two congressional districts with effective black voting majorities,'" the "'geographically non-compact'" shape of District 12. In my view, this evidence does not suffice to trigger strict scrutiny under the "demanding" test that *Miller* establishes. . . .

[T]he record reveals that two race-neutral, traditional districting criteria determined District 12's shape: the interest in ensuring that incumbents would remain residents of the districts they have previously represented; and the interest in placing predominantly rural voters in one district and predominantly urban voters in another. . . .

Unlike most States, North Carolina has not given its chief executive any power to veto enactments of its legislature. Thus, even though the voters had elected a Republican Governor, the Democratic majority in the legislature was in control of the districting process. It was the Democrats who first decided to adopt the 11-white-district plan that arguably would have violated Section 2 of the Voting Rights Act and gave rise to the Attorney General's objection under Section 5. It was also the Democrats who rejected Republican Party maps which contained two majority-minority districts because they created too many districts in which a majority of the residents were registered Republicans.

If race rather than incumbency protection had been the dominant consideration, it seems highly unlikely that the Democrats would have drawn this bizarre district rather than accepting more compact options that were clearly available. If race, rather than politics, had been the "predominant" consideration for the Democrats, they could have accepted the Republican Plan, thereby satisfying the Attorney General and avoiding any significant risk of liability as well as the attack mounted by the plaintiffs in this case. Instead, as the detailed findings of the District Court demonstrate, the legislature deliberately crafted a districting plan that would accommodate the needs of Democratic incumbents. . . .

[E]ven if I were to assume that strict scrutiny applies, and thus that it makes sense to consider the question, I would not share the majority's hesitancy in concluding that North Carolina had a "compelling interest" in drawing District 12. In my view, the record identifies not merely one, but at least three acceptable reasons that may have motivated legislators to favor the creation of two such districts. Those three reasons easily satisfy the judicially created requirement that the state legislature's decision be supported by a "compelling state interest," particularly in a case in which the alleged injury to the disadvantaged class—i.e., the majority of voters who are white—is so tenuous.

First, some legislators felt that the sorry history of race relations in North Carolina in past decades was a sufficient reason for making it easier for more black leaders to participate in the legislative process and to represent the State in the Congress of the United States. Even if that history does not provide the kind of precise guidance that will justify certain specific affirmative action programs in particular industries, it surely provides an adequate basis for a decision to facilitate the election of representatives of the previously disadvantaged minority. . . .

Second, regardless of whether Section 5 of the Act was actually violated, I believe the State's interest in avoiding the litigation that would have been necessary to overcome the Attorney General's objection to the original plan provides an acceptable reason for creating a second majority-minority district. It is entirely proper for a State whose past practices have subjected it to the pre-clearance obligation set forth in Section 5 to presume that the Attorney General's construction of the Act is correct, and to take corrective action rather than challenging him in Court. . . .

Third, regardless of the possible outcome of litigation alleging that Section 2 of the Voting Rights Act would be violated by a plan that ensured the election of white legislators in 11 of the State's 12 congressional districts, the interest in avoiding the expense and unpleasantness of such litigation was certainly legitimate and substantial. . . .

Although the Court assumes that North Carolina had a compelling interest in "avoiding liability" under Section 2, it avoids conclusively resolving that question because it holds that District 12 was not a "narrowly tailored" means of achieving that end. The majority reaches this conclusion by determining that District 12 did not "remedy" any potential violation of Section 2 that may have occurred.

In my judgment, if a State's new plan successfully avoids the potential litigation entirely, there is no reason why it must also take the form of a "remedy" for an unproven violation. Thus, the fact that no Section 2 violation has been proven in the territory that comprises District 12 does not show that the district fails to serve a compelling state interest. It shows only that a federal court, which is constrained by Article III, would not have had the power to require North Carolina to draw that district. It is axiomatic that a State should have more authority to institute a districting plan than would a federal court. . . .

It is, of course, irrelevant whether we, as judges, deem it wise policy to create majority-minority districts as a means of assuring fair and effective representation to minority voters. We have a duty to respect Congress' considered judgment that such a policy may serve to effectuate the ends of the constitutional Amendment that it is charged with enforcing. We should also respect North Carolina's conscientious effort to conform to that congressional determination. Absent some demonstration that voters are being denied fair and effective representation as a result of their race, I find no basis for this Court's intervention into a process by which federal and state actors, both black and white, are jointly attempting to resolve difficult questions of politics and race that have long plagued North Carolina. Nor do I see how our constitutional tradition can countenance the suggestion that a State may draw unsightly lines to favor farmers or city dwellers, but not to create districts that benefit the very group whose history inspired the Amendment that the Voting Rights Act was designed to implement.

Because I have no hesitation in concluding that North Carolina's decision to adopt a plan in which white voters were in the majority in only 10 of the State's 12 districts did not violate the Equal Protection Clause, I respectfully dissent.

C. CAMPAIGNS AND ELECTIONS

In its 1994–1995 term, the Court reviewed Ohio's requirement that campaign leaflets identify the individuals or organizations who prepare them in *McIntyre v. Ohio Elections Commission*, 115 S.Ct. 1511 (1995). With Chief Justice Rehnquist and Justice Scalia dissenting, Justice Stevens struck down Ohio's law against the distribution of anonymous campaign literature, and by implication similar laws in forty-eight other states. Notably, concurring Justice Thomas disagreed with the majority's method of analysis and argued that historical evidence established that the "original understanding" of the First Amendment justified striking down Ohio's law. By contrast, dissenting Justice Scalia took exception to both Stevens's and Thomas's analysis and would have upheld such campaign restrictions.

In its 1995–1996 term, the Court struck down as a violation of the First Amendment the limitations on independent campaign expenditures by political parties as set forth in the Federal Election Campaign Act of 1971 (FECA). Under FECA, political parties may not spend more than $20,000, or two cents times the voting age population of a state, in Senate races; limits on expenditures in races for the House of Representatives are about $30,000. In *Colorado Republican Federal Campaign Committee v. Federal Election Commission*, 116 S.Ct. — (1996) (excerpted below), the Court held that the limits on expenditures in Senate races were unconstitutional, but did not address the constitutionality of spending limits on congressional elections or the larger issue of the FECA's limitations on political parties' campaign expenditures made in conjunction with a candidate's campaign committee. Justice Breyer's opinion for the Court, however, was joined only by Justices O'Connor and Souter. Chief Justice Rehnquist and Justices Kennedy, Scalia, and Thomas dissented in part and would have ruled more broadly that all spending limits on political parties violate the First Amendment. Dissenting Justices Stevens and Ginsburg countered the FECA's limitations were justified by the need to combat corruption and "to protect equal access to the political arena."

Finally, the Court extended First Amendment protection and rejected arguments for political patronage in two cases, *Board of County Commissioners, Wabaunsee County, Kansas v. Umbehr*, 116 S.Ct. — (1996), and *O'Hare Truck Service, Inc. v. City of Northlake*, 116 S.Ct. — (1996). In both cases, the Court extended to independent contractors the protection extended to public employees in *Elrod v. Burns*, 427

U.S. 347 (1976), *Branti v. Finkel*, 445 U.S. 507 (1980), and *Rutan v. Republican Party of Illinois*, 497 U.S. 62 (1990) (see Vol. 1, Ch. 8). Keen Umbehr, a trash hauler for the county and an outspoken critic of the county board, had his contract terminated (so that it would not be automatically renewed) and contended that the county's retaliation for his criticisms violated the First Amendment. The Court agreed, holding that the First Amendment protects independent contractors from termination of their government contracts in retaliation for the exercise of their free speech. However, reaffirming rulings in *Connick v. Myers*, 461 U.S. 128 (1983), and *Pickering v. Board of Ed. of Township High School Dist.*, 391 U.S. 563 (1968), Justice O'Connor, in her opinion for the Court, emphasized that

> Umbehr must show that the termination of his contract was motivated by his speech on a matter of public concern, an initial showing that requires him to prove more than the mere fact that he criticized the Board members before they terminated him. If he can make that showing, the Board will have a valid defense if it can show, by a preponderance of the evidence, that, in light of their knowledge, perceptions and policies at the time of the termination, the Board members would have terminated the contract regardless of his speech. The Board will also prevail if it can persuade the District Court that the County's legitimate interests as contractor, deferentially viewed, outweigh the free speech interests at stake. And, if Umbehr prevails, evidence that the Board members discovered facts after termination that would have led to a later termination anyway, and evidence of mitigation of his loss by means of his subsequent contracts with the cities, would be relevant in assessing what remedy is appropriate.

In *O'Hare Truck Service, Inc.*, the Court extended the protections accorded in *Elrod*, *Branti*, and *Rutan* to government employees to independent contractors or regular providers of service to the government. Here, the owner of O'Hare Truck Service, Inc. refused to contribute to the mayor's reelection campaign and instead supported his opponent. After the mayor's reelection, his contract was terminated and he sued. Writing for the Court, Justice Breyer held that independent contractors, no less than public employees, may not be discharged for refusing to support a political party or its candidates. As in *Rutan* (see Vol. 1, Ch. 8), Justice Scalia dissented in *Umbehr* and *O'Hare Truck Service*; in both dissents he was joined by Justice Thomas.

Colorado Republican Federal Campaign Committee v. Federal Election Commission

116 S.Ct. — (1996)

In the spring of 1986, the Colorado Republican Federal Campaign Committee exceeded the spending limits imposed on independent campaign expenditures by political parties under the Federal Election Campaign Act of 1971 (FECA). The committee spent $15,000 for radio ads criticizing Democratic Congressman Timothy Wirth, at a time when his Republican challenger for the Senate had still not been selected. Under the FECA, political parties may not spend more than $20,000, or "2 cents multiplied by the voting age population of the State," in Senate races; independent expenditures on races for the House of Representatives are limited to about $30,000. When officials in the Democratic Party complained to the Federal Election Commission, the Colorado Committee countered that the spending limits violate the First Amendment. A federal district court interpreted the FECA's provisions narrowly and inapplicable to the circumstances here, but a federal appellate court disagreed, holding that the limitations did apply and did not violate the First Amendment. The Colorado Committee appealed that decision to the Supreme Court.

The Court's decision was seven to two and opinion announced by Justice Breyer. Justice Kennedy filed an opinion concurring in the judgment and dissenting in part, which Chief Justice Rehnquist and Justice Scalia joined. Justice Thomas likewise filed a separate opinion in part dissenting. Justice Stevens, joined by Justice Ginsburg, dissented.

Justice BREYER announced the judgment of the Court and delivered an opinion, in which Justice O'CONNOR and Justice SOUTER join.

We granted *certiorari* primarily to consider the Colorado Party's argument that the Party Expenditure Provision violates the First Amendment "either facially or as applied." For reasons we shall discuss . . . below, we consider only the latter question—whether the Party Expenditure Provision as applied here violates the First Amendment. We conclude that it does.

The summary judgment record indicates that the expenditure in question is what this Court in *Buckley* [v. *Valeo*, 424 U.S. 1 (1976),] called an "independent" expenditure, not a "coordinated" expenditure that other provisions of FECA treat as a kind of campaign "contribution." The record describes how the expenditure was made. . . . And we therefore treat the expenditure, for constitutional purposes, as an "independent" expenditure, not an indirect campaign contribution.

So treated, the expenditure falls within the scope of the Court's precedents that extend First Amendment protection to independent expenditures. Beginning with *Buckley,* the Court's cases have found a "fundamental constitutional difference between money spent to advertise one's views independently of the candidate's campaign and money contributed to the candidate to be spent on his campaign." [*Federal Election Comm'n v. National Conservative Political Action Comm.,* 470 U.S. 182 (1981) (*NCPAC*)]. This difference has been grounded in the observation that restrictions on contributions impose "only a marginal restriction upon the contributor's ability to engage in free communication," *Buckley,* because the symbolic communicative value of a contribution bears little relation to its size, and because such limits leave "persons free to engage in independent political expression, to associate actively through volunteering their services, and to assist to a limited but nonetheless substantial extent in supporting candidates and committees with financial resources." At the same time, reasonable contribution limits directly and materially advance the Government's interest in preventing exchanges of large financial contributions for political favors.

In contrast, the Court has said that restrictions on independent expenditures significantly impair the ability of individuals and groups to engage in direct political advocacy and "represent substantial . . . restraints on the quantity and diversity of political speech." And at the same time, the Court has concluded that limitations on independent expenditures are less directly related to preventing corruption, since "the absence of prearrangement and coordination of an expenditure with the candidate . . . not only undermines the value of the expenditure to the candidate, but also alleviates the danger that expenditures will be given as a quid pro quo for improper commitments from the candidate."

Given these established principles, we do not see how a provision that limits a political party's independent expenditures can escape their controlling effect. A political party's independent expression not only reflects its members' views about the philosophical and governmental matters that bind them together, it also seeks to convince others to join those members in a practical democratic task, the task of creating a government that voters can instruct and hold responsible for subsequent success or failure. The independent expression of a political party's views is "core" First Amendment activity no less than is the independent expression of individuals, candidates, or other political committees.

We are not aware of any special dangers of corruption associated with political parties that tip the constitutional balance in a different direction. When this Court considered, and held unconstitutional, limits that FECA had set on certain independent expenditures by political action committees, it reiterated *Buckley*'s observation that "the absence of prearrangement and coordination" does not eliminate, but it does help to "alleviate," any "danger" that a candidate will understand the expenditure as an effort to obtain a "quid pro quo." *NCPAC.* The same is true of independent party expenditures. . . .

We therefore believe that this Court's prior case law controls the outcome here. We do not see how a Constitution that grants to individuals, candidates, and ordinary political committees the right to make unlimited independent expenditures could deny the same right to political parties. Having concluded this, we need not consider the Party's further claim that the statute's "in connection with" language, and the FEC's interpretation of that language, are unconstitutionally vague. . . .

The Colorado Party and supporting *amici* have argued a broader question than we have decided, for they have claimed that, in the special case of political parties, the First Amendment forbids congressional efforts to limit coordinated expenditures as well as independent expenditures. Because the expenditure before us is an independent expenditure we have not reached this broader question in deciding the Party's "as applied" challenge. . . .

Justice STEVENS, with whom Justice GINSBURG joins, dissenting.

I am persuaded that three interests provide a constitutionally sufficient predicate for federal limits on spending by political parties. First, such limits serve the interest in avoiding both the appearance and the reality of a corrupt political process. . . .

Second, these restrictions supplement other spending limitations embodied in the Act, which are likewise designed to prevent corruption. Individuals and certain organizations are permitted to contribute up to $1,000 to a candidate. Since the same donors can give up to $5,000 to party committees, if there were no limits on party spending, their contributions could be spent to benefit the candidate and thereby circumvent the $1,000 cap. We have recognized the legitimate interest in blocking similar attempts to undermine the policies of the Act.

Finally, I believe the Government has an important interest in leveling the electoral playing field by constraining the cost of federal campaigns. . . .

Justice KENNEDY, with whom the CHIEF JUSTICE and Justice SCALIA join, concurring in the judgment and dissenting in part.

In agreement with Justice THOMAS, I would hold that the Colorado Republican Party, in its pleadings in the District Court and throughout this litigation, has preserved its claim that the constraints imposed by the Federal Election Campaign Act of 1971 (FECA), both on its face and as interpreted by the Federal Elections Commission (FEC), violate the First Amendment.

In the plurality's view, the FEC's conclusive presumption that all political party spending relating to identified candidates is "coordinated" cannot be squared with the First Amendment. The plurality finds the presumption invalid, and I agree with much of the reasoning behind that conclusion. The quarrel over the FEC's presumption is beside the point, however, for under the statute it is both burdensome and quite unrealistic for a political party to attempt the expenditure of funds on a candidate's behalf (or against other candidates) without running afoul of FECA's spending limitations. . . .

We had no occasion in *Buckley* to consider possible First Amendment objections to limitations on spending by parties. While our cases uphold contribution limitations on individuals and associations, political party spending "in cooperation, consultation, or concert with" a candidate does not fit within our description of "contributions" in *Buckley*. In my view, we should not transplant the reasoning of cases upholding ordinary contribution limitations to a case involving FECA's restrictions on political party spending.

The First Amendment embodies a "profound national commitment to the principle that debate on public issues should be uninhibited, robust, and wide-open." *New York Times Co. v. Sullivan*, 376 U.S. 254 (1964). Political parties have a unique role in serving this principle; they exist to advance their members' shared political beliefs. A party performs this function, in part, by "identifying the people who constitute the association, and . . . limiting the association to those people only." *Democratic Party of United States v. Wisconsin ex rel. La Follette*, 450 U.S. 107 (1981). Having identified its members, however, a party can give effect to their views only by selecting and supporting candidates. A political party has its own traditions and principles that transcend the interests of individual candidates and campaigns; but in the context of particular elections, candidates are necessary to make the party's message known and effective, and vice versa. . . .

We have a constitutional tradition of political parties and their candidates engaging in joint First Amendment activity; we also have a practical identity of interests between the two entities during an election. Party spending "in cooperation, consultation, or concert with" a candidate therefore is indistinguishable in substance from expenditures by the candidate or his campaign committee. We held in *Buckley* that the First Amendment does not permit regulation of the latter, and it should not permit this regulation of the former. Congress may have authority, consistent with the First Amendment, to restrict undifferentiated political party contributions which satisfy the constitutional criteria we discussed in *Buckley*, but that type of regulation is not at issue here. . . .

Justice THOMAS, concurring in the judgment and dissenting in part, with whom the CHIEF JUSTICE and Justice SCALIA join.

I agree that petitioners' rights under the First Amendment have been violated, but I think we should reach the facial challenge in this case in order to make clear the circumstances under which political parties may engage in political speech without running afoul of 2 U.S.C. Section 441a(d)(3). In resolving that challenge, I would reject the framework established by *Buckley v. Valeo*, 424 U.S. 1 (1976) (*per curiam*), for analyzing the constitutionality of campaign finance laws and hold that Section 441a(d)(3)'s limits on independent and coordinated expenditures fail strict scrutiny. But even under *Buckley*, Section 441a(d)(3) cannot stand, because the anti-corruption rationale that we have relied upon in sustaining other campaign finance laws is inapplicable where political parties are the subject of such regulation. . . .

Were I convinced that the *Buckley* framework rested on a principled distinction between contributions and expenditures, which I am not, I would nevertheless conclude that Section 441a(d)(3)'s limits on political parties violate the First Amendment. Under *Buckley* and its progeny, a substantial threat of corruption must exist before a law purportedly aimed at the prevention of corruption will be sustained against First Amendment attack. Just as some of the monetary limits in the *Buckley* line of cases were held to be invalid because the government interest in stemming corruption was inadequate under the circumstances to justify the restrictions on speech, so too is Section 441a(d)(3) invalid. . . .

In sum, there is only a minimal threat of "corruption," as we have understood that term, when a political party spends to support its candidate or to oppose his competitor, whether or not that expenditure is made in concert with the candidate. Parties and candidates have traditionally worked together to achieve their common goals, and when they engage in that work, there is no risk to the Republic. To the contrary, the danger to the Republic lies in Government suppression of such activity. Under *Buckley* and our subsequent cases, Section 441a(d)(3)'s heavy burden on First Amendment rights is not justified by the threat of corruption at which it is assertedly aimed.

VOLUME TWO

3

ECONOMIC RIGHTS AND AMERICAN CAPITALISM

C. THE "TAKINGS CLAUSE" AND JUST COMPENSATION

Since the mid-1980s the Rehnquist Court has periodically revisited challenges to environmental, recreational, and other kinds of land-use regulations. Business groups and conservative organizations have pressed for an expansive reading of the Fifth Amendment's guarantee that "private property [shall not] be taken for public use, without just compensation." The "takings clause," however, has yet to be so expansively read by the Court as to threaten most land-use legislation. Within the Court, Justice Scalia has championed the broadest reading of the clause, but proven unable to command a majority for going very far in applying the clause as a limitation on governmental regulation. The most important and widely watched case, *Lucas v. South Carolina Coastal Council*, 505 U.S. 1003 (1992) (in Vol. 2, Ch. 3), raised a challenge to South Carolina's law forbidding the rebuilding of homes on beachfront property after Hurricane Hugo struck its coastline. Writing for the Court, Justice Scalia was only able to win agreement that in order to trigger the takings clause, regulations must deprive property owners of the entire economic value of their property. Since the vast majority of regulations do not deprive owners of 100 percent of their property's value, *Lucas* was a hollow victory for those seeking an expansive use of the takings clause.

Despite the ruling in *Lucas*, the Rehnquist Court once again revisited the issue in its 1993–1994 term in *Dolan v. City of Tigard*, 114 S.Ct. 2309 (1994). That case presented a takings-clause challenge to city officials of Tigard, Oregon, who, as a condition for granting a building permit, required a storeowner to dedicate part of the property to public use. Specifically, Dolan was required to set aside about one-tenth of her 1.7-acre property as a public green, storm drainage channel, and path for bicyclers and pedestrians.

In *Dolan*, the Court split five to four in holding that the city had inadequately justified its requirements for a flood plain and a pathway. Writing for a bare majority, Chief Justice Rehnquist held that when government makes such determinations affecting private property, it must show a "rough proportionality" between their land-use restrictions and the harm to be prevented. Notably, though, the chief justice reaffirmed that government may simply ban all development in flood plains and that "no precise mathematical calculation" was required to justify land-use restrictions. As a result of the ruling in *Dolan*, state and local governments must satisfy a two-pronged test: first, they must show that their restrictions serve a "legitimate public purpose" and, second, when imposing their restrictions they must undertake "some sort of individualized determination" establishing a "rough proportionality" between the restrictions and the harms to be averted. In a sharply worded dissent, joined by Justices Ginsburg and Blackmun, Justice Stevens took strong exception to the majority's heightened review of and new requirements on land-use regulations. In a separate opinion, Justice Souter dissented as well.

In addition, the Rehnquist Court confronted for the fourth time in the last five years a business's challenge to large punitive damage awards by juries under the due process clause; see *Honda Motor Co. v. Oberg*, 114 S.Ct. 2331 (1994), in the next chapter.

Finally, in its 1995–1996 term the Court broke with its recent pattern of favoring takings clause claims. Writing for a bare majority, Chief Justice Rehnquist rebuffed the contention that the government violates the due process clause of the Fourteenth Amendment and the Fifth Amendment's takings clause when it undertakes the forfeiture of an innocent person's property that was used in an illegal activity, in *Bennis v. Michigan*, 116 S.Ct. 994 (1996). As further discussed in the next chapter, Justices Breyer, Kennedy, Souter, and Stevens dissented.

Dolan v. City of Tigard
114 S.Ct. 2309 (1994)

Florence Dolan applied to the city planning commission for approval to expand her store and pave her parking lot. Under a state comprehensive land-management program, the commission held that her permit was conditioned on her dedicating part of her property to (1) a public greenway along Fanno Creek to minimize flooding that would be exacerbated by the increases in impervious surfaces associated with her development and (2) a pedestrian/bicycle pathway intended to relieve traffic congestion in the central business district of Tigard. Dolan objected and appealed the commission's denial of her request for variances from those requirements to the Land Use Board of Appeals (LUBA). She argued that the requirements were not related to the proposed development and therefore constituted an uncompensated taking of her property under the Fifth Amendment. The board, however, found a reasonable relationship between her proposed development and the requirement to dedicate land for a greenway, since the larger building and paved lot would increase the impervious surfaces and thus the runoff into the creek, and alleviating the impact of increased traffic from the development by providing a pathway as an alternative means of transportation. Both a state appellate court and the Oregon state supreme court affirmed the board's ruling and Dolan appealed to the Supreme Court.

The Court's decision was five to four. Chief Justice Rehnquist announced the majority's opinion, which Justices O'Connor, Kennedy, Scalia, and Thomas joined. Justice Stevens filed a dissenting opinion joined by Justices Ginsburg and Blackmun. Justice Souter dissented in a separate opinion.

CHIEF JUSTICE REHNQUIST delivered the opinion of the Court.

We granted *certiorari* to resolve a question left open by our decision in *Nollan v. California Coastal Comm'n*, 483 U.S. 825 (1987), of what is the required degree of connection between the exactions imposed by the city and the projected impacts of the proposed development. . . .

The Commission made a series of findings concerning the relationship between the dedicated conditions and the projected impacts of petitioner's project. First, the Commission noted that "it is reasonable to assume that customers and employees of the future uses of this site could utilize a pedestrian/bicycle pathway adjacent to this development for their transportation and recreational needs." The Commission noted that the site plan has provided for bicycle parking in a rack in front of the proposed building and "it is reasonable to expect that some of the users of the bicycle parking provided for by the site plan will use the pathway adjacent to Fanno Creek if it is constructed." In addition, the Commission found that creation of a convenient, safe pedestrian/bicycle pathway system as an alternative means of transportation "could offset some of the traffic demand on [nearby] streets and lessen the increase in traffic congestion." . . .

Petitioner appealed to the Land Use Board of Appeals (LUBA) on the ground that the city's dedication requirements were not related to the proposed development, and, therefore, those requirements constituted an uncompensated taking of their property under the Fifth Amendment. . . .

The Takings Clause of the Fifth Amendment of the United States Constitution, made applicable to the States through the Fourteenth Amendment, *Chicago, B. & Q. R. Co. v. Chicago*, 166 U.S. 226 (1897), provides: "Nor shall private property be taken for public use, without just compensation." One of the principal purposes of the Takings Clause is "to bar Government from forcing some people alone to bear public burdens which, in all fairness and justice, should be borne by the public as a whole." *Armstrong v. United States*, 364 U.S. 40 (1960). Without question, had the city simply required petitioner to dedicate a strip of land along Fanno Creek for public use, rather than conditioning the grant of her permit to redevelop her property on such a dedication, a taking would have occurred. Such public access would deprive petitioner of the right to exclude others, "one of the most essential sticks in the bundle of rights that are commonly characterized as property." *Kaiser Aetna v. United States*, 444 U.S. 164 (1979).

On the other side of the ledger, the authority of state and local governments to engage in land-use planning has been sustained against constitutional challenge as long ago as our decision in *Euclid v. Ambler Realty Co.*, 272 U.S. 365 (1926). . . . The sort of land-use regulations discussed in the cases just cited, however, differ in two relevant particulars from the present case. First, they involved essentially legislative determinations classifying entire areas of the city, whereas here the city made an adjudicative decision to condition petitioner's application for a building permit on an individual parcel. Second, the conditions imposed were not simply a limitation on the use petitioner might make of her own parcel, but a requirement that she deed portions of the property to the city. In *Nollan*, we held that governmental authority to exact such a condition was circumscribed by the Fifth and Fourteenth Amendments. Under the well-settled doctrine of "unconstitutional conditions," the government may not require a person to give up a constitutional right—here the right to receive just compensation when property is taken for a public use—in exchange for a discretionary benefit conferred by the government where the property sought has little or no relationship to the benefit. . . .

In evaluating petitioner's claim, we must first determine whether the "essential nexus" exists between the "legitimate state interest" and the permit condition exacted by the city. *Nollan*. If we find that a nexus exists, we must then decide the required degree of connection between the exactions and the projected impact of the proposed development. We were not required to reach this question in *Nollan*, because we concluded that the connection did not meet even the loosest standard. Here, however, we must decide this question. . . .

Undoubtedly, the prevention of flooding along Fanno Creek and the reduction of traffic congestion in the Central Business District qualify as the type of legitimate public purposes we have upheld. It seems equally obvious that a nexus exists between preventing flooding along Fanno Creek and limiting development within the creek's 100-year floodplain. Petitioner proposes to double the size of her retail store and to pave her now gravel parking lot, thereby expanding the impervious surface on the property and increasing the amount of stormwater runoff into Fanno Creek. The same may be said for the city's attempt to reduce traffic congestion by providing for alternative means of transportation. . . .

The second part of our analysis requires us to determine whether the degree of the exactions demanded by the city's permit conditions bear the required relationship to the projected impact of petitioner's proposed development. Here the Oregon Supreme Court deferred to what it termed the "city's unchallenged factual findings" supporting the dedication conditions and found them to be reasonably related to the impact of the expansion of petitioner's business.

The city required that petitioner dedicate "to the city as Greenway all portions of the site that fall within the existing 100-year floodplain [of

Fanno Creek] . . . and all property 15 feet above [the floodplain] boundary." In addition, the city demanded that the retail store be designed so as not to intrude into the greenway area. The city relies on the Commission's rather tentative findings that increased stormwater flow from petitioner's property "can only add to the public need to manage the [floodplain] for drainage purposes" to support its conclusion that the "requirement of dedication of the floodplain area on the site is related to the applicant's plan to intensify development on the site." . . .

The question for us is whether these findings are constitutionally sufficient to justify the conditions imposed by the city on petitioner's building permit. Since state courts have been dealing with this question a good deal longer than we have, we turn to representative decisions made by them. . . .

We think the "reasonable relationship" test adopted by a majority of the state courts is closer to the federal constitutional norm than either of those previously discussed. But we do not adopt it as such. . . . We think a term such as "rough proportionality" best encapsulates what we hold to be the requirement of the Fifth Amendment. No precise mathematical calculation is required, but the city must make some sort of individualized determination that the required dedication is related both in nature and extent to the impact of the proposed development. . . .

If petitioner's proposed development had somehow encroached on existing greenway space in the city, it would have been reasonable to require petitioner to provide some alternative greenway space for the public either on her property or elsewhere. But that is not the case here. We conclude that the findings upon which the city relies do not show the required reasonable relationship between the floodplain easement and the petitioner's proposed new building. With respect to the pedestrian/bicycle pathway, we have no doubt that the city was correct in finding that the larger retail sales facility proposed by petitioner will increase traffic on the streets of the Central Business District. The city estimates that the proposed development would generate roughly 435 additional trips per day. . . . But on the record before us, the city has not met its burden of demonstrating that the additional number of vehicle and bicycle trips generated by the petitioner's development reasonably relate to the city's requirement for a dedication of the pedestrian/bicycle pathway easement. The city simply found that the creation of the pathway "could offset some of the traffic demand . . . and lessen the increase in traffic congestion."

No precise mathematical calculation is required, but the city must make some effort to quantify its findings in support of the dedication for the pedestrian/bicycle pathway beyond the conclusory statement that it could offset some of the traffic demand generated. . . . The city's goals of reducing flooding hazards and traffic congestion, and providing for public greenways, are laudable, but there are outer limits to how this may be done.

Justice STEVENS, with whom Justice BLACKMUN and Justice GINSBURG join, dissenting.

The Court is correct in concluding that the city may not attach arbitrary conditions to a building permit or to a variance even when it can rightfully deny the application outright. I also agree that state court decisions dealing with ordinances that govern municipal development plans provide useful guidance in a case of this kind. Yet the Court's description of the doctrinal underpinnings of its decision, the phrasing of its fledgling test of "rough proportionality," and the application of that test to this case run contrary to the traditional treatment of these cases and break considerable and unpropitious new ground.

Candidly acknowledging the lack of federal precedent for its exercise in rulemaking, the Court purports to find guidance in 12 "representative" state court decisions. To do so is certainly appropriate. The state cases the Court consults, however, either fail to support or decidedly undermine the Court's conclusions in key respects. . . .

It is not merely state cases, but our own cases as well, that require the analysis to focus on the impact of the city's action on the entire parcel of private property. In *Penn Central Transportation Co. v. New York City*, 438 U.S. 104 (1978), we stated that takings jurisprudence "does not divide a single parcel into discrete segments and attempt to determine whether rights in a particular segment have been entirely abrogated." Instead, this Court focuses "both on the character of the action and on the nature and extent of the interference with rights in the parcel as a whole." *Andrus v. Allard*, 444 U.S. 51 (1979), reaffirmed the nondivisibility principle outlined in *Penn Central*, stating that "at least where an owner possesses a full 'bundle' of property rights, the destruction of one 'strand' of the bundle is not a taking, because the aggregate must be viewed in its entirety." . . .

The Court has made a serious error by abandoning the traditional presumption of constitutionality and imposing a novel burden of proof on a city implementing an admittedly valid comprehensive land use plan. Even more consequential than its incorrect disposition of this case, however, is the Court's resurrection of a species of substantive due process analysis that it firmly rejected decades ago.

The Court begins its constitutional analysis by citing *Chicago, B. & Q. R. Co. v. Chicago*, 166 U.S. 226 (1897), for the proposition that the Takings Clause of the Fifth Amendment is "applicable to the States through the Fourteenth Amendment." That opinion, however, contains no mention of either the Takings Clause or the Fifth Amendment; it held that the protection afforded by the Due Process Clause of the Fourteenth Amendment extends to matters of substance as well as procedure, and that the substance of "the due process of law enjoined by the Fourteenth Amendment requires compensation to be made or adequately secured to the owner of private property taken for public use under the authority of a State." *Chicago, B. & Q. R. Co.* It applied the same kind of substantive due process analysis more frequently identified with a better known case that accorded similar substantive protection to a baker's liberty interest in working 60 hours a week and 10 hours a day. See *Lochner v. New York*, 198 U.S. 45 (1905).

Later cases have interpreted the Fourteenth Amendment's substantive protection against uncompensated deprivations of private property by the States as though it incorporated the text of the Fifth Amendment's Takings Clause. There was nothing problematic about that interpretation in cases enforcing the Fourteenth Amendment against state action that involved the actual physical invasion of private property. Justice HOLMES charted a significant new course, however, when he opined that a state law making it "commercially impracticable to mine certain coal" had "very nearly the same effect for constitutional purposes as appropriating or destroying it." *Pennsylvania Coal Co. v. Mahon,* 260 U.S. 393 (1922). The so-called "regulatory takings" doctrine that the HOLMES dictum kindled has an obvious kinship with the line of substantive due process cases that *Lochner* exemplified. Besides having similar ancestry, both doctrines are potentially open-ended sources of judicial power to invalidate state economic regulations that Members of this Court view as unwise or unfair.

This case inaugurates an even more recent judicial innovation than the regulatory takings doctrine: the application of the "unconstitutional conditions" label to a mutually beneficial transaction between a property owner and a city. The Court tells us that the city's refusal to grant Dolan a discretionary benefit infringes her right to receive just compensation for the property interests that she has refused to dedicate to the city "where the property sought has little or no relationship to the benefit." Although it is well settled that a government cannot deny a benefit on a basis that infringes constitutionally protected interests—"especially [one's] interest in freedom of speech," *Perry v. Sindermann,* 408 U.S. 593 (1972)—the "unconstitutional conditions" doctrine provides an inadequate framework in which to analyze this case.

Dolan has no right to be compensated for a taking unless the city acquires the property interests that she has refused to surrender. Since no taking has yet occurred, there has not been any infringement of her constitutional right to compensation. . . .

In its application of what is essentially the doctrine of substantive due process, the Court confuses the past with the present. On November 13, 1922, the village of Euclid, Ohio, adopted a zoning ordinance that effectively confiscated 75 percent of the value of property owned by the Ambler Realty Company. Despite its recognition that such an ordinance "would have been rejected as arbitrary and oppressive" at an earlier date, the Court (over the dissent of Justices VAN DEVANTER, MCREYNOLDS, and BUTLER) upheld the ordinance. Today's majority should heed the words of Justice SUTHERLAND:

"Such regulations are sustained, under the complex conditions of our day, for reasons analogous to those which justify traffic regulations, which, before the advent of automobiles and rapid transit street railways, would have been condemned as fatally arbitrary and unreasonable. And in this there is no inconsistency, for while the meaning of constitutional guaranties never varies, the scope of their application must expand or contract to meet the new and different conditions which are constantly coming within the field of their operation. In a changing world, it is impossible that it should be otherwise." [*Euclid v. Ambler Realty Co.*], 272 U.S. 365 (1926).

In our changing world one thing is certain: uncertainty will characterize predictions about the impact of new urban developments on the risks of floods, earthquakes, traffic congestion, or environmental harms. When there is doubt concerning the magnitude of those impacts, the public interest in averting them must outweigh the private interest of the commercial entrepreneur. If the government can demonstrate that the conditions it has imposed in a land-use permit are rational, impartial and conducive to fulfilling the aims of a valid land-use plan, a strong presumption of validity should attach to those conditions. The burden of demonstrating that those conditions have unreasonably impaired the economic value of the proposed improvement belongs squarely on the shoulders of the party challenging the state action's constitutionality. That allocation of burdens has served us well in the past. The Court has stumbled badly today by reversing it.

4

THE NATIONALIZATION OF
THE BILL OF RIGHTS

B. THE RISE AND RETREAT OF THE
"DUE PROCESS REVOLUTION"

The Rehnquist Court has generally rebuffed attempts to have it read broadly the Fifth and Fourteenth Amendments' due process clauses, both in the direction of extending their procedural safeguards and in legitimating new substantive liberty interests. In *Sandin v. Conner*, 115 U.S. 2293 (1995), for instance, Chief Justice Rehnquist commanded a bare majority for rejecting a prison inmate's claim that officials deprived him of procedural due process when refusing to allow him to present witnesses during a disciplinary hearing that resulted in his isolated confinement for alleged misconduct. When distinguishing prior rulings, the chief justice also cautioned lower federal courts against the creation of "liberty" interests and involvement in the day-to-day management of prisons. Justices Breyer, Ginsburg, Souter, and Stevens dissented. However, there have been a couple of exceptions to such rulings. In *Foucha v. United States*, 504 U.S. 71 (1992) (see Vol. 2, Ch. 4), a bare majority struck down Louisiana's law permitting the continued institutionalization of an individual who was criminally acquitted by reason of insanity and who subsequently regained sanity but was still deemed to pose a potential threat to society.

In 1993, then, another bare majority in *United States v. James Daniel Good Real Property*, 114 S.Ct. 492 (1993) (see below), held that convicted drug dealers must be given a hearing before the government seizes their property under forfeiture laws. Notably, the ruling in *James Daniel Good Real Property* was also the third time that a majority of the Rehnquist Court rejected the government's arguments for expansive powers to seize the property of convicted drug dealers as part of its "war on drugs." In *Alexander v. United States*, 113 S.Ct. 2766 (1993), and *Austin v. United States*, 113 S.Ct. 2801 (1993) (see Vol. 2, Ch. 9), the Court held that such seizures are subject to the limitations of the Eighth Amendment's bar against "excessive fines," which prevents the government from going after huge real estate parcels for comparatively small offenses.

For the fifth time in six years the Court also granted a case attacking large punitive damage awards as a denial of substantive and procedural due process. In *Pacific Mutual Life Insurance Company v. Haslip*, 499 U.S. 1 (1991), voting eight to one, the justices rejected such a challenge to large jury awards. Dissenting Justice O'Connor was the only one willing to thrust the Court into this area of litigation and to expand judicial review over common law jury awards. When in the 1993–1994 term the Court for the third time rejected a due process challenge to another large punitive damage award, in *TXO Production Corp. v. Alliance Resources Corp.*, 509 U.S. 443 (1993) (in Vol. 2, Ch. 4), however, Justice O'Connor's dissent was joined by two others, Justices Souter and White.

In its 1993–1994 term the Rehnquist Court again took up the matter of large damage awards in *Honda Motor Co. v. Oberg*, 114 S.Ct. 2331 (1994). There the Court reviewed a due process challenge to Oregon's law barring trial and appellate court judges from questioning juries about the size of their punitive damage awards. Oregon's law, which is the only one of its kind, barred judicial review of jury awards "unless the court can affirmatively say there is no evidence to support the verdict." The case stemmed from an accident on an all-terrain vehicle manufactured by Honda and a subsequent personal injury lawsuit in which a jury awarded over five million dollars in punitive damages. Attorneys for Honda appealed that award on the ground that the due process clause should limit excessive punitive damage awards.

By a vote of seven to two, the Court struck down Oregon's limitation on judicial review of jury awards as a violation of due process. Writing for the majority, Justice Stevens wrote broadly about guarding against excessive punitive damage awards. "Punitive damages pose an acute danger of arbitrary deprivation of property," he said, adding that there are constitutional limitations on punitive damage awards that are "grossly excessive." But as in prior rulings, Justice Stevens stopped short of indicating what those limitations are or how to draw them. In a concurring opinion, Justice Scalia emphasized that this was a procedural due process case. Justice Ginsburg, joined by Chief Justice Rehnquist, dissented and argued that Oregon's procedures for instructing juries on awarding punitive damages were constitutionally adequate.

In its 1994–1995 term, then, the Court granted a carmaker's appeal of another punitive damages award. In this case, *BMW of North America v. Gore*, 116 S.Ct. 1589 (1996) (excerpted below), a bare majority of the Court held that due process forbids punitive damage awards that are "grossly out of proportion to the severity of the offense." But the four dissenters—Chief Justice Rehnquist and Justices Ginsburg, Scalia, and Thomas—took strong exception to the majority's activism and intrusion into an area that, they countered, traditionally has been (and still ought to be) left to state legislatures.

Finally, in its 1995–1996 term, the Court also considered another due process challenge to forfeiture laws, which authorize the seizure of private property that has been used for illegal activities or which was purchased with money unlawfully obtained, such as by dealing in drugs. Although such laws have been instrumental to the "war on drugs" and major money-makers for state and federal governments, the Court has limited their application in recent years (see Vol. 2, Ch. 4). An unresolved issue presented in the case granted review, *Bennis v. Michigan*, 116 S.Ct. 994 (1996), was whether the due process clause bars the government's taking of an innocent person's property under state forfeiture laws; most forfeiture provisions in federal law exempt innocent persons. Tina Bennis's husband was arrested for having oral sex with a prostitute in her 1977 Pontiac. Subsequently, the county prosecutor seized and sold Bennis's car under Michigan's nuisance law, which authorizes the forfeiture of vehicles used for lewdness or prostitution. Bennis in turn appealed to the Court which granted review.

Writing for the majority in *Bennis*, Chief Justice Rehnquist rejected Mrs. Bennis's arguments that the forfeiture of an innocent person's property violated due process and the Fifth Amendment's takings clause. Drawing on nineteenth-century admiralty law upholding the government's taking possession of vessels carrying illegal goods, he concluded that, "actions of the kind at issue are 'too firmly fixed in the punitive and remedial jurisprudence of the country to be now displaced.' The State here sought to deter illegal activity that contributes to neighborhood deterioration and unsafe streets. The Bennis automobile, it is conceded, facilitated and was used in criminal activity." By contrast, the four dissenters thought otherwise. Joined by Justices Breyer and Souter, Justice Stevens pointed out that,

> The logic of the Court's analysis would permit the States to exercise virtually unbridled power to confiscate vast amounts of property where professional criminals have engaged in illegal acts. Some airline passengers have marijuana cigarettes in their luggage; some hotel guests are thieves; some spectators at professional sports events carry concealed weapons; and some hitchhikers are prostitutes. The State surely may impose strict obligations on the owners of airlines, hotels, stadiums, and vehicles to exercise a high degree of care to prevent others from making illegal use of their property, but neither logic nor history supports the Court's apparent assumption that their complete innocence imposes no constitutional impediment to the seizure of their property simply because it provided the locus for a criminal transaction.

Justice Kennedy also dissented in a separate opinion.

United States v. James Daniel Good Real Property
114 S.Ct. 492 (1993)

Almost five years after police found drugs in James Daniel Good's home and he pleaded guilty to violating Hawaii's drug laws, the federal government sought the forfeiture of his house and land under federal law. The government did so on the ground that his property had been used in the commission of a federal drug offense. Following an *ex parte* proceeding (at which Good was not present), a federal magistrate issued a warrant authorizing the seizure of Good's property. Subsequently, without prior notice or an adversary proceeding, the government seized Good's property. Good challenged the government's actions, arguing that he was deprived of his property without due process of law.

The Court's decision was five to four. Justice Kennedy announced the majority's opinion, which Justices Blackmun, Stevens, Souter, and Ginsburg joined. Chief Justice Rehnquist filed an opinion in part concurring and dissenting, which Justices O'Connor and Scalia joined. Separate opinions concurring and dissenting in part were also filed by Justices O'Connor and Thomas.

Justice KENNEDY delivered the opinion of the Court.

The Due Process Clause of the Fifth Amendment guarantees that "no person shall . . . be deprived of life, liberty, or property, without due process of law." Our precedents establish the general rule that individuals must receive notice and an opportunity to be heard before the Government deprives them of property.

The Government does not, and could not, dispute that the seizure of Good's home and four-acre parcel deprived him of property interests protected by the Due Process Clause. By the Government's own submission, the seizure gave it the right to charge rent, to condition occupancy, and even to evict the occupants. Instead, the Government argues that it afforded Good all the process the Constitution requires. The Government makes two separate points in this regard. First, it contends that compliance with the Fourth Amendment suffices when the Government seizes property for purposes of forfeiture. In the alternative, it argues that the seizure of real property under the drug forfeiture laws justifies an exception to the usual due process requirement of preseizure notice and hearing. . . .

Though the Fourth Amendment places limits on the Government's power to seize property for purposes of forfeiture, it does not provide the sole measure of constitutional protection that must be afforded property owners in forfeiture proceedings. So even assuming that the Fourth Amendment were satisfied in this case, it remains for us to determine whether the seizure complied with our well-settled jurisprudence under the Due Process Clause. Whether *ex parte* seizures of forfeitable property satisfy the Due Process Clause is a question we last confronted in *Calero-Toledo v. Pearson Yacht Leasing Co.*, 416 U.S. 663 (1974), which held that the Government could seize a yacht subject to civil forfeiture without affording prior notice or hearing. Central to our analysis in *Calero-Toledo* was the fact that a yacht was the "sort [of property] that could be removed to another jurisdiction, destroyed, or concealed, if advance warning of confiscation were given." The ease with which an owner could frustrate the Government's interests in the forfeitable property created a "'special need for very prompt action'" that justified the postponement of notice and hearing until after the seizure.

We had no occasion in *Calero-Toledo* to decide whether the same considerations apply to the forfeiture of real property, which, by its very nature, can be neither moved nor concealed. In fact, when *Calero-Toledo* was decided, both the Puerto Rican statute and the federal forfeiture statute upon which it was modeled authorized the forfeiture of personal property only. It was not until 1984, ten years later, that Congress amended [federal law] to authorize the forfeiture of real property.

The right to prior notice and a hearing is central to the Constitution's command of due process. . . . We tolerate some exceptions to the general rule requiring predeprivation notice and hearing, but only in "'extraordinary situations where some valid governmental interest is at stake that justifies postponing the hearing until after the event.'" Whether the seizure of real property for purposes of civil forfeiture justifies such an exception requires an examination of the competing interests at stake, along with the promptness and adequacy of later proceedings. The three-part inquiry set forth in *Mathews v. Eldridge*, 424 U.S. 319 (1976), provides guidance in this regard. The *Mathews* analysis requires us to consider the private interest affected by the official action; the risk of an erroneous deprivation of that interest through the procedures used, as well as the probable value of additional safeguards; and the Government's interest, including the administrative burden that additional procedural requirements would impose.

Good's right to maintain control over his home, and to be free from governmental interference, is a private interest of historic and continuing importance. The seizure deprived Good of valuable rights of ownership, including the right of sale, the right of occupancy, the right to unrestricted use and enjoyment, and the right to receive rents. All that the seizure left him, by the Government's own submission, was the right to bring a claim for the return of title at some unscheduled future hearing. . . .

The purpose of an adversary hearing is to ensure the requisite neutrality that must inform all governmental decisionmaking. That protection is of particular importance here, where the Government has a direct pecuniary interest in the outcome of the proceeding. Moreover, the availability of a postseizure hearing may be no recompense for losses caused by erroneous seizure. Given the congested civil dockets in federal courts, a claimant may not receive an adversary hearing until many months after the seizure. And even if the ultimate judicial decision is that the claimant was an innocent owner, or that the Government lacked probable cause, this determination, coming months after the seizure, "would not cure the temporary deprivation that an earlier hearing might have prevented."

This brings us to the third consideration under *Mathews*, "the Government's interest, including the function involved and the fiscal and administrative burdens that the additional or substitute procedural requirement would entail." The governmental interest we consider here is not some general interest in forfeiting property but the specific interest in seizing real property before the forfeiture hearing. The question in the civil forfeiture context is whether *ex parte* seizure is justified by a pressing need for prompt action. We find no pressing need here.

In the usual case, the Government thus has various means, short of seizure, to protect its legitimate interests in forfeitable real property. There is no reason to take the additional step of asserting control over the property without first affording notice and an adversary hearing.

Requiring the Government to postpone seizure until after an adversary hearing creates no significant administrative burden. A claimant is already entitled to an adversary hearing before a final judgment of forfeiture. No extra hearing would be required in the typical case, since the Government can wait until after the forfeiture judgment to seize the property. From an administrative standpoint it makes little difference whether that hearing is held before or after the seizure. And any harm that results from delay is minimal in comparison to the injury occasioned by erroneous seizure. . . .

CHIEF JUSTICE REHNQUIST, with whom Justices SCALIA and O'CONNOR join, concurring in part and dissenting in part.

The Court applies the three-factor balancing test for evaluating procedural due process claims set out in *Mathews v. Eldridge*, 424 U.S. 319 (1976), to reach its unprecedented holding. I reject the majority's expansive application of *Mathews*. . . .

The Court's fixation on *Mathews* sharply conflicts with both historical practice and the specific textual source of the Fourth Amendment's "reasonableness" inquiry. The Fourth Amendment strikes a balance between the people's security in their persons, houses, papers, and effects and the public interest in effecting searches and seizures for law enforcement purposes. Compliance with the standards and procedures prescribed by the Fourth Amendment constitutes all the "process" that is "due" to respondent Good under the Fifth Amendment in the forfeiture context. . . .

BMW of North America v. Gore
116 S.Ct. 1589 (1996)

In 1990, Dr. Ira Gore, Jr. bought a black BMW sports sedan for $40,750.88 from an authorized BMW dealer in Birmingham, Alabama. After driving the car for nine months, he took the car to "Slick Finish" in order to make it look "'snazzier than it normally would appear.'" When Mr. Slick detected evidence that the car had been repainted, Dr. Gore, convinced that he had been cheated, sued BMW of North

America (BMW), alleging that the failure to disclose that the car had been repainted constituted suppression of a material fact about the car. At the trial, BMW admitted it adopted a nationwide policy in 1983 concerning cars damaged in the course of manufacture or transportation. If the cost of repairing the damage exceeded three percent of the car's suggested retail price, the car was placed in company service and then sold as used. If the repair cost did not exceed three percent of the retail price, however, the car was sold as new without advising the dealer about any repairs. Because the $601.37 cost of repainting Dr. Gore's car was less than two percent of its retail price, BMW had not disclosed the damage or repair to the Birmingham dealer.

Dr. Gore contended that his repainted car was worth less than a car that had not been refinished. To prove his actual damages of $4,000, he relied on the testimony of a former BMW dealer, who estimated that the value of a repainted BMW was approximately ten percent less than the value of a new car that had not been damaged and repaired. To support his claim for punitive damages, Dr. Gore introduced evidence that BMW had sold 983 refinished cars as new, without disclosing that they had been repainted at a cost of more than $300 per vehicle, since 1983. Using the actual damage estimate of $4,000 per vehicle, Gore's attorney argued that a punitive award of four million dollars was an appropriate penalty.

Following the jury's award of four million dollars to Dr. Gore, BMW appealed to the Alabama supreme court. While that court rejected BMW's claim that the punitive damages award exceeded the constitutionally permissible amount, it nonetheless ruled in BMW's favor on one critical point: the state supreme court found that the jury improperly computed the amount of punitive damages by multiplying Dr. Gore's compensatory damages by the number of similar sales in other jurisdictions. Thereupon, the court held that two million dollars was "a constitutionally reasonable punitive damages award in this case," whereupon BMW appealed to the U.S. Supreme Court on the ground that the punitive damages award was excessive and violated the due process clause of the Fourteenth Amendment.

The Court's decision was five to four. Justice Stevens delivered the opinion for the Court and Justice Breyer filed a concurring opinion. Justices Scalia and Ginsburg filed separate dissenting opinions and were joined, respectively, by Justice Thomas and Chief Justice Rehnquist.

Justice STEVENS delivered the opinion of the Court.

The Due Process Clause of the Fourteenth Amendment prohibits a State from imposing a "'grossly excessive'" punishment on a tort-feasor. *TXO Production Corp. v. Alliance Resources Corp.*, 509 U.S. 443 (1993). . . .

Punitive damages may properly be imposed to further a State's legitimate interests in punishing unlawful conduct and deterring its repetition. *Gertz v. Robert Welch, Inc.*, 418 U.S. 323 (1974). In our federal system, States necessarily have considerable flexibility in determining the level of punitive damages that they will allow in different classes of cases and in any particular case. Most States that authorize exemplary damages afford the jury similar latitude, requiring only that the damages awarded be reasonably necessary to vindicate the State's legitimate interests in punishment and deterrence. Only when an award can fairly be categorized as "grossly excessive" in relation to these interests does it enter the zone of arbitrariness that violates the Due Process Clause of the Fourteenth Amendment. For that reason, the federal excessiveness inquiry appropriately begins with an identification of the state interests that a punitive award is designed to serve. . . .

No one doubts that a State may protect its citizens by prohibiting deceptive trade practices and by requiring automobile distributors to disclose presale repairs that affect the value of a new car. But the States need not, and in fact do not, provide such protection in a uniform manner. Some States rely on the judicial process to formulate and enforce an appropriate disclosure requirement by applying principles of contract and tort law. Other States have enacted various forms of legislation that define the disclosure obligations of automobile manufacturers, distributors, and dealers. The result is a patchwork of rules representing the diverse policy judgments of lawmakers in 50 States. . . .

We think it follows from . . . principles of state sovereignty and comity that a State may not impose economic sanctions on violators of its laws with the intent of changing the tort-feasors' lawful conduct in other States. Before this Court Dr. Gore argued that the large punitive damages award was necessary to induce BMW to change the nationwide policy that it adopted in 1983. But by attempting to alter BMW's nationwide policy, Alabama would be infringing on the policy choices of other States. . . .

In this case, we accept the Alabama Supreme Court's interpretation of the jury verdict as reflecting a computation of the amount of punitive damages "based in large part on conduct that happened in other jurisdictions." As the Alabama Supreme Court noted, neither the jury nor the trial court was presented with evidence that any of BMW's out-of-state conduct was unlawful. . . . The Alabama Supreme Court therefore properly eschewed reliance on BMW's out-of-state conduct, and based its remitted award solely on conduct that occurred within Alabama. The award must be analyzed in the light of the same conduct, with consideration given only to the interests of Alabama consumers, rather than those of the entire Nation. When the scope of the interest in punishment and deterrence that an Alabama court may appropriately consider is properly limited, it is apparent—for reasons that we shall now address—that this award is grossly excessive.

Elementary notions of fairness enshrined in our constitutional jurisprudence dictate that a person receive fair notice not only of the conduct that will subject him to punishment but also of the severity of the penalty that a State may impose. Three guideposts, each of which indicates that BMW did not receive adequate notice of the magnitude of the sanction that Alabama might impose for adhering to the nondisclosure policy adopted in 1983, lead us to the conclusion that the $2 million award against BMW is grossly excessive: the degree of reprehensibility of the nondisclosure; the disparity between the harm or potential harm suffered by Dr. Gore and his punitive damages award; and the difference between this remedy and the civil penalties authorized or imposed in comparable cases. . . .

In [*Pacific Mutual Life Insurance Company v.*] *Haslip*, [499 U.S. 1 (1991)], we concluded that even though a punitive damages award of "more than 4 times the amount of compensatory damages" might be "close to the line," it did not "cross the line into the area of constitutional impropriety." *TXO*, following *dicta* in *Haslip*, refined this analysis by confirming that the proper inquiry is "'whether there is a reasonable relationship between the punitive damages award and the harm likely to result from the defendant's conduct as well as the harm that actually has occurred.'" Thus, in upholding the $10 million award in *TXO*, we relied on the difference between that figure and the harm to the victim that would have ensued if the tortious plan had succeeded. That difference suggested that the relevant ratio was not more than 10 to 1.

The $2 million in punitive damages awarded to Dr. Gore by the Alabama Supreme Court is 500 times the amount of his actual harm as determined by the jury. Moreover, there is no suggestion that Dr. Gore or any other BMW purchaser was threatened with any additional potential harm by BMW's nondisclosure policy. The disparity in this case is thus dramatically greater than those considered in *Haslip* and *TXO*.

Of course, we have consistently rejected the notion that the constitutional line is marked by a simple mathematical formula, even one that compares actual and potential damages to the punitive award. . . .

Comparing the punitive damages award and the civil or criminal penalties that could be imposed for comparable misconduct provides a third indicium of excessiveness. . . . The maximum civil penalty authorized by the Alabama Legislature for a violation of its Deceptive Trade Practices Act is $2,000; other States authorize more severe sanctions, with the maxima ranging from $5,000 to $10,000. Significantly, some statutes draw a distinction between first offenders and recidivists; thus, in New York the penalty is $50 for a first offense and $250 for subsequent offenses. None of these statutes would provide an out-of-state distributor with fair notice that the first violation— or, indeed, the first 14 violations—of its provisions might subject an offender to a multimillion dollar penalty. Moreover, at the time BMW's policy was first challenged, there does not appear to have been any judicial decision in Alabama or elsewhere indicating that application of that policy might give rise to such severe punishment.

The sanction imposed in this case cannot be justified on the ground that it was necessary to deter future misconduct without considering whether less drastic remedies could be expected to achieve that goal. The fact that a multimillion dollar penalty prompted a change in policy sheds no light on the question whether a lesser deterrent would have adequately protected the interests of Alabama consumers. In the absence of a history of noncompliance with known statutory requirements, there is no basis for assuming that a more modest sanction would not have been sufficient to motivate full compliance with the disclosure requirement imposed by the Alabama Supreme Court in this case. . . .

As in *Haslip*, we are not prepared to draw a bright line marking the limits of a constitutionally acceptable punitive damages award. Unlike that case, however, we are fully convinced that the grossly excessive award imposed in this case transcends the constitutional limit. . . .

Justice SCALIA, with whom Justice THOMAS joins, dissenting.

Today we see the latest manifestation of this Court's recent and increasingly insistent "concern about punitive damages that 'run wild.' " *Haslip*. Since the Constitution does not make that concern any of our business, the Court's activities in this area are an unjustified incursion into the province of state governments.

In earlier cases that were the prelude to this decision, I set forth my view that a state trial procedure that commits the decision whether to impose punitive damages, and the amount, to the discretion of the jury, subject to some judicial review for "reasonableness," furnishes a defendant with all the process that is "due." I do not regard the Fourteenth Amendment's Due Process Clause as a secret repository of substantive guarantees against "unfairness"—neither the unfairness of an excessive civil compensatory award, nor the unfairness of an "unreasonable" punitive award. What the Fourteenth Amendment's procedural guarantee assures is an opportunity to contest the reasonableness of a damages judgment in state court; but there is no federal guarantee a damages award actually be reasonable. . . .

Justice GINSBURG, with whom the CHIEF JUSTICE joins, dissenting.

The Court, I am convinced, unnecessarily and unwisely ventures into territory traditionally within the States' domain, and does so in the face of reform measures recently adopted or currently under consideration in legislative arenas. The Alabama Supreme Court, in this case, endeavored to follow this Court's prior instructions; and, more recently, Alabama's highest court has installed further controls on awards of punitive damages. I would therefore leave the state court's judgment undisturbed, and resist unnecessary intrusion into an area dominantly of state concern. . . .

THE DEVELOPMENT OF LAW

Rulings on Substantive and Procedural Due Process

Case	Vote	Ruling
Weiss v. United States, 114 S.Ct. 752 (1994)	9:0	Unanimously rejected a du process challenge to the wa military judges in courts mar

tial are appointed and given fixed tenures.

| Albright v. Oliver, 114 S.Ct. 807 (1994) | 7:2 | Rejected a substantive du process claim that the initi ation of a baseless crimina |

prosecution, based on perjured testimony that the accused was selling drug when the alleged drug was in fact baking soda, provides a basis for a con stitutional tort action against state officials. Justices Stevens and Blackmu dissented.

| United States v. Carlton, 114 S.Ct. 2018 (1994) | 9:0 | Held that Congress's retro active application of a 198 amendment to the Interna |

Revenue Service Code pertaining to estate tax deductions had a rational basi and did not violate due process.

| Honda Motor Co. v. Oberg, 114 S.Ct. 2331 (1994) | 7:2 | Writing for the Court, Jus tice Stevens held that du process requires that jur |

awards of punitive damages be reviewable by courts. Justice Ginsburg an Chief Justice Rehnquist dissented.

| Bennis v. Michigan, 116 S.Ct. 994 (1996) | 5:4 | Writing for the majority Chief Justice Rehnquist re jected the claim that govern |

ment violates due process and the Fifth Amendment's takings clause when i undertakes the forfeiture of an innocent person's property that was used in a illegal activity. Justices Breyer, Kennedy, Souter, and Stevens dissented.

Cooper v. Oklahoma, 116 S.Ct. 1373   9:0   Justice Stevens struck dow
(1996)   Oklahoma's law presumin
                                                           that a defendant is competen
to stand trial unless he proves incompetence by "clear and convincing evi
dence." Finding that the state's presumption and procedures violated "funda
mental fairness" and imposed an onerous burden in violation of due process
Justice Stevens reaffirmed that states may presume a defendant's competenc
and require proof of incompetence based on the lower standard of "the prepon
derance of the evidence."

United States v. Armstrong, 116   8:1   Writing for the Court, Chie
S.Ct. 1480 (1996)   Justice Rehnquist reversed
                                                      lower federal court holdin
that several black defendants charged with drug-trafficking had met the thres
hold requirement for arguing that federal prosecutors engaged in the selectiv
prosecution of blacks and for requiring the government to turn over records o
its prosecutorial policies and practices. Their attorneys presented evidence tha
all of the defendants in twenty-four crack cocaine cases resolved in 1991 wer
black. However, the chief justice held that lower courts should defer to th
government's interests in prosecutorial discretion and that, under the federa
rules of evidence and the equal protection component of the Fifth ̕Amend
ment's due process clause, claimants must demonstrate that a federa
prosecution policy "had a discriminatory effect and that it was motivated by
discriminatory purpose." Here no evidence had been presented showing "dif
ferent treatment of similarly situated persons"; more specifically, no evidenc
was presented that non-blacks who could have been prosecuted for dru
offenses were not prosecuted. Justice Stevens dissented, arguing that court
should have greater leeway in determining whether a threshold showing o
selective prosecution had been made.

BMW of North America v. Gore, 116   5:4   Writing for the Court, Justic
S.Ct. 1589 (1996)   Stevens held that a punitiv
                                                            damages award that was 50
times the amount of the actual damages was "grossly excessive" and violate
the Fourteenth Amendment's due process clause. Chief Justice Rehnquist an
Justices Scalia, Ginsburg, and Thomas dissented.

Montana v. Egelhoff, 116 S.Ct. —   5:4   Writing for a plurality, Jus
(1996)   tice Scalia held that due pro
                                                              cess was not violated by
Montana law instructing juries that an accused's intoxicated condition shoul
not be considered in determining the mental state of a person accused of deli
berate homicide. In a concurring opinion, Justice Ginsburg argued that state
have broad authority to define criminal offenses and may decide that intoxi
cated and sober persons are equally culpable for committing criminal acts
Justices O'Connor, Stevens, Souter, and Breyer dissented.

5

FREEDOM OF EXPRESSION AND ASSOCIATION

A. JUDICIAL APPROACHES TO THE FIRST AMENDMENT

In its 1994–1995 term, the Court considered a First Amendment challenge to a controversial ban on federal employees' receiving honoraria for giving speeches and publishing articles and books. In *United States v. National Treasury Employees Union*, 115 S.Ct. 1003 (1995), the federal government appealed an appellate court's holding that the ban, imposed under the Ethics Reform Act of 1989, violates federal workers' free speech rights under the First Amendment. On appeal, a majority of the justices agreed with the lower court's ruling. Writing for the Court, Justice Stevens explained that

Federal employees who write for publication in their spare time have made significant contributions to the marketplace of ideas. They include literary giants like Nathaniel Hawthorne and Herman Melville, who were employed by the Customs Service; Walt Whitman, who worked for the Departments of Justice and Interior; and Bret Harte, an employee of the mint. Respondents have yet to make comparable contributions to American culture, but they share with these great artists important characteristics that are relevant to the issue we confront.

Even though respondents work for the Government, they have not relinquished "the First Amendment rights they would otherwise enjoy as citizens to comment on matters of public interest." *Pickering v. Board of Ed. of Township High School Dist.*, 391 U.S. 563 (1968). They seek compensation for their expressive activities in their capacity as citizens, not as Government employees. . . . With few exceptions, the content of respondents' messages has nothing to do with their jobs and does not even arguably have any adverse impact on the efficiency of the offices in which they work. They do not address audiences composed of co-workers or supervisors; instead, they write or speak for segments of the general public. Neither the character of the authors, the subject matter of their expression, the effect of the content of their expression on their official duties, nor the kind of audiences they address has any relevance to their employment. . . .

The large-scale disincentive to Government employees' expression also imposes a significant burden on the public's right to read and hear what the employees would otherwise have written and said. We have no way to measure the true cost of that burden, but we cannot ignore the risk that it might deprive us of the work of a future Melville or Hawthorne. The honoraria ban imposes the kind of burden that abridges speech under the First Amendment.

By contrast, Chief Justice Rehnquist, joined by Justices Scalia and Thomas, dissented because the Court's majority, in the words of the chief justice, "understates the weight which should be accorded to the governmental justifications for the honoraria ban and overstates the amount of speech which actually will be deterred." In a separate opinion, Justice O'Connor dissented in part and concurred in the judgment.

In another decision bearing on the First Amendment rights of public workers, in *Waters v. Churchill*, 114 S.Ct. 1878 (1994), the Court, on the one hand, reaffirmed the broad power of federal, state, and local governments to restrict their employees' speech. But on the other hand, the Court ruled for the first time that the First Amendment confers a procedural guarantee requiring employers to conduct some kind of investigation into the basis for disciplining or firing employees for speech deemed to be insubordinate. Cheryl Churchill was fired from her position as a nurse in a city hospital after administrators were told by other nurses that she had criticized the obstetrics department and denigrated her supervisors, while Churchill claimed that she was simply raising concerns about patient care and staff shortages.

Writing for the majority in *Waters*, Justice O'Connor reaffirmed that "the extra power the government has in this area comes from the nature of the government's mission as an employer. When someone who is paid a salary so that she will contribute to an agency's effective operation begins to do or say things that detract from the agency's effective operation, the government employer must have some power to restrain her." Only dissenting Justices Blackmun and Stevens thought otherwise. They charged the Court's majority with "underestimat[ing] the importance of freedom of speech for the more than 18 million civilian employees of this country's federal, state, and local governments, and subordinat[ing] that freedom to an abstract interest in bureaucratic efficiency."

Justice O'Connor's opinion for the Court, however, proceeded to hold that government employers disciplining or firing employees for their speech "must tread with a certain amount of care" and conduct an investigation into the basis for their action. The First Amendment,

O'Connor ruled, contains a procedural safeguard against the erroneous punishment of protected speech, though that safeguard depends on each case and consideration of its costs versus the risks posed for employees' free speech. No specific kind of investigation must be conducted or is constitutionally required, the justice concluded, when declining to lay down further guidelines. "Many different courses of action will necessarily be reasonable," O'Connor added, depending on a case-by-case analysis. In so holding, Justice O'Connor picked up the votes of Justices Blackmun and Stevens but lost those of Justices Scalia, Kennedy, and Thomas. In a separate opinion joined by the latter justices, Scalia countered that the First Amendment imposed no such procedural requirement and sharply attacked O'Connor's analysis as unprecedented, ambiguous, and certain to burden government employers and the courts.

Finally, in its 1996–1997 term, the Court will hear a challenge to Arizona's law making English the official language and requiring state employees to conduct business in English only. In 1988, Arizona amended its state constitution to make English the official language; twenty-three other states have similar laws. Arizona's law was challenged as a violation of the First Amendment's guarantee for free speech by a state employee, Maria-Kelly Yniquez, who handled medical malpractice claims against the state and who spoke both Spanish and English to claimants, depending on their need. A federal district and appellate court invalidated the law. By a six-to-five vote, the U.S. Court of Appeals for the Ninth Circuit ruled that Arizona's law violated government workers' free speech and because it "significantly interferes with the ability of the non-English speaking populace of Arizona to receive information and ideas." Writing for the majority and relying on a 1923 Supreme Court ruling in *Meyer v. State of Nebraska*, 262 U.S. 390 (1923), which struck down a state law forbidding the teaching of German in schools, Judge Stephen Reinhardt observed, "The protection of the Constitution extends to all, to those who speak other languages as well as those born with English on the tongue." Because the state governor decided not to appeal the decisions, a citizens group, Arizonans for Official English, which had originally sponsored the amendment, intervened in the suit and appealed the Ninth Circuit's decision to the Supreme Court, which granted review of the case, *Arizonans for Official English v. Arizona*.

D. COMMERCIAL SPEECH

In two rulings handed down during its 1993–1994 term, the Court dealt with issues arising from the application of its commercial speech doctrine. *Ibanez v. Florida Department of Professional Regulation, Board of Accountancy*, 114 S.Ct. 2084 (1994) involved a First Amendment challenge to Florida's ban on the use of the appellations "CPA" (certified public accountant) and "CFP" (certified financial planner) on business cards and letterheads and in telephone listings. By a vote of seven to two, the justices continued a two-decade-old trend towards according commercial speech greater First Amendment protection. Writing for the majority, Justice Ginsburg reaffirmed that states may "ban such speech only if it is false, deceptive, or misleading." Restrictions on such advertising must "directly and materially advance a substantial state interest in a manner no more extensive than necessary to serve [the state's] interest." Here, the Court's majority rejected Florida's claim that the use of "CPA" in advertisements was "inherently misleading" as insubstantial and outweighed by the First Amendment. By contrast, dissenting Justice O'Connor, along with Chief Justice Rehnquist, contended that, "States may prohibit inherently misleading speech entirely."

In *City of Ladue v. Gilleo*, 114 S.Ct. 2038 (1994), the Court heard an appeal of a federal appellate court's striking down of a municipal ordinance banning the posting of all signs, except for real estate sale signs, on private property. Since its founding in 1936, Ladue, Missouri, banned all signs, with the exception of "For Sale" signs, in order to preserve the city's "unique aesthetic character." But in December 1990, shortly after the United States' clash with Iraq, an anti-war protester, Margaret Gilleo, ran afoul of the ordinance by placing an 8-1/2-by-11-inch sign, "For Peace in Gulf," in a second-floor window of her home after two other similar signs she posted on her front lawn disappeared mysteriously. Gilleo in turn challenged the constitutionality of Ladue's ordinance in court and won, whereupon the city appealed to the Supreme Court.

When announcing the Court's decision in *City of Ladue*, Justice Stevens struck down the city's ordinance in a sweeping opinion that went beyond the lower courts' analysis rejecting Ladue's justification for its ban on noncommercial signs. The lower courts had held that Ladue's ordinance was flawed in giving favored status to commercial, as opposed to political, speech and was thus underinclusive. By contrast, Justice Stevens took the position that the ordinance was over-inclusive and too restrictive. In his words:

> Ladue has almost completely foreclosed a venerable means of communication that is both unique and important. It has totally foreclosed that medium to political, religious, or personal messages. Signs that react to a local happening or express a view on a controversial issue both reflect and animate change in the life of a community. Often placed on lawns or in windows, residential signs play an important part in political campaigns, during which they are displayed to signal the resident's support for particular candidates, parties, or causes. They may not afford the same opportunities for conveying complex ideas as do other media, but residential signs have long been an important and distinct medium of expression. . . .

Residential signs are an unusually cheap and convenient form of communication. Especially for persons of modest means or limited mobility, a yard or window sign may have no practical substitute. Even for the affluent, the added costs in money or time of taking out a newspaper advertisement, handing out leaflets on the street, or standing in front of one's house with a hand-held sign may make the difference between participating and not participating in some public debate. Furthermore, a person who puts up a sign at her residence often intends to reach neighbors, an audience that could not be reached nearly as well by other means.

A special respect for individual liberty in the home has long been part of our culture and our law; that principle has special resonance when the government seeks to constrain a person's ability to speak there. Most Americans would be understandably dismayed, given that tradition, to learn that it was illegal to display from their window an 8-by-11-inch sign expressing their political views. Whereas the government's need to mediate among various competing uses, including expressive ones, for public streets and facilities is constant and unavoidable, its need to regulate temperate speech from the home is surely much less pressing.

Our decision that Ladue's ban on almost all residential signs violates the First Amendment by no means leaves the City powerless to address the ills that may be associated with residential signs. It bears mentioning that individual residents themselves have strong incentives to keep their own property values up and to prevent "visual clutter" in their own yards and neighborhoods—incentives markedly different from those of persons who erect signs on others' land, in others' neighborhoods, or on public property. Residents' self-interest diminishes the danger of the "unlimited" proliferation of residential signs that concerns the City of Ladue. We are confident that more temperate measures could in large part satisfy Ladue's stated regulatory needs without harm to the First Amendment rights of its citizens. As currently framed, however, the ordinance abridges those rights.

In its 1994–1995 term, the justices decided two more commercial speech cases. One, *Rubin v. Coors Brewing Co.*, 115 S.Ct. 1585 (1995), raised a challenge to a 1935 federal statute imposing labeling restrictions on the alcohol content of malt beverages. Federal alcohol labeling rules are conflicting, somewhat confusing, and run contrary to those in ten states which require beer bottles to show alcohol levels. Under federal law, the disclosure of alcohol is required on distilled spirits and wine, while the alcohol content of beer may be shown on billboards but not on bottle labels. The federal government defended the labeling restrictions on the ground that they were necessary to prevent "strength wars" in advertising by beer producers, but an appellate court disagreed and struck down the restrictions. Writing for a unanimous Court, Justice Thomas affirmed the lower court's decision, finding that the law and the government's interest in suppressing "strength wars" failed the test set forth in *Central Hudson Gas & Electric Corp. v. Public Service Comm'n of N.Y.*, 447 U.S. 557 (1980) (see Vol 2., Ch. 5), that the government's interest in restricting commercial speech must be "substantial" and "not be more extensive than is necessary to serve that interest."

The other case invited a reconsideration of *Bates v. Arizona State Bar*, 433 U.S. 350 (1977), which first extended First Amendment protection to the advertising of legal services. At issue in *Florida Bar v. Went For It*, 115 S.Ct. 2371 (1995), was the constitutionality of two restrictions approved by the Florida state supreme court in 1991 and struck down by a federal appellate court. The rules prohibited personal injury lawyers from making written solicitations to victims or victims' relatives within thirty days of an accident or natural disaster, as well as from accepting referrals of clients from a referral service. By a five-to-four vote, the justices upheld those restrictions. Writing for the majority, Justice O'Connor explained that,

> It is now well established that lawyer advertising is commercial speech and, as such, is accorded a measure of First Amendment protection. Such First Amendment protection, of course, is not absolute. We have always been careful to distinguish commercial speech from speech at the First Amendment's core.... Mindful of these concerns, we engage in "intermediate" scrutiny of restrictions on commercial speech, analyzing them under the framework set forth in *Central Hudson Gas & Electric Corp. v. Public Service Comm'n of N.Y.*, 447 U.S. 557 (1980). Under *Central Hudson*, the government may freely regulate commercial speech that concerns unlawful activity or is misleading. Commercial speech that falls into neither of those categories, like the advertising at issue here, may be regulated if the government satisfies a test consisting of three related prongs: first, the government must assert a substantial interest in support of its regulation; second, the government must demonstrate that the restriction on commercial speech directly and materially advances that interest; and third, the regulation must be "narrowly drawn."
>
> "Unlike rational basis review, the *Central Hudson* standard does not permit us to supplant the precise interests put forward by the State with other suppositions," *Edenfield v. Fane*, 507 U.S. 761 (1993). The Florida Bar asserts that it has a substantial interest in protecting the privacy and tranquillity of personal injury victims and their loved ones against intrusive, unsolicited contact by lawyers. This interest obviously factors into the Bar's paramount (and repeatedly professed) objective of curbing activities that "negatively affect the administration of justice." Because direct mail solicitations in the wake of accidents are perceived by the public as intrusive, the Bar argues, the reputation of the legal profession in the eyes of Floridians has suffered commensurately. The regulation, then, is an effort to protect the flagging reputations of Florida lawyers by preventing them from engaging in conduct that, the Bar maintains, "'is universally regarded as deplorable and beneath common decency because of its intrusion upon the special vulnerability and private grief of victims or their families.'"
>
> We have little trouble crediting the Bar's interest as substantial. . . . Under *Central Hudson*'s second prong, the State must demonstrate that the challenged regulation "advances the Government's interest 'in a direct and material way.'" *Rubin v. Coors Brewing Co.* [115 S.Ct. 1585] (1995). . . . The

anecdotal record mustered by the Bar is noteworthy for its breadth and detail. With titles like "Scavenger Lawyers" and "Solicitors Out of Bounds," newspaper editorial pages in Florida have burgeoned with criticism of Florida lawyers who send targeted direct mail to victims shortly after accidents. . . . In light of this showing—which respondents at no time refuted, save by the conclusory assertion that the rule lacked "any factual basis"—we conclude that the Bar has satisfied the second prong of the *Central Hudson* test. . . .

Passing to *Central Hudson*'s third prong, we examine the relationship between the Florida Bar's interests and the means chosen to serve them. With respect to this prong, the differences between commercial speech and noncommercial speech are manifest. "What our decisions require," instead, "is a 'fit' between the 'legislature's ends and the means chosen to accomplish those ends,' a fit that is not necessarily perfect, but reasonable; that represents not necessarily the single best disposition but one whose scope is 'in proportion to the interest served,' that employs not necessarily the least restrictive means but . . . a means narrowly tailored to achieve the desired objective." . . . Respondents levy a great deal of criticism, echoed in the dissent, at the scope of the Bar's restriction on targeted mail. "By prohibiting written communications to all people, whatever their state of mind," respondents charge, the rule "keeps useful information from those accident victims who are ready, willing and able to utilize a lawyer's advice." This criticism may be parsed into two components. First, the rule does not distinguish between victims in terms of the severity of their injuries. According to respondents, the rule is unconstitutionally overinclusive insofar as it bans targeted mailings even to citizens whose injuries or grief are relatively minor. Second, the rule may prevent citizens from learning about their legal options, particularly at a time when other actors—opposing counsel and insurance adjusters—may be clamoring for victims' attentions. Any benefit arising from the Bar's regulation, respondents implicitly contend, is outweighed by these costs.

We are not persuaded by respondents' allegations of constitutional infirmity. We find little deficiency in the ban's failure to distinguish among injured Floridians by the severity of their pain or the intensity of their grief. Indeed, it is hard to imagine the contours of a regulation that might satisfy respondents on this score. Rather than drawing difficult lines on the basis that some injuries are "severe" and some situations appropriate (and others, presumably, inappropriate) for grief, anger, or emotion, the Florida Bar has crafted a ban applicable to all postaccident or disaster solicitations for a brief 30-day period. Unlike respondents, we do not see "numerous and obvious less-burdensome alternatives" to Florida's short temporal ban. The Bar's rule is reasonably well-tailored to its stated objective of eliminating targeted mailings whose type and timing are a source of distress to Floridians, distress that has caused many of them to lose respect for the legal profession. Respondents' second point would have force if the Bar's rule were not limited to a brief period and if there were not many other ways for injured Floridians to learn about the availability of legal representation during that time. . . .

Speech by professionals obviously has many dimensions. There are circumstances in which we will accord speech by attorneys on public issues and matters of legal representation the strongest protection our Constitution has to offer. This case, however, concerns pure commercial advertising, for which we have always reserved a lesser degree of protection under the First Amendment. Particularly because the standards and conduct of state-licensed lawyers have traditionally been subject to extensive regulation by the States, it is all the more appropriate that we limit our scrutiny of state regulations to a level commensurate with the "subordinate position" of commercial speech in the scale of First Amendment values.

By contrast, the four dissenters in *Went For It* sharply disagreed with Justice O'Connor's analysis and application of the *Central Hudson* test. Writing for Justices Stevens, Souter, and Ginsburg, Justice Kennedy charged,

It is most ironic that, for the first time since *Bates v. [Arizona State Bar]*, the Court now orders a major retreat from the constitutional guarantees for commercial speech in order to shield its own profession from public criticism. Obscuring the financial aspect of the legal profession from public discussion through direct mail solicitation, at the expense of the least sophisticated members of society, is not a laudable constitutional goal. There is no authority for the proposition that the Constitution permits the State to promote the public image of the legal profession by suppressing information about the profession's business aspects. If public respect for the profession erodes because solicitation distorts the idea of the law as most lawyers see it, it must be remembered that real progress begins with more rational speech, not less. . . .

Today's opinion is a serious departure, not only from our prior decisions involving attorney advertising, but also from the principles that govern the transmission of commercial speech. The Court's opinion reflects a newfound and illegitimate confidence that it, along with the Supreme Court of Florida, knows what is best for the Bar and its clients. Self-assurance has always been the hallmark of a censor. That is why under the First Amendment the public, not the State, has the right and the power to decide what ideas and information are deserving of their adherence. . . .

Finally, during its 1995–1996 term, the Court handed down a major ruling on commercial speech with broad implications for the government's regulation of advertisements for alcohol, tobacco, and other "vices." Justice Stevens's opinion for the Court in *44 Liquormart, Inc. v. Rhode Island* (excerpted below) reconsidered a number of precedents when striking down Rhode Island's ban on advertising the price of liquor.

During its 1996–1997 term, yet another commercial speech will be heard, though this one, *Glickman v. Willeman Brothers*, No. 95-1184, poses a twist for the developing doctrine. At issue is the Agriculture Department's almost sixty-year-old policy of requiring growers of certain products to pay for a portion of industrywide advertising. The regulation was adopted under the Agricultural Marketing Agreement

Act of 1937 on the assumption that such generic advertising would help certain industries increase consumer demand for their products. In 1987, however, growers of California peaches, nectarines, and plums challenged the constitutionality of the regulation on the ground that their forced participation in the program was a kind of compelled speech that violated the First Amendment. The Court of Appeals for the Ninth Circuit agreed and the government appealed to the Supreme Court.

44 Liquormart, Inc. v. Rhode Island
116 S.Ct. 1495 (1996)

In 1956, the state of Rhode Island enacted two prohibitions against advertising the retail price of alcoholic drinks. The first prohibits "advertising in any manner whatsoever" of the price of alcoholic drinks, with the exception of price tags, and the second categorically forbids any ads making "reference to the price of any alcoholic beverages." In 1991, complaints from competitors about an ad placed by 44 Liquormart in a newspaper generated enforcement proceedings under the statute. Notably, the ad did not state the price of any alcoholic beverages and, indeed, noted that "State law prohibits advertising liquor prices." Rather, the ad listed 44 Liquormart's low prices for peanuts, potato chips, and Schweppes mixers; it also identified various brands of packaged liquor as well as including the word "WOW" in large letters next to pictures of vodka and rum bottles. Subsequently, after being fined $400, 44 Liquormart filed a suit seeking a declaratory judgment that the state's restrictions violated the First Amendment. A federal district court agreed that the advertising ban was unconstitutional because it did not "directly advance" the government's interest in reducing alcohol consumption and was "more extensive than necessary to serve that interest." But a federal appellate court reversed and 44 Liquormart appealed to the Supreme Court.

The Court's decision was unanimous and opinion delivered by Justice Stevens. Justices Scalia, Thomas, and O'Connor filed concurring opinions.

Justice STEVENS delivered the opinion of the Court with respect to Parts I, II, and VII, in which Justices Scalia, Kennedy, Souter, Thomas, and Ginsburg joined; the opinion of the Court with respect to Part VIII, in which Justices Scalia, Kennedy, Souter, and Ginsburg joined; an opinion with respect to Parts III and V, in which Justices Kennedy, Souter, and Ginsburg joined; an opinion with respect to Part VI, in which Justices Kennedy, Thomas, and Ginsburg joined; and an opinion with respect to Part IV, in which Justices Kennedy and Ginsburg joined.

III

Advertising has been a part of our culture throughout our history. Even in colonial days, the public relied on "commercial speech" for vital information about the market. Early newspapers displayed advertisements for goods and services on their front pages, and town criers called out prices in public squares. Indeed, commercial messages played such a central role in public life prior to the Founding that Benjamin Franklin authored his early defense of a free press in support of his decision to print, of all things, an advertisement for voyages to Barbados.

It was not until the 1970's, however, that this Court held that the First Amendment protected the dissemination of truthful and nonmisleading commercial messages about lawful products and services. In *Bigelow v. Virginia*, 421 U.S. 809 (1975), we held that it was error to assume that commercial speech was entitled to no First Amendment protection or that it was without value in the marketplace of ideas. The following Term in *Virginia Bd. of Pharmacy v. Virginia Citizens Consumer Council, Inc.*, 425 U.S. 748 (1976), we expanded on our holding in *Bigelow* and held that the State's blanket ban on advertising the price of prescription drugs violated the First Amendment. *Virginia Pharmacy Bd.* reflected the conclusion that the same interest that supports regulation of potentially misleading advertising, namely the public's interest in receiving accurate commercial information, also supports an interpretation of the First Amendment that provides constitutional protection for the dissemination of accurate and nonmisleading commercial messages. . . . The opinion further explained that a State's paternalistic assumption that the public will use truthful, nonmisleading commercial information unwisely cannot justify a decision to suppress it. . . .

At the same time, our early cases recognized that the State may regulate some types of commercial advertising more freely than other forms of protected speech. Specifically, we explained that the State may require commercial messages to "appear in such a form, or include such additional information, warnings, and disclaimers, as are necessary to prevent its being deceptive," *Virginia Pharmacy Bd.*, and that it may restrict some forms of aggressive sales practices that have the potential to exert "undue influence" over consumers. See *Bates v. State Bar of Ariz.*, 433 U.S. 350 (1977). . . .

In *Central Hudson Gas & Electric Corp. v. Public Service Commission of New York*, 447 U.S. 557 (1980), we took stock of our developing commercial speech jurisprudence. In that case, we considered a regulation "completely" banning all promotional advertising by electric utilities. Our decision acknowledged the special features of commercial speech but identified the serious First Amendment concerns that attend blanket advertising prohibitions that do not protect consumers from commercial harms. . . . In reaching its conclusion, the majority explained that although the special nature of commercial speech may require less than strict review of its regulation, special concerns arise from "regulations that entirely suppress commercial speech in order to pursue a nonspeech-related policy." In those

circumstances, "a ban on speech could screen from public view the underlying governmental policy." As a result, the Court concluded that "special
care" should attend the review of such blanket bans, and it pointedly
remarked that "in recent years this Court has not approved a blanket ban on
commercial speech unless the speech itself was flawed in some way, either
because it was deceptive or related to unlawful activity."

IV

When a State regulates commercial messages to protect consumers from
misleading, deceptive, or aggressive sales practices, or requires the disclosure of beneficial consumer information, the purpose of its regulation is
consistent with the reasons for according constitutional protection to
commercial speech and therefore justifies less than strict review. However,
when a State entirely prohibits the dissemination of truthful, nonmisleading
commercial messages for reasons unrelated to the preservation of a fair
bargaining process, there is far less reason to depart from the rigorous
review that the First Amendment generally demands.

Sound reasons justify reviewing the latter type of commercial speech
regulation more carefully. Most obviously, complete speech bans, unlike
content-neutral restrictions on the time, place, or manner of expression are
particularly dangerous because they all but foreclose alternative means of
disseminating certain information. . . .

It is the State's interest in protecting consumers from "commercial harms"
that provides "the typical reason why commercial speech can be subject to
greater governmental regulation than noncommercial speech." *Cincinnati v.
Discovery Network, Inc.*, 507 U.S. 410 (1993). Yet bans that target truthful,
nonmisleading commercial messages rarely protect consumers from such
harms. Instead, such bans often serve only to obscure an "underlying
governmental policy" that could be implemented without regulating speech.
Central Hudson. In this way, these commercial speech bans not only hinder
consumer choice, but also impede debate over central issues of public
policy.

Precisely because bans against truthful, nonmisleading commercial speech
rarely seek to protect consumers from either deception or overreaching, they
usually rest solely on the offensive assumption that the public will respond
"irrationally" to the truth. The First Amendment directs us to be especially
skeptical of regulations that seek to keep people in the dark for what the
government perceives to be their own good. That teaching applies equally to
state attempts to deprive consumers of accurate information about their
chosen products: "The commercial market-place, like other spheres of our
social and cultural life, provides a forum where ideas and information
flourish. Some of the ideas and information are vital, some of slight worth.
But the general rule is that the speaker and the audience, not the
government, assess the value of the information presented." . . .

V

The State argues that the price advertising prohibition should nevertheless
be upheld because it directly advances the State's substantial interest in
promoting temperance, and because it is no more extensive than necessary.

Although there is some confusion as to what Rhode Island means by temperance, we assume that the State asserts an interest in reducing alcohol consumption. . . .

Although the record suggests that the price advertising ban may have some impact on the purchasing patterns of temperate drinkers of modest means, the State has presented no evidence to suggest that its speech prohibition will significantly reduce market-wide consumption. . . . In addition, as the District Court noted, the State has not identified what price level would lead to a significant reduction in alcohol consumption, nor has it identified the amount that it believes prices would decrease without the ban. Thus, the State's own showing reveals that any connection between the ban and a significant change in alcohol consumption would be purely fortuitous. . . .

The State also cannot satisfy the requirement that its restriction on speech be no more extensive than necessary. It is perfectly obvious that alternative forms of regulation that would not involve any restriction on speech would be more likely to achieve the State's goal of promoting temperance. As the State's own expert conceded, higher prices can be maintained either by direct regulation or by increased taxation. Per capita purchases could be limited as is the case with prescription drugs. Even educational campaigns focused on the problems of excessive, or even moderate, drinking might prove to be more effective.

As a result, even under the less than strict standard that generally applies in commercial speech cases, the State has failed to establish a "reasonable fit" between its abridgment of speech and its temperance goal. It necessarily follows that the price advertising ban cannot survive the more stringent constitutional review that *Central Hudson* itself concluded was appropriate for the complete suppression of truthful, nonmisleading commercial speech.

VI

The State responds by arguing that it merely exercised appropriate "legislative judgment" in determining that a price advertising ban would best promote temperance. Relying on the *Central Hudson* analysis set forth in *Posadas de Puerto Rico Associates v. Tourism Co. of P.R.*, 478 U.S. 328 (1986), and *United States v. Edge Broadcasting Co.*, 509 U.S. — (1993), Rhode Island first argues that, because expert opinions as to the effectiveness of the price advertising ban "go both ways," the Court of Appeals correctly concluded that the ban constituted a "reasonable choice" by the legislature. The State next contends that precedent requires us to give particular deference to that legislative choice because the State could, if it chose, ban the sale of alcoholic beverages outright. Finally, the State argues that deference is appropriate because alcoholic beverages are so-called "vice" products. We consider each of these contentions in turn.

The State's first argument fails to justify the speech prohibition at issue. Our commercial speech cases recognize some room for the exercise of legislative judgment. However, Rhode Island errs in concluding that *Edge* and *Posadas* establish the degree of deference that its decision to impose a price advertising ban warrants. . . . [In] *Posadas*, a five-Member majority held that, under the *Central Hudson* test, it was "up to the legislature" to choose to reduce gambling by suppressing in-state casino advertising rather than engaging in educational speech. Rhode Island argues that this logic demonstrates the constitutionality of its own decision to ban price advertising in lieu of raising taxes or employing some other less speech-restrictive means of promoting temperance.

The reasoning in *Posadas* does support the State's argument, but, on reflection, we are now persuaded that *Posadas* erroneously performed the First Amendment analysis. The casino advertising ban was designed to keep truthful, nonmisleading speech from members of the public for fear that they would be more likely to gamble if they received it. As a result, the advertising ban served to shield the State's antigambling policy from the public scrutiny that more direct, nonspeech regulation would draw.

Given our longstanding hostility to commercial speech regulation of this type, *Posadas* clearly erred in concluding that it was "up to the legislature" to choose suppression over a less speech-restrictive policy. The *Posadas* majority's conclusion on that point cannot be reconciled with the unbroken line of prior cases striking down similarly broad regulations on truthful, nonmisleading advertising when non-speech-related alternatives were available.

Because the 5-to-4 decision in *Posadas* marked such a sharp break from our prior precedent, and because it concerned a constitutional question about which this Court is the final arbiter, we decline to give force to its highly deferential approach. Instead, in keeping with our prior holdings, we conclude that a state legislature does not have the broad discretion to suppress truthful, nonmisleading information for paternalistic purposes that the *Posadas* majority was willing to tolerate. We also cannot accept the State's second contention, which is premised entirely on the "greater-includes-the-lesser" reasoning endorsed toward the end of the majority's opinion in *Posadas*. There, the majority stated that "the greater power to completely ban casino gambling necessarily includes the lesser power to ban advertising of casino gambling." . . .

In *Rubin v. Coors Brewing Co.*, [115 S.Ct. 1585] (1995), the United States advanced a similar argument as a basis for supporting a statutory prohibition against revealing the alcoholic content of malt beverages on product labels. We rejected the argument, noting that the statement in the *Posadas* opinion was made only after the majority had concluded that the Puerto Rican regulation "survived the *Central Hudson* test." Further consideration persuades us that the "greater-includes-the-lesser" argument should be rejected for the additional and more important reason that it is inconsistent with both logic and well-settled doctrine.

Although we do not dispute the proposition that greater powers include lesser ones, we fail to see how that syllogism requires the conclusion that the State's power to regulate commercial activity is "greater" than its power to ban truthful, nonmisleading commercial speech. Contrary to the assumption made in *Posadas*, we think it quite clear that banning speech may sometimes prove far more intrusive than banning conduct. As a venerable proverb teaches, it may prove more injurious to prevent people from teaching others how to fish than to prevent fish from being sold. Similarly, a local ordinance banning bicycle lessons may curtail freedom far more than one that prohibits bicycle riding within city limits. In short, we reject the assumption that words are necessarily less vital to freedom than actions, or that logic somehow proves that the power to prohibit an activity is necessarily "greater" than the power to suppress speech about it. . . .

Finally, we find unpersuasive the State's contention that, under *Posadas* and *Edge*, the price advertising ban should be upheld because it targets commercial speech that pertains to a "vice" activity. The appellees premise their request for a so-called "vice" exception to our commercial speech doctrine on language in *Edge* which characterized gambling as a "vice." The respondents misread our precedent. Our decision last Term striking down an alcohol-related advertising restriction effectively rejected the very contention respondents now make. See *Rubin v. Coors Brewing Co.*

Moreover, the scope of any "vice" exception to the protection afforded by the First Amendment would be difficult, if not impossible, to define. Almost any product that poses some threat to public health or public morals might reasonably be characterized by a state legislature as relating to "vice activity." Such characterization, however, is anomalous when applied to products such as alcoholic beverages, lottery tickets, or playing cards, that may be lawfully purchased on the open market. . . . For these reasons, a "vice" label that is unaccompanied by a corresponding prohibition against the commercial behavior at issue fails to provide a principled justification for the regulation of commercial speech about that activity.

VII

As is clear, the text of the Twenty-first Amendment supports the view that, while it grants the States authority over commerce that might otherwise be reserved to the Federal Government, it places no limit whatsoever on other constitutional provisions. Nevertheless, Rhode Island argues, and the Court of Appeals agreed, that in this case the Twenty-first Amendment tilts the First Amendment analysis in the State's favor.

In reaching its conclusion, the Court of Appeals relied on our decision in *California v. LaRue*, 409 U.S. 109 (1972). In *LaRue*, five Members of the Court relied on the Twenty-first Amendment to buttress the conclusion that the First Amendment did not invalidate California's prohibition of certain grossly sexual exhibitions in premises licensed to serve alcoholic beverages. Specifically, the opinion stated that the Twenty-first Amendment required that the prohibition be given an added presumption in favor of its validity. We are now persuaded that the Court's analysis in *LaRue* would have led to precisely the same result if it had placed no reliance on the Twenty-first Amendment.

Without questioning the holding in *LaRue*, we now disavow its reasoning insofar as it relied on the Twenty-first Amendment. As we explained in a case decided more than a decade after *LaRue*, although the Twenty-first Amendment limits the effect of the dormant Commerce Clause on a State's regulatory power over the delivery or use of intoxicating beverages within its borders, "the Amendment does not license the States to ignore their obligations under other provisions of the Constitution." *Capital Cities Cable, Inc. v. Crisp*, 467 U.S. 691 (1984). That general conclusion reflects our specific holdings that the Twenty-first Amendment does not in any way diminish the force of the Supremacy Clause. We see no reason why the First

Amendment should not also be included in that list. Accordingly, we now hold that the Twenty-first Amendment does not qualify the constitutional prohibition against laws abridging the freedom of speech embodied in the First Amendment. The Twenty-first Amendment, therefore, cannot save Rhode Island's ban on liquor price advertising.

VIII

Because Rhode Island has failed to carry its heavy burden of justifying its complete ban on price advertising, we conclude that [the state's restrictions on liquor advertising] abridge speech in violation of the First Amendment as made applicable to the States by the Due Process Clause of the Fourteenth Amendment. The judgment of the Court of Appeals is therefore reversed.

Justice SCALIA, concurring in part and concurring in the judgment.

I share Justice THOMAS's discomfort with the *Central Hudson* test, which seems to me to have nothing more than policy intuition to support it. I also share Justice STEVENS' aversion towards paternalistic governmental policies that prevent men and women from hearing facts that might not be good for them. On the other hand, it would also be paternalism for us to prevent the people of the States from enacting laws that we consider paternalistic, unless we have good reason to believe that the Constitution itself forbids them. I will take my guidance as to what the Constitution forbids, with regard to a text as indeterminate as the First Amendment's preservation of "the freedom of speech," and where the core offense of suppressing particular political ideas is not at issue, from the long accepted practices of the American people.

Since I do not believe we have before us the wherewithal to declare *Central Hudson* wrong—or at least the wherewithal to say what ought to replace it—I must resolve this case in accord with our existing jurisprudence, which all except Justice THOMAS agree would prohibit the challenged regulation. I am not disposed to develop new law, or reinforce old, on this issue, and accordingly I merely concur in the judgment of the Court. I believe, however, that Justice STEVENS' treatment of the application of the Twenty-First Amendment to this case is correct, and accordingly join Parts I, II, VII, and VIII of Justice STEVENS' opinion.

Justice THOMAS, concurring in Parts I, II, VI, and VII, and concurring in the judgment.

In cases such as this, in which the government's asserted interest is to keep legal users of a product or service ignorant in order to manipulate their choices in the marketplace, the balancing test adopted in *Central Hudson* should not be applied, in my view. Rather, such an "interest" is per se illegitimate and can no more justify regulation of "commercial" speech than it can justify regulation of "noncommercial" speech. . . .

I do not see a philosophical or historical basis for asserting that "commercial" speech is of "lower value" than "noncommercial" speech. Nor do I believe that the only explanations that the Court has ever advanced for treating "commercial" speech differently from other speech can justify restricting "commercial" speech in order to keep information from legal purchasers so as to thwart what would otherwise be their choices in the marketplace.

I do not join the principal opinion's application of the *Central Hudson* balancing test because I do not believe that such a test should be applied to a restriction of "commercial" speech, at least when, as here, the asserted interest is one that is to be achieved through keeping would-be recipients of the speech in the dark. Application of the advancement-of-state-interest prong of *Central Hudson* makes little sense to me in such circumstances. Faulting the State for failing to show that its price advertising ban decreases alcohol consumption "significantly," seems to imply that if the State had been more successful at keeping consumers ignorant and thereby decreasing their consumption, then the restriction might have been upheld. This contradicts *Virginia Pharmacy Bd.*'s rationale for protecting "commercial" speech in the first instance. . . .

Although the Court took a sudden turn away from *Virginia Pharmacy Bd.* in *Central Hudson*, it has never explained why manipulating the choices of consumers by keeping them ignorant is more legitimate when the ignorance is maintained through suppression of "commercial" speech than when the same ignorance is maintained through suppression of "noncommercial" speech. The courts, including this Court, have found the *Central Hudson* "test" to be, as a general matter, very difficult to apply with any uniformity. . . . Moreover, the second prong of *Central Hudson*, as applied to the facts of that case and to those here, apparently requires judges to delineate those situations in which citizens cannot be trusted with information, and invites judges to decide whether they themselves think that consumption of a product is harmful enough that it should be discouraged. In my view, the *Central Hudson* test asks the courts to weigh incommensurables—the value of knowledge versus the value of ignorance—and to apply contradictory premises—that informed adults are the best judges of their own interests, and that they are not. Rather than continuing to apply a test that makes no sense to me when the asserted state interest is of the type involved here, I would return to the reasoning and holding of *Virginia Pharmacy Bd.* Under that decision, these restrictions fall.

Justice O'CONNOR, with whom the CHIEF JUSTICE, Justice SOUTER, and Justice BREYER join, concurring in the judgment.

I agree with the Court that Rhode Island's price-advertising ban is invalid. I would resolve this case more narrowly, however, by applying our established *Central Hudson* test to determine whether this commercial-speech regulation survives First Amendment scrutiny.

Under that test, we first determine whether the speech at issue concerns lawful activity and is not misleading, and whether the asserted governmental interest is substantial. If both these conditions are met, we must decide whether the regulation "directly advances the governmental interest asserted, and whether it is not more extensive than is necessary to serve that interest." *Central Hudson.* . . . Rhode Island's regulation fails the final prong; that is, its ban is more extensive than necessary to serve the State's interest. . . .

Rhode Island offers one, and only one, justification for its ban on price advertising. Rhode Island says that the ban is intended to keep alcohol prices high as a way to keep consumption low. . . .

The fit between Rhode Island's method and this particular goal is not reasonable. If the target is simply higher prices generally to discourage consumption, the regulation imposes too great, and unnecessary, a prohibition on speech in order to achieve it. The State has other methods at its disposal—methods that would more directly accomplish this stated goal without intruding on sellers' ability to provide truthful, nonmisleading information to customers. . . .

Respondents point for support to *Posadas de Puerto Rico Associates,* where, applying the *Central Hudson* test, we upheld the constitutionality of a Puerto Rico law that prohibited the advertising of casino gambling aimed at residents of Puerto Rico, but permitted such advertising aimed at tourists. . . . It is true that *Posadas* accepted as reasonable, without further inquiry, Puerto Rico's assertions that the regulations furthered the government's interest and were no more extensive than necessary to serve that interest. Since *Posadas,* however, this Court has examined more searchingly the State's professed goal, and the speech restriction put into place to further it, before accepting a State's claim that the speech restriction satisfies First Amendment scrutiny. The closer look that we have required since *Posadas* comports better with the purpose of the analysis set out in *Central Hudson,* by requiring the State to show that the speech restriction directly advances its interest and is narrowly tailored. Under such a closer look, Rhode Island's price-advertising ban clearly fails to pass muster. Because Rhode Island's regulation fails even the less stringent standard set out in *Central Hudson,* nothing here requires adoption of a new analysis for the evaluation of commercial speech regulation. . . . Because we need go no further, I would not here undertake the question whether the test we have employed since *Central Hudson* should be displaced. . . .

F. REGULATING THE BROADCAST AND CABLE MEDIA

In 1992, Congress overrode a presidential veto to enact the Cable Television Consumer Protection and Competition Act. That legislation subjects the cable industry to rate regulation by the Federal Communications Commission (FCC) and by municipal franchising authorities; prohibits municipalities from awarding exclusive franchises to cable operators; imposes various restrictions on cable programmers that are affiliated with cable operators; and directs the FCC to develop and promulgate regulations imposing minimum technical standards for cable operators. In *Turner Broadcasting System, Inc. v. Federal Communications Commission*, 114 S.Ct. 2445 (1994), the constitutionality of two "must-carry provisions" was challenged as a violation of the First Amendment. Section 4 of the act requires cable companies to carry "local commercial television stations," other than those qualifying as "noncommercial educational" stations under Section 5, that operate within the same television market as the cable system. Cable systems with more than twelve active channels and more than three hundred subscribers are required to set aside up to one-third of their channels for commercial broadcast stations that request carriage. Cable systems with more than three hundred subscribers but only twelve or fewer active channels must carry the signals of three commercial broadcast stations. Section 5 of the act imposes similar requirements regarding the carriage of local public broadcast television stations.

Attorneys for the cable industry argued that the regulations effectively dictated what kinds of programs are carried and wrongly favored local broadcasters over other programmers or speakers. As a result of the must-carry regulations some cable systems dropped C-SPAN, for instance, in favor of local broadcasters. By contrast, lawyers for the FCC defended the regulations as within Congress's power to protect local broadcasters' ability to compete for viewing audiences and advertising.

Writing for the Court, Justice Kennedy held for the first time that the First Amendment extends protection to the cable industry and requires heightened judicial review of any regulations or restrictions in light of the differences between broadcast and cable technologies. On that issue the justices were unanimous. But Justice Kennedy commanded only four other votes—those of the chief justice and Justices Stevens, Blackmun, and Souter—on the central issue of the constitutionality of the must-carry provisions. On that issue a bare majority declined to strike down the regulations and remanded the case back to the lower court for reconsideration of the basis for the regulations. In Justice Kennedy's words:

> [T]he must-carry provisions are not designed to favor or disadvantage speech of any particular content. Rather, they are meant to protect broadcast television from what Congress determined to be unfair competition by cable systems. In enacting the provisions, Congress sought to preserve the existing structure of the Nation's broadcast television medium while permitting the concomitant expansion and development of cable television, and, in particular, to ensure that broadcast television remains available as a source of video programming for those without cable. Appellants' ability to hypothesize a content-based purpose for these provisions rests on little more than speculation and does not cast doubt upon the content-neutral character of must-carry. Indeed, "it is a familiar principle of constitutional law that this

Court will not strike down an otherwise constitutional statute on the basis of an alleged illicit legislative motive." *United States v. O'Brien*, 391 U.S. 367 (1968) (citing *McCray v. United States*, 195 U.S. 27 (1904)). . . .

Under *O'Brien*, a content-neutral regulation will be sustained if "it furthers an important or substantial governmental interest; if the governmental interest is unrelated to the suppression of free expression; and if the incidental restriction on alleged First Amendment freedoms is no greater than is essential to the furtherance of that interest." To satisfy this standard, a regulation need not be the least speech-restrictive means of advancing the Government's interests. "Rather, the requirement of narrow tailoring is satisfied 'so long as the . . . regulation promotes a substantial government interest that would be achieved less effectively absent the regulation.'" Narrow tailoring in this context requires, in other words, that the means chosen do not "burden substantially more speech than is necessary to further the government's legitimate interests."

Congress declared that the must-carry provisions serve three interrelated interests: (1) preserving the benefits of free, over-the-air local broadcast television, (2) promoting the widespread dissemination of information from a multiplicity of sources, and (3) promoting fair competition in the market for television programming. None of these interests is related to the "suppression of free expression," *O'Brien*, or to the content of any speakers' messages. And viewed in the abstract, we have no difficulty concluding that each of them is an important governmental interest.

That the Government's asserted interests are important in the abstract does not mean, however, that the must-carry rules will in fact advance those interests. When the Government defends a regulation on speech as a means to redress past harms or prevent anticipated harms, it must do more than simply "posit the existence of the disease sought to be cured." It must demonstrate that the recited harms are real, not merely conjectural, and that the regulation will in fact alleviate these harms in a direct and material way.

Thus, in applying *O'Brien* scrutiny we must ask first whether the Government has adequately shown that the economic health of local broadcasting is in genuine jeopardy and in need of the protections afforded by must-carry. Assuming an affirmative answer to the foregoing question, the Government still bears the burden of showing that the remedy it has adopted does not "burden substantially more speech than is necessary to further the government's legitimate interests." On the state of the record developed thus far, and in the absence of findings of fact from the District Court, we are unable to conclude that the Government has satisfied either inquiry.

In an opinion dissenting in part and joined by Justices Scalia, Ginsburg, and Thomas, however, Justice O'Connor contended that the must-carry provisions were content-based and thus

an impermissible restraint on the cable operators' editorial discretion as well as on the cable programmers' speech. For reasons related to the content of speech, the rules restrict the ability of cable operators to put on the programming they prefer, and require them to include programming they would rather avoid. . . . Assuming *arguendo* that the provisions are justified with reference to the content-neutral interests in fair competition and preservation of free television, they nonetheless restrict too much speech that does not implicate these interests.

Finally, in its 1995–1996 term, the Court took up a challenge by cable programmers to regulations on the programming of "patently offensive" sex-related material on cable television. The Court, however, was badly fragmented in deciding *Denver Area Educational Telecommunications Consortium, Inc. v. Federal Communications Commission,* 116 S.Ct. — (1996) (excerpted below). Shifting pluralities joined only parts of Justice Breyer's opinion for the Court, upholding the act's provision authorizing cable operators to forbid programmers for privately "leased cable channels" from programming "patently offensive" material but striking down two other regulations—one provided the same authorization for cable operators with respect to "public, educational, and governmental channels," and the other had required cable operators to isolate "patently offensive" programming on a single channel and require viewers to request access in advance and in writing.

Denver Area Educational Telecommunications Consortium, Inc. v. Federal Communications Commission
116 S.Ct. — (1996)

In 1992, Congress enacted and the president signed into law the Cable Television Consumer Protection and Competition Act. Subsequently, three of its provisions, regulating "patently offensive" sex-related material, were challenged by cable programmers. Section 10(a), which applies to privately "leased cable channels," permits cable operators to prohibit programmers from programming material that the "operator reasonably believes describes or depicts sexual or excretory activities or organs in a patently offensive way." Section 10(c) does the same with respect to "public, educational, or governmental channels." Section 10(b), furthermore, required cable operators to isolate "patently offensive" programming on a single channel and to block access to the channel unless a viewer requested access in advance and in writing. A federal appellate court upheld all three provisions and the cable programmers appealed to the Supreme Court.

The Court's decision was announced by Justice Breyer, but his opinion was joined in parts by only pluralities of other justices. Justices Stevens and Souter filed concurring opinions. Justice O'Connor filed an opinion in part concurring and dissenting. Justice Kennedy filed an opinion concurring in part and dissenting in part, which Justice Ginsburg joined. Justice Thomas filed an opinion concurring in the

judgment in part and dissenting in part, which Chief Justice Rehnquist
and Justice Scalia joined.

Justice BREYER announced the judgment of the Court and delivered
the opinion of the Court with respect to Part III, an opinion with respect
to Parts I, II, and V, in which Justice STEVENS, Justice O'CONNOR,
and Justice SOUTER join, and an opinion with respect to Parts IV and
VI, in which Justice Stevens and Justice SOUTER join.

We conclude that the first provision—that permits the operator to decide
whether or not to broadcast such programs on leased access channels—is
consistent with the First Amendment. The second provision, that requires
leased channel operators to segregate and to block that programming, and
the third provision, applicable to public, educational, and governmental
channels, violate the First Amendment, for they are not appropriately tailored to achieve the basic, legitimate objective of protecting children from
exposure to "patently offensive" material.

                                    I

A "leased channel" is a channel that federal law requires a cable system
operator to reserve for commercial lease by unaffiliated third parties. . . .
In 1992, in an effort to control sexually explicit programming conveyed
over access channels, Congress enacted the three provisions before us. The
first two provisions relate to leased channels. The first says: "This
subsection shall permit a cable operator to enforce prospectively a written
and published policy of prohibiting programming that the cable operator
reasonably believes describes or depicts sexual or excretory activities or
organs in a patently offensive manner as measured by contemporary
community standards." Section 10(a)(2).
The second provision, applicable only to leased channels, requires cable
operators to segregate and to block similar programming if they decide to
permit, rather than to prohibit, its broadcast. The provision tells the Federal
Communications Commission (FCC or Commission) to promulgate regulations that will (a) require "programmers to inform cable operators if the
programming would be indecent as defined by Commission regulations"; (b)
require "cable operators to place" such material "on a single channel"; and
(c) require "cable operators to block such single channel unless the
subscriber requests access to such channel in writing." 1992 Act, Section
10(b)(1). The Commission issued regulations defining the material at issue
in terms virtually identical to those we have already set forth, namely as
descriptions or depictions of "sexual or excretory activities or organs in a
patently offensive manner" as measured by the cable viewing community.
The regulations require the cable operators to place this material on a single
channel and to block it (say, by scrambling). They also require the system
operator to provide access to the blocked channel "within 30 days" of a
subscriber's written request for access and to re-block it within 30 days of a
subscriber's request to do so.

The third provision is similar to the first provision, but applies only to public access channels. The relevant statutory section instructs the FCC to promulgate regulations that will "enable a cable operator of a cable system to prohibit the use, on such system, of any channel capacity of any public, educational, or governmental access facility for any programming which contains obscene material, sexually explicit conduct, or material soliciting or promoting unlawful conduct." Section 10(c). . . .

II

We turn initially to the provision that permits cable system operators to prohibit "patently offensive" (or "indecent") programming transmitted over leased access channels. Section 10(a). . . .

We recognize that the First Amendment, the terms of which apply to governmental action, ordinarily does not itself throw into constitutional doubt the decisions of private citizens to permit, or to restrict, speech—and this is so ordinarily even where those decisions take place within the framework of a regulatory regime such as broadcasting. Were that not so, courts might have to face the difficult, and potentially restrictive, practical task of deciding which, among any number of private parties involved in providing a program (for example, networks, station owners, program editors, and program producers), is the "speaker" whose rights may not be abridged, and who is the speech-restricting "censor." Furthermore, as this Court has held, the editorial function itself is an aspect of "speech," see *Turner [Broadcasting System, Inc. v. Federal Communications Commission,* 114 S.Ct. 2445 (1994)], and a court's decision that a private party, say, the station owner, is a "censor," could itself interfere with that private "censor's" freedom to speak as an editor. . . .

Like the petitioners, Justices KENNEDY and THOMAS would have us decide this case simply by transferring and applying literally categorical standards this Court has developed in other contexts. For Justice KENNEDY, leased access channels are like a common carrier, cablecast is a protected medium, strict scrutiny applies, Section 10(a) fails this test, and, therefore, Section 10(a) is invalid. For Justice THOMAS, the case is simple because the cable operator who owns the system over which access channels are broadcast, like a bookstore owner with respect to what it displays on the shelves, has a predominant First Amendment interest. Both categorical approaches suffer from the same flaws: they import law developed in very different contexts into a new and changing environment, and they lack the flexibility necessary to allow government to respond to very serious practical problems without sacrificing the free exchange of ideas the First Amendment is designed to protect.

The history of this Court's First Amendment jurisprudence, however, is one of continual development, as the Constitution's general command . . . has been applied to new circumstances requiring different adaptations of prior principles and precedents. The essence of that protection is that Congress may not regulate speech except in cases of extraordinary need and with the exercise of a degree of care that we have not elsewhere required. . . . At the same time, our cases have not left Congress or the States powerless to address the most serious problems. See, e.g., *Chaplinsky v. New Hampshire,*

315 U.S. 568 (1942); *Young v. American Mini Theaters, Inc.*, 427 U.S. 50 (1976); *FCC v. Pacifica Foundation*, 438 U.S. 726 (1978). . . .

[We decide this case] narrowly, by closely scrutinizing Section 10(a) to assure that it properly addresses an extremely important problem, without imposing, in light of the relevant interests, an unnecessarily great restriction on speech. The importance of the interest at stake here—protecting children from exposure to patently offensive depictions of sex; the accommodation of the interests of programmers in maintaining access channels and of cable operators in editing the contents of their channels; the similarity of the problem and its solution to those at issue in *Pacifica*; and the flexibility inherent in an approach that permits private cable operators to make editorial decisions, lead us to conclude that Section 10(a) is a sufficiently tailored response to an extraordinarily important problem.

First, the provision before us comes accompanied with an extremely important justification, one that this Court has often found compelling—the need to protect children from exposure to patently offensive sex-related material. *Ginsberg v. New York*, 390 U.S. 629 (1968); *New York v. Ferber*, 458 U.S. 747 (1982).

Second, the provision arises in a very particular context—congressional permission for cable operators to regulate programming that, but for a previous Act of Congress, would have had no path of access to cable channels free of an operator's control. . . .

Third, the problem Congress addressed here is remarkably similar to the problem addressed by the FCC in *Pacifica*, and the balance Congress struck is commensurate with the balance we approved there. . . .

Cable television broadcasting, including access channel broadcasting, is as "accessible to children" as over-the-air broadcasting, if not more so. Cable television systems, including access channels, "have established a uniquely pervasive presence in the lives of all Americans." "Patently offensive" material from these stations can "confront the citizen" in the "privacy of the home," *Pacifica*, with little or no prior warning. There is nothing to stop "adults who feel the need" from finding similar programming elsewhere, say, on tape or in theaters. In fact, the power of cable systems to control home program viewing is not absolute. Over-the-air broadcasting and direct broadcast satellites already provide alternative ways for programmers to reach the home, and are likely to do so to a greater extent in the near future.

Fourth, the permissive nature of Section 10(a) means that it likely restricts speech less than, not more than, the ban at issue in *Pacifica*. The provision removes a restriction as to some speakers—namely, cable operators. Moreover, although the provision does create a risk that a program will not appear, that risk is not the same as the certainty that accompanies a governmental ban. . . .

For the reasons discussed, we conclude that Section 10(a) is consistent with the First Amendment.

III

The statute's second provision significantly differs from the first, for it does not simply permit, but rather requires, cable system operators to restrict speech—by segregating and blocking "patently offensive" sex-related material appearing on leased channels (but not on other channels). Section 10(b). In particular, as previously mentioned, this provision and its implementing regulations require cable system operators to place "patently offensive" leased channel programming on a separate channel; to block that channel; to unblock the channel within 30 days of a subscriber's written request for access; and to reblock the channel within 30 days of a subscriber's request for reblocking. Also, leased channel programmers must notify cable operators of an intended "patently offensive" broadcast up to 30 days before its scheduled broadcast date.

These requirements have obvious restrictive effects. The several up-to-30-day delays, along with single channel segregation, mean that a subscriber cannot decide to watch a single program without considerable advance planning and without letting the "patently offensive" channel in its entirety invade his household for days, perhaps weeks, at a time. These restrictions will prevent programmers from broadcasting to viewers who select programs day by day (or, through "surfing," minute by minute); to viewers who would like occasionally to watch a few, but not many, of the programs on the "patently offensive" channel; and to viewers who simply tend to judge a program's value through channel reputation, i.e., by the company it keeps. Moreover, the "written notice" requirement will further restrict viewing by subscribers who fear for their reputations should the operator, advertently or inadvertently, disclose the list of those who wish to watch the "patently offensive" channel. Further, the added costs and burdens that these requirements impose upon a cable system operator may encourage that operator to ban programming that the operator would otherwise permit to run, even if only late at night. . . .

We agree with the Government that protection of children is a "compelling interest." But we do not agree that the "segregate and block" requirements properly accommodate the speech restrictions they impose and the legitimate objective they seek to attain. Nor need we here determine whether, or the extent to which, *Pacifica* does, or does not, impose some lesser standard of review where indecent speech is at issue. . . .

Several circumstances lead us to this conclusion. For one thing, the law, as recently amended, uses other means to protect children from similar "patently offensive" material broadcast on unleased cable channels, i.e., broadcast over any of a system's numerous ordinary, or public access, channels. The law, as recently amended, requires cable operators to "scramble or . . . block" such programming on any (unleased) channel "primarily dedicated to sexually-oriented programming." Telecommunications Act of 1996. In addition, cable operators must honor a subscriber's request to block any, or all, programs on any channel to which he or she does not wish to subscribe. And manufacturers, in the future, will have to make television sets with a so-called "V-chip"—a device that will be able automatically to identify and block sexually explicit or violent programs.

Although we cannot, and do not, decide whether the new provisions are themselves lawful (a matter not before us), we note that they are significantly less restrictive than the provision here at issue. . . . They therefore inevitably lead us to ask why, if they adequately protect children from "patently offensive" material broadcast on ordinary channels, they would not offer adequate protection from similar leased channel broadcasts as well?

Alternatively, if these provisions do not adequately protect children from "patently offensive" material broadcast on ordinary channels, how could one justify more severe leased channel restrictions when (given ordinary channel programming) they would yield so little additional protection for children? . . .

The record's description and discussion of a different alternative—the "lockbox"—leads, through a different route, to a similar conclusion. The Cable Communications Policy Act of 1984 required cable operators to provide "upon the request of a subscriber, a device by which the subscriber can prohibit viewing of a particular cable service during periods selected by the subscriber." This device—the "lockbox"—would help protect children by permitting their parents to "lock out" those programs or channels that they did not want their children to see. . . . Consequently, we cannot find that the "segregate and block" restrictions on speech are a narrowly, or reasonably, tailored effort to protect children. Rather, they are overly restrictive, "sacrificing" important First Amendment interests for too "speculative a gain." For that reason they are not consistent with the First Amendment.

IV

The statute's third provision, as implemented by FCC regulation, is similar to its first provision, in that it too permits a cable operator to prevent transmission of "patently offensive" programming, in this case on public access channels. But there are four important differences.

The first is the historical background. As Justice KENNEDY points out, cable operators have traditionally agreed to reserve channel capacity for public, governmental, and educational channels as part of the consideration they give municipalities that award them cable franchises. . . .

The second difference is the institutional background that has developed as a result of the historical difference. When a "leased channel" is made available by the operator to a private lessee, the lessee has total control of programming during the leased time slot. Public access channels, on the other hand, are normally subject to complex supervisory systems of various sorts, often with both public and private elements. . . .

Third, the existence of a system aimed at encouraging and securing programming that the community considers valuable strongly suggests that a "cable operator's veto" is less likely necessary to achieve the statute's basic objective, protecting children, than a similar veto in the context of leased channels. Of course, the system of access managers and supervising boards can make mistakes, which the operator might in some cases correct with its veto power. Balanced against this potential benefit, however, is the risk that the veto itself may be mistaken; and its use, or threatened use, could prevent the presentation of programming, that, though borderline, is not "patently offensive" to its targeted audience. And this latter threat must bulk large within a system that already has publicly accountable systems for maintaining responsible programs.

Finally, our examination of the legislative history and the record before us is consistent with what common sense suggests, namely that the public/nonprofit programming control systems now in place would normally avoid, minimize, or eliminate any child-related problems concerning "patently offensive" programming. . . .

The upshot, in respect to the public access channels, is a law that could radically change present programming-related relationships among local community and nonprofit supervising boards and access managers, which relationships are established through municipal law, regulation, and contract. In doing so, it would not significantly restore editorial rights of cable operators, but would greatly increase the risk that certain categories of programming (say, borderline offensive programs) will not appear. At the same time, given present supervisory mechanisms, the need for this particular provision, aimed directly at public access channels, is not obvious. Having carefully reviewed the legislative history of the Act, the proceedings before the FCC, the record below, and the submissions of the parties and *amici* here, we conclude that the Government cannot sustain its burden of showing that Section 10(c) is necessary to protect children or that it is appropriately tailored to secure that end. Consequently, we find this third provision violates the First Amendment. . . .

Justice STEVENS, concurring.

The difference between Section 10(a) and Section 10(c) is the difference between a permit and a prohibition. The former restores the freedom of cable operators to reject indecent programs; the latter requires local franchising authorities to reject such programs. While I join the Court's opinion, I add these comments to emphasize the difference between the two provisions and to endorse the analysis in Part III-B of Justice KENNEDY's opinion even though I do not think it necessary to characterize the public access channels as public fora. Like Justice SOUTER, I am convinced that it would be unwise to take a categorical approach to the resolution of novel First Amendment questions arising in an industry as dynamic as this. Cf. *R.A.V. v. St. Paul*, 505 U.S. 377 (1992) (STEVENS, J., concurring in judgment). . . .

Justice SOUTER, concurring.

Justice KENNEDY's separate opinion . . . sees no warrant in this case for anything but a categorical and rule-based approach applying a fixed level of scrutiny, the strictest, to judge the content-based provisions of Sections 10(a), (b), and (c), and he accordingly faults the plurality opinion for declining to decide the precise doctrinal categories that should govern the issue at hand. The value of the categorical approach generally to First Amendment security prompts a word to explain why I join the Court's unwillingness to announce a definitive categorical analysis in this case. . . .

All of the relevant characteristics of cable are presently in a state of technological and regulatory flux. Recent and far-reaching legislation not only affects the technical feasibility of parental control over children's access to undesirable material, but portends fundamental changes in the competitive structure of the industry and, therefore, the ability of individual entities to act as bottlenecks to the free flow of information. As cable and telephone companies begin their competition for control over the single wire that will carry both their services, we can hardly settle rules for review of regulation on the assumption that cable will remain a separable and useful category of First Amendment scrutiny. And as broadcast, cable, and the cyber-technology of the Internet and the World Wide Web approach the day of using a common receiver, we can hardly assume that standards for judging the regulation of one of them will not have immense, but now unknown and unknowable, effects on the others.

Accordingly, in charting a course that will permit reasonable regulation in light of the values in competition, we have to accept the likelihood that the media of communication will become less categorical and more protean. Because we cannot be confident that for purposes of judging speech restrictions it will continue to make sense to distinguish cable from other technologies, and because we know that changes in these regulated technologies will enormously alter the structure of regulation itself, we should be shy about saying the final word today about what will be accepted as reasonable tomorrow. In my own ignorance I have to accept the real possibility that "if we had to decide today . . . just what the First Amendment should mean in cyberspace, . . . we would get it fundamentally wrong." Lessig, "The Path of Cyberlaw," 104 *Yale L. J.* 1743 (1995).

The upshot of appreciating the fluidity of the subject that Congress must regulate is simply to accept the fact that not every nuance of our old standards will necessarily do for the new technology, and that a proper choice among existing doctrinal categories is not obvious. Rather than definitively settling the issue now, Justice BREYER wisely reasons by direct analogy rather than by rule, concluding that the speech and the restriction at issue in this case may usefully be measured against the ones at issue in *Pacifica*. If that means it will take some time before reaching a final method of review for cases like this one, there may be consolation in recalling that 16 years passed, from *Roth v. United States*, 354 U.S. 476 (1957), to *Miller v. California*, 413 U.S. 15 (1973), before the modern obscenity rule jelled; that it took over 40 years, from *Hague v. CIO*, 307 U.S. 496 (1939), to *Perry Ed. Assn. v. Perry Local Educators' Assn.*, 460 U.S. 37 (1983), for the public forum category to settle out; and that a round half-century passed before the clear and present danger of *Schenck v. United States*, 249 U.S. 47 (1919), evolved into the modern incitement rule of *Brandenburg v. Ohio*, 395 U.S. 444 (1969).

I cannot guess how much time will go by until the technologies of communication before us today have matured and their relationships become known. But until a category of indecency can be defined both with reference to the new technology and with a prospect of durability, the job of the courts will be just what Justice BREYER does today: recognizing established First Amendment interests through a close analysis that constrains the Congress, without wholly incapacitating it in all matters of the significance apparent here, maintaining the high value of open communication, measuring the costs of regulation by exact attention to fact, and compiling a pedigree of experience with the changing subject. These are familiar judicial responsibilities in times when we know too little to risk the finality of precision, and attention to them will probably take us through the communications revolution. Maybe the judicial obligation to shoulder these responsibilities can itself be captured by a much older rule, familiar to every doctor of medicine: "First, do no harm."

Justice O'CONNOR, concurring in part and dissenting in part.

I agree that Section 10(a) is constitutional and that Section 10(b) is unconstitutional, and I join Parts I, II, III, and V, and the judgment in part. I am not persuaded, however, that the asserted "important differences" between Sections 10(a) and 10(c) are sufficient to justify striking down Section 10(c). I find the features shared by Section 10(a), which covers leased access channels, and Section 10(c), which covers public access channels, to be more significant than the differences. For that reason, I would find that Section 10(c) too withstands constitutional scrutiny. . . .

Justice KENNEDY, with whom Justice GINSBURG joins, concurring in part, concurring in the judgment in part, and dissenting in part.

Though I join Part III of the opinion (there for the Court) striking down Section 10(b) of the Act, and concur in the judgment that Section 10(c) is unconstitutional, with respect I dissent from the remainder. . . .

It is important to understand that public access channels are public forums created by local or state governments in the cable franchise. Section 10(c) does not, as the Court of Appeals thought, just return rightful First Amendment discretion to the cable operator. Cable operators have First Amendment rights, of course; restrictions on entry into the cable business may be challenged under the First Amendment, and a cable operator's activities in originating programs or exercising editorial discretion over programs others provide on its system also are protected, *Turner Broadcasting*. Yet the editorial discretion of a cable operator is a function of the cable franchise it receives from local government. The operator's right to exercise any editorial discretion over cable service disappears if its franchise is terminated. . . .

In providing public access channels under their franchise agreements, cable operators therefore are not exercising their own First Amendment rights. They serve as conduits for the speech of others. Section 10(c) thus restores no power of editorial discretion over public access channels that the cable operator once had; the discretion never existed. It vests the cable operator with a power under federal law, defined by reference to the content of speech, to override the franchise agreement and undercut the public forum the agreement creates. By enacting a law in 1992 excluding indecent programming from protection but retaining the prohibition on cable operators' editorial control over all other protected speech, the Federal Government at the same time ratified the public-forum character of public access channels but discriminated against certain speech based on its content.

The plurality refuses to analyze public access channels as public forums because it is reluctant to decide "the extent to which private property can be designated a public forum." We need not decide here any broad issue of whether private property can be declared a public forum by simple governmental decree. That is not what happens in the creation of public access channels. Rather, in return for granting cable operators easements to use public rights-of-way for their cable lines, local governments have bargained for a right to use cable lines for public access channels. . . .

Leased access channels, as distinct from public access channels, are those the cable operator must set aside for unaffiliated programmers who pay to transmit shows of their own without the cable operator's creative assistance or editorial approval. In my view, strict scrutiny also applies to Section 10(a)'s authorization to cable operators to exclude indecent programming from these channels. . . .

At a minimum, the proper standard for reviewing Sections 10(a) and (c) is strict scrutiny. The plurality gives no reason why it should be otherwise. I would hold these enactments unconstitutional because they are not narrowly tailored to serve a compelling interest. . . .

Congress does have, however, a compelling interest in protecting children from indecent speech. *Sable Communications* [*v. Federal Communications Commission*, 492 U.S. 115 (1989)], *Ginsberg v. New York, Pacifica Foundation*. . . . Sections 10(a) and (c) nonetheless are not narrowly tailored to protect children from indecent programs on access channels. First, to the extent some operators may allow indecent programming, children in localities those operators serve will be left unprotected. Partial service of a compelling interest is not narrow tailoring.

Second, to the extent cable operators prohibit indecent programming on access channels, not only children but adults will be deprived of it. The Government may not "reduce the adult population . . . to [viewing] only what is fit for children." *Butler v. Michigan*, 352 U.S. 380 (1957). . . .

Sections 10(a) and (c) present a classic case of discrimination against speech based on its content. There are legitimate reasons why the Government might wish to regulate or even restrict the speech at issue here, but Sections 10(a) and 10(c) are not drawn to address those reasons with the precision the First Amendment requires. . . .

Justice THOMAS, joined by the CHIEF JUSTICE and Justice SCALIA, concurring in the judgment in part and dissenting in part.

I agree with the plurality's conclusion that Section 10(a) is constitutionally permissible, but I disagree with its conclusion that Section 10(b) and (c) violate the First Amendment. For many years, we have failed to articulate how and to what extent the First Amendment protects cable operators, programmers, and viewers from state and federal regulation. I think it is time we did so, and I cannot go along with the plurality's assiduous attempts to avoid addressing that issue openly. . . .

The First Amendment challenge, if one is to be made, must come from the party whose constitutionally protected freedom of speech has been burdened. Viewing the federal access requirements as a whole, it is the cable operator, not the access programmer, whose speech rights have been infringed. Consequently, it is the operator, and not the programmer, whose speech has arguably been infringed by these provisions. If Congress passed a law forcing bookstores to sell all books published on the subject of

congressional politics, we would undoubtedly entertain a claim by bookstores that this law violated the First Amendment principles established in
[*Miami Herald Publishing Co. v. Tornillo*, 418 U.S. 241 (1974)] and *Pacific
Gas [& Electric Co. v. Public Utilities Comm'n of Cal.*, 475 U.S. 1 (1986)].
But I doubt that we would similarly find merit in a claim by publishers of
gardening books that the law violated their First Amendment rights. If that is
so, then the petitioners in these cases cannot reasonably assert that the Court
should strictly scrutinize the provisions at issue in a way that maximizes
their ability to speak over leased and public access channels and, by
necessity, minimizes the operators' discretion. . . .

H. SYMBOLIC SPEECH AND
SPEECH-PLUS-CONDUCT

In a major ruling on freedom of speech and speech-plus-conduct
growing out of the continuing controversy over abortion, the Rehnquist
Court confronted the issue of anti-abortion protesters' First Amendment freedoms in *Madsen v. Women's Health Center* (excerpted
below). *Madsen* presented the issue of whether a Florida trial judge's
injunction against anti-abortion protesters constituted a suppression of
their message or, as the Florida state supreme court held, aimed at
protecting constitutionally guaranteed interests in medical care and
patients' privacy. The trial judge forbade demonstrations within thirty-
six feet of abortion clinics, prohibited protesters from coming into
contact with women going into clinics within three hundred feet of the
clinics, and banned all "congregating, picketing, patrolling, [and]
demonstrating" within three hundred feet of the home of any doctors or
other personnel who worked at an abortion clinic.

Splitting six to three and five to four on different parts of the ruling,
the Court held that injunctions restraining protesters must be evaluated
for "content neutrality" and must not burden demonstrators' speech
more than necessary to achieve the government's legitimate interests,
as well as being framed in the narrowest terms to achieve its pinpoint
objective. Writing for the majority, Chief Justice Rehnquist upheld the
thirty-six-foot buffer zone around the clinic's entrances and driveway,
along with the limitations on noise around the clinic during surgery and
recovery periods. However, he rejected as too broad and as an infringement on First Amendment freedoms the injunction's (1) thirty-

six-foot buffer zone as applied to private property north and west of the clinic, (2) blanket ban on "observable images," and (3) three-hundred-foot no-approach zone around the clinic. Justice Souter filed a brief concurring opinion, and Justice Stevens filed an opinion in part concurring and dissenting. In a bitter dissent joined by Justices Kennedy and Thomas, Justice Scalia took strong exception to the majority's upholding any part of the injunction.

In its 1994–1995 term, the Court considered an appeal of a Massachusetts state court holding that the veteran groups organizing Boston's St. Patrick's Day parade could not exclude gay, lesbian, and bisexual marchers. In *Hurley v. Irish-American Gay, Lesbian, and Bisexual Group of Boston* (excerpted below), the parade's organizers contended that the parade was a private activity and they had a First Amendment right to exclude other marchers. The state court had ruled that they could not discriminate on the basis of sexual orientation and that, although privately organized, the parade was nonetheless subject to the state's public accommodation law, barring discrimination on the basis of sexual orientation. But the Supreme Court reversed in an unanimous opinion delivered by Justice Souter.

In its 1996–1997 term, the Court will revisit the issue of anti-abortion protesters' First Amendment freedoms, which it initially addressed in *Madsen v. Women's Health Center*. At issue in *Schenck v. Pro-Choice Network* is the permissibility of a court order creating a fifteen-foot buffer zone around abortion clinics, as well as around vehicles entering the clinics' driveways. The order also permits only two protesters to come within fifteen feet of patients entering the clinics, located in Buffalo and Rochester, New York. In appealing the decision of the Court of Appeals for the Second Circuit upholding the order, the Reverend Paul Schenck contends that the court order strikes at the core of the First Amendment and its "protection of unpopular and despised speech in the traditional public forum of public sidewalks and streets." Attorneys for Schenck also argue that the order runs afoul of the holding in *Madsen* that injunctions against anti-abortion protesters may "burden no more speech than necessary to serve a significant government interest." However, lawyers for the Pro-Choice Network of Western New York counter that the restrictions are justified given the anti-abortion protesters' "record of obstruction, intimidation, health risks, and contempts."

Hurley and South Boston Allied War Veterans Council v. Irish-American Gay, Lesbian, and Bisexual Group of Boston

115 S.Ct. 2338 (1995)

The pertinent facts are discussed in Justice Souter's opinion for the Court. The Court's decision was unanimous and announced by Justice Souter.

Justice SOUTER delivered the opinion of the Court.

March 17 is set aside for two celebrations in South Boston. As early as 1737, some people in Boston observed the feast of the apostle to Ireland, and since 1776 the day has marked the evacuation of royal troops and Loyalists from the city, prompted by the guns captured at Ticonderoga and set up on Dorchester Heights under General Washington's command. . . . The tradition of formal sponsorship by the city came to an end in 1947, however, when Mayor James Michael Curley himself granted authority to organize and conduct the St. Patrick's Day-Evacuation Day Parade to the petitioner South Boston Allied War Veterans Council, an unincorporated association of individuals elected from various South Boston veterans groups. . . .

1992 was the year that a number of gay, lesbian, and bisexual descendants of the Irish immigrants joined together with other supporters to form the respondent organization, GLIB, to march in the parade as a way to express pride in their Irish heritage as openly gay, lesbian, and bisexual individuals, to demonstrate that there are such men and women among those so descended, and to express their solidarity with like individuals who sought to march in New York's St. Patrick's Day Parade. Although the Council denied GLIB's application to take part in the 1992 parade, GLIB obtained a state-court order to include its contingent, which marched "uneventfully" among that year's 10,000 participants and 750,000 spectators.

In 1993, after the Council had again refused to admit GLIB to the upcoming parade, the organization and some of its members filed this suit . . ., alleging violations of the State and Federal Constitutions and of the state public accommodations law, which prohibits "any distinction, discrimination or restriction on account of . . . sexual orientation . . . relative to the admission of any person to, or treatment in any place of public accommodation, resort or amusement." . . . [T]he state trial court ruled that the parade fell within the statutory definition of a public accommodation . . . and found the Council's "final position [to be] that GLIB would be excluded because of its values and its message, i.e., its members' sexual orientation." This position, in the court's view, was not only violative of the public accommodations law but "paradoxical" as well, since "a proper celebration of St. Patrick's and Evacuation Day requires diversity and inclusiveness." [T]he court rejected the notion that GLIB's admission would trample on the Council's First Amendment rights since the court . . . found it "impossible to discern any specific expressive purpose entitling the Parade to protection under the First Amendment." . . .

Given the scope of the issues as originally joined in this case, it is worth noting some that have fallen aside in the course of the litigation, before reaching us. Although the Council presents us with a First Amendment claim, respondents do not. Neither do they press a claim that the Council's action has denied them equal protection of the laws in violation of the Fourteenth Amendment. While the guarantees of free speech and equal protection guard only against encroachment by the government and "erect no shield against merely private conduct," *Shelley v. Kraemer,* 334 U.S. 1 (1948), respondents originally argued that the Council's conduct was not purely private, but had the character of state action. The trial court's review of the city's involvement led it to find otherwise. . . . In any event, respondents have not brought that question up either in a cross-petition for *certiorari* or in their briefs filed in this Court. . . . In this Court, then, their claim for inclusion in the parade rests solely on the Massachusetts public accommodations law. . . .

Accordingly, our review of petitioners' claim that their activity is indeed in the nature of protected speech carries with it a constitutional duty to conduct an independent examination of the record as a whole. . . .

If there were no reason for a group of people to march from here to there except to reach a destination, they could make the trip without expressing any message beyond the fact of the march itself. Some people might call such a procession a parade, but it would not be much of one. . . . [W]e use the word "parade" to indicate marchers who are making some sort of collective point, not just to each other but to bystanders along the way. Indeed a parade's dependence on watchers is so extreme that nowadays, as with Bishop Berkeley's celebrated tree, "if a parade or demonstration receives no media coverage, it may as well not have happened." Parades are thus a form of expression, not just motion, and the inherent expressiveness of marching to make a point explains our cases involving protest marches. . . .

The protected expression that inheres in a parade is not limited to its banners and songs, however, for the Constitution looks beyond written or spoken words as mediums of expression. . . . Not many marches, then, are beyond the realm of expressive parades, and the South Boston celebration is not one of them. . . .

Respondents' participation as a unit in the parade was equally expressive. GLIB was formed for the very purpose of marching in it, as the trial court found, in order to celebrate its members' identity as openly gay, lesbian, and bisexual descendants of the Irish immigrants, to show that there are such individuals in the community, and to support the like men and women who sought to march in the New York parade. . . .

The Massachusetts public accommodations law under which respondents brought suit has a venerable history. At common law, innkeepers, smiths, and others who "made profession of a public employment," were prohibited from refusing, without good reason, to serve a customer. After the Civil War, the Commonwealth of Massachusetts was the first State to codify this principle to ensure access to public accommodations regardless of race. . . . Provisions like these are well within the State's usual power to enact when a legislature has reason to believe that a given group is the target of discrimination, and they do not, as a general matter, violate the First or Fourteenth Amendments. Nor is this statute unusual in any obvious way, since it does not, on its face, target speech or discriminate on the basis of its content, the focal point of its prohibition being rather on the act of discriminating against individuals in the provision of publicly available goods, privileges, and services on the proscribed grounds.

In the case before us, however, the Massachusetts law has been applied in a peculiar way. Its enforcement does not address any dispute about the participation of openly gay, lesbian, or bisexual individuals in various units admitted to the parade. The petitioners disclaim any intent to exclude homosexuals as such, and no individual member of GLIB claims to have been excluded from parading as a member of any group that the Council has approved to march. Instead, the disagreement goes to the admission of GLIB as its own parade unit carrying its own banner. Since every participating unit affects the message conveyed by the private organizers, the state courts' application of the statute produced an order essentially requiring petitioners to alter the expressive content of their parade. . . . Under this approach any contingent of protected individuals with a message would have the right to participate in petitioners' speech, so that the communication produced by the private organizers would be shaped by all those protected by the law who wished to join in with some expressive demonstration of their own. But this use of the State's power violates the fundamental rule of protection under the First Amendment, that a speaker has the autonomy to choose the content of his own message.

"Since all speech inherently involves choices of what to say and what to leave unsaid," *Pacific Gas & Electric Co. v. Public Utilities Comm'n of Cal.*, 475 U.S. 1 (1986), one important manifestation of the principle of free speech is that one who chooses to speak may also decide "what not to say." Although the State may at times "prescribe what shall be orthodox in commercial advertising" by requiring the dissemination of "purely factual and uncontroversial information," outside that context it may not compel affirmance of a belief with which the speaker disagrees. Indeed this general rule, that the speaker has the right to tailor the speech, applies not only to expressions of value, opinion, or endorsement, but equally to statements of fact the speaker would rather avoid. . . .

Petitioners' claim to the benefit of this principle of autonomy to control one's own speech is as sound as the South Boston parade is expressive. Rather like a composer, the Council selects the expressive units of the parade from potential participants, and though the score may not produce a particularized message, each contingent's expression in the Council's eyes comports with what merits celebration on that day. Even if this view gives the Council credit for a more considered judgment than it actively made, the Council clearly decided to exclude a message it did not like from the communication it chose to make, and that is enough to invoke its right as a private speaker to shape its expression by speaking on one subject while remaining silent on another. The message it disfavored is not difficult to identify. . . . But whatever the reason, it boils down to the choice of a speaker not to propound a particular point of view, and that choice is presumed to lie beyond the government's power to control. . . .

It might, of course, have been argued that a broader objective is apparent: that the ultimate point of forbidding acts of discrimination toward certain classes is to produce a society free of the corresponding biases. . . . But if this indeed is the point of applying the state law to expressive conduct, it is a decidedly fatal objective. . . . The very idea that a noncommercial speech restriction be used to produce thoughts and statements acceptable to some groups or, indeed, all people, grates on the First Amendment, for it amounts to nothing less than a proposal to limit speech in the service of orthodox expression. The Speech Clause has no more certain antithesis. While the law is free to promote all sorts of conduct in place of harmful behavior, it is not free to interfere with speech for no better reason than promoting an approved message or discouraging a disfavored one, however enlightened either purpose may strike the government. . . .

Our holding today rests not on any particular view about the Council's message but on the Nation's commitment to protect freedom of speech. . . . Accordingly, the judgment of the Supreme Judicial Court is reversed and the case remanded for proceedings not inconsistent with this opinion.

Madsen v. Women's Health Center
114 S.Ct. 2516 (1994)

In 1993, after repeated demonstrations and arrests of anti-abortion protesters, the directors of the Aware Woman Center for Choice in Melbourne, Florida, sought an injunction stopping the protesters from going on their driveway and the surrounding street, as well as from harassing women and doctors entering the clinic. Judy Madsen and several other Operation Rescue leaders named in the suit countered that such an injunction would deny them their First Amendment right of free speech. But trial judge Robert McGregor disagreed and issued an injunction creating a "buffer zone" around the clinic. The injunction forbade demonstrations within thirty-six feet of the clinic, prohibited anti-abortion protesters' contact with clinic clients and doctors, and banned "approaching, congregating, picketing, patrolling, [and] demonstrating" within three hundred feet of the home of any clinic personnel. In addition, Judge McGregor forbade in morning hours, "during surgical procedures and recovery periods," the protesters' singing, chanting, whistling, shouting, and use of bullhorns on the ground that such activities were too disruptive and threatened the women's psychological and physical well-being.

On appeal, the state supreme court upheld the injunction upon concluding that the anti-abortion protesters' tactics "placed in jeopardy the health, safety, and rights of Florida women" and "in light of the medical services provided at the clinic and Operation Rescue's past conduct." The First Amendment freedoms of the protesters were not denied, the state court reasoned, but instead merely subjected to reasonable "time, place, and manner" restrictions. By contrast, in a separate suit filed in the federal courts, the Court of Appeals for the Eleventh Circuit ruled that the injunction was an unconstitutional infringement on free speech in a "public forum." On Madsen's further appeal of the state court's ruling, the Supreme Court granted review in order to resolve the judicial conflict over the issue of the First Amendment rights of anti-abortion protesters.

The Court's decision was six to three and five to four on different parts of its ruling. Chief Justice Rehnquist delivered the majority's opinion. Justice Souter filed a concurring opinion and Justice Stevens issued an opinion in part concurring and dissenting. In a separate opinion in part concurring and dissenting, Justice Scalia was joined by Justices Kennedy and Thomas.

CHIEF JUSTICE REHNQUIST delivered the opinion of the Court.

We begin by addressing petitioners' contention that the state court's order, because it is an injunction that restricts only the speech of anti-abortion protesters, is necessarily content or viewpoint based. Accordingly, they argue, we should examine the entire injunction under the strictest standard of scrutiny. We disagree. To accept petitioners' claim would be to classify virtually every injunction as content or viewpoint based. An injunction, by its very nature, applies only to a particular group (or individuals) and regulates the activities, and perhaps the speech, of that group. It does so, however, because of the group's past actions in the context of a specific dispute between real parties. The parties seeking the injunction assert a violation of their rights; the court hearing the action is charged with fashioning a remedy for a specific deprivation, not with the drafting of a statute addressed to the general public. . . .

Our principal inquiry in determining content neutrality is whether the government has adopted a regulation of speech "without reference to the content of the regulated speech." *Ward v. Rock Against Racism*, 491 U.S. 781 (1989). We thus look to the government's purpose as the threshold consideration. Here, the state court imposed restrictions on petitioners incidental to their anti-abortion message because they repeatedly violated the court's original order. That petitioners all share the same viewpoint regarding abortion does not in itself demonstrate that some invidious content- or viewpoint-based purpose motivated the issuance of the order. It suggests only that those in the group whose conduct violated the court's order happen to share the same opinion regarding abortions being performed at the clinic. In short, the fact that the injunction covered people with a particular viewpoint does not itself render the injunction content or viewpoint based. Accordingly, the injunction issued in this case does not demand the level of heightened scrutiny. . . . And we proceed to discuss the standard which does govern.

If this were a content-neutral, generally applicable statute, instead of an injunctive order, its constitutionality would be assessed under the standard set forth in *Ward v. Rock Against Racism*, and similar cases. Given that the forum around the clinic is a traditional public forum, we would determine whether the time, place, and manner regulations were "narrowly tailored to serve a significant governmental interest." *Ward*. There are obvious differences, however, between an injunction and a generally applicable ordinance. Ordinances represent a legislative choice regarding the promotion of particular societal interests. Injunctions, by contrast, are remedies imposed for violations (or threatened violations) of a legislative or judicial decree. . . .

We believe that these differences require a somewhat more stringent application of general First Amendment principles in this context. . . . [W]hen evaluating a content-neutral injunction, we think that our standard time, place, and manner analysis is not sufficiently rigorous. We must ask instead whether the challenged provisions of the injunction burden no more speech than necessary to serve a significant government interest.

Both Justice STEVENS and Justice SCALIA disagree with the standard we announce, for policy reasons. Justice STEVENS believes that "injunctive relief should be judged by a more lenient standard than legislation," because injunctions are imposed on individuals or groups who have engaged in illegal activity. Justice SCALIA, by contrast, believes that content-neutral injunctions are "at least as deserving of strict scrutiny as a statutory, content-based restriction." Justice SCALIA bases his belief on the danger that injunctions, even though they might not "attack content as content," may be used to suppress particular ideas; that individual judges should not be trusted to impose injunctions in this context; and that an injunction is procedurally more difficult to challenge than a statute. We believe that consideration of all of the differences and similarities between statutes and injunctions supports, as a matter of policy, the standard we apply here. . . .

We begin with the 36-foot buffer zone. . . . The 36-foot buffer zone protecting the entrances to the clinic and the parking lot is a means of protecting unfettered ingress to and egress from the clinic, and ensuring that petitioners do not block traffic on Dixie Way. The state court seems to have had few other options to protect access given the narrow confines around the clinic. As the Florida Supreme Court noted, Dixie Way is only 21 feet wide in the area of the clinic. The state court was convinced that allowing the petitioners to remain on the clinic's sidewalk and driveway was not a viable option in view of the failure of the first injunction to protect access. And allowing the petitioners to stand in the middle of Dixie Way would obviously block vehicular traffic.

The need for a complete buffer zone near the clinic entrances and driveway may be debatable, but some deference must be given to the state court's familiarity with the facts and the background of the dispute between the parties even under our heightened review. Moreover, one of petitioners' witnesses during the evidentiary hearing before the state court conceded that the buffer zone was narrow enough to place petitioners at a distance of no greater than 10 to 12 feet from cars approaching and leaving the clinic. Protesters standing across the narrow street from the clinic can still be seen and heard from the clinic parking lots. We also bear in mind the fact that the state court originally issued a much narrower injunction, providing no buffer zone, and that this order did not succeed in protecting access to the clinic. The failure of the first order to accomplish its purpose may be taken into consideration in evaluating the constitutionality of the broader order. On balance, we hold that the 36-foot buffer zone around the clinic entrances and driveway burdens no more speech than necessary to accomplish the governmental interest at stake.

Justice SCALIA's dissent argues that a videotape made of demonstrations at the clinic represents "what one must presume to be the worst of the activity justifying the injunction." This seems to us a gratuitous assumption. The videotape was indeed introduced by respondents, presumably because they thought it supported their request for the second injunction. But witnesses also testified as to relevant facts in a 3-day evidentiary hearing, and the state court was therefore not limited to Justice SCALIA's rendition of what he saw on the videotape to make its findings in support of the second injunction. Indeed, petitioners themselves studiously refrained from challenging the factual basis for the injunction both in the state courts and here. Before the Florida Supreme Court, petitioners stated that "the Amended Permanent Injunction contains fundamental error on its face. The sole question presented by this appeal is a question of law, and for purposes of this appeal [petitioners] are assuming, *arguendo*, that a factual basis exists to grant injunctive relief." Petitioners argued against including the factual record as an appendix in the Florida Supreme Court, and never certified a full record. We must therefore judge this case on the assumption that the evidence and testimony presented to the state court supported its findings that the presence of protesters standing, marching, and demonstrating near the clinic's entrance interfered with ingress to and egress from the clinic despite the issuance of the earlier injunction.

The inclusion of private property on the back and side of the clinic in the 36-foot buffer zone raises different concerns. . . . Patients and staff wishing to reach the clinic do not have to cross the private property abutting the clinic property on the north and west, and nothing in the record indicates that petitioners' activities on the private property have obstructed access to the clinic. Nor was evidence presented that protesters located on the private property blocked vehicular traffic on Dixie Way. Absent evidence that petitioners standing on the private property have obstructed access to the clinic, blocked vehicular traffic, or otherwise unlawfully interfered with the clinic's operation, this portion of the buffer zone fails to serve the significant government interests relied on by the Florida Supreme Court. We hold that on the record before us the 36-foot buffer zone as applied to the private property to the north and west of the clinic burdens more speech than necessary to protect access to the clinic.

In response to high noise levels outside the clinic, the state court restrained the petitioners from "singing, chanting, whistling, shouting, yelling, use of bullhorns, auto horns, sound amplification equipment or other sounds or images observable to or within earshot of the patients inside the clinic" during the hours of 7:30 a.m. through noon on Mondays through Saturdays. We must, of course, take account of the place to which the regulations apply in determining whether these restrictions burden more speech than necessary. We have upheld similar noise restrictions in the past, and as we noted in upholding a local noise ordinance around public schools, "the nature of a place, 'the pattern of its normal activities, dictate the kinds of regulations . . . that are reasonable.'" *Grayned v. City of Rockford*, 408 U.S. 104

(1972). . . . We hold that the limited noise restrictions imposed by the state court order burden no more speech than necessary to ensure the health and well-being of the patients at the clinic. The First Amendment does not demand that patients at a medical facility undertake Herculean efforts to escape the cacophony of political protests. "If overamplified loudspeakers assault the citizenry, government may turn them down." *Grayned.* That is what the state court did here, and we hold that its action was proper.

The same, however, cannot be said for the "images observable" provision of the state court's order. Clearly, threats to patients or their families, however communicated, are proscribable under the First Amendment. But rather than prohibiting the display of signs that could be interpreted as threats or veiled threats, the state court issued a blanket ban on all "images observable." This broad prohibition on all "images observable" burdens more speech than necessary to achieve the purpose of limiting threats to clinic patients or their families. Similarly, if the blanket ban on "images observable" was intended to reduce the level of anxiety and hypertension suffered by the patients inside the clinic, it would still fail. The only plausible reason a patient would be bothered by "images observable" inside the clinic would be if the patient found the expression contained in such images disagreeable. But it is much easier for the clinic to pull its curtains than for a patient to stop up her ears, and no more is required to avoid seeing placards through the windows of the clinic. This provision of the injunction violates the First Amendment.

The state court ordered that petitioners refrain from physically approaching any person seeking services of the clinic "unless such person indicates a desire to communicate" in an area within 300 feet of the clinic. But it is difficult, indeed, to justify a prohibition on all uninvited approaches of persons seeking the services of the clinic, regardless of how peaceful the contact may be, without burdening more speech than necessary to prevent intimidation and to ensure access to the clinic. Absent evidence that the protesters' speech is independently proscribable (i.e., "fighting words" or threats), or is so infused with violence as to be indistinguishable from a threat of physical harm, this provision cannot stand.

The final substantive regulation challenged by petitioners relates to a prohibition against picketing, demonstrating, or using sound amplification equipment within 300 feet of the residences of clinic staff. The prohibition also covers impeding access to streets that provide the sole access to streets on which those residences are located. The same analysis applies to the use of sound amplification equipment here as that discussed above: the government may simply demand that petitioners turn down the volume if the protests overwhelm the neighborhood.

As for the picketing, our prior decision upholding a law banning targeted residential picketing remarked on the unique nature of the home, as "'the last citadel of the tired, the weary, and the sick.'" [*Frisby v. Schultz,* 487 U.S. 474 (1988)]. We stated that "'the State's interest in protecting the well-being, tranquillity, and privacy of the home is certainly of the highest order in a free and civilized society.'"

By contrast, the 300-foot zone would ban "general marching through residential neighborhoods, or even walking a route in front of an entire block of houses." The record before us does not contain sufficient justification for this broad a ban on picketing; it appears that a limitation on the time, duration of picketing, and number of pickets outside a smaller zone could have accomplished the desired result. . . .

In sum, we uphold the noise restrictions and the 36-foot buffer zone around the clinic entrances and driveway because they burden no more speech than necessary to eliminate the unlawful conduct targeted by the state court's injunction. We strike down as unconstitutional the 36-foot buffer zone as applied to the private property to the north and west of the clinic, the "images observable" provision, the 300-foot no-approach zone around the clinic, and the 300-foot buffer zone around the residences, because these provisions sweep more broadly than necessary to accomplish the permissible goals of the injunction. Accordingly, the judgment of the Florida Supreme Court is

Affirmed in part, and reversed in part.

Justice STEVENS, concurring in part and dissenting in part.

I agree with the Court that a different standard governs First Amendment challenges to generally applicable legislation than the standard that measures such challenges to judicial remedies for proven wrongdoing. Unlike the Court, however, I believe that injunctive relief should be judged by a more lenient standard than legislation. As the Court notes, legislation is imposed on an entire community, regardless of individual culpability. By contrast, injunctions apply solely to an individual or a limited group of individuals who, by engaging in illegal conduct, have been judicially deprived of some liberty—the normal consequence of illegal activity. Given this distinction, a statute prohibiting demonstrations within 36 feet of an abortion clinic would probably violate the First Amendment, but an injunction directed at a limited group of persons who have engaged in unlawful conduct in a similar zone might well be constitutional. . . .

Justice SCALIA, with whom Justice KENNEDY and Justice THOMAS join, concurring in the judgment in part and dissenting in part.

Because I believe that the judicial creation of a 36-foot zone in which only a particular group, which had broken no law, cannot exercise its rights of speech, assembly, and association, and the judicial enactment of a noise prohibition, applicable to that group and that group alone, are profoundly at odds with our First Amendment precedents and traditions, I dissent.

6

FREEDOM FROM AND
OF RELIGION

A. THE (DIS)ESTABLISHMENT OF RELIGION

In a number of cases in recent years, the Rehnquist Court has reconsidered the First Amendment's guarantees for religious freedom (see Vol. 2, Ch. 6). Moreover, a number of the justices have frequently expressed dissatisfaction with the three-pronged test for applying the (dis)establishment clause set forth by the Burger Court in *Lemon v. Kurtzman*, 403 U.S. 602 (1971) (in Vol. 2, Ch. 6). Under *Lemon*, governmental legislation and regulations must (1) have a secular purpose, (2) have a primary effect that neither advances nor inhibits religion, and (3) not foster an excessive governmental entanglement with religion. But Chief Justice Rehnquist and Justice Scalia, in particular, have pushed for a greater accommodation of religion by the government and for overruling *Lemon*. Still, even with its changing composition, the Court has been unable to agree on whether to jettison or to adhere to *Lemon*, as well as on how and when to apply the test. As a result, the Court's rulings on the (dis)establishment clause have been fragmented, confusing, and have invited continued litigation.

In spite of calls from within and without the Court to overturn *Lemon*, in *Lee v. Weisman*, 505 U.S. 577 (1992) (in Vol. 2, Ch. 6), a bare majority declined to do so, when holding that school-sponsored prayers at graduation ceremonies run afoul of the (dis)establishment clause. In the 1993–1994 term, then, in two more cases the Court declined to reexamine *Lemon*. In *Lamb's Chapel v. Center Moriches Union Free School District*, 113 S.Ct. 2141 (1993) (in Vol. 2, Ch. 6), the Court unanimously held that the denial by a school district of a religious group's use of public school facilities for meetings after school hours violated the First Amendment. And in *Zobrest v. Catalina Foothills School District*, 509 U.S. 1 (1993) (in Vol. 2, Ch. 6), a bare majority ruled that there is no bar against public funding for a sign-language interpeter for a deaf student who attends a religious school.

Once again, in its 1993–1994 term, the Court was asked to jettison *Lemon* in *Board of Education of Kiryas Joel v. Grumet*, 114 S.Ct. 2481 (1994) (excerpted below). Notably, though, the Court declined again to abandon *Lemon*. Dividing six to three when striking down New York's law creating a special school district for Kiryas Joel, Justice Souter's opinion for the Court twice noted approvingly the ruling in *Lemon*. His opinion in parts, however, commanded only a plurality of the justices. Justice Blackmun issued a brief concurring opinion strongly supporting the *Lemon* test, while Justice O'Connor's concurring opinion, again, suggested that *Lemon* should be abandoned. Joined by Chief Justice Rehnquist and Justice Thomas, dissenting Justice Scalia also renewed his call for abandoning *Lemon*.

After granting so many cases involving the (dis)establishment clause in recent years and failing to reach agreement on whether to jettison the *Lemon* test in favor of some alternative, in its 1994–1995 term the justices notably declined to grant some appeals of rulings that a few years ago would have almost certainly been granted review. A case in point, *City of San Diego v. Paulson*, 115 S.Ct. 311 (1994), was an appeal of the Court of Appeals for the Ninth Circuit's ruling in *Ellis v. City of La Mesa*, 990 F.2d 1518 (1992), that a forty-three-foot cross, a San Diego landmark for over forty years, could no longer stand on public property because it violated the First Amendment's (dis)establishment clause. Yet the Court denied review and left the ruling intact.

However, the Court granted review and heard arguments during its 1994–1995 term in two other important cases that enabled it to consider the interrelationships among First Amendment doctrines for free speech, the (dis)establishment of religion, and religious freedom. In the so-called *"Wide Awake"* case, *Rosenberger v. The Rector and Visitors of the University of Virginia* (excerpted below), the editor of a university Christian student group's magazine sued the university over its policy, based on the (dis)establishment clause's prohibition of governmental sponsorship of religion, denying student-activity funds for the magazine, while at the same time subsidizing Jewish and Muslim student publications as "cultural activities." Rosenberger contended that the university's policy was discriminatory and a violation of the First Amendment guarantees for free speech and religious exercise. A bare majority of the Court agreed. Writing for the Court, Justice Kennedy held that discrimination against the expression of religious viewpoints violates the First Amendment's guarantee for free speech and that that amendment's (dis)establishment clause did not compel or justify the university's policy. By contrast, the four dissenters thought otherwise. Joined by Justices Stevens, Ginsburg, and Breyer, dissenting Justice Souter countered that for the first time the Court had approved direct governmental expenditures for religious activities, which ran afoul of the First Amendment's (dis)establishment clause.

The other case, *Capitol Square Review Board v. Pinette*, 115 S.Ct. 2440 (1995), appealed lower court decisions rejecting Cleveland, Ohio's Capitol Square Review Board's argument that it could, on the basis of the (dis)establishment clause, deny permission for the Klu Klux Klan to display at Christmastime a ten-foot cross in a public park across from the state capitol. The KKK, represented by the American Civil Liberties Union, argued that the lower courts correctly enforced the First Amendment guarantee for free speech, arguing that "the Government can neither favor some religious expressions over others nor discriminate against unpopular political views in a public forum." By contrast, the American Jewish Congress sided with Cleveland's review board in arguing that the guarantee for free speech should not automatically defeat all arguments in support of governmental policies based on the First Amendment's (dis)establishment clause.

In *Pinette* the Court's majority also held that the display of the cross was private religious speech protected by the First Amendment's free speech clause. But parts of Justice Scalia's opinion were joined only by a plurality of justices—Justices Kennedy and Thomas, along with Chief Justice Rehnquist. In a separate opinion joined by Justices Souter and Breyer, Justice O'Connor reasserted her "endorsement test" for determining the application of the First Amendment's (dis)establishment clause and that, based on the facts in case, that clause was not abridged. Dissenting Justices Stevens and Ginsburg, however, defended the view that the (dis)establishment clause compels a strict separation of the state from religion.

Board of Education of Kiryas Joel Village School District v. Grumet

114 S.Ct. 2481 (1994)

In response to a ruling by a bare majority of the Supreme Court in *Aguilar v. Felton*, 473 U.S. 402 (1985), forbidding public school teachers from offering remedial classes for handicapped children attending religious schools, the New York legislature created a special school district, governed by the Board of Education of Kiryas Joel, in Orange County, New York. Kiryas Joel is a community inhabited solely by Hasidic Jews of the Satmar sect, one of the most orthodox and conservative Jewish sects. All other Jewish children in the district attended private religious schools. But Kiryas Joel did not want to send two hundred handicapped children to public schools in the county because that might expose them to stress and possible ridicule for their clothes, use of Yiddish, and other traditional practices. In 1989, the state legislature created a special public school district for Kiryas Joel's handicapped children. The following year, Louis Grumet, the director of the New York State School Boards, challenged the constitutionality of the special school district as a violation of the First Amendment's (dis)establishment clause. Lower state courts and the New York Court of Appeals agreed that the special district failed to pass the tests set forth in *Lemon v. Kurtzman*, 403 U.S. 602 (1971) (in Vol. 2, Ch. 6), specifically, those requiring that legislation have a primary effect that neither advances nor inhibits religion. The school district thereupon appealed to the Supreme Court.

The Court's decision was six to three. Justice Souter announced the majority's opinion, which Justices Blackmun, Stevens, O'Connor, and Ginsburg joined in Parts I, II-B, II-C, and III, and which Justices Blackmun, Stevens, and Ginsburg joined in Part II-A. Justices Blackmun, Stevens, Kennedy, and O'Connor filed separate concurring opinions. Justice Scalia filed a dissenting opinion, which Chief Justice Rehnquist and Justice Thomas joined.

Justice SOUTER delivered the opinion of the Court.

The question is whether the Act creating the separate school district violates the Establishment Clause of the First Amendment, binding on the States through the Fourteenth Amendment. Because this unusual act is tantamount to an allocation of political power on a religious criterion and neither presupposes nor requires governmental impartiality toward religion, we hold that it violates the prohibition against establishment. . . .

II

"A proper respect for both the Free Exercise and the Establishment Clauses compels the State to pursue a course of 'neutrality' toward religion," *Committee for Public Ed. & Religious Liberty v. Nyquist*, 413 U.S. 756 (1973), favoring neither one religion over others nor religious adherents collectively over nonadherents. Chapter 748, the statute creating the Kiryas Joel Village School District, departs from this constitutional command by delegating the State's discretionary authority over public schools to a group defined by its character as a religious community, in a legal and historical context that gives no assurance that governmental power has been or will be exercised neutrally.

Larkin v. Grendel's Den, Inc., 459 U.S. 116 (1982), provides an instructive comparison with the litigation before us. There, the Court was requested to strike down a Massachusetts statute granting religious bodies veto power over applications for liquor licenses. Under the statute, the governing body of any church, synagogue, or school located within 500 feet of an applicant's premises could, simply by submitting written objection, prevent the Alcohol Beverage Control Commission from issuing a license. In spite of the State's valid interest in protecting churches, schools, and like institutions from "'the hurly-burly' associated with liquor outlets," the Court found that in two respects the statute violated "the wholesome 'neutrality' of which this

Court's cases speak," *School Dist. of Abington v. Schempp*, 374 U.S. 203 (1963). The Act brought about a "'fusion of governmental and religious functions'" by delegating "important, discretionary governmental powers" to religious bodies, thus impermissibly entangling government and religion. And it lacked "any 'effective means of guaranteeing' that the delegated power '[would] be used exclusively for secular, neutral, and nonideological purposes;'" this, along with the "significant symbolic benefit to religion" associated with "the mere appearance of a joint exercise of legislative authority by Church and State," led the Court to conclude that the statute had a "'primary' and 'principal' effect of advancing religion." Comparable constitutional problems inhere in the statute before us.

A

Larkin presented an example of united civic and religious authority, an establishment rarely found in such straightforward form in modern America. The Establishment Clause problem presented by Chapter 748 is more subtle, but it resembles the issue raised in *Larkin* to the extent that the earlier case teaches that a State may not delegate its civic authority to a group chosen according to a religious criterion. Authority over public schools belongs to the State, and cannot be delegated to a local school district defined by the State in order to grant political control to a religious group. What makes this litigation different from *Larkin* is the delegation here of civic power to the "qualified voters of the village of Kiryas Joel," as distinct from a religious leader such as the village rov, or an institution of religious government like the formally constituted parish council in *Larkin*. In light of the circumstances of this case, however, this distinction turns out to lack constitutional significance.

It is, first, not dispositive that the recipients of state power in this case are a group of religious individuals united by common doctrine, not the group's leaders or officers. Although some school district franchise is common to all voters, the State's manipulation of the franchise for this district limited it to Satmars, giving the sect exclusive control of the political subdivision. In the circumstances of this case, the difference between thus vesting state power in the members of a religious group as such instead of the officers of its sectarian organization is one of form, not substance. It is true that religious people (or groups of religious people) cannot be denied the opportunity to exercise the rights of citizens simply because of their religious affiliations or commitments, for such a disability would violate the right to religious free exercise, see *McDaniel v. Paty*, 435 U.S. 618 (1978), which the First Amendment guarantees as certainly as it bars any establishment. But *McDaniel*, which held that a religious individual could not, because of his religious activities, be denied the right to hold political office, is not in point here. That individuals who happen to be religious may hold public office does not mean that a state may deliberately delegate discretionary power to an individual, institution, or community on the ground of religious identity. If New York were to delegate civic authority to "the Grand Rebbe," *Larkin* would obviously require invalidation (even though under *McDaniel* the Grand Rebbe may run for, and serve on his local school board), and the same is true if New York delegates political authority by reference to religious belief. Where "fusion" is an issue, the difference lies in the distinction between a government's purposeful delegation on the basis of religion and a delegation on principles neutral to religion, to individuals whose religious identities are incidental to their receipt of civic authority.

Of course, Chapter 748 delegates power not by express reference to the religious belief of the Satmar community, but to residents of the "territory of the village of Kiryas Joel." Thus the second (and arguably more important) distinction between this case and *Larkin* is the identification here of the group to exercise civil authority in terms not expressly religious. But our analysis does not end with the text of the statute at issue, see *Church of Lukumi Babalu Aye, Inc. v. Hialeah*, 508 U.S. 520 (1993); *Wallace v. Jaffree*, 472 U.S. 38 (1985); *Gomillion v. Lightfoot*, 364 U.S. 339 (1960), and the context here persuades us that Chapter 748 effectively identifies these recipients of governmental authority by reference to doctrinal adherence, even though it does not do so expressly. We find this to be the better view of the facts because of the way the boundary lines of the school district divide residents according to religious affiliation, under the terms of an unusual and special legislative act.

It is undisputed that those who negotiated the village boundaries when applying the general village incorporation statute drew them so as to exclude all but Satmars, and that the New York Legislature was well aware that the village remained exclusively Satmar in 1989 when it adopted Chapter 748. The significance of this fact to the state legislature is indicated by the further fact that carving out the village school district ran counter to customary districting practices in the State. Indeed, the trend in New York is not toward dividing school districts but toward consolidating them. . . .

The origin of the district in a special act of the legislature, rather than the State's general laws governing school district reorganization, is likewise anomalous. . . . Because the district's creation ran uniquely counter to state practice, following the lines of a religious community where the customary and neutral principles would not have dictated the same result, we have good reasons to treat this district as the reflection of a religious criterion for identifying the recipients of civil authority. Not even the special needs of the children in this community can explain the legislature's unusual Act, for the State could have responded to the concerns of the Satmar parents without implicating the Establishment Clause, as we explain in some detail further on. We therefore find the legislature's Act to be substantially equivalent to defining a political subdivision and hence the qualification for its franchise by a religious test, resulting in a purposeful and forbidden "fusion of governmental and religious functions." *Larkin v. Grendel's Den.*

B

The fact that this school district was created by a special and unusual Act of the legislature also gives reason for concern whether the benefit received by the Satmar community is one that the legislature will provide equally to other religious (and nonreligious) groups. This is the second malady the *Larkin* Court identified in the law before it, the absence of an "effective means of guaranteeing" that governmental power will be and has been neutrally employed. But whereas in *Larkin* it was religious groups the Court thought might exercise civic power to advance the interests of religion (or religious adherents), here the threat to neutrality occurs at an antecedent stage. . . .

The general principle that civil power must be exercised in a manner neutral to religion is one the *Larkin* Court recognized, although it did not discuss the specific possibility of legislative favoritism along religious lines because the statute before it delegated state authority to any religious group assembled near the premises of an applicant for a liquor license, as well as to a further category of institutions not identified by religion. But the principle is well grounded in our case law, as we have frequently relied explicitly on the general availability of any benefit provided religious groups or individuals in turning aside Establishment Clause challenges. . . . Here the benefit flows only to a single sect, but aiding this single, small religious group causes no less a constitutional problem than would follow from aiding a sect with more members or religion as a whole, and we are forced to conclude that the State of New York has violated the Establishment Clause.

C

In finding that Chapter 748 violates the requirement of governmental neutrality by extending the benefit of a special franchise, we do not deny that the Constitution allows the state to accommodate religious needs by alleviating special burdens. Our cases leave no doubt that in commanding neutrality the Religion Clauses do not require the government to be oblivious to impositions that legitimate exercises of state power may place on religious belief and practice. Rather, there is "ample room under the Establishment Clause for 'benevolent neutrality which will permit religious exercise to exist without sponsorship and without interference,'" *Corporation of Presiding Bishop of Church of Jesus Christ of Latter-day Saints v. Amos,* 483 U.S. 327 (1987). The fact that Chapter 748 facilitates the practice of religion is not what renders it an unconstitutional establishment.

But accommodation is not a principle without limits, and what petitioners seek is an adjustment to the Satmars' religiously grounded preferences that our cases do not countenance. Prior decisions have allowed religious communities and institutions to pursue their own interests free from governmental interference, but we have never hinted that an otherwise unconstitutional delegation of political power to a religious group could be saved as a religious accommodation. Petitioners' proposed accommodation singles out a particular religious sect for special treatment, and whatever the limits of permissible legislative accommodations may be, compare *Texas Monthly, Inc. v. Bullock,* [489 U.S. 1 (1989)], (striking down law exempting only religious publications from taxation), with *Corporation of Presiding Bishop v. Amos* (upholding law exempting religious employers from Title VII), it is clear that neutrality as among religions must be honored.

This conclusion does not, however, bring the Satmar parents, the Monroe-Woodbury school district, or the State of New York to the end of the road in seeking ways to respond to the parents' concerns. Just as the Court in *Larkin* observed that the State's interest in protecting religious meeting places could be "readily accomplished by other means," there are several alternatives here for providing bilingual and bicultural special education to Satmar children. Such services can perfectly well be offered to village children through the Monroe-Woodbury Central School District. Since the Satmars do not claim that separatism is religiously mandated, their children may receive bilingual and bicultural instruction at a public school already run by the Monroe-Woodbury district. Or if the educationally appropriate offering by Monroe-Woodbury should turn out to be a separate program of bilingual and bicultural education at a neutral site near one of the village's parochial schools, this Court has already made it clear that no Establishment Clause difficulty would inhere in such a scheme, administered in accordance with neutral principles that would not necessarily confine special treatment to Satmars. . . .

III

Justice CARDOZO once cast the dissenter as "the gladiator making a last stand against the lions." B. CARDOZO, *Law and Literature* 34 (1931). Justice SCALIA's dissent is certainly the work of a gladiator, but he thrusts at lions of his own imagining. We do not disable a religiously homogeneous group from exercising political power conferred on it without regard to religion. Unlike the states of Utah and New Mexico (which were laid out according to traditional political methodologies taking account of lines of latitude and longitude and topographical features), the reference line chosen for the Kiryas Joel Village School District was one purposely drawn to separate Satmars from non-Satmars. Nor do we impugn the motives of the New York Legislature, which no doubt intended to accommodate the Satmar community without violating the Establishment Clause; we simply refuse to ignore that the method it chose is one that aids a particular religious community, as such, rather than all groups similarly interested in separate schooling. . . .

Our job, of course, would be easier if the dissent's position had prevailed with the Framers and with this Court over the years. An Establishment Clause diminished to the dimensions acceptable to Justice SCALIA could be enforced by a few simple rules, and our docket would never see cases requiring the application of a principle like neutrality toward religion as well as among religious sects. But that would be as blind to history as to precedent, and the difference between Justice SCALIA and the Court accordingly turns on the Court's recognition that the Establishment Clause does comprehend such a principle and obligates courts to exercise the judgment necessary to apply it.

In this case we are clearly constrained to conclude that the statute before us fails the test of neutrality. It delegates a power this Court has said "ranks at the very apex of the function of a State," *Wisconsin v. Yoder*, 406 U.S. 205 (1972), to an electorate defined by common religious belief and practice, in a manner that fails to foreclose religious favoritism. It therefore crosses the line from permissible accommodation to impermissible establishment. The judgment of the Court of Appeals of the State of New York is accordingly

Affirmed.

Justice O'CONNOR, concurring in part and concurring in the judgment.

We have time and again held that the government generally may not treat people differently based on the God or gods they worship, or don't worship. This emphasis on equal treatment is, I think, an eminently sound approach. In my view, the Religion Clauses—the Free Exercise Clause, the Establishment Clause, the Religious Test Clause, Art. VI, cl. 3, and the Equal Protection Clause as applied to religion—all speak with one voice on this point: Absent the most unusual circumstances, one's religion ought not affect one's legal rights or duties or benefits. As I have previously noted, "the Establishment Clause is infringed when the government makes adherence to religion relevant to a person's standing in the political community." *Wallace v. Jaffree*, 472 U.S. 38 (1985) (O'CONNOR, J., concurring in judgment).

That the government is acting to accommodate religion should generally not change this analysis. What makes accommodation permissible, even praiseworthy, is not that the government is making life easier for some particular religious group as such. Rather, it is that the government is accommodating a deeply held belief. Accommodations may thus justify treating those who share this belief differently from those who do not; but they do not justify discriminations based on sect. A state law prohibiting the consumption of alcohol may exempt sacramental wines, but it may not exempt sacramental wine use by Catholics but not by Jews. A draft law may exempt conscientious objectors, but it may not exempt conscientious objectors whose objections are based on theistic belief (such as Quakers) as opposed to nontheistic belief (such as Buddhists) or atheistic belief.

Experience proves that the Establishment Clause, like the Free Speech Clause, cannot easily be reduced to a single test. There are different categories of Establishment Clause cases, which may call for different approaches. Some cases, like this one, involve government actions targeted at particular individuals or groups, imposing special duties or giving special benefits. Cases involving government speech on religious topics, seem to me to fall into a different category and to require an analysis focusing on whether the speech endorses or disapproves of religion, rather than on whether the government action is neutral with regard to religion. Another category encompasses cases in which the government must make decisions about matters of religious doctrine and religious law. These cases, which often arise in the application of otherwise neutral property or contract principles to religious institutions, involve complicated questions not present in other situations. Government delegations of power to religious bodies may make up yet another category. As *Larkin* itself suggested, government impartiality towards religion may not be enough in such situations: A law that bars all alcohol sales within some distance of a church, school, or hospital may be valid, but an equally evenhanded law that gives each institution discretionary power over the sales may not be. Of course, there may well be additional categories, or more opportune places to draw the lines between the categories.

As the Court's opinion today shows, the slide away from *Lemon*'s unitary approach is well under way. A return to *Lemon*, even if possible, would likely be futile, regardless of where one stands on the substantive Establishment Clause questions. I think a less unitary approach provides a better structure for analysis. If each test covers a narrower and more homogeneous area, the tests may be more precise and therefore easier to apply. There may be more opportunity to pay attention to the specific nuances of each area. There might also be, I hope, more consensus on each of the narrow tests than there has been on a broad test. And abandoning the *Lemon* framework need not mean abandoning some of the insights that the test reflected, nor the insights of the cases that applied it. . . .

Justice SCALIA, with whom the CHIEF JUSTICE and Justice THOMAS join, dissenting.

The Court today finds that the Powers That Be, up in Albany, have conspired to effect an establishment of the Satmar Hasidim. I do not know who would be more surprised at this discovery: the Founders of our Nation or Grand Rebbe Joel Teitelbaum, founder of the Satmar. The Grand Rebbe would be astounded to learn that after escaping brutal persecution and coming to America with the modest hope of religious toleration for their ascetic form of Judaism, the Satmar had become so powerful, so closely allied with Mammon, as to have become an "establishment" of the Empire State. And the Founding Fathers would be astonished to find that the Establishment Clause—which they designed "to insure that no one powerful sect or combination of sects could use political or governmental power to punish dissenters," *Zorach v. Clauson*, 343 U.S. 306 (1952) (BLACK, J., dissenting)—has been employed to prohibit characteristically and admirably American accommodation of the religious practices (or more precisely, cultural peculiarities) of a tiny minority sect. I, however, am not surprised. Once this Court has abandoned text and history as guides, nothing prevents it from calling religious toleration the establishment of religion. . . .

For his thesis that New York has unconstitutionally conferred governmental authority upon the Satmar sect, Justice SOUTER relies extensively, and virtually exclusively, upon *Larkin v. Grendel's Den, Inc.*, 459 U.S. 116 (1982). Justice SOUTER believes that the present case "resembles" *Grendel's Den* because that case "teaches that a state may not delegate its civic authority to a group chosen according to a religious criterion." That misdescribes both what that case taught (which is that a state may not delegate its civil authority to a church), and what this case involves (which is a group chosen according to cultural characteristics). The statute at issue there gave churches veto power over the State's authority to grant a liquor license to establishments in the vicinity of the church. The Court had little difficulty finding the statute unconstitutional.

Justice SOUTER concedes that *Grendel's Den* "presented an example of united civic and religious authority, an establishment rarely found in such straightforward form in modern America." The uniqueness of the case stemmed from the grant of governmental power directly to a religious institution, and the Court's opinion focused on that fact, remarking that the transfer of authority was to "churches" (10 times), the "governing body of churches" (twice), "religious institutions" (twice) and "religious bodies" (once). Astonishingly, however, Justice SOUTER dismisses the difference between a transfer of government power to citizens who share a common religion as opposed to "the officers of its sectarian organization"—the critical factor that made *Grendel's Den* unique and "rare"—as being "one of form, not substance."

Justice SOUTER's steamrolling of the difference between civil authority held by a church, and civil authority held by members of a church, is breathtaking. To accept it, one must believe that large portions of the civil authority exercised during most of our history were unconstitutional, and that much more of it than merely the Kiryas Joel School District is unconstitutional today. The history of the populating of North America is in no small measure the story of groups of people sharing a common religious and cultural heritage striking out to form their own communities. It is preposterous to suggest that the civil institutions of these communities, separate from their churches, were constitutionally suspect. And if they were, surely Justice SOUTER cannot mean that the inclusion of one or two nonbelievers in the community would have been enough to eliminate the constitutional vice. If the conferral of governmental power upon a religious institution as such (rather than upon American citizens who belong to the religious institution) is not the test of *Grendel's Den* invalidity, there is no reason why giving power to a body that is overwhelmingly dominated by the members of one sect would not suffice to invoke the Establishment Clause. That might have made the entire States of Utah and New Mexico unconstitutional at the time of their admission to the Union, and would undoubtedly make many units of local government unconstitutional today. [A census taken in 1906, 10 years after statehood was granted to Utah, and 6 years before it was granted to New Mexico, showed that in Utah 87.7% of all church members were Mormon, and in New Mexico 88.7% of all church members were Roman Catholic.]

Justice SOUTER's position boils down to the quite novel proposition that any group of citizens (say, the residents of Kiryas Joel) can be invested with political power, but not if they all belong to the same religion. Of course such disfavoring of religion is positively antagonistic to the purposes of the Religion Clauses, and we have rejected it before. In *McDaniel v. Paty*, 435 U.S. 618 (1978), we invalidated a state constitutional amendment that would have permitted all persons to participate in political conventions, except ministers. We adopted James Madison's view that the State could not "'punish a religious profession with the privation of a civil right.'" I see no reason why it is any less pernicious to deprive a group rather than an individual of its rights simply because of its religious beliefs. . . .

I turn, next, to Justice SOUTER's second justification for finding an establishment of religion: his facile conclusion that the New York Legislature's creation of the Kiryas Joel School District was religiously motivated. But in the Land of the Free, democratically adopted laws are not so easily impeached by unelected judges. To establish the unconstitutionality of a facially neutral law on the mere basis of its asserted religiously preferential (or discriminatory) effects—or at least to establish it in conformity with our precedents—Justice SOUTER "must be able to show the absence of a neutral, secular basis" for the law. *Gillette v. United States*, 401 U.S. 437 (1971). . . .

Since the obvious presence of a neutral, secular basis renders the asserted preferential effect of this law inadequate to invalidate it, Justice SOUTER is required to come forward with direct evidence that religious preference was the objective. His case could scarcely be weaker. It consists, briefly, of this: The People of New York created the Kiryas Joel Village School District in order to further the Satmar religion, rather than for any proper secular purpose, because (1) they created the district in an extraordinary manner— by special Act of the legislature, rather than under the State's general laws governing school-district reorganization; (2) the creation of the district ran counter to a State trend towards consolidation of school districts; and (3) the District includes only adherents of the Satmar religion. On this indictment, no jury would convict.

One difficulty with the first point is that it is not true. There was really nothing so "special" about the formation of a school district by an Act of the New York Legislature. The State has created both large school districts, and small specialized school districts for institutionalized children, through these special Acts. But in any event all that the first point proves, and the second point as well (countering the trend toward consolidation), is that New York regarded Kiryas Joel as a special case, requiring special measures. I should think it obvious that it did, and obvious that it should have. But even if the New York Legislature had never before created a school district by special statute (which is not true), and even if it had done nothing but consolidate school districts for over a century (which is not true), how could the departure from those past practices possibly demonstrate that the legislature had religious favoritism in mind? It could not. To be sure, when there is no special treatment there is no possibility of religious favoritism; but it is not logical to suggest that when there is special treatment there is proof of religious favoritism.

Justice SOUTER's case against the statute comes down to nothing more, therefore, than his third point: the fact that all the residents of the Kiryas Joel Village School District are Satmars. But all its residents also wear unusual dress, have unusual civic customs, and have not much to do with people who are culturally different from them. (The Court recognizes that "the Satmars prefer to live together 'to facilitate individual religious observance and maintain social, cultural and religious values,' but that it is not 'against their religion' to interact with others." On what basis does Justice SOUTER conclude that it is the theological distinctiveness rather than the cultural distinctiveness that was the basis for New York State's decision? The normal assumption would be that it was the latter, since it was not theology but dress, language, and cultural alienation that posed the educational problem for the children. Justice SOUTER not only does not adopt the logical assumption, he does not even give the New York Legislature the benefit of the doubt. . . . In other words, we know the legislature must have been motivated by the desire to favor the Satmar Hasidim religion, because it could have met the needs of these children by a method that did not place the Satmar Hasidim in a separate school district. This is not a rational argument proving religious favoritism; it is rather a novel Establishment Clause principle to the effect that no secular objective may be pursued by a means that might also be used for religious favoritism if some other means is available.) . . .

When a legislature acts to accommodate religion, particularly a minority sect, "it follows the best of our traditions." The Constitution itself contains an accommodation of sorts. Article VI, cl. 3, prescribes that executive, legislative and judicial officers of the Federal and State Governments shall bind themselves to support the Constitution "by Oath or Affirmation." Although members of the most populous religions found no difficulty in swearing an oath to God, Quakers, Moravians, and Mennonites refused to take oaths based on Matthew 5:34's injunction "swear not at all." The option of affirmation was added to accommodate these minority religions and enable their members to serve in government. Congress, from its earliest sessions, passed laws accommodating religion by refunding duties paid by specific churches upon the importation of plates for the printing of Bibles, vestments, and bells. Congress also exempted church property from the tax assessments it levied on residents of the District of Columbia; and all 50 States have had similar laws. . . .

In today's opinion, however, the Court seems uncomfortable with this aspect of our constitutional tradition. Although it acknowledges the concept of accommodation, it quickly points out that it is "not a principle without limits," and then gives reasons why the present case exceeds those limits, reasons which simply do not hold water. "We have never hinted," the Court says, "that an otherwise unconstitutional delegation of political power to a religious group could be saved as a religious accommodation." Putting aside the circularity inherent in referring to a delegation as "otherwise unconstitutional" when its constitutionality turns on whether there is an accommodation, if this statement is true, it is only because we have never hinted that delegation of political power to citizens who share a particular religion could be unconstitutional. This is simply a replay of the argument we rejected in Part II.

The second and last reason the Court finds accommodation impermissible is, astoundingly, the mere risk that the State will not offer accommodation to a similar group in the future, and that neutrality will therefore not be preserved. . . .

Contrary to the Court's suggestion, I do not think that the Establishment Clause prohibits formally established "state" churches and nothing more. I have always believed, and all my opinions are consistent with the view, that the Establishment Clause prohibits the favoring of one religion over others. In this respect, it is the Court that attacks lions of straw. What I attack is the Court's imposition of novel "up front" procedural requirements on state legislatures. Making law (and making exceptions) one case at a time, whether through adjudication or through highly particularized rulemaking or legislation, violates, *ex ante*, no principle of fairness, equal protection, or neutrality, simply because it does not announce in advance how all future cases (and all future exceptions) will be disposed of. If it did, the manner of proceeding of this Court itself would be unconstitutional. It is presumptuous for this Court to impose—out of nowhere—an unheard-of prohibition against proceeding in this manner upon the Legislature of New York State. I never heard of such a principle, nor has anyone else, nor will it ever be heard of again. Unlike what the New York Legislature has done, this is a special rule to govern only the Satmar Hasidim. . . .

Rosenberger v. The Rector and Visitors of the University of Virginia
115 S.Ct. 2510 (1995)

In 1990, Ronald Rosenberger and several other undergraduates at the University of Virginia formed Wide Awake Productions (WAP) and qualified under the university's guidelines as a "Contracted Independent Organization" (CIO), which entitled it to access to the university's facilities, including computer terminals. WAP was established "to publish a magazine of philosophical and religious expression," "to facilitate discussion which fosters an atmosphere of sensitivity to and tolerance of Christian viewpoints," and "to provide a unifying focus for Christians of multicultural backgrounds." In particular, WAP published *Wide Awake: A Christian Perspective*, a paper devoted to offering "a Christian perspective on both personal and community issues, especially those relevant to college students at the University of Virginia." The editors committed the paper to a twofold mission: "to challenge Christians to live, in word and deed, according to the faith they proclaim and to encourage students to consider what a personal relationship with Jesus Christ means."

Under the university's guidelines, some CIOs are also entitled to apply for funds from the Student Activities Fund (SAF). Funded by a mandatory fourteen-dollar fee per semester from each student, the purpose of the SAF is to support a broad range of extracurricular student activities that "are related to the educational purpose of the University." Under the guidelines, the SAF must be administered "in a manner consistent with the educational purpose of the University as well as with state and federal law." The SAF, for instance, may not pay for "religious activities." The Student Council has the initial authority to disburse the funds, but its actions are subject to review by a faculty body.

The university's guidelines recognize eleven categories of student groups that may seek payment to third-party contractors because they "are related to the educational purpose of the University of Virginia." One category includes "student news, information, opinion, entertainment, or academic communications media groups." The guidelines also specify, however, that the costs of certain activities of CIOs that are otherwise eligible for funding will not be reimbursed by the SAF. The student activities which are excluded from SAF support are religious activities, philanthropic contributions and activities, political activities, activities that would jeopardize the university's tax-exempt status, those which involve payment of honoraria or similar fees, or social entertainment or related expenses. The prohibition on "political activities" is defined so that it is limited to electioneering and lobbying.

The guidelines provide that "these restrictions on funding political activities are not intended to preclude funding of any otherwise eligible student organization which ... espouses particular positions or ideological viewpoints, including those that may be unpopular or are not generally accepted." A "religious activity," by contrast, is defined as any activity that "primarily promotes or manifests a particular belief in or about a deity or an ultimate reality."

A few months after receiving CIO status, WAP requested the SAF to pay its printer $5,862 for the costs of printing *Wide Awake*. The appropriations committee of the Student Council denied WAP's request on the ground that *Wide Awake* was a "religious activity" within the meaning of the university's guidelines; that is, *Wide Awake* "promoted or manifested a particular belief in or about a deity or an ultimate reality." WAP appealed to the full Student Council, but that appeal was denied.

Rosenberger and other editors of *Wide Awake* subsequently filed a suit in federal district court. They alleged that refusal to fund *Wide Awake* on the basis of its religious editorial viewpoint violated their rights to freedom of speech and press, to the free exercise of religion, and to equal protection of the law. The district court, however, disagreed and ruled that the university's funding the newspaper would violate the First Amendment's (dis)establishment clause. The Court of Appeals for the Fourth Circuit affirmed, upon concluding that the university had a "compelling interest in maintaining strict separation of church and state," whereupon Rosenberger appealed to the Supreme Court, which granted review.

The Court's decision was five to four and opinion delivered by Justice Kennedy. Justices O'Connor and Thomas filed separate concurrences. Justice Souter filed a dissenting opinion, which was joined by Justices Stevens, Ginsburg, and Breyer.

Justice KENNEDY delivered the opinion of the Court.

It is axiomatic that the government may not regulate speech based on its substantive content or the message it conveys. Other principles follow from this precept. In the realm of private speech or expression, government regulation may not favor one speaker over another. Discrimination against speech because of its message is presumed to be unconstitutional. These rules informed our determination that the government offends the First Amendment when it imposes financial burdens on certain speakers based on the content of their expression. *Simon & Schuster, Inc. v. Members of N.Y. State Crime Victims Bd.*, 502 U.S. 105 (1991). When the government targets not subject matter but particular views taken by speakers on a subject, the violation of the First Amendment is all the more blatant. See *R. A. V. v. St. Paul*, 505 U.S. 377 (1992). Viewpoint discrimination is thus an egregious form of content discrimination. The government must abstain from regulating speech when the specific motivating ideology or the opinion or perspective of the speaker is the rationale for the restriction.

These principles provide the framework forbidding the State from exercising viewpoint discrimination, even when the limited public forum is one of its own creation. In a case involving a school district's provision of school facilities for private uses, we declared that "there is no question that the District, like the private owner of property, may legally preserve the property under its control for the use to which it is dedicated." *Lamb's Chapel v. Center Moriches Union Free School Dist.,* [113 S.Ct. 2141] (1993). The necessities of confining a forum to the limited and legitimate purposes for which it was created may justify the State in reserving it for certain groups or for the discussion of certain topics. Once it has opened a limited forum, however, the State must respect the lawful boundaries it has itself set. The State may not exclude speech where its distinction is not "reasonable in light of the purpose served by the forum," nor may it discriminate against speech on the basis of its viewpoint. Thus, in determining whether the State is acting to preserve the limits of the forum it has created so that the exclusion of a class of speech is legitimate, we have observed a distinction between, on the one hand, content discrimination, which may be permissible if it preserves the purposes of that limited forum, and, on the other hand, viewpoint discrimination, which is presumed impermissible when directed against speech otherwise within the forum's limitations.

The SAF is a forum more in a metaphysical than in a spatial or geographic sense, but the same principles are applicable. The most recent and most apposite case is our decision in *Lamb's Chapel.* There, a school district had opened school facilities for use after school hours by community groups for a wide variety of social, civic, and recreational purposes. The district, however, had enacted a formal policy against opening facilities to groups for religious purposes. Invoking its policy, the district rejected a request from a group desiring to show a film series addressing various child-rearing questions from a "Christian perspective." There was no indication in the record in *Lamb's Chapel* that the request to use the school facilities was "denied for any reason other than the fact that the presentation would have been from a religious perspective." Our conclusion was unanimous: "It discriminates on the basis of viewpoint to permit school property to be used for the presentation of all views about family issues and child-rearing except those dealing with the subject matter from a religious standpoint."

The University does acknowledge (as it must in light of our precedents) that "ideologically driven attempts to suppress a particular point of view are presumptively unconstitutional in funding, as in other contexts," but insists that this case does not present that issue because the Guidelines draw lines based on content, not viewpoint. As we have noted, discrimination against one set of views or ideas is but a subset or particular instance of the more general phenomenon of content discrimination. And, it must be acknowledged, the distinction is not a precise one. It is, in a sense, something of an understatement to speak of religious thought and discussion as just a viewpoint, as distinct from a comprehensive body of thought. The nature of our origins and destiny and their dependence upon the existence of a divine being have been subjects of philosophic inquiry throughout human history. We conclude, nonetheless, that here, as in *Lamb's Chapel,* viewpoint discrimination is the proper way to interpret the University's objections to *Wide Awake*. By the very terms of the SAF prohibition, the University does not exclude religion as a subject matter but selects for disfavored treatment those student journalistic efforts with religious editorial viewpoints. Religion may be a vast area of inquiry, but it also provides, as it did here, a specific premise, a perspective, a standpoint from which a variety of subjects may be discussed and considered. The prohibited perspective, not the general subject matter, resulted in the refusal to make third-party payments, for the subjects discussed were otherwise within the approved category of publications. . . .

The University's denial of WAP's request for third-party payments in the present case is based upon viewpoint discrimination not unlike the discrimination the school district relied upon in *Lamb's Chapel* and that we found invalid. The church group in *Lamb's Chapel* would have been qualified as a social or civic organization, save for its religious purposes. Furthermore, just as the school district in *Lamb's Chapel* pointed to nothing but the religious views of the group as the rationale for excluding its message, so in this case the University justifies its denial of SAF participation to WAP on the ground that the contents of *Wide Awake* reveal an avowed religious perspective. . . .

The University tries to escape the consequences of our holding in *Lamb's Chapel* by urging that this case involves the provision of funds rather than access to facilities. The University begins with the unremarkable proposition that the State must have substantial discretion in determining how to allocate scarce resources to accomplish its educational mission. Citing our decisions in *Rust v. Sullivan*, 500 U.S. 173 (1991), *Regan v. Taxation with Representation of Wash.*, 461 U.S. 540 (1983), and *Widmar v. Vincent*, 454 U.S. 263 (1981), the University argues that content-based funding decisions are both inevitable and lawful. . . .

To this end the University relies on our assurance in *Widmar v. Vincent*. There, in the course of striking down a public university's exclusion of religious groups from use of school facilities made available to all other student groups, we stated: "Nor do we question the right of the University to make academic judgments as to how best to allocate scarce resources." The quoted language in *Widmar* was but a proper recognition of the principle that when the State is the speaker, it may make content-based choices. When the University determines the content of the education it provides, it is the University speaking, and we have permitted the government to regulate the content of what is or is not expressed when it is the speaker or when it enlists private entities to convey its own message. In the same vein, in *Rust v. Sullivan*, we upheld the government's prohibition on abortion-related advice applicable to recipients of federal funds for family planning counseling. There, the government did not create a program to encourage private speech but instead used private speakers to transmit specific information pertaining to its own program. We recognized that when the government appropriates public funds to promote a particular policy of its own it is entitled to say what it wishes. When the government disburses public funds to private entities to convey a governmental message, it may take legitimate and appropriate steps to ensure that its message is neither garbled nor distorted by the grantee.

It does not follow, however, and we did not suggest in *Widmar*, that viewpoint-based restrictions are proper when the University does not itself speak or subsidize transmittal of a message it favors but instead expends funds to encourage a diversity of views from private speakers. A holding that the University may not discriminate based on the viewpoint of private persons whose speech it facilitates does not restrict the University's own speech, which is controlled by different principles. For that reason, the University's reliance on *Regan v. Taxation with Representation of Wash.* is inapposite as well. *Regan* involved a challenge to Congress' choice to grant tax deductions for contributions made to veterans' groups engaged in lobbying, while denying that favorable status to other charities which pursued lobbying efforts. Although acknowledging that the Government is not required to subsidize the exercise of fundamental rights, we reaffirmed the requirement of viewpoint neutrality in the Government's provision of financial benefits by observing that "the case would be different if Congress were to discriminate invidiously in its subsidies in such a way as to 'aim at the suppression of dangerous ideas.'" *Regan* relied on a distinction based on preferential treatment of certain speakers—veterans' organizations—and not a distinction based on the content or messages of those groups' speech. The University's regulation now before us, however, has a speech-based restriction as its sole rationale and operative principle.

The distinction between the University's own favored message and the private speech of students is evident in the case before us. The University itself has taken steps to ensure the distinction in the agreement each CIO must sign. The University declares that the student groups eligible for SAF support are not the University's agents, are not subject to its control, and are not its responsibility. Having offered to pay the third-party contractors on behalf of private speakers who convey their own messages, the University may not silence the expression of selected viewpoints.

The University urges that, from a constitutional standpoint, funding of speech differs from provision of access to facilities because money is scarce and physical facilities are not. Beyond the fact that in any given case this proposition might not be true as an empirical matter, the underlying premise that the University could discriminate based on viewpoint if demand for space exceeded its availability is wrong as well. The government cannot justify viewpoint discrimination among private speakers on the economic fact of scarcity. . . .

The Guideline invoked by the University to deny third-party contractor payments on behalf of WAP effects a sweeping restriction on student thought and student inquiry in the context of University-sponsored publications. The prohibition on funding on behalf of publications that "primarily promote or manifest a particular belief in or about a deity or an ultimate reality," in its ordinary and commonsense meaning, has a vast potential reach. The term "promotes" as used here would comprehend any writing advocating a philosophic position that rests upon a belief in a deity or ultimate reality. And the term "manifests" would bring within the scope of the prohibition any writing that is explicable as resting upon a premise which presupposes the existence of a deity or ultimate reality. Were the prohibition applied with much vigor at all, it would bar funding of essays by hypothetical student contributors named Plato, Spinoza, and Descartes. And if the regulation covers, as the University says it does, those student journalistic efforts which primarily manifest or promote a belief that there is no deity and no ultimate reality, then undergraduates named Karl Marx, Bertrand Russell, and Jean-Paul Sartre would likewise have some of their major essays excluded from student publications. If any manifestation of beliefs in first principles disqualifies the writing, as seems to be the case, it is indeed difficult to name renowned thinkers whose writings would be accepted, save perhaps for articles disclaiming all connection to their ultimate philosophy. Plato could contrive perhaps to submit an acceptable essay on making pasta or peanut butter cookies, provided he did not point out their (necessary) imperfections.

Based on the principles we have discussed, we hold that the regulation invoked to deny SAF support, both in its terms and in its application to these petitioners, is a denial of their right of free speech guaranteed by the First Amendment. It remains to be considered whether the violation following from the University's action is excused by the necessity of complying with the Constitution's prohibition against state establishment of religion. We turn to that question. . . .

A central lesson of our decisions is that a significant factor in upholding governmental programs in the face of Establishment Clause attack is their neutrality towards religion. We have decided a series of cases addressing the receipt of government benefits where religion or religious views are implicated in some degree. The first case in our modern Establishment Clause jurisprudence was *Everson v. Board of Ed. of Ewing*, 330 U.S. 1 (1947). There we cautioned that in enforcing the prohibition against laws respecting establishment of religion, we must "be sure that we do not inadvertently prohibit [the government] from extending its general state law benefits to all its citizens without regard to their religious belief." We have held that the guarantee of neutrality is respected, not offended, when the government, following neutral criteria and evenhanded policies, extends benefits to recipients whose ideologies and viewpoints, including religious ones, are broad and diverse. More than once have we rejected the position that the Establishment Clause even justifies, much less requires, a refusal to extend free speech rights to religious speakers who participate in broad-reaching government programs neutral in design. See *Lamb's Chapel*, [*Board of Ed. of Westside Community Schools v.*] *Mergens*, [496 U.S. 226 (1990)], *Widmar*.

The governmental program here is neutral toward religion. . . . The University's SAF Guidelines have a separate classification for, and do not make third-party payments on behalf of, "religious organizations," which are those "whose purpose is to practice a devotion to an acknowledged ultimate reality or deity." The category of support here is for "student news, information, opinion, entertainment, or academic communications media groups," of which *Wide Awake* was 1 of 15 in the 1990 school year. WAP did not seek a subsidy because of its Christian editorial viewpoint; it sought funding as a student journal, which it was. . . .

It does not violate the Establishment Clause for a public university to grant access to its facilities on a religion-neutral basis to a wide spectrum of student groups, including groups which use meeting rooms for sectarian activities, accompanied by some devotional exercises. This is so even where the upkeep, maintenance, and repair of the facilities attributed to those uses is paid from a student activities fund to which students are required to contribute. The government usually acts by spending money. Even the provision of a meeting room, as in *Mergens* and *Widmar*, involved governmental expenditure, if only in the form of electricity and heating or cooling costs. . . . There is no difference in logic or principle, and no difference of constitutional significance, between a school using its funds to operate a facility to which students have access, and a school paying a third-party contractor to operate the facility on its behalf. The latter occurs here. The University provides printing services to a broad spectrum of student newspapers qualified as CIOs by reason of their officers and membership. Any benefit to religion is incidental to the government's provision of secular services for secular purposes on a religion-neutral basis. Printing is a routine, secular, and recurring attribute of student life.

To obey the Establishment Clause, it was not necessary for the University to deny eligibility to student publications because of their viewpoint. The neutrality commanded of the State by the separate Clauses of the First Amendment was compromised by the University's course of action. The viewpoint discrimination inherent in the University's regulation required public officials to scan and interpret student publications to discern their underlying philosophic assumptions respecting religious theory and belief. That course of action was a denial of the right of free speech and would risk fostering a pervasive bias or hostility to religion, which could undermine the very neutrality the Establishment Clause requires. There is no Establishment Clause violation in the University's honoring its duties under the Free Speech Clause.

The judgment of the Court of Appeals must be, and is, reversed.

Justice O'CONNOR, concurring.

When two bedrock principles so conflict, understandably neither can provide the definitive answer. Reliance on categorical platitudes is unavailing. Resolution instead depends on the hard task of judging—sifting through the details and determining whether the challenged program offends the Establishment Clause. Such judgment requires courts to draw lines, sometimes quite fine, based on the particular facts of each case. . . .

So it is in this case. The nature of the dispute does not admit of categorical answers, nor should any be inferred from the Court's decision today. Instead, certain considerations specific to the program at issue lead me to conclude that by providing the same assistance to *Wide Awake* that it does to other publications, the University would not be endorsing the magazine's religious perspective.

First, the student organizations, at the University's insistence, remain strictly independent of the University. . . . Second, financial assistance is distributed in a manner that ensures its use only for permissible purposes. A student organization seeking assistance must submit disbursement requests; if approved, the funds are paid directly to the third-party vendor and do not pass through the organization's coffers. . . . Third, assistance is provided to the religious publication in a context that makes improbable any perception of government endorsement of the religious message. *Wide Awake* does not exist in a vacuum. It competes with 15 other magazines and newspapers for advertising and readership. The widely divergent viewpoints of these many purveyors of opinion, all supported on an equal basis by the University, significantly diminishes the danger that the message of any one publication is perceived as endorsed by the University. . . .

Finally, although the question is not presented here, I note the possibility that the student fee is susceptible to a Free Speech Clause challenge by an objecting student that she should not be compelled to pay for speech with which she disagrees. While the Court does not resolve the question here, the existence of such an opt-out possibility not available to citizens generally provides a potential basis for distinguishing proceeds of the student fees in this case from proceeds of the general assessments in support of religion that lie at the core of the prohibition against religious funding, and from government funds generally. Unlike moneys dispensed from state or federal treasuries, the Student Activities Fund is collected from students who themselves administer the fund and select qualifying recipients only from among those who originally paid the fee. . . . The Student Activities Fund, then, represents not government resources, whether derived from tax revenue, sales of assets, or otherwise, but a fund that simply belongs to the students.

The Court's decision today therefore neither trumpets the supremacy of the neutrality principle nor signals the demise of the funding prohibition in Establishment Clause jurisprudence. . . . When bedrock principles collide, they test the limits of categorical obstinacy and expose the flaws and dangers of a Grand Unified Theory that may turn out to be neither grand nor unified. The Court today does only what courts must do in many Establishment Clause cases—focus on specific features of a particular government action to ensure that it does not violate the Constitution. By withholding from *Wide Awake* assistance that the University provides generally to all other student publications, the University has discriminated on the basis of the magazine's religious viewpoint in violation of the Free Speech Clause. . . .

Justice SOUTER, with whom Justice STEVENS, Justice GINS-BURG, and Justice BREYER join, dissenting.

The Court today, for the first time, approves direct funding of core religious activities by an arm of the State. It does so, however, only after erroneous treatment of some familiar principles of law implementing the First Amendment's Establishment and Speech Clauses, and by viewing the very funds in question as beyond the reach of the Establishment Clause's funding restrictions as such. Because there is no warrant for distinguishing among public funding sources for purposes of applying the First Amendment's prohibition of religious establishment, I would hold that the University's refusal to support petitioners' religious activities is compelled by the Establishment Clause. I would therefore affirm. . . .

The Court's difficulties will be all the more clear after a closer look at *Wide Awake* than the majority opinion affords. The character of the magazine is candidly disclosed on the opening page of the first issue, where the editor-in-chief announces *Wide Awake*'s mission in a letter to the readership signed, "Love in Christ": it is "to challenge Christians to live, in word and deed, according to the faith they proclaim and to encourage students to consider what a personal relationship with Jesus Christ means." The masthead of every issue bears St. Paul's exhortation, that "the hour has come for you to awake from your slumber, because our salvation is nearer now than when we first believed. Romans 13:11."

Each issue of *Wide Awake* contained in the record makes good on the editor's promise and echoes the Apostle's call to accept salvation. . . . Even featured essays on facially secular topics become platforms from which to call readers to fulfill the tenets of Christianity in their lives. . . .

This writing is . . . [a] straightforward exhortation to enter into a relationship with God as revealed in Jesus Christ, and to satisfy a series of moral obligations derived from the teachings of Jesus Christ. These are not the words of "student news, information, opinion, entertainment, or academic communication. . ." (in the language of the University's funding criterion), but the words of "challenge [to] Christians to live, in word and deed, according to the faith they proclaim and . . . to consider what a personal relationship with Jesus Christ means" (in the language of *Wide Awake*'s founder). The subject is not the discourse of the scholar's study or the seminar room, but of the evangelist's mission station and the pulpit. It is nothing other than the preaching of the word, which (along with the sacraments) is what most branches of Christianity offer those called to the religious life.

Using public funds for the direct subsidization of preaching the word is categorically forbidden under the Establishment Clause, and if the Clause was meant to accomplish nothing else, it was meant to bar this use of public money. Evidence on the subject antedates even the Bill of Rights itself, as may be seen in the writings of Madison, whose authority on questions about the meaning of the Establishment Clause is well settled. Four years before the First Congress proposed the First Amendment, Madison gave his opinion on the legitimacy of using public funds for religious purposes, in the Memorial and Remonstrance Against Religious Assessments, which played the central role in ensuring the defeat of the Virginia tax assessment bill in 1786 and framed the debate upon which the Religion Clauses stand: "Who does not see that . . . the same authority which can force a citizen to contribute three pence only of his property for the support of any one establishment, may force him to conform to any other establishment in all cases whatsoever?" James Madison, Memorial and Remonstrance Against Religious Assessments. . . .

The principle against direct funding with public money is patently violated by the contested use of today's student activity fee. Like today's taxes generally, the fee is Madison's threepence. The University exercises the power of the State to compel a student to pay it, and the use of any part of it for the direct support of religious activity thus strikes at what we have repeatedly held to be the heart of the prohibition on establishment.

The Court, accordingly, has never before upheld direct state funding of the sort of proselytizing published in *Wide Awake* and, in fact, has categorically condemned state programs directly aiding religious activity, *School Dist. v. Ball*, [413 U.S. 756 (1973)], (striking programs providing secular instruction to nonpublic school students on nonpublic school premises because they are "indistinguishable from the provision of a direct cash subsidy to the religious school that is most clearly prohibited under the Establishment

Clause"); *Wolman v. Walter*, 433 U.S. 229 (1977) (striking field trip aid program because it constituted "an impermissible direct aid to sectarian education"); *Meek v. Pittenger*, 421 U.S. 349 (1975) (striking material and equipment loan program to nonpublic schools because of the inability to "channel aid to the secular without providing direct aid to the sectarian"); *Committee for Public Education v. Nyquist*, [413 U.S. 756 (1973)] (striking aid to nonpublic schools for maintenance and repair of facilities because "no attempt is made to restrict payments to those expenditures related to the upkeep of facilities used exclusively for secular purposes"); *Levitt v. Committee for Public Ed. & Religious Liberty*, 413 U.S. 472 (1973) (striking aid to nonpublic schools for state-mandated tests because the state had failed to "assure that the state-supported activity is not being used for religious indoctrination"); *Tilton v. Richardson*, 403 U.S. 672 (1971) (striking as insufficient a 20-year limit on prohibition for religious use in federal construction program for university facilities because unrestricted use even after 20 years "is in effect a contribution of some value to a religious body"). . . .

Why does the Court not apply this clear law to these clear facts and conclude, as I do, that the funding scheme here is a clear constitutional violation? The answer must be in part that the Court fails to confront the evidence set out in the preceding section. Throughout its opinion, the Court refers uninformatively to *Wide Awake*'s "Christian viewpoint," or its "religious perspective," and in distinguishing funding of Wide Awake from the funding of a church, the Court maintains that "[Wide Awake] is not a religious institution, at least in the usual sense." The Court does not quote the magazine's adoption of Saint Paul's exhortation to awaken to the nearness of salvation, or any of its articles enjoining readers to accept Jesus Christ, or the religious verses, or the religious textual analyses, or the suggested prayers. And so it is easy for the Court to lose sight of what the University students and the Court of Appeals found so obvious, and to blanch the patently and frankly evangelistic character of the magazine by unrevealing allusions to religious points of view. . . .

At the heart of the Establishment Clause stands the prohibition against direct public funding, but that prohibition does not answer the questions that occur at the margins of the Clause's application. . . . In the doubtful cases (those not involving direct public funding), where there is initially room for argument about a law's effect, evenhandedness serves to weed out those laws that impermissibly advance religion by channelling aid to it exclusively. Evenhandedness is therefore a prerequisite to further enquiry into the constitutionality of a doubtful law, but evenhandedness goes no further. It does not guarantee success under Establishment Clause scrutiny.

Three cases permitting indirect aid to religion, *Mueller v. Allen*, 463 U.S. 388 (1983), *Witters v. Washington Dept. of Services for the Blind*, 474 U.S. 481 (1986), and *Zobrest v. Catalina Foothills School Dist.*, 509 U.S. 1 (1993), are among the latest of those to illustrate this relevance of evenhandedness when advancement is not so obvious as to be patently unconstitutional. Each case involved a program in which benefits given to individuals on a religion-neutral basis ultimately were used by the individuals, in one way or another, to support religious institutions. In each, the fact that aid was distributed generally and on a neutral basis was a necessary condition for upholding the program at issue. But the significance of evenhandedness stopped there. We did not, in any of these cases, hold that satisfying the condition was sufficient, or dispositive. Even more importantly, we never held that evenhandedness might be sufficient to render direct aid to religion constitutional. Quite the contrary. Critical to our decisions in these cases was the fact that the aid was indirect; it reached religious institutions "only as a result of the genuinely independent and private choices of aid recipients," *Witters.* Thus, our holdings in these cases were little more than extensions of the unremarkable proposition that "a State may issue a paycheck to one of its employees, who may then donate all or part of that paycheck to a religious institution, all without constitutional barrier. . . ." *Witters.* Such "attenuated financial benefits, ultimately controlled by the private choices of individuals," we have found, are simply not within the contemplation of the Establishment Clause's broad prohibition. *Mueller.*

Evenhandedness as one element of a permissibly attenuated benefit is, of course, a far cry from evenhandedness as a sufficient condition of constitutionality for direct financial support of religious proselytization, and our cases have unsurprisingly repudiated any such attempt to cut the Establishment Clause down to a mere prohibition against unequal direct aid. And nowhere has the Court's adherence to the preeminence of the no-direct-funding principle over the principle of evenhandedness been as clear as in *Bowen v. Kendrick,* [487 U.S. 589 (1988)].

Bowen involved consideration of the Adolescent Family Life Act (AFLA), a federal grant program providing funds to institutions for counseling and educational services related to adolescent sexuality and pregnancy. At the time of the litigation, 141 grants had been awarded under the AFLA to a broad array of both secular and religiously affiliated institutions. In an Establishment Clause challenge to the Act brought by taxpayers and other interested parties, the District Court resolved the case on a pre-trial motion for summary judgment, holding the AFLA program unconstitutional both on its face and also insofar as religious institutions were involved in receiving grants under the Act. When this Court reversed on the issue of facial constitutionality under the Establishment Clause, we said that there was "no intimation in the statute that at some point, or for some grantees, religious uses are permitted." On the contrary, after looking at the legislative history and applicable regulations, we found safeguards adequate to ensure that grants would not be "used by . . . grantees in such a way as to advance religion." . . .

Bowen was no sport; its pedigree was the line of *Everson v. Board of Ed., Board of Ed. v. Allen,* [392 U.S. 236 (1968)], *Tilton v. Richardson,* [403 U.S. 672 (1971)], *Hunt v. McNair,* [413 U.S. 734 (1973)], and *Roemer v. Board of Pub. Works of Md.,* [426 U.S. 736 (1976)]. Each of these cases involved a general aid program that provided benefits to a broad array of secular and sectarian institutions on an evenhanded basis, but in none of them was that fact dispositive. . . . Instead, the central enquiry in each of these general aid cases, as in *Bowen,* was whether secular activities could be separated from the sectarian ones sufficiently to ensure that aid would flow to the secular alone.

Witters, Mueller, and *Zobrest* expressly preserve the standard thus exhibited so often. Each of these cases explicitly distinguished the indirect aid in issue from contrasting examples in the line of cases striking down direct aid, and each thereby expressly preserved the core constitutional principle that direct aid to religion is impermissible.

Since conformity with the marginal or limiting principle of evenhandedness is insufficient of itself to demonstrate the constitutionality of providing a government benefit that reaches religion, the Court must identify some further element in the funding scheme that does demonstrate its permissibility. For one reason or another, the Court's chosen element appears to be the fact that under the University's Guidelines, funds are sent to the printer chosen by *Wide Awake*, rather than to *Wide Awake* itself.

If the Court's suggestion is that this feature of the funding program brings this case into line with *Witters, Mueller,* and *Zobrest*, the Court has misread those cases, which turned on the fact that the choice to benefit religion was made by a non-religious third party standing between the government and a religious institution. Here there is no third party standing between the government and the ultimate religious beneficiary to break the circuit by its independent discretion to put state money to religious use. The printer, of course, has no option to take the money and use it to print a secular journal instead of *Wide Awake*. It only gets the money because of its contract to print a message of religious evangelism at the direction of Wide Awake, and it will receive payment only for doing precisely that. The formalism of distinguishing between payment to Wide Awake so it can pay an approved bill and payment of the approved bill itself cannot be the basis of a decision of Constitutional law. . . .

Given the dispositive effect of the Establishment Clause's bar to funding the magazine, there should be no need to decide whether in the absence of this bar the University would violate the Free Speech Clause by limiting funding as it has done. But the Court's speech analysis may have independent application, and its flaws should not pass unremarked. . . .

There is no viewpoint discrimination in the University's application of its Guidelines to deny funding to *Wide Awake*. Under those Guidelines, a "religious activity" which is not eligible for funding is "an activity which primarily promotes or manifests a particular belief(s) in or about a deity or an ultimate reality." It is clear that this is the basis on which Wide Awake Productions was denied funding. The discussion of *Wide Awake*'s content shows beyond any question that it "primarily promotes or manifests a particular belief(s) in or about a deity. . . ," in the very specific sense that its manifest function is to call students to repentance, to commitment to Jesus Christ, and to particular moral action because of its Christian character.

If the Guidelines were written or applied so as to limit only such Christian advocacy and no other evangelical efforts that might compete with it, the discrimination would be based on viewpoint. But that is not what the regulation authorizes; it applies to Muslim and Jewish and Buddhist advocacy as well as to Christian. And since it limits funding to activities promoting or manifesting a particular belief not only "in" but "about" a deity or ultimate reality, it applies to agnostics and atheists as well as it does to deists and theists (as the University maintained at oral argument, and as the Court recognizes). The Guidelines, and their application to *Wide Awake*, thus do not skew debate by funding one position but not its competitors. As understood by their application to *Wide Awake*, they simply deny funding for hortatory speech that "primarily promotes or manifests" any view on the merits of religion; they deny funding for the entire subject matter of religious apologetics.

The Court, of course, reads the Guidelines differently, but while I believe the Court is wrong in construing their breadth, the important point is that even on the Court's own construction the Guidelines impose no viewpoint discrimination. . . .

Even if the Court were indeed correct about the funding restriction's categorical breadth, the stringency of the restriction would most certainly not work any impermissible viewpoint discrimination under any prior understanding of that species of content discrimination. If a University wished to fund no speech beyond the subjects of pasta and cookie preparation, it surely would not be discriminating on the basis of someone's viewpoint, at least absent some controversial claim that pasta and cookies did not exist. The upshot would be an instructional universe without higher education, but not a universe where one viewpoint was enriched above its competitors.

The Guidelines are thus substantially different from the access restriction considered in *Lamb's Chapel*, the case upon which the Court heavily relies in finding a viewpoint distinction here. *Lamb's Chapel* addressed a school board's regulation prohibiting the after-hours use of school premises "by any group for religious purposes," even though the forum otherwise was open for a variety of social, civic, and recreational purposes. "Religious" was understood to refer to the viewpoint of a believer, and the regulation did not purport to deny access to any speaker wishing to express a non-religious or expressly antireligious point of view on any subject.

With this understanding, it was unremarkable that in *Lamb's Chapel* we unanimously determined that the access restriction, as applied to a speaker wishing to discuss family values from a Christian perspective, impermissibly distinguished between speakers on the basis of viewpoint. Equally obvious is the distinction between that case and this one, where the regulation is being applied, not to deny funding for those who discuss issues in general from a religious viewpoint, but to those engaged in promoting or opposing religious conversion and religious observances as such. If this amounts to viewpoint discrimination, the Court has all but eviscerated the line between viewpoint and content.

To put the point another way, the Court's decision equating a categorical exclusion of both sides of the religious debate with viewpoint discrimination suggests the Court has concluded that primarily religious and antireligious speech, grouped together, always provides an opposing (and not merely a related) viewpoint to any speech about any secular topic. Thus, the Court's reasoning requires a university that funds private publications about any primarily nonreligious topic also to fund publications primarily espousing adherence to or rejection of religion. But a university's decision to fund a magazine about racism, and not to fund publications aimed at urging repentance before God, does not skew the debate either about racism or the desirability of religious conversion. The Court's contrary holding amounts to a significant reformulation of our viewpoint discrimination precedents and will significantly expand access to limited-access forums.

Since I cannot see the future I cannot tell whether today's decision portends much more than making a shambles out of student activity fees in public colleges. Still, my apprehension is whetted by Chief Justice Burger's warning in *Lemon v. Kurtzman*, 403 U.S. 602 (1971): "in constitutional adjudication some steps, which when taken were thought to approach 'the verge,' have become the platform for yet further steps. A certain momentum develops in constitutional theory and it can be a 'downhill thrust' easily set in motion but difficult to retard or stop."

I respectfully dissent.

7

THE FOURTH AMENDMENT GUARANTEE AGAINST UNREASONABLE SEARCHES AND SEIZURES

A. REQUIREMENTS FOR A WARRANT AND REASONABLE SEARCHES AND SEIZURES

Although in recent years the Rehnquist Court has sharply limited the scope and application of the Fourth Amendment (see Vol. 2, Ch. 7), the justices drew a line in holding unanimously, in *Wilson v. Arkansas*, 115 S.Ct. 1914 (1995), that when police enter a home armed with search and arrest warrants, they must generally announce their presence and entry. Writing for the Court, however, Justice Thomas declined to set forth a rigid bright-line rule. Instead, he left it for the lower courts to determine under what circumstances police may reasonably enter a house without first knocking and announcing their entry. In Justice Thomas's words:

> At the time of the framing, the common law of search and seizure recognized a law enforcement officer's authority to break open the doors of a dwelling, but generally indicated that he first ought to announce his presence and authority. In this case, we hold that this common-law "knock and announce" principle forms a part of the reasonableness inquiry under the Fourth Amendment. . . .
>
> Our own cases have acknowledged that the common-law principle of announcement is "embedded in Anglo-American law," *Miller v. United States*, 357 U.S. 301 (1958), but we have never squarely held that this principle is an element of the reasonableness inquiry under the Fourth Amendment. We now so hold. . . .

This is not to say, of course, that every entry must be preceded by an announcement. The Fourth Amendment's flexible requirement of reasonableness should not be read to mandate a rigid rule of announcement that ignores countervailing law enforcement interests. . . . [B]ecause the common-law rule was justified in part by the belief that announcement generally would avoid "the destruction or breaking of any house . . . by which great damage and inconvenience might ensue," courts acknowledged that the presumption in favor of announcement would yield under circumstances presenting a threat of physical violence. . . .

We need not attempt a comprehensive catalog of the relevant countervailing factors here. For now, we leave to the lower courts the task of determining the circumstances under which an unannounced entry is reasonable under the Fourth Amendment. We simply hold that although a search or seizure of a dwelling might be constitutionally defective if police officers enter without prior announcement, law enforcement interests may also establish the reasonableness of an unannounced entry. . . .

C. THE SPECIAL PROBLEMS OF AUTOMOBILES IN A MOBILE SOCIETY

The Court unanimously rejected the contention that the standard for traffic stops should not be that of probable cause, but whether "a police officer, acting reasonably, would have made the stop for the reason given," in *Whren v. United States*, 116 S.Ct. 1769 (1996). Plainclothes policemen who were patrolling in an unmarked car a "high drug area" in the District of Columbia stopped Whren and another black man in a truck after they were observed making a sudden turn, without signaling, and then speeding off at an "unreasonable" speed. When the officer approached the truck, he observed Whren holding a bag of crack cocaine and arrested him. At his trial, Whren's attorney sought to suppress the evidence on the ground that the officer did not have probable cause to believe that he was engaged in drug-dealing and that the traffic violation was merely a pretext for stopping the truck. The trial judge rejected that claim and Whren was convicted and sentenced to fourteen years in prison. An appellate court affirmed that decision. Writing for the Court, Justice Scalia reaffirmed that stopping and detaining a motorist upon probable cause that the driver violated traffic laws does not violate the Fourth Amendment, even if a reasonable officer without some additional law enforcement interest would not have stopped the motorist.

In its 1996–1997 term, the Court will decide whether the police may engage in extended questioning of drivers who are stopped for routine traffic violations without making it clear that the motorists are free to leave. Ohio appealed its state supreme court's decision invalidating a search by police of a car that was stopped for speeding. The police officer, after giving the driver back his license, asked if there were any drugs or contraband in the car. The driver said that there was nothing illegal in the car, but gave the officer permission to search the car, which turned up packets of marijuana. In its four-to-three ruling, the Ohio supreme court observed that "most people believe that they are validly in a police officer's custody as long as the officer continues to interrogate them," and therefore would not feel free to leave even when there was no reason to suspect drug possession and no basis for a search. On the basis of the Fourth Amendment's guarantee against unreasonable searches and seizures, the court concluded that "any attempt at consensual interrogation must be preceded by the phrase 'at this time you legally are free to go' or by words of similar import." In its appeal, *Ohio v. Robinette*, the state argues that the validity of such searches or interrogations should turn on an analysis of all of the circumstances, rather than a particular *Miranda*-like verbal formula.

In a related case, *Maryland v. Wilson*, the Court will decide whether police who stop cars for routine traffic violations may order the passengers out of the vehicle. In its appeal, Maryland claims that any intrusion on passengers' liberty is overridden by the state's interest in protecting police from potentially dangerous individuals.

D. OTHER GOVERNMENTAL SEARCHES IN THE ADMINISTRATIVE STATE

An important case involving students' Fourth Amendment rights and random drug testing in public schools was handed down in the 1994–1995 term. The case, *Vernonia School District 47J v. Acton* (excerpted below), appealed a decision of the Ninth Circuit Court of Appeals invalidating a school district's policy requiring all students signing up for interscholastic sports to submit to a drug test and to remain subject to random tests throughout the year. State and lower federal courts had divided on similar challenges to random drug testing in high schools and colleges. And those conflicting rulings have stood because the justices had previously declined to revisit the matter of Fourth Amendment restrictions on drug testing since handing down two rulings in 1989. In *National Treasury Employees Union v. Von Raab*, 489 U.S. 656 (1989) (see Vol. 2, Ch. 7), a bare majority approved a federal drug-testing program for public employees, and by a six-to-three vote upheld mandatory drug tests for railroad workers involved in serious accidents in *Skinner v. Railway Labor Executives' Association*, 489 U.S. 602 (1989). By a six-to-three vote in *Vernonia School District*, the Rehnquist Court reversed the lower court's decision and upheld the school district's drug-testing policy.

Vernonia School District 47J v. Acton
115 S.Ct. 2386 (1995)

The parents of James Acton, a twelve-year-old seventh-grader with no indication of drug use, challenged the constitutionality of the Vernonia School District's drug-testing policy for students participating in school athletic programs. Teachers and school officials in Vernonia, a small logging community in Oregon, noticed a sharp increase in drug use and disciplinary problems in the late 1980s. Between 1988 and 1989, for instance, the number of disciplinary referrals doubled that reported in the early 1980s. In addition, school officials later testified during the trial that student athletes were not only among the drug users but were leaders of the drug culture. As a result, in the fall of 1989, the school board approved a drug-testing policy under which athletes had to sign a form consenting to drug testing and obtain the written consent of their parents. At the beginning of each season, every student athlete was tested for drugs. Throughout the season, then, ten percent of the student athletes were randomly tested each week.

A federal district court rejected the Actons' claim that the school district's policy of random drug testing violated the Fourth Amendment's guarantee against "unreasonable searches and seizures." But the Court of Appeals for the Ninth Circuit reversed and school officials appealed to the Supreme Court.

The Court's decision was six to three and opinion delivered by Justice Scalia. Justice O'Connor filed a dissenting opinion, which was joined by Justices Stevens and Souter.

Justice SCALIA delivered the opinion of the Court.

The Fourth Amendment to the United States Constitution provides that the Federal Government shall not violate "the right of the people to be secure in their persons, houses, papers, and effects, against unreasonable searches and seizures. . . ." We have held that the Fourteenth Amendment extends this constitutional guarantee to searches and seizures by state officers, including public school officials, *New Jersey v. T. L. O.*, 469 U.S. 325 (1985). In *Skinner v. Railway Labor Executives' Assn.*, 489 U.S. 602 (1989), we held that state-compelled collection and testing of urine, such as that required by the Student Athlete Drug Policy, constitutes a "search" subject to the demands of the Fourth Amendment. See also [*National Treasury Employees Union*] v. *Von Raab*, 489 U.S. 656 (1989).

As the text of the Fourth Amendment indicates, the ultimate measure of the constitutionality of a governmental search is "reasonableness." At least in a case such as this, where there was no clear practice, either approving or disapproving the type of search at issue, at the time the constitutional provision was enacted, whether a particular search meets the reasonableness standard "'is judged by balancing its intrusion on the individual's Fourth

Amendment interests against its promotion of legitimate governmental interests.'" *Skinner*. . . . A search unsupported by probable cause can be constitutional, we have said, "when special needs, beyond the normal need for law enforcement, make the warrant and probable-cause requirement impracticable." *Griffin v. Wisconsin*, 483 U.S. 868 (1987).

We have found such "special needs" to exist in the public-school context. There, the warrant requirement "would unduly interfere with the maintenance of the swift and informal disciplinary procedures [that are] needed," and "strict adherence to the requirement that searches be based upon probable cause" would undercut "the substantial need of teachers and administrators for freedom to maintain order in the schools." *T. L. O.* The school search we approved in *T. L. O.*, while not based on probable cause, was based on individualized suspicion of wrongdoing. As we explicitly acknowledged, however, "the Fourth Amendment imposes no irreducible requirement of such suspicion." We have upheld suspicionless searches and seizures to conduct drug testing of railroad personnel involved in train accidents, *Skinner*; to conduct random drug testing of federal customs officers who carry arms or are involved in drug interdiction, *Von Raab*; and to maintain automobile checkpoints looking for illegal immigrants and contraband, and drunk drivers, *Michigan Dept. of State Police v. Sitz*, 496 U.S. 444 (1990).

The first factor to be considered is the nature of the privacy interest upon which the search here at issue intrudes. The Fourth Amendment does not protect all subjective expectations of privacy, but only those that society recognizes as "legitimate." What expectations are legitimate varies, of course, with context, depending, for example, upon whether the individual asserting the privacy interest is at home, at work, in a car, or in a public park. In addition, the legitimacy of certain privacy expectations vis-à-vis the State may depend upon the individual's legal relationship with the State. . . . Central, in our view, to the present case is the fact that the subjects of the Policy are (1) children, who (2) have been committed to the temporary custody of the State as schoolmaster. . . .

Fourth Amendment rights, no less than First and Fourteenth Amendment rights, are different in public schools than elsewhere; the "reasonableness" inquiry cannot disregard the schools' custodial and tutelary responsibility for children. For their own good and that of their classmates, public school children are routinely required to submit to various physical examinations, and to be vaccinated against various diseases. . . .

Legitimate privacy expectations are even less with regard to student athletes. School sports are not for the bashful. They require "suiting up" before each practice or event, and showering and changing afterwards. Public school locker rooms, the usual sites for these activities, are not notable for the privacy they afford. The locker rooms in Vernonia are typical: no individual dressing rooms are provided; shower heads are lined up along a wall, unseparated by any sort of partition or curtain; not even all the toilet stalls have doors. . . .

There is an additional respect in which school athletes have a reduced expectation of privacy. By choosing to "go out for the team," they voluntarily subject themselves to a degree of regulation even higher than that imposed on students generally. In Vernonia's public schools, they must submit to a preseason physical exam (James testified that his included the giving of a urine sample), they must acquire adequate insurance coverage or sign an insurance waiver, maintain a minimum grade point average, and comply with any "rules of conduct, dress, training hours and related matters as may be established for each sport by the head coach and athletic director with the principal's approval." . . .

Finally, we turn to consider the nature and immediacy of the governmental concern at issue here, and the efficacy of this means for meeting it. In both *Skinner* and *Von Raab*, we characterized the government interest motivating the search as "compelling." . . . It is a mistake, however, to think that the phrase "compelling state interest," in the Fourth Amendment context, describes a fixed, minimum quantum of governmental concern, so that one can dispose of a case by answering in isolation the question: Is there a compelling state interest here? Rather, the phrase describes an interest which appears important enough to justify the particular search at hand, in light of other factors which show the search to be relatively intrusive upon a genuine expectation of privacy. Whether that relatively high degree of government concern is necessary in this case or not, we think it is met.

That the nature of the concern is important—indeed, perhaps compelling—can hardly be doubted. Deterring drug use by our Nation's schoolchildren is at least as important as enhancing efficient enforcement of the Nation's laws against the importation of drugs, which was the governmental concern in *Von Raab*, or deterring drug use by engineers and trainmen, which was the governmental concern in *Skinner*. . . .

Taking into account all the factors we have considered above—the decreased expectation of privacy, the relative unobtrusiveness of the search, and the severity of the need met by the search—we conclude Vernonia's Policy is reasonable and hence constitutional. . . .

Justice O'CONNOR, with whom Justice STEVENS and Justice SOUTER join, dissenting.

The population of our Nation's public schools, grades 7 through 12, numbers around 18 million. By the reasoning of today's decision, the millions of these students who participate in interscholastic sports, an overwhelming majority of whom have given school officials no reason whatsoever to suspect they use drugs at school, are open to an intrusive bodily search.

In justifying this result, the Court dispenses with a requirement of individualized suspicion on considered policy grounds. First, it explains that precisely because every student athlete is being tested, there is no concern that school officials might act arbitrarily in choosing who to test. Second, a broad-based search regime, the Court reasons, dilutes the accusatory nature of the search. In making these policy arguments, of course, the Court sidesteps powerful, countervailing privacy concerns. Blanket searches, because they can involve "thousands or millions" of searches, "pose a greater threat to liberty" than do suspicion-based ones, which "affect one person at a time," *Illinois v. Krull*, 480 U.S. 340 (1987) (O'CONNOR, J., dissenting). Searches based on individualized suspicion also afford potential targets considerable control over whether they will, in fact, be searched because a person can avoid such a search by not acting in an objectively suspicious way. And given that the surest way to avoid acting suspiciously is to avoid the underlying wrongdoing, the costs of such a regime, one would think, are minimal.

But whether a blanket search is "better" than a regime based on individualized suspicion is not a debate in which we should engage. In my view, it is not open to judges or government officials to decide on policy grounds which is better and which is worse. For most of our constitutional history, mass, suspicionless searches have been generally considered per se unreasonable within the meaning of the Fourth Amendment. And we have allowed exceptions in recent years only where it has been clear that a suspicion-based regime would be ineffectual. Because that is not the case here, I dissent.

In *Carroll v. United States*, 267 U.S. 132 (1925), the Court explained that "the Fourth Amendment does not denounce all searches or seizures, but only such as are unreasonable." Applying this standard, the Court first held that a search of a car was not unreasonable merely because it was warrantless; because obtaining a warrant is impractical for an easily movable object such as a car, the Court explained, a warrant is not required. The Court also held, however, that a warrantless car search was unreasonable unless supported by some level of individualized suspicion, namely probable cause. Significantly, the Court did not base its conclusion on the express probable cause requirement contained in the Warrant Clause, which, as just noted, the Court found inapplicable. Rather, the Court rested its views on "what was deemed an unreasonable search and seizure when [the Fourth Amendment] was adopted" and "[what] will conserve public interests as well as the interests and rights of individual citizens." . . .

The *Carroll* Court's view that blanket searches are "intolerable and unreasonable" is well-grounded in history. . . . [W]hat the Framers of the Fourth Amendment most strongly opposed, with limited exceptions wholly inapplicable here, were general searches—that is, searches by general warrant, by writ of assistance, by broad statute, or by any other similar authority. . . .

The view that mass, suspicionless searches, however evenhanded, are generally unreasonable remains inviolate in the criminal law enforcement context, see *Ybarra v. Illinois*, 444 U.S. 85 (1979) (invalidating evenhanded, nonaccusatory patdown for weapons of all patrons in a tavern in which there was probable cause to think drug dealing was going on), at least where the search is more than minimally intrusive, see *Michigan Dept. of State Police v. Sitz*, 496 U.S. 444 (1990) (upholding the brief and easily avoidable detention, for purposes of observing signs of intoxication, of all motorists approaching a roadblock). . . .

Thus, it remains the law that the police cannot, say, subject to drug testing every person entering or leaving a certain drug-ridden neighborhood in order to find evidence of crime. And this is true even though it is hard to think of a more compelling government interest than the need to fight the scourge of drugs on our streets and in our neighborhoods. Nor could it be otherwise, for if being evenhanded were enough to justify evaluating a search regime under an open-ended balancing test, the Warrant Clause, which presupposes that there is some category of searches for which individualized suspicion is non-negotiable, would be a dead letter. . . .

One searches today's majority opinion in vain for recognition that history and precedent establish that individualized suspicion is "usually required" under the Fourth Amendment (regardless of whether a warrant and probable cause are also required) and that, in the area of intrusive personal searches, the only recognized exception is for situations in which a suspicion-based scheme would be likely ineffectual. Far from acknowledging anything special about individualized suspicion, the Court treats a suspicion-based regime as if it were just any run-of-the-mill, less intrusive alternative—that is, an alternative that officials may bypass if the lesser intrusion, in their reasonable estimation, is outweighed by policy concerns unrelated to practicability. . . .

The great irony of this case is that most (though not all) of the evidence the District introduced to justify its suspicionless drug-testing program consisted of first- or secondhand stories of particular, identifiable students acting in ways that plainly gave rise to reasonable suspicion of in-school drug use—and thus that would have justified a drug-related search under our *T. L. O.* decision. Small groups of students, for example, were observed by a teacher "passing joints back and forth" across the street at a restaurant before school and during school hours. Another group was caught skipping school and using drugs at one of the student's houses. Several students actually admitted their drug use to school officials (some of them being caught with marijuana pipes). . . .

In light of all this evidence of drug use by particular students, there is a substantial basis for concluding that a vigorous regime of suspicion-based testing would have gone a long way toward solving Vernonia's school drug problem while preserving the Fourth Amendment rights of James Acton and others like him. . . .

I recognize that a suspicion-based scheme, even where reasonably effective in controlling in-school drug use, may not be as effective as a mass, suspicionless testing regime. In one sense, that is obviously true—just as it is obviously true that suspicion-based law enforcement is not as effective as mass, suspicionless enforcement might be. "But there is nothing new in the realization" that Fourth Amendment protections come with a price. *Arizona v. Hicks*, 480 U.S. 321 (1987). . . .

I find unpersuasive the Court's reliance on the widespread practice of physical examinations and vaccinations, which are both blanket searches of a sort. . . . [I]t is worth noting that a suspicion requirement for vaccinations is not merely impractical; it is nonsensical, for vaccinations are not searches for anything in particular and so there is nothing about which to be suspicious. . . . It might also be noted that physical exams (and of course vaccinations) are not searches for conditions that reflect wrongdoing on the part of the student, and so are wholly nonaccusatory and have no consequences that can be regarded as punitive. These facts may explain the absence of Fourth Amendment challenges to such searches. By contrast, . . . any testing program that searches for conditions plainly reflecting serious wrongdoing can never be made wholly nonaccusatory from the student's perspective, the motives for the program notwithstanding; and for the same reason, the substantial consequences that can flow from a positive test, such as suspension from sports, are invariably—and quite reasonably—understood as punishment. . . .

I do not believe that suspicionless drug testing is justified on these facts. But even if I agreed that some such testing were reasonable here, I see two other Fourth Amendment flaws in the District's program. First, and most serious, there is virtually no evidence in the record of a drug problem at the Washington Grade School, which includes the 7th and 8th grades, and which Acton attended when this litigation began. . . . Second, even as to the high school, I find unreasonable the school's choice of student athletes as the class to subject to suspicionless testing—a choice that appears to have been driven more by a belief in what would pass constitutional muster than by a belief in what was required to meet the District's principal disciplinary concern. Reading the full record in this case, as well as the District Court's authoritative summary of it, it seems quite obvious that the true driving force behind the District's adoption of its drug-testing program was the need to combat the rise in drug-related disorder and disruption in its classrooms and around campus. I mean no criticism of the strength of that interest. On the contrary, where the record demonstrates the existence of such a problem, that interest seems self-evidently compelling. . . . The evidence of a drug-related sports injury problem at Vernonia, by contrast, was considerably weaker.

On this record, then, it seems to me that the far more reasonable choice would have been to focus on the class of students found to have violated published school rules against severe disruption in class and around campus —disruption that had a strong nexus to drug use, as the District established at trial. Such a choice would share two of the virtues of a suspicion-based regime: testing dramatically fewer students, tens as against hundreds, and giving students control, through their behavior, over the likelihood that they would be tested. . . .

Having reviewed the record here, I cannot avoid the conclusion that the District's suspicionless policy of testing all student-athletes sweeps too broadly, and too imprecisely, to be reasonable under the Fourth Amendment.

F. THE EXCLUSIONARY RULE

The Burger Court recognized a "good faith" exception to the Fourth Amendment's exclusionary rule, which otherwise requires evidence illegally obtained by police to be excluded at trial, in *United States v. Leon*, 468 U.S. 897 (1984), and *Massachusetts v. Sheppard*, 468 U.S. 981 (1984) (see Vol. 2, Ch. 7). While the Court in those and subsequent cases was urged to abandon the exclusionary rule in its entirety, in the following decade the justices have declined to do so. However, in *Arizona v. Evans* (excerpted below), the Court confronted the question of extending the "good faith" exception in a case with a technological twist brought by law enforcement's increased reliance on computerized information. By a seven-to-two vote, the Rehnquist

Court extended the "good faith" exception to the exclusionary rule to include police reliance on mistaken computer records of outstanding arrest warrants.

Arizona v. Evans
115 S.Ct. 1185 (1995)

After stopping the driver of a car going in the wrong direction on a one-way street, the Phoenix police checked their squad car computer and found that the driver had an outstanding arrest warrant, which in fact had been canceled seventeen days earlier but not entered into the police department's computerized records. Based on that mistaken finding of an outstanding warrant for the driver's arrest, the police searched the car and discovered marijuana. Subsequently, the Arizona supreme court held that the marijuana could not be introduced as evidence and refused to apply the "good faith" exception to the exclusionary rule. In the state supreme court's words, "As automation increasingly invades modern life, the potential for Orwellian mischief grows. Under such circumstances, the exclusionary rule is a 'cost' we cannot afford to be without." The state subsequently appealed that ruling and the Supreme Court granted review.

The Court's decision was seven to two and the opinion was written by Chief Justice Rehnquist. Justices O'Connor and Souter filed concurring opinions, which Justice Breyer joined. Justices Stevens and Ginsburg filed dissenting opinions.

CHIEF JUSTICE REHNQUIST delivered the opinion of the Court.

"The question whether the exclusionary rule's remedy is appropriate in a particular context has long been regarded as an issue separate from the question whether the Fourth Amendment rights of the party seeking to invoke the rule were violated by police conduct." *Illinois v. Gates*, 462 U.S. 213 (1983). The exclusionary rule operates as a judicially created remedy designed to safeguard against future violations of Fourth Amendment rights through the rule's general deterrent effect. As with any remedial device, the rule's application has been restricted to those instances where its remedial objectives are thought most efficaciously served. Where "the exclusionary rule does not result in appreciable deterrence, then, clearly, its use . . . is unwarranted." *United States v. Janis*, 428 U.S. 433 (1976).

In [*United States v.*] *Leon*, [468 U.S. 897 (1984)], we applied these principles to the context of a police search in which the officers had acted in objectively reasonable reliance on a search warrant, issued by a neutral and detached Magistrate, that later was determined to be invalid. On the basis of three factors, we determined that there was no sound reason to apply the exclusionary rule as a means of deterring misconduct on the part of judicial officers who are responsible for issuing warrants. *Illinois v. Krull*, 480 U.S. 340 (1987). First, we noted that the exclusionary rule was historically designed "to deter police misconduct rather than to punish the errors of judges and magistrates." Second, there was "no evidence suggesting that judges and magistrates are inclined to ignore or subvert the Fourth Amendment or that lawlessness among these actors requires the application of the extreme sanction of exclusion." Third, and of greatest importance, there was no basis for believing that exclusion of evidence seized pursuant to a warrant would have a significant deterrent effect on the issuing judge or magistrate. . . .

Applying the reasoning of *Leon* to the facts of this case, we conclude that the decision of the Arizona Supreme Court must be reversed. The Arizona Supreme Court['s] . . . holding is contrary to the reasoning of *Leon*. If court employees were responsible for the erroneous computer record, the exclusion of evidence at trial would not sufficiently deter future errors so as to warrant such a severe sanction. First, as we noted in *Leon*, the exclusionary rule was historically designed as a means of deterring police misconduct, not mistakes by court employees. Second, respondent offers no evidence that court employees are inclined to ignore or subvert the Fourth Amendment or that lawlessness among these actors requires application of the extreme sanction of exclusion. To the contrary, the Chief Clerk of the Justice Court testified at the suppression hearing that this type of error occurred once every three or four years.

Finally, and most important, there is no basis for believing that application of the exclusionary rule in these circumstances will have a significant effect on court employees responsible for informing the police that a warrant has been quashed. Because court clerks are not adjuncts to the law enforcement team engaged in the often competitive enterprise of ferreting out crime, they have no stake in the outcome of particular criminal prosecutions. The threat of exclusion of evidence could not be expected to deter such individuals from failing to inform police officials that a warrant had been quashed. . . .

Justice STEVENS, dissenting.

The Court seems to assume that the Fourth Amendment—and particularly the exclusionary rule, which effectuates the Amendment's commands—has the limited purpose of deterring police misconduct. Both the constitutional text and the history of its adoption and interpretation identify a more majestic conception. . . . The Fourth Amendment's Warrant Clause provides the fundamental check on official invasions of the individual's right to privacy. *Leon* stands for the dubious but limited proposition that courts should not look behind the face of a warrant on which police have relied in good faith. . . .

The Phoenix Police Department was part of the chain of information that resulted in petitioner's unlawful, warrantless arrest. We should reasonably presume that law enforcement officials, who stand in the best position to monitor such errors as occurred here, can influence mundane communication procedures in order to prevent those errors. That presumption comports with the notion that the exclusionary rule exists to deter future police misconduct systemically. The deterrent purpose extends to law enforcement as a whole, not merely to "the arresting officer." Consequently, the Phoenix officers' good faith does not diminish the deterrent value of invalidating their arrest of petitioner. . . .

[O]ne consequence of the Court's holding seems immediately obvious. Its most serious impact will be on the otherwise innocent citizen who is stopped for a minor traffic infraction and is wrongfully arrested based on erroneous information in a computer data base. . . . [I]f courts are to have any power to discourage official error of this kind, it must be through application of the exclusionary rule. . . . I respectfully dissent.

8

THE FIFTH AMENDMENT GUARANTEE AGAINST SELF-ACCUSATION

OVER THE YEARS the Court has handed down conflicting rulings on when a person is technically "in custody" and hence entitled to *Miranda* warnings and, in the absence of those warnings, entitled to have incriminating statements made during police questioning excluded as evidence at trial (see Vol. 2, Ch. 8). As a result, police have been generally given a freer hand in interrogating individuals. But shortly after hearing oral arguments in *Stansbury v. California*, 114 S.Ct. 1526 (1994), the Supreme Court unanimously drew a line at lower courts' allowing police officers' subjective views, in contrast to objective factors, to determine when a person is "in custody" for the purposes of *Miranda*.

Mr. Stansbury had responded to a knock on his door by police who were investigating a homicide and agreed to accompany them to the police station for questioning. At the station, Stansbury was questioned about his activities without being given his *Miranda* warnings, and said that he had last seen the victim about midnight when he had left the victim's trailer in his housemate's turquoise American-made car. That last detail aroused the police's suspicions, since a turquoise car had been identified as associated with the homicide. When Stansbury admitted, in response to further questioning, that he had prior convictions for rape, kidnapping, and child molestation, the police terminated their questioning and advised Stansbury of his *Miranda* rights. Stansbury thereafter declined to answer further questions, requested an attorney, and was subsequently arrested and charged with first-degree murder. His attorney later filed a pre-trial motion to suppress all of the statements he had made at the station house. But the trial court denied that motion on the ground that Stansbury was not "in custody" at the time of his questioning and therefore not entitled to *Miranda* warnings. The California state supreme court agreed and Stansbury appealed that ruling to the Supreme Court.

In a brief *per curiam* opinion reversing the state court's ruling, the Rehnquist Court held,

Our decisions make clear that the initial determination of custody depends on the objective circumstances of the interrogation, not on the subjective views harbored by either the interrogating officers or the person being questioned. In *Beckwith v. United States*, 425 U.S. 341 (1976), for example, the defendant, without being advised of his *Miranda* rights, made incriminating statements to Government agents during an interview in a private home. He later asked that *Miranda* "be extended to cover interrogation in non-custodial circumstances after a police investigation has focused on the suspect." We found his argument unpersuasive, explaining that it "was the compulsive aspect of custodial interrogation, and not the strength or content of the government's suspicions at the time the questioning was conducted, which led the Court to impose *Miranda* requirements with regard to custodial questioning." As a result, we concluded that the defendant was not entitled to *Miranda* warnings. . . .

It is well settled, then, that a police officer's subjective view that the individual under questioning is a suspect, if undisclosed, does not bear upon the question whether the individual is in custody for purposes of *Miranda*. The same principle obtains if an officer's undisclosed assessment is that the person being questioned is not a suspect. In either instance, one cannot expect the person under interrogation to probe the officer's innermost thoughts. Save as they are communicated or otherwise manifested to the person being questioned, an officer's evolving but unarticulated suspicions do not affect the objective circumstances of an interrogation or interview, and thus cannot affect the *Miranda* custody inquiry.

In another *Miranda*-related case, *Davis v. United States*, 114 S.Ct. 2350 (1994), the Court was asked to clarify what constitutes a suspect's request for an attorney and whether police must stop their questioning at the suspect's request. Robert L. Davis, a Navy sailor who was accused of murdering a man who refused to pay off a pool wager, was handcuffed to a chair during an interrogation about his whereabouts at the time of the murder. At the outset of the interrogation, Davis was informed of his *Miranda* rights but said that he did not need a lawyer. Subsequently, when told that his girlfriend had contradicted his account of where he was the night of the murder, and reminded that he had earlier admitted winning thirty dollars in a pool game with the victim, Davis said, "Maybe I should talk to a lawyer." When the questioning continued and agents sought to clarify whether he really wanted a lawyer, Davis then again contradicted his earlier request. As a result, some incriminating statements made during his interrogation were used against him at trial, and the U.S. Court of Military Appeals held that the interrogation was proper and upheld the use of self-incriminating statements.

Writing for the Court, Justice O'Connor affirmed the lower court's ruling and held that Davis's statement was not a request for counsel and that the officers were not required to seek further clarification of his statement (which they had in any event). In O'Connor's words:

> The right to counsel in *Miranda* is sufficiently important to suspects in criminal investigations, we have held, that it "requires the special protection of the knowing and intelligent waiver standard." *Edwards v. Arizona*, 451 U.S. [477 (1981)]. If the suspect effectively waives his right to counsel after receiving *Miranda* warnings, law enforcement officers are free to question him. *North Carolina v. Butler*, 441 U.S. 369 (1979). But if a suspect requests counsel at any time during the interview, he is not subject to further questioning until a lawyer has been made available or the suspect himself reinitiates conversation. . . .
>
> We decline petitioner's invitation to extend *Edwards* and require law enforcement officers to cease questioning immediately upon the making of an ambiguous or equivocal reference to an attorney. The rationale underlying *Edwards* is that the police must respect a suspect's wishes regarding his right to have an attorney present during custodial interrogation. But when the officers conducting the questioning reasonably do not know whether or not the suspect wants a lawyer, a rule requiring the immediate cessation of questioning "would transform the *Miranda* safeguards into wholly irrational obstacles to legitimate police investigative activity," *Michigan v. Mosley*, 423 U.S. 96 (1975), because it would needlessly prevent the police from questioning a suspect in the absence of counsel even if the suspect did not wish to have a lawyer present. Nothing in *Edwards* requires the provision of counsel to a suspect who consents to answer questions without the assistance of a lawyer. In *Miranda* itself, we expressly rejected the suggestion "that each police station must have a 'station house lawyer' present at all times to advise prisoners," and held instead that a suspect must be told of his right to have an attorney present and that he may not be questioned after invoking his right to counsel. We also noted that if a suspect is "indecisive in his request for counsel," the officers need not always cease questioning.
>
> We recognize that requiring a clear assertion of the right to counsel might disadvantage some suspects who—because of fear, intimidation, lack of linguistic skills, or a variety of other reasons—will not clearly articulate their right to counsel although they actually want to have a lawyer present. But the primary protection afforded suspects subject to custodial interrogation is the *Miranda* warnings themselves.

Separate concurrences were filed by Justices Scalia and Souter. Justices Blackmun, Stevens, and Ginsburg joined Justice Souter's concurring opinion, which objected to O'Connor's suggestion that the police could have disregarded Davis's statement without seeking further clarification of whether he wanted an attorney.

In its 1995 term, by a seven-to-two vote in *Thompson v. Keohane*, 116 S.Ct. — (1995), the justices reaffirmed that federal courts should independently review the question of whether a suspect was technically "in custody," and therefore entitled to *Miranda* warnings, at the time of confessing to a crime. Carl Thompson was asked to go the Alaska state troopers' headquarters in Fairbanks, Alaska, to answer questions about his former wife, who was found stabbed to death. After arriving there, he was questioned for two hours, without the benefit of being told his *Miranda* rights. Upon the troopers telling him that they were obtaining a warrant to search his home and truck, Thompson confessed. However, he was also told that he could leave and, because the troopers impounded his truck, he accepted their offer to drive him to a friend's house, where two hours later they arrested him and charged Thompson with first-degree murder. The trial court denied Thompson's motion to suppress his confession on the ground that he was not "in custody" for *Miranda* purposes. A state appellate court affirmed his conviction and the Alaska supreme court denied review. Thompson then filed a petition for a writ of *habeas corpus* in federal district, but that court denied the writ because it deemed the issue of whether he was "in custody" to be a factual question for the trial court. That decision was affirmed by the Court of Appeals for the Ninth Circuit, but vacated on appeal by the Supreme Court. Writing for the majority, Justice Ginsburg held that the question of whether a suspect is "in custody" for the purposes of *Miranda* is a "mixed question of law and fact" meriting independent review. Justice Thomas, joined by Chief Justice Rehnquist, dissented.

9

THE RIGHTS TO COUNSEL
AND OTHER PROCEDURAL
GUARANTEES

D. THE RIGHT TO AN IMPARTIAL JURY TRIAL

Duncan v. Louisiana, 391 U.S. 145 (1968) (in Vol. 2, Ch. 4), made
the Sixth Amendment right to a jury trial in all nonpetty cases applicable to the states. Petty cases were defined in *Baldwin v. New York*, 399
U.S. 66 (1970), as those carrying a potential sentence of six months' or
less imprisonment. However, in *Lewis v. United States*, 116 S.Ct. —
(1996), the Court held that a defendant has no Sixth Amendment right
to a jury trial when prosecuted in a single proceeding for multiple petty
offenses—offenses that each carry a maximum of six or less months—
even though the aggregate prison term exceeds six months. Writing for
the Court, Justice O'Connor held that, "The Sixth Amendment's
guarantee of the right to a jury trial does not extend to petty offenses,
and its scope does not change where a defendant faces a potential
aggregate prison term in excess of six months for petty offenses
charged." Although agreeing with the Court's decision, Justice
Kennedy filed a concurring opinion, joined by Justice Breyer, that
lamented, "The holding both in its doctrinal formulation and in its
practical effect is one of the most serious incursions on the right to jury
trial in the Court's history, and it cannot be squared with our
precedents." Joined by Justice Ginsburg, however, dissenting Justice
Stevens countered that, "the legislature's determination of the severity
of the charges against a defendant is properly measured by the maximum sentence authorized for the prosecution as a whole. The text of the
Sixth Amendment supports this interpretation by referring expressly to
'criminal prosecutions.'"

G. THE GUARANTEE AGAINST DOUBLE JEOPARDY

Over the last decade the Court has been reconsidering the scope of the Fifth Amendment's bar against being held in double jeopardy for the same offense, and thereby invited the litigation of such claims. In *Schiro v. Farley*, 114 S.Ct. 783 (1994), a majority of the Rehnquist Court declined an invitation to apply the double jeopardy clause to the sentencing stage of a capital case and on that basis to vacate Thomas Schiro's death sentence. Only dissenting Justices Blackmun and Stevens thought otherwise, as the latter explained:

> The jury found Thomas Schiro guilty of felony murder but not intentional murder. Thereafter, in a separate sentencing hearing, the same jury unanimously concluded that Schiro did not deserve the death penalty, presumably because he had not intended to kill. Nevertheless, without finding any aggravating circumstance, the trial judge overrode the jury's recommendation and sentenced Schiro to death. Months later, when the Indiana Supreme Court remanded the case to give the judge an opportunity to justify that sentence, the judge found that Schiro had intentionally killed his victim. That finding, like the majority's holding today, violated the central purpose of the Double Jeopardy Clause. After the issue of intent had been raised at trial and twice resolved by the jury, and long after that jury had been discharged, it was constitutionally impermissible for the trial judge to reexamine the issue. Because the death sentence rests entirely on that unauthorized finding, the law requires that it be set aside.

By contrast, writing for the majority in *Schiro,* Justice O'Connor observed that,

> Schiro urges us to treat the sentencing phase of a single prosecution as a successive prosecution for purposes of the Double Jeopardy Clause. We decline to do so. Our prior decisions are inconsistent with the argument that a first sentencing proceeding can amount to a successive prosecution. In *Stroud v. United States,* 251 U.S. 15 (1919), we held that where a defendant's murder conviction was overturned on appeal, the defendant could be resentenced after retrial. Similarly, we found no constitutional infirmity in holding a second sentencing hearing where the first sentence was improperly based on a prior conviction for which the defendant had been pardoned. *Lockhart v. Nelson,* 488 U.S. 33 (1988). If a second sentencing proceeding ordinarily does not violate the double jeopardy clause, we fail to see how an initial sentencing proceeding could do so.
>
> We have also upheld the use of prior convictions to enhance sentences for subsequent convictions, even though this means a defendant must, in a certain sense, relitigate in a sentencing proceeding conduct for which he was previously tried. *Spenser v. Texas,* 385 U.S. 554 (1967). In short, as applied to successive prosecutions, the Clause "is written in terms of potential or risk of trial and conviction, not punishment." *Pierce v. Georgia,* 398 U.S. 323 (1970).

In another ruling on the scope of the double jeopardy clause, the justices split five to four when striking down Montana's tax on illegal drugs in *Department of Revenue of Montana v. Kurth Ranch*, 114 S.Ct. 1937 (1994). Along with more than twenty other states, Montana imposed a tax on illegal drugs confiscated in drug raids. Montana's statute assessed a tax of $100 per ounce on marijuana plants and defended it as a fund-raising, not a punitive, measure. But the tax was challenged for constituting a form of double jeopardy, since it imposed an additional penalty inflicted on those convicted of possessing illegal drugs and thus unconstitutionally punished people twice for the same offense. Writing for a bare majority, Justice Stevens rejected Montana's claim that its tax was simply a revenue-raising measure. "This tax, imposed on criminals and no others, departs so far from normal revenue laws as to become a form of punishment," said Justice Stevens, who further added that,

> As a general matter, the unlawfulness of an activity does not prevent its taxation. Montana, no doubt, could collect its tax on the possession of marijuana, for example, if it had not previously punished the taxpayer for the same offense, or, indeed, if it had assessed the tax in the same proceeding that resulted in his conviction. . . . [But] this drug tax is a concoction of anomalies, too far removed in crucial respects from a standard tax assessment to escape characterization as punishment for the purpose of double jeopardy analysis.

The four dissenters, however, took strong exception to Justice Stevens's analysis. Noting that a number of states had enacted similar laws in their "war on drugs," dissenting Justice O'Connor charged that the ruling "will be felt acutely by law-abiding taxpayers, because it will seriously undermine the ability of the state and federal governments to collect recompense for the immense costs criminals impose on our society." In a separate dissenting opinion, Chief Justice Rehnquist countered that Montana's tax was comparable to other valid "sin taxes," such as those imposed on alcohol and cigarettes, which aim at raising money and discouraging certain kinds of behavior. In a third dissenting opinion, joined by Justice Thomas, Justice Scalia dismissed flat out the majority's analysis. The Fifth Amendment's double jeopardy clause, he maintained, should apply only to successive prosecutions, not successive punishments.

In its 1994–1995 term, the Court held that the double jeopardy clause does not bar prosecution for a crime even though the same criminal conduct was previously used to raise the defendant's prison sentence for a different offense. Steven Witte was indicted on marijuana charges after he was caught in a sting operation. Under federal sentencing guidelines, a judge may consider other "relevant conduct" when determining a sentence. Witte would have been eligible for six to eight years in prison on his conviction for selling marijuana. But a federal district judge held that Witte's additional cocaine transactions (for which he had not yet been but would subsequently be charged) could be considered in sentencing and thereby made him eligible for twenty years' imprisonment. Writing for the majority in *Witte v. United States*, 115 S.Ct. 2199 (1995), Justice O'Connor found no violation of the guarantee against double jeopardy. Only dissenting Justice Stevens objected that the majority's ruling "weakens the fundamental protections [of] the double jeopardy clause."

Finally, in 1995–1996 term and in spite of its earlier ruling in *Kurth Ranch*, the Court held that civil forfeiture proceedings, which since the 1980s have become common for defendants criminally convicted for drug-trafficking, do not violate the double jeopardy clause when the defendant has also been tried for the same offense on criminal charges. Writing for the Court in *United States v. Ursery*, 116 S.Ct. — (1996), Chief Justice Rehnquist held simply that civil forfeitures "do not constitute 'punishment' for purposes of the Double Jeopardy Clause."

I. INDIGENTS AND THE CRIMINAL JUSTICE SYSTEM

Writing for the Court in *Lewis v. Casey*, 116 S.Ct. — (1996), Justice Scalia reinterpreted the ruling handed down in *Bounds v. Smith*, 430 U.S. 817 (1977), to limit prison inmates' standing to sue and federal courts' remedial powers to order changes in prison law libraries and legal assistance programs so as to require fully adequate libraries and facilitate inmates' "right of access to the courts." In a concurrence, Justice Thomas questioned the basis for the ruling in *Bounds* that prisons must provide inmates with libraries so that they may make a "meaningful appeal." Justice Souter, joined by Justices Ginsburg and Breyer, filed an opinion in part concurring and in part dissenting, while Justice Stevens dissented.

10

CRUEL AND UNUSUAL PUNISHMENT

A. NONCAPITAL PUNISHMENT

While the Rehnquist Court was rather bitterly divided in rulings extending the scope of the Eighth Amendment's cruel and unusual punishment clause to conditions of imprisonment and the treatment of prisoners (see *Wilson v. Seiter*, 501 U.S. 298 (1991), and *Hudson v. McMillian*, 502 U.S. 1 (1992) in Vol. 2, Ch. 10), the justices unanimously reinstated a suit for damages brought by a transsexual inmate in *Farmer v. Brennan*, 114 S.Ct. 1970 (1994). Dee Farmer, who is serving a twenty-year sentence for credit card fraud, was born male but underwent estrogen therapy, had breast implants, and had unsuccessful surgery to remove his testicles. In prison, Farmer was raped and subsequently claimed that prison officials should not have put him with the general prison population because they should have known that a transsexual "who projects feminine characteristics" would be vulnerable to sexual assaults.

In holding for the Court that Farmer could sue for damages based on showing that prison officials exhibited "deliberate indifference" to his safety, Justice Souter observed, "Being violently assaulted in prison is simply not part of the penalty that criminal offenders pay for their offenses against society." Although concurring in the judgment in a separate opinion, Justice Thomas maintained his position that the Eighth Amendment does not extend to brutality among prisoners or inflicted by guards. As Justice Thomas put it, "Punishment, from the time of the founding through the present day, has always meant a fine, penalty or confinement inflicted upon a person by the authority of the law and the judgment and sentence of a court, for some crime or offense committed by him. . . . Because the unfortunate attack that befell petitioner was not part of his sentence, it did not constitute 'punishment' under the Eighth Amendment."

B. CAPITAL PUNISHMENT

Although the Rehnquist Court has made it easier to impose death sentences and has expedited the carrying out of capital punishment (see Vol. 2, Ch. 10), it continues to review numerous death penalty appeals each year. See "The Development of Law" box in this chapter. How far the Court's balance has shifted was underscored in the 1994–1995 term. In *Edmund v. Florida*, 458 U.S. 782 (1982), a bare majority held that the Eighth Amendment bars the execution of a person who, although participating in a crime that led to murder, did not actually kill or intend for the killing to take place. While not overruling that decision, the Rehnquist Court has made it much easier to impose the death penalty and to carry out executions. Moreover, in *Herrera v. Collins*, 506 U.S. 390 (1993), Chief Justice Rehnquist issued an equivocal opinion indicating that it was presumably unconstitutional to execute an "actually innocent" person, but holding that federal courts were not obliged to consider such claims in reviewing *habeas corpus* petitions. Subsequently, by a six-to-three vote the justices denied an appeal and the stay of the execution of Jesse D. Jacobs, who claimed it was unconstitutional to execute an innocent person. Jesse Jacobs had confessed to, but later denied, killing a woman. At his trial, the prosecutor contended that he had pulled the trigger of the gun and obtained Jacobs's conviction and death sentence. The prosecutor changed his mind, though, and charged Jacobs's sister with the same crime, as well as claiming that she had fired the fatal shot. Following his sister's conviction and sentence of ten years' imprisonment, Jacobs appealed his death sentence. In *Jacobs v. Scott*, 115 S.Ct. 711 (1995), only Justices Stevens, Ginsburg, and Breyer dissented from the Court's denial of review and stay of Jacobs's execution.

However, in another case of a death-row inmate claiming "actual innocence," a bare majority laid down a new standard for federal courts' granting *habeas corpus* relief in such cases. In *Schlup v. Delo*, 115 S.Ct. 851 (1995), Justice Stevens managed to muster four votes for holding that inmates who claim their execution would be a "miscarriage of justice" must show only that "a constitutional violation has *probably* resulted in the conviction of one who is actually innocent." That standard is less difficult than the higher one used by the lower courts, requiring a showing of "clear and convincing evidence" that "no reasonable juror" would have voted for conviction if a constitutional error had not been made in the trial. Clinton's two appointees, Justices Ginsburg and Breyer, were joined by Justices O'Connor and Souter in forming the majority. Chief Justice Rehnquist and Justices Kennedy, Scalia, and Thomas dissented.

The bare majority in *Schlup* came together in yet another decision, *Kyles v. Whitley*, 115 S.Ct. 1555 (1995), allowing another death-row inmate to challenge his conviction and sentence on the ground that prosecutors wrongly suppressed evidence favorable to his defense attorneys. At Kyles's trial, the prosecutor suppressed the following evidence: (1) an eyewitness's statements to police following the murder; (2) various statements by a police informer who was not called to testify; and (3) a computer printout of license numbers of cars parked at the crime scene on the night of the murder, which notably did not include Kyles's car. Writing for a bare majority, Justice Souter held that the cumulative effect of all the withheld evidence deprived Kyles of due process, and that a constitutional error occurs when there is a "reasonable probability" that the disclosure of exculpatory evidence would have changed the outcome of a trial. Joined by Chief Justice Rehnquist and Justices Kennedy and Thomas, dissenting Justice Scalia decried the majority's ruling as "wholly unprecedented" and complained that the Court should not have granted review in the first place. "The reality is that responsibility for factual accuracy, in capital cases as in other cases, rests elsewhere," Scalia lamented and added, "We do nothing but encourage foolish reliance to pretend otherwise." But in a concurring opinion joined by Justices Ginsburg and Breyer, Justice Stevens countered that the Court's exercise of judicial review in such cases was especially important given the "current popularity of capital punishment."

Near the end of its 1995–1996 term, the Court in an extraordinary order granted and expedited proceedings for review of *Felker v. Turpin*, a challenge to the constitutionality of the Anti-Terrorism and Effective Death Penalty Act of 1996. That legislation was signed into law by President Clinton on the anniversary of the Oklahoma bombing of a federal building, just ten days before the justices granted review of *Felker*. The law imposes tough new standards, tight time limits on appeals, and restrictions on federal courts' review of death sentences, among other things. Ellis Wayne Felker, who was sentenced to death in 1983, challenged a provision of the law requiring death-row inmates to obtain permission from a three-judge appellate court panel before filing a second petition for a writ of *habeas corpus* for a federal court's review of a state court's imposition of capital punishment. Having already completed its oral argument session for the term, a majority of the Court nonetheless granted review and scheduled oral arguments in *Felker* for June 3, 1996. The decision to grant to expedite proceedings, however, drew a bitter dissent from Justices Stevens, Ginsburg, Souter, and Breyer. They charged that it was "both unnecessary and profoundly unwise for the Court to order expedited briefing of the important questions" presented. The Court, nonetheless, unanimously upheld the act; see "The Development of Law" box below.

THE DEVELOPMENT OF LAW

Other Recent Rulings of the Rehnquist Court on
Capital Punishment

Case	Vote	Ruling

Schiro v. Farley, 114 S.Ct. 783 (1994)   7:2   Rejected a double jeopardy challenge to a death sentence and claim that the double jeopardy clause applies to the sentencing stage of a capital murder trial. Justices Blackmun and Stevens dissented.

Romano v. Oklahoma, 114 S.Ct. 2004 (1994)   5:4   Commanding a bare majority, Chief Justice Rehnquist held that the introduction as evidence in a capital trial of the judgment and death sentence in an earlier trial for another murder does not violate the Eighth Amendment or infect the sentencing determination and balancing of aggravating and mitigating factors when imposing a second death sentence. Justices Blackmun, Ginsburg, Stevens, and Souter dissented.

Simmons v. South Carolina, 114 S. Ct. 2187 (1994)   7:2   Writing for a plurality of the Court, Justice Blackmun held that during the sentencing stage of a capital trial, if the prosecution argues that the accused's future dangerousness is a factor to be considered by the jury in determining whether to impose a death sentence or life imprisonment, then due process requires that the jury also be instructed that the accused is ineligible for parole under state law. In a separate opinion, joined by Chief Justice Rehnquist and Justice Kennedy, Justice O'Connor concluded that due process requires a jury to be instructed of an accused's parole ineligibility only if the prosecution makes an issue of the defendant's future dangerousness at the sentencing stage of a murder trial. Justices Scalia and Thomas dissented.

Tuilaepa v. California, 114 S.Ct. 2630 (1994)   8:1   Writing for the Court, Justice Kennedy held that California's instructions for juries when determining whether to impose a death sentence were not unconstitutionally vague. The provisions challenged provided that juries consider, among other factors, the "circumstances of the crime of which the defendant was convicted . . . and the existence of any special circumstances found to be true," and the "presence or absence of criminal activity (involving) the use or attempted use of force or violence or the express or implied threat to use force or violence," as well as the defendant's age at the time of the crime. Justice Blackmun dissented.

Harris v. Alabama, 115 S.Ct.   8:1   Rejected a challenge to Ala-
1031 (1995)   bama's capital punishment
                                                 law on the ground that it
failed to specify the weight a judge must give to the jury's recommendation on
sentencing. Here the jury had recommended a sentence of lifetime imprisonment, but the trial judge sentenced Harris to death upon concluding that the
aggravating circumstances outweighed all of the mitigating circumstances.
Writing for the Court, Justice O'Connor rejected Harris's claim that the state's
law permitted the arbitrary imposition of capital punishment and held that the
Eighth Amendment does not require states to define the weight judges must
give to a jury's sentence recommendation. Justice Stevens dissented.

Schlup v. Delo, 115 S.Ct. 851 —   5:4   Justice Stevens laid down a
(1995)   new   standard   for   federal
                                                 courts' granting *habeas cor-*
pus relief in cases of death-row inmates claiming "actual innocence." Writing
for a bare majority, Justice Stevens held that inmates who claim their execution
would be a "miscarriage of justice" must show only that "a constitutional
violation has probably resulted in the conviction of one who is actually innocent." Chief Justice Rehnquist and Justices Kennedy, Scalia, and Thomas
dissented.

Kyles v. Whitley, 115 S.Ct. 1555   5:4   Writing for a bare majority,
(1995)   Justice   Souter   held   that
                                                 death-row inmates may chal-
lenge their convictions on the ground that the prosecution wrongly suppressed
evidence favorable to their defense when the cumulative effect of the withholding of the evidence constitutes a denial of due process and there is a "reasonable probability" that the disclosure of the exculpatory evidence would have
resulted in a different trial outcome. Chief Justice Rehnquist and Justices
Kennedy, Scalia, and Thomas dissented.

Lonchar v. Thomas, 116 S.Ct. 1293   9:0   Writing   for   a   unanimous
(1996)   Court, Justice Breyer held
                                                 that federal courts must take
seriously death-row inmates' first petition for *habeas corpus* review of their
convictions, and thereby limited lower courts' discretion to dismiss such
petitions without reviewing the merits of claims to constitutional violations.
Here a lower court had dismissed Lonchar's petition because he had refused to
complete it for nearly nine years after his sentence, until the day of his scheduled execution.

Loving v. United States, 116 S.Ct. 9:0   Writing   for   a   unanimous
— (1996)   Court, Justice Kennedy re-
                                                 buffed a challenge to a death
sentence imposed under the Uniform Code of Military Justice on the ground
that Congress had unconstitutionally delegated its power to the president when
in 1983 President Ronald Reagan prescribed, in order to bring the code into
conformity with the Court's Eighth Amendment jurisprudence, the aggravating
factors to be considered in capital murder cases.

Felker v. Turpin, 116 S.Ct. — (1996)   9:0   Writing for a unanimous Court, Chief Justice Rehnquist upheld the provisions of the Anti-Terrorism and Effective Death Penalty Act of 1996. That law limits state prisoners' filing second or successive applications for writs of *habeas corpus* if no new claim is presented. The act also creates a "gatekeeping" mechanism in requiring a three-judge panel to review an inmate's second or successive *habeas* application and authorizes their denial without the possibility of further appeal. Attorneys for Ellis Felker, a death-row inmate, challenged the law on the ground that it unconstitutionally restricts the Court's appellate jurisdiction. The Court, however, upheld the restrictions on the filing of second or successive *habeas* applications on the ground that the Court still retained original jurisdiction over such applications. In a concurring opinion joined by Justices Souter and Breyer, Justice Stevens emphasized as well that the law does not limit the Court's appellate jurisdiction under the All Writs Act.

11

THE RIGHT OF PRIVACY

A. PRIVACY AND REPRODUCTIVE FREEDOM

The Court is now entering a second generation of litigation stemming from the controversy over abortion that was sparked by the landmark ruling in *Roe v. Wade*, 410 U.S. 113 (1973) (see Vol. 2, Ch. 11). In the wake of the Rehnquist Court's controversial abortion ruling in *Planned Parenthood of Southeastern Pennsylvania v. Casey*, 505 U.S. 833 (1992) (see Vol. 2, Ch. 11), lower courts have become split in applying *Casey*'s "undue burden" test to restrictive abortion laws. Yet the Court has refused to clarify its analysis and declined to grant a number of appeals of lower court rulings striking down or upholding restrictions on women seeking abortions. By a six-to-three vote and without explanation, the Court denied review of *Ada v. Guam Society of Obstetricians & Gynecologists*, 506 U.S. 1011 (1992), in which the governor of the Territory of Guam appealed the Ninth Circuit's invalidation of Guam's 1990 law banning virtually all abortions. The Court also denied review of *Edwards v. Sojourner T.*, 507 U.S. 972 (1993), which appealed the Eleventh Circuit's striking down Louisiana's 1991 ban on all abortions except those necessary to save a woman's life or in cases of rape or incest. While those lower court rulings striking down very restrictive abortion laws were left standing, the Court also denied review of appeals of the Fifth Circuit's upholding provisions of Mississippi's anti-abortion law. By denying review in *Barnes v. Moore*, 506 U.S. 1020 (1992), the Court left undisturbed the appellate court's analysis that under *Casey* Mississippi could require women seeking an abortion to wait twenty-four hours after giving their informed consent and after having their doctors explain the medical risks of abortion, describe the stage of fetal development, discuss pregnancy prevention and alternatives to abortion, and notify them "that the father is liable to assist in the support of her child." Mississippi's requirement that unmarried women under the age of eighteen obtain both of their

216

parents' permission before having an abortion was also upheld by the Fifth Circuit, and the Court declined to review that decision in *Barnes v. Mississippi*, 114 S.Ct. 468 (1993), as well. Mississippi's parental consent requirement, however, permits an unmarried teenager in extraordinary circumstances to obtain a judge's permission to have an abortion if she demonstrates maturity and it is not in her best interest to tell her parents about her desire to have an abortion.

There remains little doubt, though, the Court will revisit the controversy over *Casey's* undue burden test, particularly since the balance on the Court shifted with Justice Ginsburg's filling the seat of Justice White, who dissented in *Roe* and sided with the minority in *Casey*. Almost two years after *Casey* upheld Pennsylvania's restrictions on abortion, during which time there remained a lower court's stay on the enforcement of those restrictions, Justice Souter refused to grant a further stay. He did so in his capacity as the justice assigned to handle matters coming from the court of appeals for the Third Circuit, in a rather extraordinary six-page opinion in *Planned Parenthood of Southeastern Pennsylvania v. Casey*, 114 S.Ct. 909 (1994). At issue is the contention of abortion clinics that informed consent and twenty-four-hour waiting period requirements, though upheld in *Casey*, may operate to create an undue burden for women who must take time off from work and who have to travel great distances to an abortion clinic. That argument was accepted by the court of appeals for the Eighth Circuit in 1993, when it barred North Dakota's twenty-four-hour waiting period requirement from taking effect because of the burdens it imposed on women seeking abortions at the state's sole abortion clinic in Fargo, North Dakota. Justice Souter cited approvingly that ruling and noted, "The letter of our *Casey* opinion is not entirely hard-edged." Moreover, Justice Souter emphasized that "litigants are free to challenge similar restrictions in other jurisdictions."

The issue of the impact of restrictive abortion laws and the application of the "undue burden" test has continued to dog the Court, but the justices have declined to grant a case review and to hand down a decision clarifying the matter. In a 1993 concurring opinion, in *Fargo Women's Health Organization v. Schafer*, 507 U.S. 1013 (1993), though, Justice O'Connor, joined only by Justice Souter, observed that, in her view, "a law restricting abortions constitutes an undue burden, and hence is invalid, if in a large fraction of the cases in which the law is relevant, it will operate as a substantial obstacle to a woman's choice to undergo an abortion."

Almost three years later in the 1995–1996 term, the issue still haunted the justices. Yet the Court denied review in *Janklow v. Planned Parenthood*, 116 S.Ct. 1582 (1996). In this case, South Dakota's governor appealed a ruling of the Court of Appeals for the Eighth Circuit striking down a 1993 provision requiring unmarried women under the age of eighteen to obtain their parents' consent in order to obtain an abortion and which failed to provide, as an alternative to the parental consent requirement, a so-called "judicial bypass" provision. At issue was whether a federal court may invalidate a restrictive anti-abortion law because of its effect, or "undue burden," on a "large fraction" of women, or whether it must be shown that there are no possible circumstances under which the law could have constitutional application. The latter standard was laid down in *United States v. Salerno*, 481 U.S. 739 (1987), a case challenging a federal bail law. In a separate memorandum to the Court's denial of review in *Janklow*, Justice Stevens defended the Court's refusal to follow *Salerno* and cited approvingly Justice O'Connor's 1993 opinion in *Fargo Women's Health Organization*. By contrast, in an opinion dissenting from the denial of review and joined by Chief Justice Rehnquist and Justice Thomas, Justice Scalia decried the Court's denial of a case that "virtually cries out for our review." And he lamented that the Court's continued refusal to confront the issue "serves only one rational purpose: it makes our abortion ad hoc nullification machine as stealthful as possible."

By a five-to-four vote, however, in *Leavitt v. Jane*, 116 S.Ct. — (1996), the Court summarily reversed a decision of the Court of Appeals for the Tenth Circuit. At issue was Utah's 1991 restrictions on mid- and late-term abortions. That legislation established two sets of regulations. First, with respect to pregnancies of twenty weeks or less, abortions were permitted only under five circumstances: (1) to save the woman's life; when the pregnancy is due to (2) rape or (3) incest, and the rape or incest was reported to law enforcement officials; (4) when the attending physician determines that an abortion is necessary to prevent "grave damage" to the woman's medical health; or (5) to prevent the birth of a child "born with grave defects." Second, with respect to pregnancies of more than twenty weeks, abortions were permitted only under three of the above circumstances, namely, (1), (4), and (5); thus, late-term abortions for women who have suffered rape or incest would not be permitted. A federal district struck down the restriction on early and mid-term abortions, but held that the restrictions on late-term abortions were severable and constitutionally enforceable. The appellate court reversed on the ground that the two sets of restrictions were not severable. But in a brief *per curiam*, the Supreme Court disagreed, holding that the appellate court erred in ruling that the restrictions were severable and, without addressing the merits, remanded the case for further consideration. In a bitter dissent, joined by Justices Ginsburg, Souter, and Breyer, Justice Stevens attacked the majority for second-guessing the appellate court and for summarily deciding the case.

Other cases stemming from the controversy over abortion revolve around attempts to bring lawsuits against anti-abortion protesters and demonstrators who have intimidated women, blockaded abortion clinics, and even engaged in fire bombings and shootings of doctors. In *Bray v. Alexandria Women's Health Clinic*, 506 U.S. 263 (1993) (in Vol. 2, Ch. 11), the Rehnquist Court was bitterly split five to four in holding that the Civil Rights Act of 1871 does not give federal judges jurisdiction to enjoin the activities of anti-abortion protesters. However, in *National Organization for Women v. Scheidler*, 114 S.Ct. 798 (1994), the Court unanimously agreed that anti-abortion protesters could be sued for conspiracy and damages under the Racketeer Influenced and Corrupt Organizations (RICO) Act. Notably, though, in a concurring opinion joined by Justice Kennedy, Justice Souter indicated that the ruling in *Scheidler* did not preclude further consideration of the First Amendment claims of anti-abortion protesters.

In the same week that *Scheidler* came down, the justices also announced that they would finally grant review of a case involving anti-abortion protesters' claims of the First Amendment when fighting restrictions imposed on their protests and demonstrations. Courts throughout the country had been divided on that issue, raised in *Madsen v. Women's Health Center*, 114 S.Ct. 2516 (1994). *Madsen* is excerpted here in Volume 2, Chapter 5.

In its 1996–1997 term, the Court will revisit the issue of anti-abortion protesters' First Amendment freedoms raised in *Schenck v. Pro-Choice Network*. At issue in that case is the permissibility of a court order creating a fifteen-foot buffer zone around abortion clinics, as well as around vehicles entering the clinics' driveways. The order also permits only two protesters to come within fifteen feet of patients entering the clinics, located in Buffalo and Rochester, New York. In appealing the decision of the Court of Appeals for the Second Circuit, upholding the order, the Reverend Paul Schenck contends that the court order strikes at the core of the First Amendment and its "protection of unpopular and despised speech in the traditional public forum of public sidewalks and streets." Attorneys for Schenck also argue that the order runs afoul of the holding in *Madsen* that injunctions against anti-abortion protesters may "burden no more speech than necessary to serve a significant government interest."

12

THE EQUAL PROTECTION
OF THE LAWS

B. RACIAL DISCRIMINATION IN EDUCATION

In the decades-old controversy over school desegregation, the Rehnquist Court turned a corner in *Freeman v. Pitts*, 503 U.S. 467 (1992)
(see Vol. 2, Ch. 12), giving lower courts greater leeway to withdraw judicial supervision of desegregation efforts and signaling an end to the
Brown era, which was inaugurated by the landmark ruling in *Brown v.
Board of Ed. of Topeka, Kansas,* 347 U.S. 483 (1954) (in Vol. 2, Ch.
12). In *Missouri v. Jenkins,* 115 S.Ct. 2038 1995), the Court continued
to grapple with the issue of guidelines for lower courts withdrawing
from efforts to force greater integration.

Although not breaking any new ground or laying down new guidelines in *Missouri v. Jenkins,* a bare majority reiterated its view that
lower courts should disengage from desegregation efforts. Writing for
the Court, Chief Justice Rehnquist held that a federal district court had
exceeded its remedial powers in ordering the state to (1) fund salary
increases for virtually all teachers and staff within the Kansas City,
Missouri, School District (KCMSD); and (2) to continue to fund
remedial "quality education" programs because student achievement
scores were still "at or below national norms at many grade levels." In
order to eliminate the vestiges of past discrimination and to make the
KCMSD's schools, which have over ninety percent black student
enrollments, more attractive to white students in surrounding suburbs,
the district court also created a magnet school district with expanded
educational opportunities and facilities. However, drawing on *Milliken
v. Bradley,* 418 U.S. 717 (1974) (see Vol. 2, Ch. 12), Chief Justice
Rehnquist ruled that that "*inter*district goal [of encouraging further
integration through magnet schools and greater funding] is beyond the
scope of the *intra*district violation" of prior racial discrimination. The
chief justice also rejected the lower court's use of educational test
scores as a legitimate measure of the progress of integration. In

remanding the case back to the lower court to determine whether judicial supervision of the school district should be terminated, the chief justice further admonished, "The district court must bear in mind that its end purpose is not only to remedy the violation to the extent practicable, but also to restore state and local authorities to the control of a school system that is operating in compliance with the Constitution." Justices O'Connor and Thomas filed separate concurring opinions. The latter's was, notably, a highly personal twenty-seven-page opinion taking issue with the lower court's presumption that predominantly black school districts are inferior and should be made more attractive for white students.

By contrast, the four dissenters—Justices Souter, Stevens, Ginsburg, and Breyer—countered that the majority had overreached in ruling on issues such as the use of student achievement scores, and firmly rejected the majority's conclusion that lower courts possess no authority to order improvements in school districts so as to make them more attractive to white students. While also joining Justice Souter's opinion for the dissenters, Justice Ginsburg added a few words of her own in a separate dissent. "Given the deep, inglorious history of segregation in Missouri," in her words, "to curtail desegregation at this time and in this manner is an action at once too swift and too soon."

C. AFFIRMATIVE ACTION AND REVERSE DISCRIMINATION

The Rehnquist Court made it much more difficult for states and localities to defend affirmative-action programs in *City of Richmond v. J. A. Croson Co.*, 488 U.S. 469 (1989), and easier for white-owned business to attack the constitutionality of such programs in *Northeastern Florida Chapter of the Associated General Contractors of America v. City of Jacksonville, Florida*, 113 S.Ct. 2297 (1993) (both cases are excerpted in Vol. 2, Ch. 12). Notably, in its 1994–1995 term the Court then denied review of a decision of the appellate court for the Fourth Circuit, in *Podbersky v. Kirwin*, 38 F.3d 147 (1994), which struck down the University of Maryland's affirmative-action program for admissions. Approximately twelve percent of the university's student body is black, while the statewide population is twenty-four percent. Thus the university provided forty annual scholarships for blacks as a remedy for past discrimination and to encourage the recruitment of blacks. But in declining to review the appellate court's ruling, the Rehnquist Court further signaled its opposition to such programs and invited challenges to similar programs in more than half of the colleges in the country.

However, in 1990 a bare majority of the Court held, in *Metro Broadcasting, Inc. v. Federal Communications Commission*, 497 U.S. 547

(1990) (see Vol. 2, Ch. 12), that Congress has broader latitude than states and localities when authorizing affirmative-action programs, even without showing a close remedial nexus to past discrimination. Yet the only justice on the bench from the time of that decision remains Justice Stevens. The other four justices—Justices Brennan, Marshall, White, and Blackmun—composing the majority in *Metro Broadcasting* subsequently retired and were replaced, respectively, by Justices Souter, Thomas, Ginsburg, and Breyer. With the Court's composition so dramatically changed in four short years, not surprisingly the Rehnquist Court decided to revisit the controversial issue of Congress's power to enact affirmative-action programs in *Adarand Constructors, Inc. v. Pena* (excerpted below). There a bare majority of the Rehnquist Court, in an opinion announced by Justice O'Connor, held both that the "strict scrutiny" standard applied in *Croson* to affirmative action programs adopted by state and local governments applies no less to federal programs, and overruled *Metro Broadcasting*.

Adarand Constructors, Inc. v. Pena
115 S.Ct. 2097 (1995)

Adarand Constructors, Inc., a Colorado-based highway company specializing in guardrail work, submitted a low bid to Mountain Gravel, which had received a contract from the Department of Transportation (DoT) for a construction project. But Gonzales Construction Company, a Hispanic–American-owned company, was selected for the work instead. Mountain Gravel picked the latter company over Adarand because the Small Business Act made it a matter of federal policy to encourage subcontracting to "small business concerns owned and controlled by socially and economically disadvantaged individuals." The act defines "socially disadvantaged individuals" as "those who have been subject to racial or ethnic prejudice or cultural bias." The act also established the goal of participation of small businesses "owned or controlled by socially and economically disadvantaged individuals" at "not less than 5 percent of the total value of all prime contract and subcontract awards for each fiscal year." In addition, the Surface Transportation and Uniform Relocation Assistance Act of 1987 (STURAA), a DoT appropriations measure, stipulates that "not less than 10 percent" of appropriated funds "be expended with small business concerns owned and controlled by socially and economically disadvantaged individuals."

After losing the subcontract to Gonzales Construction Company, Adarand filed a suit in federal district court, contending that the federal laws and policy presumptions governing the DoT's subcontracting guidelines violated the Fourteenth Amendment's equal protection clause. The district court rejected Adarand's claims. A federal appellate court affirmed that decision on the basis of *Fullilove v. Klutznick*, 448 U.S. 448 (1980), and *Metro Broadcasting v. Federal Communications Commission*, 497 U.S. 547 (1990), whereupon Adarand appealed to the Supreme Court.

The Court's ruling was five to four and opinion announced by Justice O'Connor. Justices Scalia and Thomas filed concurring opinions. Justices Stevens and Souter filed dissenting opinions, as did Justice Ginsburg, who was joined by Justice Breyer.

Justice O'CONNOR announced the judgment of the Court and delivered an opinion with respect to Parts I, II, III-A, III-B, III-D, and IV, which is for the Court except insofar as it might be inconsistent with the views expressed in Justice SCALIA's concurrence, and an opinion with respect to Part III-C in which Justice KENNEDY joins.

III

Adarand's claim arises under the Fifth Amendment to the Constitution, which provides that "No person shall . . . be deprived of life, liberty, or property, without due process of law." Although this Court has always understood that Clause to provide some measure of protection against arbitrary treatment by the Federal Government, it is not as explicit a guarantee of equal treatment as the Fourteenth Amendment, which provides that "No State shall . . . deny to any person within its jurisdiction the equal protection of the laws." Our cases have accorded varying degrees of significance to the difference in the language of those two Clauses. We think it necessary to revisit the issue here.

A

Through the 1940s, this Court had routinely taken the view in non-race-related cases that, "unlike the Fourteenth Amendment, the Fifth contains no equal protection clause and it provides no guaranty against discriminatory legislation by Congress." *Detroit Bank v. United States*, 317 U.S. 329 (1943). When the Court first faced a Fifth Amendment equal protection challenge to a federal racial classification, it adopted a similar approach, with most unfortunate results. In *Hirabayashi v. United States*, 320 U.S. 81 (1943), the Court considered a curfew applicable only to persons of Japanese ancestry. The Court observed—correctly—that "distinctions between citizens solely because of their ancestry are by their very nature odious to a free people whose institutions are founded upon the doctrine of equality," and that "racial discriminations are in most circumstances irrelevant and therefore prohibited." But it also cited *Detroit Bank* for the proposition that the Fifth Amendment "restrains only such discriminatory legislation by Congress as amounts to a denial of due process," and upheld the curfew because "circumstances within the knowledge of those charged with the responsibility for maintaining the national defense afforded a rational basis for the decision which they made." Eighteen months later, the Court again approved wartime measures directed at persons of Japanese ancestry. *Korematsu v. United States*, 323 U.S. 214 (1944), concerned an order that completely excluded such persons from particular areas. . . .

In *Bolling v. Sharpe*, 347 U.S. 497 (1954), the Court for the first time explicitly questioned the existence of any difference between the obligations of the Federal Government and the States to avoid racial classifications. *Bolling* did note that "the 'equal protection of the laws' is a more explicit safeguard of prohibited unfairness than 'due process of law.'" But *Bolling* then concluded that, "in view of [the] decision that the Constitution prohibits the states from maintaining racially segregated public schools, it would be unthinkable that the same Constitution would impose a lesser duty on the Federal Government."

Bolling's facts concerned school desegregation, but its reasoning was not so limited. The Court's observations that "distinctions between citizens solely because of their ancestry are by their very nature odious," *Hirabayashi*, and that "all legal restrictions which curtail the civil rights of a single racial group are immediately suspect," *Korematsu*, carry no less force in the context of federal action than in the context of action by the States—indeed, they first appeared in cases concerning action by the Federal Government. . . . Later cases in contexts other than school desegregation did not distinguish between the duties of the States and the Federal Government to avoid racial classifications. . . .

B

Most of the cases discussed above involved classifications burdening groups that have suffered discrimination in our society. In 1978, the Court confronted the question whether race-based governmental action designed to benefit such groups should also be subject to "the most rigid scrutiny." *Regents of Univ. of California v. Bakke*, 438 U.S. 265 [(1978)], involved an equal protection challenge to a state-run medical school's practice of reserving a number of spaces in its entering class for minority students. The petitioners argued that "strict scrutiny" should apply only to "classifications that disadvantage 'discrete and insular minorities.'" *Bakke* did not produce an opinion for the Court, but Justice POWELL's opinion announcing the Court's judgment rejected the argument. In a passage joined by Justice WHITE, Justice POWELL wrote that "the guarantee of equal protection cannot mean one thing when applied to one individual and something else when applied to a person of another color." He concluded that "racial and ethnic distinctions of any sort are inherently suspect and thus call for the most exacting judicial examination." . . .

Two years after *Bakke*, the Court faced another challenge to remedial race-based action, this time involving action undertaken by the Federal Government. In *Fullilove v. Klutznick*, 448 U.S. 448 (1980), the Court upheld Congress' inclusion of a 10% set-aside for minority-owned businesses in the Public Works Employment Act of 1977. As in *Bakke*, there was no opinion for the Court. Chief Justice BURGER, in an opinion joined by

Justices WHITE and POWELL, observed that "any preference based on racial or ethnic criteria must necessarily receive a most searching examination to make sure that it does not conflict with constitutional guarantees." That opinion, however, "did not adopt, either expressly or implicitly, the formulas of analysis articulated in such cases as [Bakke]." It employed instead a two-part test which asked, first, "whether the objectives of the legislation are within the power of Congress," and second, "whether the limited use of racial and ethnic criteria, in the context presented, is a constitutionally permissible means for achieving the congressional objectives." It then upheld the program under that test, adding at the end of the opinion that the program also "would survive judicial review under either 'test' articulated in the several Bakke opinions." . . .

In Wygant v. Jackson Board of Ed., 476 U.S. 267 (1986), the Court considered a Fourteenth Amendment challenge to another form of remedial racial classification. The issue in Wygant was whether a school board could adopt race-based preferences in determining which teachers to lay off. Justice POWELL's plurality opinion observed that "the level of scrutiny does not change merely because the challenged classification operates against a group that historically has not been subject to governmental discrimination," and stated the two-part inquiry as "whether the layoff provision is supported by a compelling state purpose and whether the means chosen to accomplish that purpose are narrowly tailored." In other words, "racial classifications of any sort must be subjected to 'strict scrutiny.'" . . .

The Court's failure to produce a majority opinion in Bakke, Fullilove, and Wygant left unresolved the proper analysis for remedial race-based governmental action.

The Court resolved the issue, at least in part, in 1989. [City of] Richmond v. J. A. Croson Co., 488 U.S. 469 (1989), concerned a city's determination that 30% of its contracting work should go to minority-owned businesses. A majority of the Court in Croson held that "the standard of review under the Equal Protection Clause is not dependent on the race of those burdened or benefited by a particular classification," and that the single standard of review for racial classifications should be "strict scrutiny." The Court also thought it "obvious that [the] program is not narrowly tailored to remedy the effects of prior discrimination."

With Croson, the Court finally agreed that the Fourteenth Amendment requires strict scrutiny of all race-based action by state and local governments. But Croson of course had no occasion to declare what standard of review the Fifth Amendment requires for such action taken by the Federal Government. . . .

Despite lingering uncertainty in the details, however, the Court's cases through Croson had established three general propositions with respect to governmental racial classifications. First, skepticism: "any preference based on racial or ethnic criteria must necessarily receive a most searching examination," Wygant. Second, consistency: "the standard of review under the Equal Protection Clause is not dependent on the race of those burdened or benefited by a particular classification," Croson. And third, congruence: "equal protection analysis in the Fifth Amendment area is the same as that under the Fourteenth Amendment," Buckley v. Valeo, 424 U.S. [1 (1976)]. Taken together, these three propositions lead to the conclusion that any person, of whatever race, has the right to demand that any governmental actor subject to the Constitution justify any racial classification subjecting that person to unequal treatment under the strictest judicial scrutiny. . . .

A year later, however, the Court took a surprising turn. *Metro Broadcasting, Inc. v. [Federal Communications Commission]*, 497 U.S. 547 (1990), involved a Fifth Amendment challenge to two race-based policies of the Federal Communications Commission. In *Metro Broadcasting*, the Court repudiated the long-held notion that "it would be unthinkable that the same Constitution would impose a lesser duty on the Federal Government" than it does on a State to afford equal protection of the laws, *Bolling*. It did so by holding that "benign" federal racial classifications need only satisfy intermediate scrutiny, even though *Croson* had recently concluded that such classifications enacted by a State must satisfy strict scrutiny. "Benign" federal racial classifications, the Court said, "—even if those measures are not 'remedial' in the sense of being designed to compensate victims of past governmental or societal discrimination—are constitutionally permissible to the extent that they serve important governmental objectives within the power of Congress and are substantially related to achievement of those objectives." The Court did not explain how to tell whether a racial classification should be deemed "benign," other than to express "confidence that an 'examination of the legislative scheme and its history' will separate benign measures from other types of racial classifications."

Applying this test, the Court first noted that the FCC policies at issue did not serve as a remedy for past discrimination. Proceeding on the assumption that the policies were nonetheless "benign," it concluded that they served the "important governmental objective" of "enhancing broadcast diversity," and that they were "substantially related" to that objective. It therefore upheld the policies.

By adopting intermediate scrutiny as the standard of review for congressionally mandated "benign" racial classifications, *Metro Broadcasting* departed from prior cases in two significant respects. First, it turned its back on *Croson*'s explanation of why strict scrutiny of all governmental racial classifications is essential: "Absent searching judicial inquiry into the justification for such race-based measures, there is simply no way of determining what classifications are 'benign' or 'remedial' and what classifications are in fact motivated by illegitimate notions of racial inferiority or simple racial politics. Indeed, the purpose of strict scrutiny is to 'smoke out' illegitimate uses of race by assuring that the legislative body is pursuing a goal important enough to warrant use of a highly suspect tool. The test also ensures that the means chosen 'fit' this compelling goal so closely that there is little or no possibility that the motive for the classification was illegitimate racial prejudice or stereotype." *Croson*. We adhere to that view today, despite the surface appeal of holding "benign" racial classifications to a lower standard, because "it may not always be clear that a so-called preference is in fact benign," *Bakke*.

Second, *Metro Broadcasting* squarely rejected one of the three propositions established by the Court's earlier equal protection cases, namely, congruence between the standards applicable to federal and state racial classifications, and in so doing also undermined the other two—skepticism of all racial classifications, and consistency of treatment irrespective of the race of the burdened or benefited group. Under *Metro Broadcasting*, certain racial classifications ("benign" ones enacted by the Federal Government) should be treated less skeptically than others; and the race of the benefited group is critical to the determination of which standard of review to apply. *Metro Broadcasting* was thus a significant departure from much of what had come before it.

The three propositions undermined by *Metro Broadcasting* all derive from the basic principle that the Fifth and Fourteenth Amendments to the Constitution protect persons, not groups. . . . Accordingly, we hold today that all racial classifications, imposed by whatever federal, state, or local governmental actor, must be analyzed by a reviewing court under strict scrutiny. In other words, such classifications are constitutional only if they are narrowly tailored measures that further compelling governmental interests. To the extent that *Metro Broadcasting* is inconsistent with that holding, it is overruled. . . .

C

It is worth pointing out the difference between the applications of *stare decisis* in this case and in *Planned Parenthood of Southeastern Pa. v. Casey,* [505 U.S. 833] (1992). *Casey* explained how considerations of *stare decisis* inform the decision whether to overrule a long-established precedent that has become integrated into the fabric of the law. Overruling precedent of that kind naturally may have consequences for "the ideal of the rule of law." In addition, such precedent is likely to have engendered substantial reliance, as was true in *Casey* itself. But in this case, as we have explained, we do not face a precedent of that kind, because *Metro Broadcasting* itself departed from our prior cases—and did so quite recently. By refusing to follow *Metro Broadcasting*, then, we do not depart from the fabric of the law; we restore it. . . .

D

Our action today makes explicit what Justice POWELL thought implicit in the *Fullilove* lead opinion: federal racial classifications, like those of a State, must serve a compelling governmental interest, and must be narrowly tailored to further that interest. Of course, it follows that to the extent (if any) that *Fullilove* held federal racial classifications to be subject to a less rigorous standard, it is no longer controlling. But we need not decide today whether the program upheld in *Fullilove* would survive strict scrutiny as our more recent cases have defined it. . . .

Finally, we wish to dispel the notion that strict scrutiny is "strict in theory, but fatal in fact." *Fullilove.* The unhappy persistence of both the practice and the lingering effects of racial discrimination against minority groups in this country is an unfortunate reality, and government is not disqualified from acting in response to it. As recently as 1987, for example, every Justice of this Court agreed that the Alabama Department of Public Safety's "pervasive, systematic, and obstinate discriminatory conduct" justified a narrowly tailored race-based remedy. See *United States v. Paradise*, 480 U.S. [149 (1987)]. When race-based action is necessary to further a compelling interest, such action is within constitutional constraints if it satisfies the "narrow tailoring" test this Court has set out in previous cases. . . .

Accordingly, the judgment of the Court of Appeals is vacated, and the case is remanded for further proceedings consistent with this opinion.

Justice SCALIA, concurring in part and concurring in the judgment.

I join the opinion of the Court, except Part III-C, and except insofar as it may be inconsistent with the following: In my view, government can never have a "compelling interest" in discriminating on the basis of race in order to "make up" for past racial discrimination in the opposite direction. Individuals who have been wronged by unlawful racial discrimination should be made whole; but under our Constitution there can be no such thing as either a creditor or a debtor race. That concept is alien to the Constitution's focus upon the individual, see Amdt. 14, Sec. 1 ("Nor shall any State . . . deny to any person" the equal protection of the laws), and its rejection of dispositions based on race, see Amdt. 15, Sec. 1 (prohibiting abridgment of the right to vote "on account of race") or based on blood, see Art. III, Sec. 3 ("No Attainder of Treason shall work Corruption of Blood"); Art. I, Sec. 9 ("No Title of Nobility shall be granted by the United States"). To pursue the concept of racial entitlement—even for the most admirable and benign of purposes—is to reinforce and preserve for future mischief the way of thinking that produced race slavery, race privilege and race hatred. In the eyes of government, we are just one race here. It is American. . . .

Justice THOMAS, concurring in part and concurring in the judgment.

I agree with the majority's conclusion that strict scrutiny applies to all government classifications based on race. I write separately, however, to express my disagreement with the premise underlying Justice STEVENS' and Justice GINSBURG's dissents: that there is a racial paternalism exception to the principle of equal protection. I believe that there is a "moral [and] constitutional equivalence" between laws designed to subjugate a race and those that distribute benefits on the basis of race in order to foster some current notion of equality. Government cannot make us equal; it can only recognize, respect, and protect us as equal before the law. . . .

Justice STEVENS, with whom Justice GINSBURG joins, dissenting.

Instead of deciding this case in accordance with controlling precedent, the Court today delivers a disconcerting lecture about the evils of governmental racial classifications. For its text the Court has selected three propositions, represented by the bywords "skepticism," "consistency," and "congruence." I shall comment on each of these propositions, then add a few words about *stare decisis*, and finally explain why I believe this Court has a duty to affirm the judgment of the Court of Appeals.

The Court's concept of skepticism is, at least in principle, a good statement of law and of common sense. Undoubtedly, a court should be wary of a governmental decision that relies upon a racial classification. . . . But, as the opinions in *Fullilove* demonstrate, substantial agreement on the standard to be applied in deciding difficult cases does not necessarily lead to agreement on how those cases actually should or will be resolved. In my judgment, because uniform standards are often anything but uniform, we should evaluate the Court's comments on "consistency," "congruence," and *stare decisis* with the same type of skepticism that the Court advocates for the underlying issue.

The Court's concept of "consistency" assumes that there is no significant difference between a decision by the majority to impose a special burden on the members of a minority race and a decision by the majority to provide a benefit to certain members of that minority notwithstanding its incidental burden on some members of the majority. In my opinion that assumption is untenable. There is no moral or constitutional equivalence between a policy that is designed to perpetuate a caste system and one that seeks to eradicate racial subordination. Invidious discrimination is an engine of oppression, subjugating a disfavored group to enhance or maintain the power of the majority. Remedial race-based preferences reflect the opposite impulse: a desire to foster equality in society. . . .

To illustrate the point, consider our cases addressing the Federal Government's discrimination against Japanese Americans during World War II, *Hirabayashi* and *Korematsu*. The discrimination at issue in those cases was invidious because the Government imposed special burdens—a curfew and exclusion from certain areas on the West Coast—on the members of a minority class defined by racial and ethnic characteristics. Members of the same racially defined class exhibited exceptional heroism in the service of our country during that War. Now suppose Congress decided to reward that service with a federal program that gave all Japanese-American veterans an extraordinary preference in Government employment. Cf. *Personnel Administrator of Mass. v. Feeney*, 442 U.S. 256 (1979). If Congress had done so, the same racial characteristics that motivated the discriminatory burdens in *Hirabayashi* and *Korematsu* would have defined the preferred class of veterans. Nevertheless, "consistency" surely would not require us to describe the incidental burden on everyone else in the country as "odious" or "invidious" as those terms were used in those cases. We should reject a concept of "consistency" that would view the special preferences that the National Government has provided to Native Americans since 1834 as comparable to the official discrimination against African Americans that was prevalent for much of our history.

The consistency that the Court espouses would disregard the difference between a "No Trespassing" sign and a welcome mat. It would treat a Dixiecrat Senator's decision to vote against Thurgood Marshall's confirmation in order to keep African Americans off the Supreme Court as on a par with President Johnson's evaluation of his nominee's race as a positive factor. It would equate a law that made black citizens ineligible for military service with a program aimed at recruiting black soldiers. An attempt by the majority to exclude members of a minority race from a regulated market is fundamentally different from a subsidy that enables a relatively small group of newcomers to enter that market. An interest in "consistency" does not justify treating differences as though they were similarities. . . .

Nothing is inherently wrong with applying a single standard to fundamentally different situations, as long as that standard takes relevant differences into account. For example, if the Court in all equal protection cases were to insist that differential treatment be justified by relevant characteristics of the members of the favored and disfavored classes that provide a legitimate basis for disparate treatment, such a standard would treat dissimilar cases differently while still recognizing that there is, after all, only one Equal Protection Clause. See *Cleburne v. Cleburne Living Center, Inc.*, 473 U.S. 432 (1985). Under such a standard, subsidies for disadvantaged businesses may be constitutional though special taxes on such businesses would be invalid. But a single standard that purports to equate remedial preferences with invidious discrimination cannot be defended in the name of "equal protection."

Moreover, the Court may find that its new "consistency" approach to race-based classifications is difficult to square with its insistence upon rigidly separate categories for discrimination against different classes of individuals. For example, as the law currently stands, the Court will apply "intermediate scrutiny" to cases of invidious gender discrimination and "strict scrutiny" to cases of invidious race discrimination, while applying the same standard for benign classifications as for invidious ones. If this remains the law, then today's lecture about "consistency" will produce the anomalous result that the Government can more easily enact affirmative-action programs to remedy discrimination against women than it can enact affirmative-action programs to remedy discrimination against African Americans—even though the primary purpose of the Equal Protection Clause was to end discrimination against the former slaves. When a court becomes preoccupied with abstract standards, it risks sacrificing common sense at the altar of formal consistency. . . .

The Court's concept of "congruence" assumes that there is no significant difference between a decision by the Congress of the United States to adopt an affirmative-action program and such a decision by a State or a municipality. In my opinion that assumption is untenable. It ignores important practical and legal differences between federal and state or local decision-makers.

These differences have been identified repeatedly and consistently both in opinions of the Court and in separate opinions authored by members of today's majority. Thus, in *Metro Broadcasting*, in which we upheld a federal program designed to foster racial diversity in broadcasting, we identified the special "institutional competence" of our National Legislature. "It is of overriding significance in these cases," we were careful to emphasize, "that the FCC's minority ownership programs have been specifically approved—indeed, mandated—by Congress." We recalled the several opinions in *Fullilove* that admonished this Court to "'approach our task with appropriate deference to the Congress, a co-equal branch charged by the Constitution with the power to 'provide for the . . . general Welfare of the United States' and 'to enforce, by appropriate legislation, the equal protection guarantees of the Fourteenth Amendment.'"

The majority in *Metro Broadcasting* and the plurality in *Fullilove* were not alone in relying upon a critical distinction between federal and state programs. . . . In her plurality opinion in *Croson*, Justice O'CONNOR also emphasized the importance of this distinction when she responded to the City's argument that *Fullilove* was controlling. She wrote: "What appellant ignores is that Congress, unlike any State or political subdivision, has a specific constitutional mandate to enforce the dictates of the Fourteenth Amendment. The power to 'enforce' may at times also include the power to define situations which Congress determines threaten principles of equality and to adopt prophylactic rules to deal with those situations. The Civil War Amendments themselves worked a dramatic change in the balance between congressional and state power over matters of race."

An additional reason for giving greater deference to the National Legislature than to a local law-making body is that federal affirmative-action programs represent the will of our entire Nation's elected representatives, whereas a state or local program may have an impact on nonresident entities who played no part in the decision to enact it. Thus, in the state or local context, individuals who were unable to vote for the local representatives who enacted a race-conscious program may nonetheless feel the effects of that program. This difference recalls the goals of the Commerce Clause, U.S. Const., Art. I, Sec. 8, cl. 3, which permits Congress to legislate on certain matters of national importance while denying power to the States in this area for fear of undue impact upon out-of-state residents.

Our opinion in *Metro Broadcasting* relied on several constitutional provisions to justify the greater deference we owe to Congress when it acts with respect to private individuals. In the programs challenged in this case, Congress has acted both with respect to private individuals and, as in *Fullilove*, with respect to the States themselves. When Congress does this, it draws its power directly from Sec. 5 of the Fourteenth Amendment. That section reads: "The Congress shall have power to enforce, by appropriate legislation, the provisions of this article." One of the "provisions of this article" that Congress is thus empowered to enforce reads: "No State shall make or enforce any law which shall abridge the privileges or immunities of citizens of the United States; nor shall any State deprive any person of life, liberty, or property, without due process of law; nor deny to any person within its jurisdiction the equal protection of the laws." U.S. Const., Amdt. 14, Sec. 1. The Fourteenth Amendment directly empowers Congress at the same time it expressly limits the States. This is no accident. It represents our Nation's consensus, achieved after hard experience throughout our sorry history of race relations, that the Federal Government must be the primary defender of racial minorities against the States, some of which may be inclined to oppress such minorities. A rule of "congruence" that ignores a purposeful "incongruity" so fundamental to our system of government is unacceptable.

The Court's concept of *stare decisis* treats some of the language we have used in explaining our decisions as though it were more important than our actual holdings. In my opinion that treatment is incorrect. . . . In the Court's view, our decision in *Metro Broadcasting* was inconsistent with the rule announced in *Croson*. But two decisive distinctions separate those two cases. First, *Metro Broadcasting* involved a federal program, whereas

Croson involved a city ordinance. *Metro Broadcasting* thus drew primary support from *Fullilove*, which predated *Croson* and which *Croson* distinguished on the grounds of the federal-state dichotomy that the majority today discredits. Although members of today's majority trumpeted the importance of that distinction in *Croson*, they now reject it in the name of "congruence." It is therefore quite wrong for the Court to suggest today that overruling *Metro Broadcasting* merely restores the status quo ante, for the law at the time of that decision was entirely open to the result the Court reached. Today's decision is an unjustified departure from settled law.

Second, *Metro Broadcasting*'s holding rested on more than its application of "intermediate scrutiny." Indeed, I have always believed that, labels notwithstanding, the FCC program we upheld in that case would have satisfied any of our various standards in affirmative-action cases—including the one the majority fashions today. What truly distinguishes *Metro Broadcasting* from our other affirmative-action precedents is the distinctive goal of the federal program in that case. Instead of merely seeking to remedy past discrimination, the FCC program was intended to achieve future benefits in the form of broadcast diversity. Reliance on race as a legitimate means of achieving diversity was first endorsed by Justice POWELL in *Bakke*. . . .

The Court's suggestion that it may be necessary in the future to overrule *Fullilove* in order to restore the fabric of the law is even more disingenuous than its treatment of *Metro Broadcasting*. For the Court endorses the "strict scrutiny" standard that Justice POWELL applied in *Bakke*, and acknowledges that he applied that standard in *Fullilove* as well. Moreover, Chief Justice BURGER also expressly concluded that the program we considered in *Fullilove* was valid under any of the tests articulated in *Bakke*, which of course included Justice POWELL's. The Court thus adopts a standard applied in *Fullilove* the same time it questions that case's continued vitality and accuses it of departing from prior law. . . .

The Court's holding in *Fullilove* surely governs the result in this case. The Public Works Employment Act of 1977, which this Court upheld in *Fullilove*, is different in several critical respects from the portions of the Small Business Act (SBA), and the Surface Transportation and Uniform Relocation Assistance Act of 1987 (STURAA), challenged in this case. Each of those differences makes the current program designed to provide assistance to disadvantaged business enterprises (DBE's) significantly less objectionable than the 1977 categorical grant of $400 million in exchange for a 10% set-aside in public contracts to "a class of investors defined solely by racial characteristics." *Fullilove*. In no meaningful respect is the current scheme more objectionable than the 1977 Act. Thus, if the 1977 Act was constitutional, then so must be the SBA and STURAA. Indeed, even if my dissenting views in *Fullilove* had prevailed, this program would be valid.

Unlike the 1977 Act, the present statutory scheme does not make race the sole criterion of eligibility for participation in the program. Race does give rise to a rebuttable presumption of social disadvantage which, at least under STURAA, gives rise to a second rebuttable presumption of economic disadvantage. But a small business may qualify as a DBE, by showing that it is both socially and economically disadvantaged, even if it receives neither of these presumptions. Thus, the current preference is more inclusive than the 1977 Act because it does not make race a necessary qualification.

More importantly, race is not a sufficient qualification. Whereas a millionaire with a long history of financial successes, who was a member of numerous social clubs and trade associations, would have qualified for a preference under the 1977 Act merely because he was an Asian American or an African American, neither the SBA nor STURAA creates any such anomaly. The DBE program excludes members of minority races who are not, in fact, socially or economically disadvantaged. The presumption of social disadvantage reflects the unfortunate fact that irrational racial prejudice—along with its lingering effects—still survives. The presumption of economic disadvantage embodies a recognition that success in the private sector of the economy is often attributable, in part, to social skills and relationships. Unlike the 1977 set-asides, the current preference is designed to overcome the social and economic disadvantages that are often associated with racial characteristics. If, in a particular case, these disadvantages are not present, the presumptions can be rebutted. The program is thus designed to allow race to play a part in the decisional process only when there is a meaningful basis for assuming its relevance. In this connection, I think it is particularly significant that the current program targets the negotiation of subcontracts between private firms. The 1977 Act applied entirely to the award of public contracts, an area of the economy in which social relationships should be irrelevant and in which proper supervision of government contracting officers should preclude any discrimination against particular bidders on account of their race. In this case, in contrast, the program seeks to overcome barriers of prejudice between private parties—specifically, between general contractors and subcontractors. The SBA and STURAA embody Congress' recognition that such barriers may actually handicap minority firms seeking business as subcontractors from established leaders in the industry that have a history of doing business with their golfing partners. Indeed, minority subcontractors may face more obstacles than direct, intentional racial prejudice: they may face particular barriers simply because they are more likely to be new in the business and less likely to know others in the business. Given such difficulties, Congress could reasonably find that a minority subcontractor is less likely to receive favors from the entrenched businesspersons who award subcontracts only to people with whom—or with whose friends—they have an existing relationship. This program, then, if in part a remedy for past discrimination, is most importantly a forward-looking response to practical problems faced by minority subcontractors. . . .

My skeptical scrutiny of the Court's opinion leaves me in dissent. The majority's concept of "consistency" ignores a difference, fundamental to the idea of equal protection, between oppression and assistance. The majority's concept of "congruence" ignores a difference, fundamental to our constitutional system, between the Federal Government and the States. And the majority's concept of *stare decisis* ignores the force of binding precedent. I would affirm the judgment of the Court of Appeals.

Justice GINSBURG, with whom Justice BREYER joins, dissenting.

The statutes and regulations at issue, as the Court indicates, were adopted by the political branches in response to an "unfortunate reality": "the unhappy persistence of both the practice and the lingering effects of racial discrimination against minority groups in this country." The United States suffers from those lingering effects because, for most of our Nation's history, the idea that "we are just one race" (SCALIA, J.) was not embraced. For generations, our lawmakers and judges were unprepared to say that there is in this land no superior race, no race inferior to any other. In *Plessy v. Ferguson*, 163 U.S. 537 (1896), not only did this Court endorse the oppressive practice of race segregation, but even Justice HARLAN, the advocate of a "color-blind" Constitution, stated: "The white race deems itself to be the dominant race in this country. And so it is, in prestige, in achievements, in education, in wealth and in power. So, I doubt not, it will continue to be for all time, if it remains true to its great heritage and holds fast to the principles of constitutional liberty." (HARLAN, J., dissenting).

Not until *Loving v. Virginia*, 388 U.S. 1 (1967), which held unconstitutional Virginia's ban on interracial marriages, could one say with security that the Constitution and this Court would abide no measure "designed to maintain White Supremacy."

The divisions in this difficult case should not obscure the Court's recognition of the persistence of racial inequality and a majority's acknowledgment of Congress' authority to act affirmatively, not only to end discrimination, but also to counteract discrimination's lingering effects. Those effects, reflective of a system of racial caste only recently ended, are evident in our workplaces, markets, and neighborhoods. Job applicants with identical resumes, qualifications, and interview styles still experience different receptions, depending on their race. White and African-American consumers still encounter different deals. People of color looking for housing still face discriminatory treatment by landlords, real estate agents, and mortgage lenders. Minority entrepreneurs sometimes fail to gain contracts though they are the low bidders, and they are sometimes refused work even after winning contracts. Bias both conscious and unconscious, reflecting traditional and unexamined habits of thought, keeps up barriers that must come down if equal opportunity and nondiscrimination are ever genuinely to become this country's law and practice. Given this history and its practical consequences, Congress surely can conclude that a carefully designed affirmative action program may help to realize, finally, the "equal protection of the laws" the Fourteenth Amendment has promised since 1868. . . .

For a classification made to hasten the day when "we are just one race," however, the lead opinion has dispelled the notion that "strict scrutiny" is "'fatal in fact.'" Properly, a majority of the Court calls for review that is searching, in order to ferret out classifications in reality malign, but masquerading as benign. The Court's once lax review of sex-based classifications demonstrates the need for such suspicion. Today's decision thus usefully reiterates that the purpose of strict scrutiny "is precisely to distinguish legitimate from illegitimate uses of race in governmental decisionmaking," "to 'differentiate between' permissible and impermissible govern mental use of race," to distinguish "'between a "No Trespassing" sign and a welcome mat.'" . . .

While I would not disturb the programs challenged in this case, and would leave their improvement to the political branches, I see today's decision as one that allows our precedent to evolve, still to be informed by and responsive to changing conditions.

D. NONRACIAL CLASSIFICATIONS AND THE EQUAL PROTECTION OF THE LAWS

(1) Gender-Based Discrimination

In a sweeping and unanimous decision, in *Harris v. Forklift Systems, Inc.*, 114 S.Ct. 367 (1993), which will make it easier for individuals to prove sexual harassment in the workplace, the Supreme Court held that under Title VII of the Civil Rights Act of 1964, individuals need not meet the high standard of proving "psychological injury." In *Meritor Savings Bank v. Vinson*, 477 U.S. 57 (1986) (see Vol. 2, Ch. 12), the Court held that the Civil Rights Act forbids harassment in the workplace, along with discrimination in the hiring and firing of employees. But lower courts were divided over the standards for proving harassment. Writing for the Court, Justice O'Connor explained that judges and juries have substantial leeway to decide whether sexual advances, insults, and other discriminatory conduct constitute harassment. In Justice O'Connor's words:

Title VII of the Civil Rights Act of 1964 makes it "an unlawful employment practice for an employer . . . to discriminate against any individual with respect to his compensation, terms, conditions, or privileges of employment, because of such individual's race, color, religion, sex, or national origin." As we made clear in *Meritor Savings Bank v. Vinson*, 477 U.S. 57 (1986), this language "is not limited to 'economic' or 'tangible' discrimination. The phrase 'terms, conditions, or privileges of employment' evinces a congressional intent 'to strike at the entire spectrum of disparate treatment of men and women' in employment," which includes requiring people to work in a discriminatorily hostile or abusive environment. When the workplace is permeated with "discriminatory intimidation, ridicule, and insult," that is "sufficiently severe or pervasive to alter the conditions of the victim's employment and create an abusive working environment," Title VII is violated.

This standard, which we reaffirm today, takes a middle path between making actionable any conduct that is merely offensive and requiring the conduct to cause a tangible psychological injury. . . . But Title VII comes into play before the harassing conduct leads to a nervous breakdown. A discriminatorily abusive work environment, even one that does not seriously affect employees' psychological well-being, can and often will detract from employees' job performance, discourage employees from remaining on the job, or keep them from advancing in their careers. Moreover, even without regard to these tangible effects, the very fact that the discriminatory conduct was so severe or pervasive that it created a work environment abusive to employees because of their race, gender, religion, or national origin offends Title VII's broad rule of workplace equality. The appalling conduct alleged in *Meritor*, and the reference in that case to environments "'so heavily polluted with discrimination as to destroy completely the emotional and psychological stability of minority group workers,'" merely present some especially egregious examples of harassment. They do not mark the boundary of what is actionable. . . .

Title VII bars conduct that would seriously affect a reasonable person's psychological well-being, but the statute is not limited to such conduct. So long as the environment would reasonably be perceived, and is perceived, as hostile or abusive, *Meritor, supra*, there is no need for it also to be psychologically injurious.

In another important ruling, the Court split six to three in *J. E. B. v. Alabama ex rel. T. B.*, 511 U.S. 127 (1994), when extending its earlier rulings barring the exclusion of jurors from serving on juries on the basis of race to gender discrimination in jury selection. Writing for the majority, Justice Blackmun held that such gender discrimination violates the Fourteenth Amendment and requires "heightened judicial scrutiny," while dissenting Chief Justice Rehnquist and Justices Scalia and Thomas sharply disagreed.

Finally, in its 1995–1996 term, the Court struck down Virginia's creation of a separate all-female institute as a remedy for a lower court's finding that the state's all-male Virginia Military Institute violated the Fourteenth Amendment in *United States v. Virginia* (excerpted below).

United States v. Virginia
116 S.Ct. — (1996)

The Virginia Military Institute (VMI) is a state-run, all-male military college, employing an "adversative," military-like training program aimed at producing "citizen-soldiers, educated and honorable men" suited for leadership in civilian or military life. In 1990, the Bush administration's Department of Justice challenged the all-male policy as a violation of the Fourteenth Amendment's Equal Protection Clause. As a result of that suit, the Court of Appeals for the Fourth Circuit held that, although VMI's single-gender education was pedagogically justifiable, the Fourteenth Amendment required the state to either admit females into VMI or, alternatively, create a similar program for females. Virginia responded by creating a parallel program for women—the Virginia Women's Institute for Leadership (VWIL)—at the private, all-female Mary Baldwin College. A task force determined that the mission of VWIL would be the same as that of VMI, but instead of adopting VMI's "adversative method," it de-emphasized harsh military methods and instituted a structured environment emphasizing leadership and training. When this plan was in turn challenged, the district court upheld it and the appellate court affirmed, whereupon the Department of Justice appealed to the Supreme Court.

The Court's decision was seven to one and opinion delivered by Justice Ginsburg. Chief Justice Rehnquist filed a concurring opinion and Justice Scalia a dissent. Justice Thomas did not participate in the decision.

Justice GINSBURG delivered the opinion of the Court.

Virginia's public institutions of higher learning include an incomparable military college, Virginia Military Institute (VMI). The United States maintains that the Constitution's equal protection guarantee precludes Virginia from reserving exclusively to men the unique educational opportunities VMI affords. We agree. . . .

The cross-petitions in this case present two ultimate issues. First, does Virginia's exclusion of women from the educational opportunities provided by VMI—extraordinary opportunities for military training and civilian leadership development—deny to women "capable of all of the individual activities required of VMI cadets" the equal protection of the laws guaranteed by the Fourteenth Amendment? Second, if VMI's "unique" situation—as Virginia's sole single-sex public institution of higher education—offends the Constitution's equal protection principle, what is the remedial requirement?

We note, once again, the core instruction of this Court's pathmarking decisions in *J.E.B. v. Alabama ex rel. T.B.*, 511 U.S. 127 (1994), and *Mississippi Univ. for Women [v. Hogan]*, 458 U.S. [718 (1982)]: Parties who seek to defend gender-based government action must demonstrate an "exceedingly persuasive justification" for that action.

Today's skeptical scrutiny of official action denying rights or opportunities based on sex responds to volumes of history. As a plurality of this Court acknowledged a generation ago, "our Nation has had a long and unfortunate history of sex discrimination." *Frontiero v. Richardson*, 411 U.S. 677 (1973). Through a century plus three decades and more of that history, women did not count among voters composing "We the People"; not until 1920 did women gain a constitutional right to the franchise. And for a half century thereafter, it remained the prevailing doctrine that government, both federal and state, could withhold from women opportunities accorded men so long as any "basis in reason" could be conceived for the discrimination.

In 1971, for the first time in our Nation's history, this Court ruled in favor of a woman who complained that her State had denied her the equal protection of its laws. *Reed v. Reed*, 404 U.S. 71 [(1971)] (holding unconstitutional Idaho Code prescription that, among " 'several persons claiming and equally entitled to administer [a decedent's estate], males must be preferred to females' "). Since *Reed*, the Court has repeatedly recognized that neither federal nor state government acts compatibly with the equal protection principle when a law or official policy denies to women, simply because they are women, full citizenship stature—equal opportunity to aspire, achieve, participate in and contribute to society based on their individual talents and capacities.

Without equating gender classifications, for all purposes, to classifications based on race or national origin, the Court, in post-*Reed* decisions, has carefully inspected official action that closes a door or denies opportunity to women (or to men). To summarize the Court's current directions for cases of official classification based on gender: Focusing on the differential treatment or denial of opportunity for which relief is sought, the reviewing court must determine whether the proffered justification is "exceedingly persuasive." The burden of justification is demanding and it rests entirely on the State. See *Mississippi Univ. for Women*. The State must show "at least that the [challenged] classification serves 'important governmental objectives and that the discriminatory means employed' are 'substantially related to the achievement of those objectives.'" Ibid. The justification must be genuine, not hypothesized or invented post hoc in response to litigation. And it must not rely on overbroad generalizations about the different talents, capacities, or preferences of males and females. See *Weinberger v. Wiesenfeld*, 420 U.S. 636 (1975); *Califano v. Goldfarb*, 430 U.S. 199 (1977) (STEVENS, J., concurring in judgment).

The heightened review standard our precedent establishes does not make sex a proscribed classification. Supposed "inherent differences" are no longer accepted as a ground for race or national origin classifications. See *Loving v. Virginia*, 388 U.S. 1 (1967). Physical differences between men and women, however, are enduring: "The two sexes are not fungible; a community made up exclusively of one [sex] is different from a community composed of both." *Ballard v. United States*, 329 U.S. 187 (1946).

"Inherent differences" between men and women, we have come to appreciate, remain cause for celebration, but not for denigration of the members of either sex or for artificial constraints on an individual's opportunity. Sex classifications may be used to compensate women "for particular economic disabilities [they have] suffered," *Califano v. Webster*, 430 U.S. 313 (1977) (*per curiam*), to "promote equal employment opportunity," see *California Federal Sav. & Loan Assn. v. Guerra*, 479 U.S. 272 (1987), to advance full development of the talent and capacities of our Nation's people. But such classifications may not be used, as they once were, to create or perpetuate the legal, social, and economic inferiority of women.

Measuring the record in this case against the review standard just described, we conclude that Virginia has shown no "exceedingly persuasive justification" for excluding all women from the citizen-soldier training afforded by VMI. We therefore affirm the Fourth Circuit's initial judgment, which held that Virginia had violated the Fourteenth Amendment's Equal Protection Clause. Because the remedy proffered by Virginia—the Mary Baldwin VWIL program—does not cure the constitutional violation, i.e., it does not provide equal opportunity, we reverse the Fourth Circuit's final judgment in this case.

The Fourth Circuit initially held that Virginia had advanced no state policy by which it could justify, under equal protection principles, its determination "to afford VMI's unique type of program to men and not to women." Virginia challenges that "liability" ruling and asserts two justifications in defense of VMI's exclusion of women. First, the Commonwealth contends, "single-sex education provides important educational benefits," and the option of single-sex education contributes to "diversity in educational approaches." Second, the Commonwealth argues, "the unique VMI method of character development and leadership training," the school's adversative approach, would have to be modified were VMI to admit women. We consider these two justifications in turn.

[I]t is not disputed that diversity among public educational institutions can serve the public good. But Virginia has not shown that VMI was established, or has been maintained, with a view to diversifying, by its categorical exclusion of women, educational opportunities within the State. . . .

Mississippi Univ. for Women is immediately in point. There the State asserted, in justification of its exclusion of men from a nursing school, that it was engaging in "educational affirmative action" by "compensating for discrimination against women." Undertaking a "searching analysis," the Court found no close resemblance between "the alleged objective" and "the actual purpose underlying the discriminatory classification." Pursuing a similar inquiry here, we reach the same conclusion.

Neither recent nor distant history bears out Virginia's alleged pursuit of diversity through single-sex educational options. In 1839, when the State established VMI, a range of educational opportunities for men and women was scarcely contemplated. Higher education at the time was considered dangerous for women; reflecting widely held views about women's proper place, the Nation's first universities and colleges—for example, Harvard in Massachusetts, William and Mary in Virginia—admitted only men. VMI was not at all novel in this respect: In admitting no women, VMI followed the lead of the State's flagship school, the University of Virginia, founded in 1819. . . .

In 1879, the State Senate resolved to look into the possibility of higher education for women, recognizing that Virginia "'has never, at any period of her history,'" provided for the higher education of her daughters, though she "'has liberally provided for the higher education of her sons.'" Despite this recognition, no new opportunities were instantly open to women.

Virginia eventually provided for several women's seminaries and colleges. Farmville Female Seminary became a public institution in 1884. Two women's schools, Mary Washington College and James Madison University, were founded in 1908; another, Radford University, was founded in 1910. By the mid-1970's, all four schools had become coeducational.

Debate concerning women's admission as undergraduates at the main university continued well past the century's midpoint. Familiar arguments were rehearsed. If women were admitted, it was feared, they "would encroach on the rights of men; there would be new problems of government, perhaps scandals; the old honor system would have to be changed; standards would be lowered to those of other coeducational schools; and the glorious reputation of the university, as a school for men, would be trailed in the dust."

Ultimately, in 1970, "the most prestigious institution of higher education in Virginia," the University of Virginia, introduced coeducation and, in 1972, began to admit women on an equal basis with men. A three-judge Federal District Court confirmed: "Virginia may not now deny to women, on the basis of sex, educational opportunities at the Charlottesville campus that are not afforded in other institutions operated by the State."

Virginia describes the current absence of public single-sex higher education for women as "an historical anomaly." But the historical record indicates action more deliberate than anomalous: First, protection of women against higher education; next, schools for women far from equal in resources and stature to schools for men; finally, conversion of the separate schools to coeducation. The state legislature, prior to the advent of this controversy, had repealed "all Virginia statutes requiring individual institutions to admit only men or women." And in 1990, an official commission, "legislatively established to chart the future goals of higher education in Virginia," reaffirmed the policy "of affording broad access" while maintaining "autonomy and diversity" (Report of the Virginia Commission on the University of the 21st Century). . . .

Our 1982 decision in *Mississippi Univ. for Women* prompted VMI to reexamine its male-only admission policy. Virginia relies on that reexamination as a legitimate basis for maintaining VMI's single-sex character. A Mission Study Committee, appointed by the VMI Board of Visitors, studied the problem from October 1983 until May 1986, and in that month counseled against "change of VMI status as a single-sex college." Whatever internal purpose the Mission Study Committee served—and however well-meaning the framers of the report—we can hardly extract from that effort any state policy evenhandedly to advance diverse educational options. As the District Court observed, the Committee's analysis "primarily focused on anticipated difficulties in attracting females to VMI," and the report, overall, supplied "very little indication of how the conclusion was reached."

In sum, we find no persuasive evidence in this record that VMI's male-only admission policy "is in furtherance of a state policy of 'diversity.'"

. . . A purpose genuinely to advance an array of educational options, as the Court of Appeals recognized, is not served by VMI's historic and constant plan—a plan to "afford a unique educational benefit only to males." However "liberally" this plan serves the State's sons, it makes no provision whatever for her daughters. That is not equal protection.

Virginia next argues that VMI's adversative method of training provides educational benefits that cannot be made available, unmodified, to women. Alterations to accommodate women would necessarily be "radical," so "drastic," Virginia asserts, as to transform, indeed "destroy," VMI's program. Neither sex would be favored by the transformation, Virginia maintains: Men would be deprived of the unique opportunity currently available to them; women would not gain that opportunity because their participation would "eliminate the very aspects of [the] program that distinguish [VMI] from . . . other institutions of higher education in Virginia." . . .

The United States does not challenge any expert witness estimation on average capacities or preferences of men and women. Instead, the United States emphasizes that time and again since this Court's turning point decision in *Reed v. Reed*, 404 U.S. 71 (1971), we have cautioned reviewing courts to take a "hard look" at generalizations or "tendencies" of the kind pressed by Virginia, and relied upon by the District Court. State actors controlling gates to opportunity, we have instructed, may not exclude qualified individuals based on "fixed notions concerning the roles and abilities of males and females." *Mississippi Univ. for Women.*

It may be assumed, for purposes of this decision, that most women would not choose VMI's adversative method. . . . The issue, however, is not whether "women—or men—should be forced to attend VMI"; rather, the question is whether the State can constitutionally deny to women who have the will and capacity, the training and attendant opportunities that VMI uniquely affords.

The notion that admission of women would downgrade VMI's stature, destroy the adversative system and, with it, even the school, is a judgment hardly proved, a prediction hardly different from other "self-fulfilling prophecies," once routinely used to deny rights or opportunities. When women first sought admission to the bar and access to legal education, concerns of the same order were expressed. For example, in 1876, the Court of Common Pleas of Hennepin County, Minnesota, explained why women were thought ineligible for the practice of law. Women train and educate the young, the court said, which "forbids that they shall bestow that time (early and late) and labor, so essential in attaining to the eminence to which the true lawyer should ever aspire. It cannot therefore be said that the opposition of courts to the admission of females to practice . . . is to any extent the outgrowth of . . . 'old fogyism[.]' . . . It arises rather from a comprehension of the magnitude of the responsibilities connected with the successful practice of law, and a desire to grade up the profession." *In re Application of Martha Angle Dorsett to Be Admitted to Practice as Attorney and Counselor at Law* (Minn. C.P. Hennepin Cty., 1876). . . .

Women's successful entry into the federal military academies, and their participation in the Nation's military forces, indicate that Virginia's fears for the future of VMI may not be solidly grounded. The State's justification for excluding all women from "citizen-soldier" training for which some are qualified, in any event, cannot rank as "exceedingly persuasive," as we have explained and applied that standard. Virginia and VMI trained their argument on "means" rather than "end," and thus misperceived our precedent. Single-sex education at VMI serves an "important governmental objective," they maintained, and exclusion of women is not only "substantially related," it is essential to that objective. By this notably circular argument, the "straightforward" test *Mississippi Univ. for Women* described, was bent and bowed. . . .

In the second phase of the litigation, Virginia presented its remedial plan—maintain VMI as a male-only college and create VWIL as a separate program for women. The plan met District Court approval. The Fourth Circuit, in turn, deferentially reviewed the State's proposal and decided that the two single-sex programs directly served Virginia's reasserted purposes: single-gender education, and "achieving the results of an adversative method in a military environment." . . . The United States challenges this "remedial" ruling as pervasively misguided.

A remedial decree, this Court has said, must closely fit the constitutional violation; it must be shaped to place persons unconstitutionally denied an opportunity or advantage in "the position they would have occupied in the absence of [discrimination]." See *Milliken v. Bradley*, 433 U.S. 267 (1977) [*Milliken II*]. The constitutional violation in this case is the categorical exclusion of women from an extraordinary educational opportunity afforded men. A proper remedy for an unconstitutional exclusion, we have explained, aims to "eliminate [so far as possible] the discriminatory effects of the past" and to "bar like discrimination in the future." *Louisiana v. United States*, 380 U.S. 145 (1965).

Virginia chose not to eliminate, but to leave untouched, VMI's exclusionary policy. For women only, however, Virginia proposed a separate program, different in kind from VMI and unequal in tangible and intangible facilities. Having violated the Constitution's equal protection requirement, Virginia was obliged to show that its remedial proposal "directly addressed and related to" the violation, the equal protection denied to women ready, willing, and able to benefit from educational opportunities of the kind VMI offers. Virginia described VWIL as a "parallel program," and asserted that VWIL shares VMI's mission of producing "citizen-soldiers" and VMI's goals of providing "education, military training, mental and physical discipline, character . . . and leadership development." If the VWIL program could not "eliminate the discriminatory effects of the past," could it at least "bar like discrimination in the future"? A comparison of the programs said to be "parallel" informs our answer. . . .

VWIL affords women no opportunity to experience the rigorous military training for which VMI is famed. Instead, the VWIL program "deemphasizes" military education, and uses a "cooperative method" of education "which reinforces self-esteem."

VWIL students participate in ROTC and a "largely ceremonial" Virginia Corps of Cadets, but Virginia deliberately did not make VWIL a military institute. . . . VWIL students receive their "leadership training" in seminars, externships, and speaker series, episodes and encounters lacking the "physical rigor, mental stress, . . . minute regulation of behavior, and indoctrination in desirable values" made hallmarks of VMI's citizen-soldier training. Kept away from the pressures, hazards, and psychological bonding characteristic of VMI's adversative training, VWIL students will not know the "feeling of tremendous accomplishment" commonly experienced by VMI's successful cadets.

Virginia maintains that these methodological differences are "justified pedagogically," based on "important differences between men and women in learning and developmental needs," "psychological and sociological differences" Virginia describes as "real" and "not stereotypes." The Task Force charged with developing the leadership program for women, drawn from the staff and faculty at Mary Baldwin College, "determined that a military model and, especially VMI's adversative method, would be wholly inappropriate for educating and training most women."

As earlier stated, generalizations about "the way women are," estimates of what is appropriate for most women, no longer justify denying opportunity to women whose talent and capacity place them outside the average description. Notably, Virginia never asserted that VMI's method of education suits most men. It is also revealing that Virginia accounted for its failure to make the VWIL experience "the entirely militaristic experience of VMI" on the ground that VWIL "is planned for women who do not necessarily expect to pursue military careers." By that reasoning, VMI's "entirely militaristic" program would be inappropriate for men in general or as a group, for "only about 15% of VMI cadets enter career military service."

In contrast to the generalizations about women on which Virginia rests, we note again these dispositive realties: VMI's "implementing methodology" is not "inherently unsuitable to women;" "some women . . . do well under [the] adversative model;" "some women, at least, would want to attend [VMI] if they had the opportunity;" "some women are capable of all of the individual activities required of VMI cadets," and "can meet the physical standards [VMI] now imposes on men." It is on behalf of these women that the United States has instituted this suit, and it is for them that a remedy must be crafted, a remedy that will end their exclusion from a state-supplied educational opportunity for which they are fit, a decree that will "bar like discrimination in the future." *Louisiana.*

In myriad respects other than military training, VWIL does not qualify as VMI's equal. VWIL's student body, faculty, course offerings, and facilities hardly match VMI's. Nor can the VWIL graduate anticipate the benefits associated with VMI's 157-year history, the school's prestige, and its influential alumni network. . . .

Virginia, in sum, while maintaining VMI for men only, has failed to provide any "comparable single-gender women's institution." Instead, the Commonwealth has created a VWIL program fairly appraised as a "pale shadow" of VMI in terms of the range of curricular choices and faculty stature, funding, prestige, alumni support and influence.

Virginia's VWIL solution is reminiscent of the remedy Texas proposed 50 years ago, in response to a state trial court's 1946 ruling that, given the equal protection guarantee, African Americans could not be denied a legal education at a state facility. See *Sweatt v. Painter*, 339 U.S. 629 (1950). Reluctant to admit African Americans to its flagship University of Texas Law School, the State set up a separate school for Herman Sweatt and other black law students. As originally opened, the new school had no independent faculty or library, and it lacked accreditation. Nevertheless, the state trial and appellate courts were satisfied that the new school offered Sweatt opportunities for the study of law "substantially equivalent to those offered by the State to white students at the University of Texas." . . .

More important than the tangible features, the Court emphasized, are "those qualities which are incapable of objective measurement but which make for greatness" in a school, including "reputation of the faculty, experience of the administration, position and influence of the alumni, standing in the community, traditions and prestige." Facing the marked differences reported in the *Sweatt* opinion, the Court unanimously ruled that Texas had not shown "substantial equality in the [separate] educational opportunities" the State offered. Accordingly, the Court held, the Equal Protection Clause required Texas to admit African Americans to the University of Texas Law School. In line with *Sweatt*, we rule here that Virginia has not shown substantial equality in the separate educational opportunities the State supports at VWIL and VMI. . . .

The Fourth Circuit plainly erred in exposing Virginia's VWIL plan to a deferential analysis, for "all gender-based classifications today" warrant "heightened scrutiny." Valuable as VWIL may prove for students who seek the program offered, Virginia's remedy affords no cure at all for the opportunities and advantages withheld from women who want a VMI education and can make the grade. In sum, Virginia's remedy does not match the constitutional violation; the State has shown no "exceedingly persuasive justification" for withholding from women qualified for the experience premier training of the kind VMI affords. . . .

A generation ago, "the authorities controlling Virginia higher education," despite long established tradition, agreed "to innovate and favorably entertained the [then] relatively new idea that there must be no discrimination by sex in offering educational opportunity." Commencing in 1970, Virginia opened to women "educational opportunities at the Charlottesville campus that [were] not afforded in other [State-operated] institutions." A federal court approved the State's innovation, emphasizing that the University of Virginia "offered courses of instruction . . . not available elsewhere." The court further noted: "There exists at Charlottesville a 'prestige' factor [not paralleled in] other Virginia educational institutions."

VMI, too, offers an educational opportunity no other Virginia institution provides, and the school's "prestige"—associated with its success in developing "citizen-soldiers"—is unequaled. Virginia has closed this facility to its daughters and, instead, has devised for them a "parallel program," with a faculty less impressively credentialed and less well paid, more limited course offerings, fewer opportunities for military training and for scientific specialization. Cf. *Sweatt.* VMI, beyond question, "possesses to a far greater degree" than the VWIL program "those qualities which are incapable of objective measurement but which make for greatness in a . . . school," including "position and influence of the alumni, standing in the community, traditions and prestige." Women seeking and fit for a VMI-quality education cannot be offered anything less, under the State's obligation to afford them genuinely equal protection. . . .

For the reasons stated, the initial judgment of the Court of Appeals is affirmed, the final judgment of the Court of Appeals is reversed, and the case is remanded for further proceedings consistent with this opinion.

It is so ordered.

CHIEF JUSTICE REHNQUIST, concurring in judgment.

The Court holds first that Virginia violates the Equal Protection Clause by maintaining the Virginia Military Institute's (VMI's) all-male admissions policy, and second that establishing the Virginia Women's Institute for Leadership (VWIL) program does not remedy that violation. While I agree with these conclusions, I disagree with the Court's analysis and so I write separately.

Two decades ago in *Craig v. Boren*, 429 U.S. 190 (1976), we announced that "to withstand constitutional challenge, . . . classifications by gender must serve important governmental objectives and must be substantially related to achievement of those objectives." We have adhered to that standard of scrutiny ever since. While the majority adheres to this test today, it also says that the State must demonstrate an " 'exceedingly persuasive justification'" to support a gender-based classification. It is unfortunate that the Court thereby introduces an element of uncertainty respecting the appropriate test.

While terms like "important governmental objective" and "substantially related" are hardly models of precision, they have more content and specificity than does the phrase "exceedingly persuasive justification." That phrase is best confined, as it was first used, as an observation on the difficulty of meeting the applicable test, not as a formulation of the test itself. To avoid introducing potential confusion, I would have adhered more closely to our traditional, "firmly established," [*Mississippi Univ. for Women v.*] *Hogan*; *Heckler* [*v. Mathews*], 465 U.S. 728 (1984), standard that a gender-based classification "must bear a close and substantial relationship to important governmental objectives." [*Personnel Administrator of Mass. v.*] *Feeney*, 442 U.S. 256 (1979).

Even if diversity in educational opportunity were the State's actual objective, the State's position would still be problematic. The difficulty with its position is that the diversity benefited only one sex; there was single-sex public education available for men at VMI, but no corresponding single-sex public education available for women. When *Hogan* placed Virginia on notice that VMI's admissions policy possibly was unconstitutional, VMI could have dealt with the problem by admitting women; but its governing body felt strongly that the admission of women would have seriously harmed the institution's educational approach. Was there something else the State could have done to avoid an equal protection violation? Since the State did nothing, we do not have to definitively answer that question. . . .

The dissent criticizes me for "disregarding the four all-women's private colleges in Virginia (generously assisted by public funds)." The private women's colleges are treated by the State exactly as all other private schools are treated, which includes the provision of tuition-assistance grants to Virginia residents. Virginia gives no special support to the women's single-sex education. But obviously, the same is not true for men's education. Had the State provided the kind of support for the private women's schools that it provides for VMI, this may have been a very different case. For in so doing, the State would have demonstrated that its interest in providing a single-sex education for men, was to some measure matched by an interest in providing the same opportunity for women.

Virginia offers a second justification for the single-sex admissions policy: maintenance of the adversative method. I agree with the Court that this justification does not serve an important governmental objective. A State does not have substantial interest in the adversative methodology unless it is pedagogically beneficial. While considerable evidence shows that a single-sex education is pedagogically beneficial for some students, and hence a State may have a valid interest in promoting that methodology, there is no similar evidence in the record that an adversative method is pedagogically beneficial or is any more likely to produce character traits than other methodologies. . . .

In the end, the women's institution Virginia proposes, VWIL, fails as a remedy, because it is distinctly inferior to the existing men's institution and will continue to be for the foreseeable future. VWIL simply is not, in any sense, the institution that VMI is. In particular, VWIL is a program appended to a private college, not a self-standing institution; and VWIL is substantially underfunded as compared to VMI. I therefore ultimately agree with the Court that Virginia has not provided an adequate remedy.

Justice SCALIA, dissenting.

I shall devote most of my analysis to evaluating the Court's opinion on the basis of our current equal-protection jurisprudence, which regards this Court as free to evaluate everything under the sun by applying one of three tests: "rational basis" scrutiny, intermediate scrutiny, or strict scrutiny. These tests are no more scientific than their names suggest, and a further element of randomness is added by the fact that it is largely up to us which test will be applied in each case. Strict scrutiny, we have said, is reserved for state "classifications based on race or national origin and classifications affecting fundamental rights," *Clark v. Jeter*, 486 U.S. 456 (1988). It is my position that the term "fundamental rights" should be limited to "interests traditionally protected by our society," *Michael H. v. Gerald D.*, 491 U.S. 110 (1989) (plurality opinion of SCALIA, J.); but the Court has not accepted that view, so that strict scrutiny will be applied to the deprivation of whatever sort of right we consider "fundamental." We have no established criterion for "intermediate scrutiny" either, but essentially apply it when it seems like a good idea to load the dice. So far it has been applied to content-neutral restrictions that place an incidental burden on speech, to disabilities attendant to illegitimacy, and to discrimination on the basis of sex.

I have no problem with a system of abstract tests such as rational-basis, intermediate, and strict scrutiny (though I think we can do better than applying strict scrutiny and intermediate scrutiny whenever we feel like it). Such formulas are essential to evaluating whether the new restrictions that a changing society constantly imposes upon private conduct comport with that "equal protection" our society has always accorded in the past. But in my view the function of this Court is to preserve our society's values regarding (among other things) equal protection, not to revise them; to prevent backsliding from the degree of restriction the Constitution imposed upon democratic government, not to prescribe, on our own authority, progressively higher degrees. For that reason it is my view that, whatever abstract tests we may choose to devise, they cannot supersede—and indeed ought to be crafted so as to reflect—those constant and unbroken national traditions that embody the people's understanding of ambiguous constitutional texts. More specifically, it is my view that "when a practice not expressly prohibited by the text of the Bill of Rights bears the endorsement of a long tradition of open, widespread, and unchallenged use that dates back to the beginning of the Republic, we have no proper basis for striking it down." *Rutan v. Republican Party of Ill.*, 497 U.S. 62 (1990) (SCALIA, J., dissenting). The same applies, *mutatis mutandis*, to a practice asserted to be in violation of the post-Civil War Fourteenth Amendment.

The all-male constitution of VMI comes squarely within such a governing tradition. Founded by the Commonwealth of Virginia in 1839 and continuously maintained by it since, VMI has always admitted only men. . . . In other words, the tradition of having government-funded military schools for men is as well rooted in the traditions of this country as the tradition of sending only men into military combat. The people may decide to change the one tradition, like the other, through democratic processes; but the assertion that either tradition has been unconstitutional through the centuries is not law, but politics-smuggled-into-law.

To reject the Court's disposition today, however, it is not necessary to accept my view that the Court's made-up tests cannot displace longstanding national traditions as the primary determinant of what the Constitution means. It is only necessary to apply honestly the test the Court has been applying to sex-based classifications for the past two decades. It is well settled, as Justice O'CONNOR stated some time ago for a unanimous Court, that we evaluate a statutory classification based on sex under a standard that lies "between the extremes of rational basis review and strict scrutiny." *Clark v. Jeter.* We have denominated this standard "intermediate scrutiny" and under it have inquired whether the statutory classification is "substantially related to an important governmental objective."

Before I proceed to apply this standard to VMI, I must comment upon the manner in which the Court avoids doing so. . . .

Only the amorphous "exceedingly persuasive justification" phrase, and not the standard elaboration of intermediate scrutiny, can be made to yield this conclusion that VMI's single-sex composition is unconstitutional because there exist several women (or, one would have to conclude under the Court's reasoning, a single woman) willing and able to undertake VMI's program. Intermediate scrutiny has never required a least-restrictive-means analysis, but only a "substantial relation" between the classification and the state interests that it serves. Thus, in *Califano v. Webster*, 430 U.S. 313 (1977), we upheld a congressional statute that provided higher Social Security benefits for women than for men. We reasoned that "women . . . as such have been unfairly hindered from earning as much as men," but we did not require proof that each woman so benefited had suffered discrimination or that each disadvantaged man had not; it was sufficient that even under the former congressional scheme "women on the average received lower retirement benefits than men." The reasoning in our other intermediate-scrutiny cases has similarly required only a substantial relation between end and means, not a perfect fit. . . . There is simply no support in our cases for the notion that a sex-based classification is invalid unless it relates to characteristics that hold true in every instance. . . .

The question to be answered, I repeat, is whether the exclusion of women from VMI is "substantially related to an important governmental objective."

It is beyond question that Virginia has an important state interest in providing effective college education for its citizens. That single-sex instruction is an approach substantially related to that interest should be evident enough from the long and continuing history in this country of men's and women's colleges. But beyond that, as the Court of Appeals here stated: "That single-gender education at the college level is beneficial to both sexes is a fact established in this case." . . .

The potential of today's decision for widespread disruption of existing institutions lies in its application to private single-sex education. Government support is immensely important to private educational institutions. Mary Baldwin College—which designed and runs VWIL—notes that private institutions of higher education in the 1990–1991 school year derived approximately 19 percent of their budgets from federal, state, and local government funds, not including financial aid to students. Charitable status under the tax laws is also highly significant for private educational institutions, and it is certainly not beyond the Court that rendered today's decision to hold that a donation to a single-sex college should be deemed contrary to public policy and therefore not deductible if the college discriminates on the basis of sex. See *Bob Jones Univ. v. United States*, 461 U.S. 574 (1983). . . .

The only hope for state-assisted single-sex private schools is that the Court will not apply in the future the principles of law it has applied today. That is a substantial hope, I am happy and ashamed to say. After all, did not the Court today abandon the principles of law it has applied in our earlier sex-classification cases? And does not the Court positively invite private colleges to rely upon our ad-hocery by assuring them this case is "unique"? I would not advise the foundation of any new single-sex college (especially an all-male one) with the expectation of being allowed to receive any government support; but it is too soon to abandon in despair those single-sex colleges already in existence. It will certainly be possible for this Court to write a future opinion that ignores the broad principles of law set forth today, and that characterizes as utterly dispositive the opinion's perceptions that VMI was a uniquely prestigious all-male institution, conceived in chauvinism, etc., etc. I will not join that opinion.

(2) Discrimination against Gays and Lesbians

Romer v. Evans
116 S.Ct. 1620 (1996)

In November 1992, voters in Colorado approved an amendment to the state constitution that forbids localities from enacting ordinances outlawing discrimination against homosexuals. Known as Amendment 2, the "No Protected Status Based on Homosexual, Lesbian, or Bisexual Orientation Amendment" provides that

> Neither the State of Colorado, through any of its branches or departments, nor any of its agencies, political subdivisions, municipalities or school districts, shall enact, adopt or enforce any statute, regulation, ordinance or policy whereby homosexual, lesbian or bisexual orientation, conduct, practices or relationships shall constitute or otherwise be the basis of or entitle any person or class of persons to have or claim any minority status quota preferences, protected status or claim of discrimination. This Section of the Constitution shall be in all respects self-executing.

Richard G. Evans and several local government officials immediately filed a suit to enjoin the enforcement of the amendment on the grounds that it was unconstitutional. A state trial court subsequently agreed and Governor Roy Romer appealed.

In 1993, the Colorado State Supreme Court interpreted precedents of the U.S. Supreme Court to hold that "the Equal Protection Clause of the United States Constitution protects the fundamental right to participate equally in the political process," and "that any legislation or state constitutional amendment which infringes on this right by 'fencing out' an independently identifiable class of persons must be subject to strict judicial scrutiny." *Evans v. Romer*, 854 P.2d 1270 (Colo. 1993) (*Evans I*). On that basis, the state supreme court affirmed the trial court's decision and remanded the case back to the trial court to determine whether Amendment 2 was supported by a compelling state interest and narrowly tailored to serve that interest. Subsequently, government officials offered six "compelling" state interests for the amendment: (1) deterring factionalism; (2) preserving the integrity of the state's political functions; (3) preserving the ability of the state to remedy discrimination against suspect classes; (4) preventing the government from interfering with personal, familial, and religious privacy; (5) preventing government from subsidizing the political objectives of a special interest group; and (6) promoting the physical and psychological well-being of Colorado children.

For a second time, however, the trial court rejected most of the rationales as not compelling state interests and concluded the government's interests in preventing interference with personal privacy and religious liberty, although compelling, were not narrowly tailored enough. Accordingly, the trial court issued a permanent injunction against the enforcement of Amendment 2. Besides appealing *Evans I* to the U.S. Supreme Court, which denied review, Governor Romer appealed the trial court's second ruling on the amendment to the Colorado state supreme court. On appeal in *Evans II*, attorneys for the state argued that: (1) the legal standard set forth in *Evans I* for assessing the constitutionality of Amendment 2 should be reconsidered; (2) Amendment 2 was supported by several compelling state interests and was narrowly tailored to meet those interests; (3) that the unconstitutional provisions of Amendment 2 were severable from the remainder; and (4) Amendment 2 was a valid exercise of state power under the Tenth Amendment to the United States Constitution. However, in 1994 in *Evans II,* the Colorado state supreme court rejected those arguments and, once again, held that Amendment 2 was unconstitutional. Subsequently, Colorado's governor, Roy Romer, appealed to the Supreme Court.

The Court's decision was six to three. Justice Kennedy delivered the opinion for the Court and Justice Scalia filed a dissent, which was joined by Chief Justice Rehnquist and Justice Thomas.

Justice KENNEDY delivered the opinion of the Court.

One century ago, the first Justice HARLAN admonished this Court that the Constitution "neither knows nor tolerates classes among citizens." *Plessy v. Ferguson*, 163 U.S. 537 (1896) (dissenting opinion). Unheeded then, those words now are understood to state a commitment to the law's neutrality where the rights of persons are at stake. The Equal Protection Clause enforces this principle and today requires us to hold invalid a provision of Colorado's Constitution. . . .

The State's principal argument in defense of Amendment 2 is that it puts gays and lesbians in the same position as all other persons. So, the State says, the measure does no more than deny homosexuals special rights. This reading of the amendment's language is implausible. We rely not upon our own interpretation of the amendment but upon the authoritative construction of Colorado's Supreme Court. The state court, deeming it unnecessary to determine the full extent of the amendment's reach, found it invalid even on a modest reading of its implications. The critical discussion of the amendment, set out in *Evans I*, is as follows: "The immediate objective of Amendment 2 is, at a minimum, to repeal existing statutes, regulations, ordinances, and policies of state and local entities that barred discrimination based on sexual orientation. . . .

The change that Amendment 2 works in the legal status of gays and lesbians in the private sphere is far-reaching, both on its own terms and when considered in light of the structure and operation of modern anti-discrimination laws. That structure is well illustrated by contemporary statutes and ordinances prohibiting discrimination by providers of public accommodations. "At common law, innkeepers, smiths, and others who 'made profession of a public employment,' were prohibited from refusing, without good reason, to serve a customer." *Hurley v. Irish-American Gay, Lesbian and Bisexual Group of Boston, Inc.* [115 S.Ct. 2338] (1995). The duty was a general one and did not specify protection for particular groups. The common law rules, however, proved insufficient in many instances, and it was settled early that the Fourteenth Amendment did not give Congress a general power to prohibit discrimination in public accommodations, *Civil Rights Cases*, 109 U.S. 3 (1883). In consequence, most States have chosen to counter discrimination by enacting detailed statutory schemes. Colorado's state and municipal laws typify this emerging tradition of statutory protection and follow a consistent pattern. . . .

These statutes and ordinances also depart from the common law by enumerating the groups or persons within their ambit of protection. Enumeration is the essential device used to make the duty not to discriminate concrete and to provide guidance for those who must comply. . . .

Amendment 2 bars homosexuals from securing protection against the injuries that these public-accommodations laws address. That in itself is a severe consequence, but there is more. Amendment 2, in addition, nullifies specific legal protections for this targeted class in all transactions in housing, sale of real estate, insurance, health and welfare services, private education, and employment. . . .

Amendment 2's reach may not be limited to specific laws passed for the benefit of gays and lesbians. It is a fair, if not necessary, inference from the broad language of the amendment that it deprives gays and lesbians even of the protection of general laws and policies that prohibit arbitrary discrimination in governmental and private settings. At some point in the systematic administration of these laws, an official must determine whether homosexuality is an arbitrary and thus forbidden basis for decision. Yet a decision to that effect would itself amount to a policy prohibiting discrimination on the basis of homosexuality, and so would appear to be no more valid under Amendment 2 than the specific prohibitions against discrimination the state court held invalid. . . .

The Fourteenth Amendment's promise that no person shall be denied the equal protection of the laws must co-exist with the practical necessity that most legislation classifies for one purpose or another, with resulting disadvantage to various groups or persons. We have attempted to reconcile the principle with the reality by stating that, if a law neither burdens a fundamental right nor targets a suspect class, we will uphold the legislative classification so long as it bears a rational relation to some legitimate end. See, e.g., *Heller v. Doe*, 509 U.S. — (1993).

Amendment 2 fails, indeed defies, even this conventional inquiry. First, the amendment has the peculiar property of imposing a broad and undifferentiated disability on a single named group, an exceptional and, as we shall explain, invalid form of legislation. Second, its sheer breadth is so discontinuous with the reasons offered for it that the amendment seems inexplicable by anything but animus toward the class that it affects; it lacks a rational relationship to legitimate state interests.

Taking the first point, even in the ordinary equal protection case calling for the most deferential of standards, we insist on knowing the relation between the classification adopted and the object to be attained. The search for the link between classification and objective gives substance to the Equal Protection Clause; it provides guidance and discipline for the legislature, which is entitled to know what sorts of laws it can pass; and it marks the limits of our own authority. In the ordinary case, a law will be sustained if it can be said to advance a legitimate government interest, even if the law seems unwise or works to the disadvantage of a particular group, or if the rationale for it seems tenuous. By requiring that the classification bear a rational relationship to an independent and legitimate legislative end, we ensure that classifications are not drawn for the purpose of disadvantaging the group burdened by the law.

Amendment 2 confounds this normal process of judicial review. It is at once too narrow and too broad. It identifies persons by a single trait and then denies them protection across the board. The resulting disqualification of a class of persons from the right to seek specific protection from the law is unprecedented in our jurisprudence.

It is not within our constitutional tradition to enact laws of this sort. Central both to the idea of the rule of law and to our own Constitution's guarantee of equal protection is the principle that government and each of its parts remain open on impartial terms to all who seek its assistance. "'Equal protection of the laws is not achieved through indiscriminate imposition of inequalities.'" *Sweatt v. Painter*, 339 U.S. 629 (1950) (quoting *Shelley v. Kraemer*, 334 U.S. 1 (1948)). Respect for this principle explains why laws singling out a certain class of citizens for disfavored legal status or general hardships are rare. A law declaring that in general it shall be more difficult for one group of citizens than for all others to seek aid from the government is itself a denial of equal protection of the laws in the most literal sense. "The guaranty of 'equal protection of the laws is a pledge of the protection of equal laws.'" *Skinner v. Oklahoma ex rel. Williamson*, 316 U.S. 535 (1942) (quoting *Yick Wo v. Hopkins*, 118 U.S. 356 (1886)).

Davis v. Beason, 133 U.S. 333 (1890), not cited by the parties but relied upon by the dissent, is not evidence that Amendment 2 is within our constitutional tradition, and any reliance upon it as authority for sustaining the amendment is misplaced. In *Davis*, the Court approved an Idaho territorial statute denying Mormons, polygamists, and advocates of polygamy the right to vote and to hold office because, as the Court construed the statute, it "simply excludes from the privilege of voting, or of holding any office of honor, trust or profit, those who have been convicted of certain offences, and those who advocate a practical resistance to the laws of the Territory and justify and approve the commission of crimes forbidden by it." To the extent *Davis* held that persons advocating a certain practice may be denied the right to vote, it is no longer good law. *Brandenburg v. Ohio*, 395 U.S. 444 (1969) (*per curiam*). To the extent it held that the groups designated in the statute may be deprived of the right to vote because of their status, its ruling could not stand without surviving strict scrutiny, a most doubtful outcome. To the extent *Davis* held that a convicted felon may be denied the right to vote, its holding is not implicated by our decision and is unexceptionable.

A second and related point is that laws of the kind now before us raise the inevitable inference that the disadvantage imposed is born of animosity toward the class of persons affected. Even laws enacted for broad and ambitious purposes often can be explained by reference to legitimate public policies which justify the incidental disadvantages they impose on certain persons. Amendment 2, however, in making a general announcement that gays and lesbians shall not have any particular protections from the law, inflicts on them immediate, continuing, and real injuries that outrun and belie any legitimate justifications that may be claimed for it. We conclude that, in addition to the far-reaching deficiencies of Amendment 2 that we have noted, the principles it offends, in another sense, are conventional and venerable; a law must bear a rational relationship to a legitimate government purpose, and Amendment 2 does not.

The primary rationale the State offers for Amendment 2 is respect for other citizens' freedom of association, and in particular the liberties of landlords or employers who have personal or religious objections to homosexuality. Colorado also cites its interest in conserving resources to fight discrimination against other groups. The breadth of the Amendment is so far removed from these particular justifications that we find it impossible to credit them. We cannot say that Amendment 2 is directed to any identifiable legitimate purpose or discrete objective. It is a status-based enactment divorced from any factual context from which we could discern a relationship to legitimate state interests; it is a classification of persons undertaken for its own sake, something the Equal Protection Clause does not permit. "Class legislation . . . [is] obnoxious to the prohibitions of the Fourteenth Amendment. . . ." *Civil Rights Cases.*

We must conclude that Amendment 2 classifies homosexuals not to further a proper legislative end but to make them unequal to everyone else. This Colorado cannot do. A State cannot so deem a class of persons a stranger to its laws. Amendment 2 violates the Equal Protection Clause, and the judgment of the Supreme Court of Colorado is affirmed.

It is so ordered.

Justice SCALIA, with whom the CHIEF JUSTICE and Justice THOMAS join, dissenting.

The Court has mistaken a Kulturkampf ["culture war"] for a fit of spite. The constitutional amendment before us here is not the manifestation of a "'bare . . . desire to harm'" homosexuals, but is rather a modest attempt by seemingly tolerant Coloradans to preserve traditional sexual mores against the efforts of a politically powerful minority to revise those mores through use of the laws. That objective, and the means chosen to achieve it, are not only unimpeachable under any constitutional doctrine hitherto pronounced (hence the opinion's heavy reliance upon principles of righteousness rather than judicial holdings); they have been specifically approved by the Congress of the United States and by this Court.

In holding that homosexuality cannot be singled out for disfavorable treatment, the Court contradicts a decision, unchallenged here, pronounced only 10 years ago, see *Bowers v. Hardwick*, 478 U.S. 186 (1986), and places the prestige of this institution behind the proposition that opposition to homosexuality is as reprehensible as racial or religious bias. Whether it is or not is precisely the cultural debate that gave rise to the Colorado constitutional amendment (and to the preferential laws against which the amendment was directed). Since the Constitution of the United States says nothing about this subject, it is left to be resolved by normal democratic means, including the democratic adoption of provisions in state constitutions. This Court has no business imposing upon all Americans the resolution favored by the elite class from which the Members of this institution are selected, pronouncing that "animosity" toward homosexuality, is evil. I vigorously dissent. . . .

[T]he principle underlying the Court's opinion is that one who is accorded equal treatment under the laws, but cannot as readily as others obtain preferential treatment under the laws, has been denied equal protection of the laws. If merely stating this alleged "equal protection" violation does not suffice to refute it, our constitutional jurisprudence has achieved terminal silliness.

The central thesis of the Court's reasoning is that any group is denied equal protection when, to obtain advantage (or, presumably, to avoid disadvantage), it must have recourse to a more general and hence more difficult level of political decisionmaking than others. The world has never heard of such a principle, which is why the Court's opinion is so long on emotive utterance and so short on relevant legal citation. And it seems to me most unlikely that any multilevel democracy can function under such a principle. For whenever a disadvantage is imposed, or conferral of a benefit is prohibited, at one of the higher levels of democratic decisionmaking (i.e., by the state legislature rather than local government, or by the people at large in the state constitution rather than the legislature), the affected group has (under this theory) been denied equal protection. To take the simplest of examples, consider a state law prohibiting the award of municipal contracts to relatives of mayors or city councilmen. Once such a law is passed, the group composed of such relatives must, in order to get the benefit of city contracts, persuade the state legislature—unlike all other citizens, who need only persuade the municipality. It is ridiculous to consider this a denial of equal protection, which is why the Court's theory is unheard of.

The Court might reply that the example I have given is not a denial of equal protection only because the same "rational basis" (avoidance of corruption) which renders constitutional the substantive discrimination against relatives (i.e., the fact that they alone cannot obtain city contracts) also automatically suffices to sustain what might be called the electoral-procedural discrimination against them (i.e., the fact that they must go to the state level to get this changed). This is of course a perfectly reasonable response, and would explain why "electoral-procedural discrimination" has not hitherto been heard of: a law that is valid in its substance is automatically valid in its level of enactment. But the Court cannot afford to make this argument, for as I shall discuss next, there is no doubt of a rational basis for the substance of the prohibition at issue here. The Court's entire novel theory rests upon the proposition that there is something special—something that cannot be justified by normal "rational basis" analysis—in making a disadvantaged group (or a nonpreferred group) resort to a higher decisionmaking level. That proposition finds no support in law or logic.

I turn next to whether there was a legitimate rational basis for the substance of the constitutional amendment—for the prohibition of special protection for homosexuals. It is unsurprising that the Court avoids discussion of this question, since the answer is so obviously yes. The case most relevant to the issue before us today is not even mentioned in the Court's opinion: In *Bowers v. Hardwick*, 478 U.S. 186 (1986), we held that the Constitution does not prohibit what virtually all States had done from the founding of the Republic until very recent years—making homosexual conduct a crime. That holding is unassailable, except by those who think that the Constitution changes to suit current fashions. But in any event it is a given in the present case: Respondents' briefs did not urge overruling *Bowers*, and at oral argument respondents' counsel expressly disavowed any intent to seek such overruling. If it is constitutionally permissible for a State to make homosexual conduct criminal, surely it is constitutionally permissible for a State to enact other laws merely disfavoring homosexual conduct. And *a fortiori* it is constitutionally permissible for a State to adopt a provision not even disfavoring homosexual conduct, but merely prohibiting all levels of state government from bestowing special protections upon homosexual conduct. Respondents (who, unlike the Court, cannot afford the luxury of ignoring inconvenient precedent) counter *Bowers* with the argument that a greater-includes-the-lesser rationale cannot justify Amendment 2's application to individuals who do not engage in homosexual acts, but are merely of homosexual "orientation." Some courts of appeals have concluded that, with respect to laws of this sort at least, that is a distinction without a difference.

But assuming that, in Amendment 2, a person of homosexual "orientation" is someone who does not engage in homosexual conduct but merely has a tendency or desire to do so, *Bowers* still suffices to establish a rational basis for the provision. If it is rational to criminalize the conduct, surely it is rational to deny special favor and protection to those with a self-avowed tendency or desire to engage in the conduct. Indeed, where criminal sanctions are not involved, homosexual "orientation" is an acceptable stand-in for homosexual conduct. . . .

Moreover, even if the provision regarding homosexual "orientation" were invalid, respondents' challenge to Amendment 2—which is a facial challenge—must fail. "A facial challenge to a legislative Act is, of course, the most difficult challenge to mount successfully, since the challenger must establish that no set of circumstances exists under which the Act would be valid." *United States v. Salerno*, 481 U.S. 739 (1987). It would not be enough for respondents to establish (if they could) that Amendment 2 is unconstitutional as applied to those of homosexual "orientation"; since, under *Bowers*, Amendment 2 is unquestionably constitutional as applied to those who engage in homosexual conduct, the facial challenge cannot succeed. Some individuals of homosexual "orientation" who do not engage in homosexual acts might successfully bring an as-applied challenge to Amendment 2, but so far as the record indicates, none of the respondents is such a person.

The foregoing suffices to establish what the Court's failure to cite any case remotely in point would lead one to suspect: No principle set forth in the Constitution, nor even any imagined by this Court in the past 200 years, prohibits what Colorado has done here. But the case for Colorado is much stronger than that. What it has done is not only unprohibited, but eminently reasonable, with close, congressionally approved precedent in earlier constitutional practice.

First, as to its eminent reasonableness. The Court's opinion contains grim, disapproving hints that Coloradans have been guilty of "animus" or "animosity" toward homosexuality, as though that has been established as Unamerican. Of course it is our moral heritage that one should not hate any human being or class of human beings. But I had thought that one could consider certain conduct reprehensible—murder, for example, or polygamy, or cruelty to animals—and could exhibit even "animus" toward such conduct. Surely that is the only sort of "animus" at issue here: moral disapproval of homosexual conduct, the same sort of moral disapproval that produced the centuries-old criminal laws that we held constitutional in *Bowers*. The Colorado amendment does not, to speak entirely precisely, prohibit giving favored status to people who are homosexuals; they can be favored for many reasons—for example, because they are senior citizens or members of racial minorities. But it prohibits giving them favored status because of their homosexual conduct—that is, it prohibits favored status for homosexuality. But though Coloradans are, as I say, entitled to be hostile toward homosexual conduct, the fact is that the degree of hostility reflected by Amendment 2 is the smallest conceivable. The Court's portrayal of Coloradans as a society fallen victim to pointless, hate-filled "gay-bashing" is so false as to be comical. Colorado not only is one of the 25 States that have repealed their antisodomy laws, but was among the first to do so. But the society that eliminates criminal punishment for homosexual acts does not necessarily abandon the view that homosexuality is morally wrong and socially harmful;

often, abolition simply reflects the view that enforcement of such criminal laws involves unseemly intrusion into the intimate lives of citizens.

There is a problem, however, which arises when criminal sanction of homosexuality is eliminated but moral and social disapprobation of homosexuality is meant to be retained. The Court cannot be unaware of that problem; it is evident in many cities of the country, and occasionally bubbles to the surface of the news, in heated political disputes over such matters as the introduction into local schools of books teaching that homosexuality is an optional and fully acceptable "alternate lifestyle." The problem (a problem, that is, for those who wish to retain social disapprobation of homosexuality) is that, because those who engage in homosexual conduct tend to reside in disproportionate numbers in certain communities, and of course care about homosexual-rights issues much more ardently than the public at large, they possess political power much greater than their numbers, both locally and statewide. Quite understandably, they devote this political power to achieving not merely a grudging social toleration, but full social acceptance, of homosexuality.

By the time Coloradans were asked to vote on Amendment 2, their exposure to homosexuals' quest for social endorsement was not limited to newspaper accounts of happenings in places such as New York, Los Angeles, San Francisco, and Key West. Three Colorado cities—Aspen, Boulder, and Denver—had enacted ordinances that listed "sexual orientation" as an impermissible ground for discrimination, equating the moral disapproval of homosexual conduct with racial and religious bigotry. The phenomenon had even appeared statewide: the Governor of Colorado had signed an executive order pronouncing that "in the State of Colorado we recognize the diversity in our pluralistic society and strive to bring an end to discrimination in any form," and directing state agency-heads to "ensure non-discrimination" in hiring and promotion based on, among other things, "sexual orientation." I do not mean to be critical of these legislative successes; homosexuals are as entitled to use the legal system for reinforcement of their moral sentiments as are the rest of society. But they are subject to being countered by lawful, democratic countermeasures as well.

That is where Amendment 2 came in. It sought to counter both the geographic concentration and the disproportionate political power of homosexuals by (1) resolving the controversy at the statewide level, and (2) making the election a single-issue contest for both sides. It put directly, to all the citizens of the State, the question: Should homosexuality be given special protection? They answered no. The Court today asserts that this most democratic of procedures is unconstitutional. Lacking any cases to establish that facially absurd proposition, it simply asserts that it must be unconstitutional, because it has never happened before. . . .

What the Court says is even demonstrably false at the constitutional level. The Eighteenth Amendment to the Federal Constitution, for example, deprived those who drank alcohol not only of the power to alter the policy of prohibition locally or through state legislation, but even of the power to alter it through state constitutional amendment or federal legislation. The Establishment Clause of the First Amendment prevents theocrats from having their way by converting their fellow citizens at the local, state, or federal statutory level; as does the Republican Form of Government Clause prevent monarchists.

But there is a much closer analogy, one that involves precisely the effort by the majority of citizens to preserve its view of sexual morality statewide, against the efforts of a geographically concentrated and politically powerful minority to undermine it. The constitutions of the States of Arizona, Idaho, New Mexico, Oklahoma, and Utah to this day contain provisions stating that polygamy is "forever prohibited." Polygamists, and those who have a polygamous "orientation," have been "singled out" by these provisions for much more severe treatment than merely denial of favored status; and that treatment can only be changed by achieving amendment of the state constitutions. The Court's disposition today suggests that these provisions are unconstitutional, and that polygamy must be permitted in these States on a state-legislated, or perhaps even local-option, basis—unless, of course, polygamists for some reason have fewer constitutional rights than homosexuals.

The United States Congress, by the way, required the inclusion of these antipolygamy provisions in the constitutions of Arizona, New Mexico, Oklahoma, and Utah, as a condition of their admission to statehood. Thus, this "singling out" of the sexual practices of a single group for statewide, democratic vote—so utterly alien to our constitutional system, the Court would have us believe—has not only happened, but has received the explicit approval of the United States Congress.

I cannot say that this Court has explicitly approved any of these state constitutional provisions; but it has approved a territorial statutory provision that went even further, depriving polygamists of the ability even to achieve a constitutional amendment, by depriving them of the power to vote. *Davis v. Beason*, 133 U.S. 333 (1890). To the extent, if any, that this opinion permits the imposition of adverse consequences upon mere abstract advocacy of polygamy, it has of course been overruled by later cases. See *Brandenburg v. Ohio*, 395 U.S. 444 (1969) (*per curiam*). But the proposition that polygamy can be criminalized, and those engaging in that crime deprived of the vote, remains good law. *Beason* rejected the argument that "such discrimination is a denial of the equal protection of the laws." . . .

This Court cited *Beason* with approval as recently as 1993, in an opinion authored by the same Justice who writes for the Court today. That opinion said: "Adverse impact will not always lead to a finding of impermissible targeting. For example, a social harm may have been a legitimate concern of government for reasons quite apart from discrimination. . . . See, e.g., . . . *Davis v. Beason*, 133 U.S. 333 (1890)." *Church of Lukumi Babalu Aye, Inc. v. Hialeah*, 508 U.S. 520 (1993). It remains to be explained how Section 501 of the Idaho Revised Statutes was not an "impermissible targeting" of polygamists, but (the much more mild) Amendment 2 is an "impermissible targeting" of homosexuals. Has the Court concluded that the perceived social harm of polygamy is a "legitimate concern of government," and the perceived social harm of homosexuality is not?

I strongly suspect that the answer to the last question is yes, which leads me to the last point I wish to make: The Court today, announcing that Amendment 2 "defies . . . conventional [constitutional] inquiry," and "confounds [the] normal process of judicial review," employs a constitutional theory heretofore unknown to frustrate Colorado's reasonable effort to preserve traditional American moral values. The Court's stern disapproval of "animosity" towards homosexuality might be compared with what an earlier Court (including the revered Justices HARLAN and BRADLEY) said in *Murphy v. Ramsey*, 114 U.S. 15 (1885), rejecting a constitutional challenge to a United States statute that denied the franchise in federal territories to those who engaged in polygamous cohabitation:

"Certainly no legislation can be supposed more wholesome and necessary in the founding of a free, self-governing commonwealth, fit to take rank as one of the co-ordinate States of the Union, than that which seeks to establish it on the basis of the idea of the family, as consisting in and springing from the union for life of one man and one woman in the holy estate of matrimony; the sure foundation of all that is stable and noble in our civilization; the best guaranty of that reverent morality which is the source of all beneficent progress in social and political improvement."

I would not myself indulge in such official praise for heterosexual monogamy, because I think it no business of the courts (as opposed to the political branches) to take sides in this culture war.

But the Court today has done so, not only by inventing a novel and extravagant constitutional doctrine to take the victory away from traditional forces, but even by verbally disparaging as bigotry adherence to traditional attitudes. To suggest, for example, that this constitutional amendment springs from nothing more than " 'a bare . . . desire to harm a politically unpopular group,' " is nothing short of insulting. (It is also nothing short of preposterous to call "politically unpopular" a group which enjoys enormous influence in American media and politics, and which, as the trial court here noted, though composing no more than 4% of the population had the support of 46% of the voters on Amendment 2.)

When the Court takes sides in the culture wars, it tends to be with the knights rather than the villeins—and more specifically with the Templars, reflecting the views and values of the lawyer class from which the Court's Members are drawn. How that class feels about homosexuality will be evident to anyone who wishes to interview job applicants at virtually any of the Nation's law schools. The interviewer may refuse to offer a job because the applicant is a Republican; because he is an adulterer; because he went to the wrong prep school or belongs to the wrong country club; because he eats snails; because he is a womanizer; because she wears real-animal fur; or even because he hates the Chicago Cubs. But if the interviewer should wish not to be an associate or partner of an applicant because he disapproves of the applicant's homosexuality, then he will have violated the pledge which the Association of American Law Schools requires all its member-schools to exact from job interviewers: "assurance of the employer's willingness" to hire homosexuals. This law-school view of what "prejudices" must be stamped out may be contrasted with the more plebeian attitudes that apparently still prevail in the United States Congress, which has been unresponsive to repeated attempts to extend to homosexuals the protections of federal civil rights laws, and which took the pains to exclude them specifically from the Americans With Disabilities Act of 1990.

Today's opinion has no foundation in American constitutional law, and barely pretends to. The people of Colorado have adopted an entirely reasonable provision which does not even disfavor homosexuals in any substantive sense, but merely denies them preferential treatment. Amendment 2 is designed to prevent piecemeal deterioration of the sexual morality favored by a majority of Coloradans, and is not only an appropriate means to that legitimate end, but a means that Americans have employed before. Striking it down is an act, not of judicial judgment, but of political will. I dissent.

(4) Alienage and Age

Writing for a unanimous Court in *O'Connor v. Consolidated Coin Caterers*, 116 S.Ct. 1307 (1996), Justice Scalia ruled that a fifty-six-year-old sales manager, who was fired and replaced by a forty-year-old, could bring a suit for age discrimination under the federal Age Discrimination in Employment Act. O'Connor's claim had been dismissed by an appellate court, but in reversing the lower court's decision Justice Scalia held that it is not relevant whether an employee's replacement is under forty. Rather, what is relevant in such suits is evidence that an employee was fired because of his or her age. In the words of the justice, "There can be no greater inference of age discrimination when a 40-year-old is replaced by a 39-year-old than when a 56-year-old is replaced by a 40-year-old."

INDEX OF CASES

Cases printed in boldface are excerpted on the page printed in italic .